D0870387

Graphical Applications with Tcl and Tk, 2e

Eric Foster-Johnson

A Division of Henry Holt and Company, Inc.

M&T Books
A Division of MIS:Press, Inc.
A Subsidiary of Henry Holt and Company, Inc.
115 West 18th Street
New York, New York 10011
http://www.mispress.com

Copyright © 1997 by Eric Foster-Johnson

Printed in the United States of America

All rights reserved. No part of this book may be reproduced or transmitted in any form or by any means, electronic or mechanical, including photocopying, recording, or by any information storage and retrieval system, without prior written permission from the Publisher. Contact the Publisher for information on foreign rights.

Limits of Liability and Disclaimer of Warranty

The Author and Publisher of this book have used their best efforts in preparing the book and the programs contained in it. These efforts include the development, research, and testing of the theories and programs to determine their effectiveness.

The Author and Publisher make no warranty of any kind, expressed or implied, with regard to these programs or the documentation contained in this book. The Author and Publisher shall not be liable in any event for incidental or consequential damages in connection with, or arising out of, the furnishing, performance, or use of these programs.

All products, names and services are trademarks or registered trademarks of their respective companies.

Second Edition—1997

Library of Congress Cataloging-in-Publication Data

Johnson, Eric F.
   Graphical applications with Tcl & Tk / Eric Foster-Johnson --
2nd ed.
   p.   cm.
      ISBN 1-55851-569-0
      1. Computer graphics 2. Tcl (Computer program language) 3. Tk toolkit.
   I. Title.
   T385.J618   1997
   005.13'3—dc21   97-30960
                                                                    CIP

MIS:Press and M&T Books are available at special discounts for bulk purchases for sales promotions, premiums, and fundraising. Special editions or book excerpts can also be created to specification.

For details contact: Special Sales Director
                            MIS:Press and M&T Books
                            Divisions of Henry Holt and Company, Inc.
                            115 West 18th Street
                            New York, New York 10011

10 9 8 7 6 5 4 3 2 1

Associate Publisher: *Paul Farrell*   Production Editor: *Justin C. Nisbet*
Executive Editor: *Shari Chappell*   Copy Editor: *Sara Black*
Editor: *Laura Lewin*   Copy Edit Manager: *Karen Tongish*

CONTENTS

Contents

Contents

Contents

Chapter 8: Bitmaps, Images and the canvas Widget 449

Section II: Advanced Applications 509

Chapter 9: Tcl Tricks and Traps: Handling Errors and Debugging 511

Contents

x

Contents

Section III: Embedding Tcl in Your C and C++ Applications 695

Chapter 15: Embedding Tcl in Your Applications 697

Chapter 16: Extending Tcl 723

Appendix A: For More Information 779

Appendix B: Installing Tcl And Tk 785

Appendix C: How to Use the CD-ROM 793

Index 795

DEDICATION

To Norma, and many years together.

INTRODUCTION

What Is Tcl?

Tcl, the **Tool Command Language** (pronounced *tickle*), has captured the hearts and minds of tens of thousands of software developers worldwide. It's an easy-to-learn scripting language that runs under Windows (3.1 and 95), Windows NT, UNIX, and the Macintosh OS.

An associated add-on toolkit, **Tk** (short for *toolkit*), allows you to quickly create graphical applications without delving into arcane subjects such as Win32, Quickdraw, Object Linking and Embedding, or Motif and the X toolkit intrinsics. With a surprisingly small amount of code, you can quickly develop graphical applications.

This newly expanded and updated book will help you quickly get up to speed creating cross-platform applications with Tcl/Tk.

Since the first edition of this book was published, the Tcl community has continued to grow, and new versions with great new features have appeared. This edition covers many of these new Tcl features, including:

- Standard file, color, and message dialog boxes.
- Windows native widgets.
- Networking commands for cross-platform communication.
- Vast improvements in the Windows version of Tcl/Tk.
- A Web plug-in allows for Tcl "applets."
- A new C programmer's API.
- Many new Tcl/Tk commands that make your tasks even easier.

This book covers these new features and includes a number of new and expanded chapters. Much of the new material comes from questions from readers of the first edition. I've tried to expand areas that seem to confuse newcomers to Tcl/Tk.

Among the new chapters, Chapter 13 covers Tcl and the Web, including how to write miniature applications, or applets. In Tcl, these are called **tclets** and they work with the Tcl browser plug-in. Chapter 12 covers networking commands in Tcl, which allow you to create cross-platform applications that can communicate with each other.

Chapters 15 and 16 offers expanded coverage of Tcl's C language API, and Chapter 7 covers a host of new dialog boxes, including those for file and color selection. That's just the tip of the iceberg. You'll find coverage of HTML, CGI scripts, more interface standards, cursors, finishing applications, the grid layout manager, and scads of advice based on practical experience using Tcl/Tk on Windows and UNIX.

Why Use Tcl?

There are a number of reasons for the great success of Tcl.

- **Tcl is a scripting language**. While there are a few Tcl compilers, the vast majority of Tcl users run their programs as scripts. Scripts are easier to develop than full-fledged C or C++ programs because scripting languages such as Tcl tend to stand at a higher level than low-level languages such as C, so you simply have less to do. Furthermore, because the language is interpreted, you get a really quick turnaround when testing your code. You don't have to compile and you don't have to link; all you have to do is execute the Tcl interpreter and run your script.

- **Tcl is easy to learn**. After reading just a few chapters, you'll be ready to go out into the world and write Tcl applications. It shouldn't take you more than a few hours to pick up the basics of the language, as covered in Chapter 2 or the Tk toolkit, introduced in Chapter 3.

- **Tcl works on many different platforms**. Ported to just about every version of UNIX, from Hewlett-Packard's HP-UX to Silicon Graphics' Irix, from SCO Unix to Linux, Tcl works well in the UNIX environment, particularly because developing graphical applications on UNIX under Motif tends to be a troublesome task.

  On the Windows side, versions of Tcl exist for Windows 3.1, Window 95, and Windows NT. The latest versions of Tcl also run on Apple's Macintosh platform.

You can write complicated scripts in Tcl and execute them on multiple platforms with the same results.

- **You can embed Tcl in your programs**. As you'll find in Chapter 15, the Tcl interpreter is merely a C function that you can link into your applications. This means that you can use Tcl as the application language in your program. For example, if you're developing a spreadsheet program, you can use Tcl as the built-in macro language.

- Tcl also works well as a testing framework for object-oriented programs, as shown in Chapter 16. You can write Tcl commands that create new C++ objects and then create commands for these new objects that exercise methods and test your code. You'll find more coverage of this technique in Chapter 16.

- **Tcl is easy to extend**. As you'll see in Chapter 15, you can easily add commands to Tcl, extending the language. In fact, if you're embedding Tcl in your applications, chances are you'll need to add a number of commands that pertain to your application. This is one of the major uses of Tcl.

- **Tcl is free**. Yup, you can get all this for free on the Internet or from a number of on-line services. This book comes with a CD-ROM that contains the Tcl source code (and binaries for Windows), so you should be up and ready in just a few minutes.

- **Tcl works well with the Internet**. Tcl includes a number of built-in features that make working with World Wide Web pages easier. The text widget, for example, supports tags that help you create hypertext links in your text. Tcl is also good for CGI scripts, the code that Web pages execute for imagemaps and data retrieval.

All these great reasons should be enough to convince you to get on the Tcl bandwagon and program away.

When to Use Tcl

But all is not roses with Tcl. There are definitely circumstances in which Tcl is appropriate and those in which it is not.

Tcl, as an interpreted language, suffers performance losses because each statement is read in, parsed, and then executed at runtime. You can find a few Tcl compilers that improve this situation somewhat, but because so much of the language is text oriented (even numbers are stored as text strings), the language suffers from some inherent speed problems. (I should note, however, that in most graphical applications, the speed of the interpreter is not an issue when compared to the time it takes to create windows, draw menus, and so on.) Recent advances in Tcl allow the interpreter to compile Tcl statements to internal byte codes. These byte codes execute much faster, but Tcl is still an interpreted language and that means you suffer a performance hit.

Tcl provides only the weakest tools for building complex data structures. Tcl treats most data items as merely text. Just look at the bizarre way you must simulate multidimensional arrays (as shown in Chapter 2). You can interpret text as a number, but the focus of Tcl is clearly on text and lists of text items.

Part of the beauty of Tcl, however, is that you can choose how much of the application should be written in Tcl and how much should be written in C or C++ (or whatever other programming language you use). For example, if your application does a lot of heavy computations, you can create new Tcl commands to perform the computations in C or C++, inside the syntactic sugar of your new Tcl commands.

Tcl is also strong in text and list processing. Tcl manages the memory for strings and lists, which is one of the most troublesome areas for C programmers to handle properly.

Tcl is also a very effective command language because it provides most of the handy utility functions of shell scripts to go through directories and sort the file names, execute commands, and so on.

In this book, the focus is on developing graphical applications using Tcl and Tk on both the Windows and UNIX platforms. Because graphical programs are so hard to create, you'll soon see for yourself the advantages of the speedy Tcl development model.

This book is not a reference. It does not provide mind-numbing lists of every possible option; that's what the free on-line reference documentation is for. Instead, my goal is to provide you with a tutorial to help you get going with Tcl/Tk applications. When you've finished this book, you won't need a tutorial any more, and the on-line reference material should suffice.

There are some differences between Tcl for UNIX and Tcl for Windows. Many of these differences lie in the commands you can type in shell windows (called **DOS prompt windows** for PC users). Because Tcl makes it very easy to execute shell commands and because these shell commands differ between UNIX and Windows, there are bound to be some differences. In this book, you'll find some symbols to help you sort out these differences:

The Windows icon identifies information that pertains to Windows.

The UNIX icon, as you'd expect, identifies information that pertains to UNIX.

The cross-platform icon identifies special areas of concern to those writing portable applications.

In Chapter 1, you'll find a basic introduction to Tcl and Tk in which you'll create the obligatory "Hello World" program with two very short lines of Tcl code.

Chapter 2 introduces the basic syntax of Tcl, covering variables, arrays, flow control, and procedures.

Chapter 3 introduces most of the Tk widgets and shows you how to start creating graphical applications, which is the focus of this book.

Chapter 4 covers creating menus, menu bars and the style guide requirements for Windows and UNIX applications.

Just about every application requires some form of text editing, even if it's only for a single-line text entry field. Chapter 5 delves into this topic with the `entry` and `text` widgets. The `text` widget forms the base of what could be a quickly-created HTML Web page browsing widget.

Chapter 6 goes on to discuss lists, `listbox` widgets, lists of files and lists of directories.

Chapter 7 rounds out the discussion of Tcl basics by covering dialog windows, such as error and warning dialog boxes.

Chapter 8 reaches into Tk's strangest bag of tricks and covers the `canvas` widget. In one sense, the `canvas` widget is merely a place to draw graphics items such as lines and arcs. In another sense, though, you can embed windows in the canvas and bind events to these items, turning the canvas widget into a complicated application window. Chapter 8 also covers bitmaps and images in Tk, including built-in support for GIF images.

The advanced applications section starts with Chapter 9, which concentrates on how to debug Tcl and Tk applications. This chapter shows how to track down problems and what help is available to correct the source of the trouble.

Because Tcl is a scripting language, most of your scripts need to execute existing applications on your Windows or UNIX system. Tcl provides a number of commands for launching other applications, as shown in Chapter 10.

Chapter 11 covers on-line help, an essential part of any graphical application, with special emphasis on HTML, the *lingua franca* of the World Wide Web.

Chapter 12 covers how your Tcl applications can communicate with other Tcl applications and other kinds of programs.

Chapter 13 extends the coverage of the Web, delving into Tcl's use of Common Gateway Interface (CGI) scripts and Tcl applets.

Chapter 14 rounds out the discussion by tackling odds and ends you'll need to create robust finished applications.

Chapters 15 and 16 cover how to embed the Tcl interpreter as an application language within your programs, as well as how to extend the Tcl language from C functions. If you embed Tcl in a spreadsheet program, for example, you need to extend the base set of Tcl commands with commands to access the cells in the spreadsheet.

Tcl is an ever-changing language. John Ousterhout, the creator of Tcl, and his team keep adding neat new features every day. You can get new versions on the Internet, or use the version that accompanies this book on CD-

ROM. You'll quickly find that Tcl and Tk give you the tools to rapidly develop graphical applications.

If you're using older versions of Tcl/Tk, you really should upgrade to the latest versions. Since the first edition of this book was published, Tcl has been updated many times, with two major releases.

Tcl 7.6 and Tk 4.2 provides:

- Windows native message dialog boxes.
- File open dialog box that uses the native dialog box on Windows 95 and a fairly good emulation of the Windows 95 file dialog box on UNIX.
- New file commands allow you to copy and remove files, so you no longer have to exec **cp** and **rm** on UNIX. These commands work across all Tcl platforms, helping your scripts become more portable.

Tcl 8.0 and Tk 8.0 provides:

- Windows native widgets such as checkbuttons and radiobuttons.
- Generic font implementation aids cross-platform scripts.
- Many fixes for Windows.
- A byte-code compiler that speeds up most complicated Tcl scripts.

You'll find Tcl/Tk 8.0 on the CD-ROM that comes with this book.

What's Been Done with Tcl

Applications written with Tcl and Tk provide a good idea of what you can do with this powerful scripting language. You may also get some ideas for your own Tcl scripts.

TkDesk is the best Tcl/Tk application I've seen (Figure I.1). Acting as a file manager on UNIX, it allows you to browse directories on disk and launch commands, thus automating many difficult UNIX constructs.

Figure I.1 The TkDesk file manager, by Christian Bolik.

Like many great Tcl/Tk applications, TkDesk combines C and C++ code with Tcl/Tk. Tcl was designed to be embedded within C programs, as shown in Chapter 15.

Ical is a desktop calendar, also on UNIX. (Because Tcl supported only UNIX for many years, many Tcl applications run only on UNIX.) With Ical, you can enter tasks you need to do and appointments you need to keep, as shown in Figure I.2.

TkZip is a program for managing ZIP files on UNIX and Linux, as shown in Figure I.3. While WinZip provides a very useful interface to ZIP files on Windows, nothing like WinZip has been available on UNIX until TkZip.

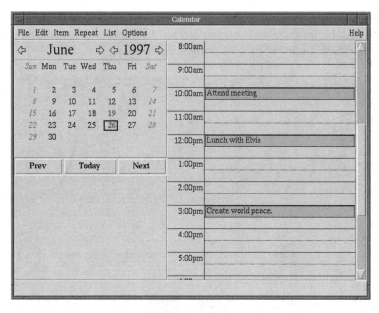

Figure I.2 The Ical desktop calendar, by Sanjay Ghemawat.

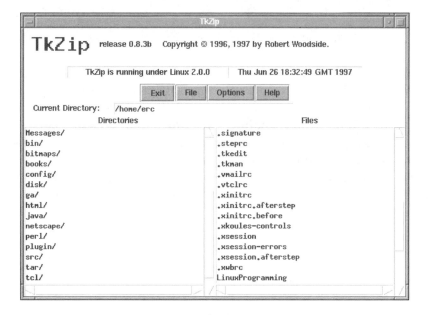

Figure I.3 TkZip on Linux.

The oddly named TkRat is a handy e-mail program that provides great support for e-mail attachments. The *rat* in TkRat is short for *Ratatosk*, a squirrel from Norse mythology. Figure I.4 shows TkRat.

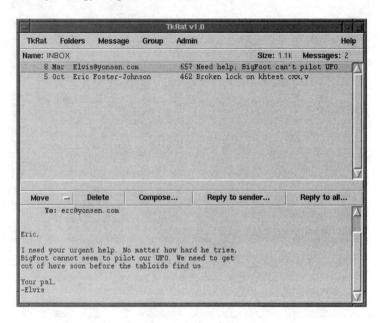

Figure I.4 The TkRat mailer, by Martin Forssen.

To help you develop Tcl code, particularly on Windows or MacOS systems, you may find TkCon handy. TkCon is an enhanced console window that helps you debug Tcl/Tk applications. On UNIX, you normally run your Tcl applications from a shell window. All error output and standard output messages from your C code goes to the shell window. Under Windows or MacOS, though, you don't have this shell to hide many of these messages (except on Windows NT if it is specially linked as a Console application). The Tcl console window helps a bit in this regard, but TkCon, shown in Figure I.5, provides even more.

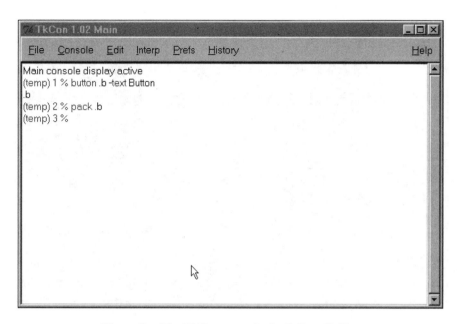

Figure I.5 The TkCon console, by Jeffrey Hobbs.

 You need to load Tk from the Interps menu before creating graphical applications in TkCon.

N O T E

Another handy development tool is Visual Tcl, a graphical interface builder. Written entirely in Tcl/Tk, this tool is helpful for developing interfaces with Tcl/Tk on any Tcl-supported platform. You can use Visual Tcl to create dialog windows, place widgets, and control attributes of the interface, as shown in Figure I.6.

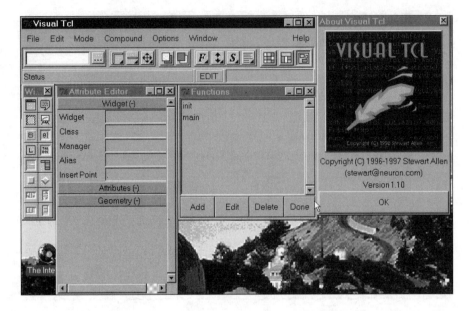

Figure I.6 The Visual Tcl interface builder, by Stewart Allen.

There are at least three completely different projects that use the name Visual Tcl, including a package from the Santa Cruz Operation. As you might expect, this causes a lot of confusion. The Visual Tcl mentioned here is a freeware GUI builder from Stewart Allen.

N O T E

UNIX developers who track versions of their software (and if you don't, you should) can benefit from **tkxcd**, a graphical file comparison program built on top of the UNIX utility called **diff**. **tkxcd**, shown in Figure I.7, presents an interface similar to that of Pure Atria's **xcleardiff**.

Other useful development tools include **tkdiff**, another graphical **diff** application; **tkCVS**, a front end to the Concurrent Version System; and **gdbtk**, a Tcl/Tk graphical interface to the **gdb** debugger.

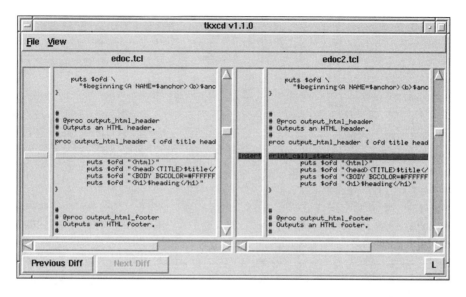

Figure I.7 The **tkxcd diff** program by John Quillan.

I hope the pictures in this section inspire you to take your Tcl/Tk applications to new heights.

Now you're ready to start creating graphical applications with Tcl/Tk. If you haven't yet installed Tcl, jump ahead to Appendix B, which covers this process for Windows and UNIX systems. Otherwise, go to Chapter 1.

Contacting the Author

The best way to reach me is through my Web page on the Internet, located at **http://www.pconline.com/~erc/**. My Web pages also provide extra information on Tcl/Tk as well as a list of frequently asked questions about Tcl/Tk usage on Windows, a document I maintain and distribute over the Internet. You can send me e-mail at **erc@pconline.com**.

Writing Applications in Tcl/Tk

This first section introduces all the basics you need to create graphical applications with Tcl and Tk.

Chapter 1 gets the whole thing rolling. **Chapter 2** delves into the basic syntax of Tcl, the Tool Command Language. You'll use the commands introduced in this chapter in every Tcl script to come.

Chapter 3 starts with graphical applications and the widgets provided by the Tk extension to Tcl. It covers the basic widgets required of all Tcl applications. This continues in **Chapter 4** on menus and **Chapter 5** on text editing and string commands.

Chapter 6 picks up with lists, listbox widgets, files and directories. **Chapter 7** delves into dialog boxes, covering crucial parts of your interface such as file open dialogs, font and search/replace dialogs.

The Tcl canvas widget, covered in **Chapter 8**, allows you to create drawing items such as lines and arcs. You can go much further, though, with the canvas widget and include text items and embed any Tk widget into the canvas. You'll find the canvas great for displaying charts of data, creating graphical file managers, and a host of other purposes. Chapter 8 also delves into bitmaps and images, including Tk support for GIF imagery.

CHAPTER 1

Your First Tcl Programs

This chapter covers:

- Starting to program in Tcl
- Basic Tcl syntax
- A few quirks of how Tcl works
- How to look up reference information on Tcl and Tk commands
- Creating a Tcl script file
- Double-clicking on script files on Windows
- Turning a Tcl script into a UNIX command
- Using the `source` command to load Tcl scripts

What Is a Tcl Program?

A Tcl program is simply a bunch of commands. Like a DOS batch file or UNIX shell script, all you need to do is place commands one after another. There is no `main` function, so familiar to C programmers, nor is there a `WinMain`. There are just commands.

Some key points to remember are that, because Tcl is an interpreted language, every single command is text. You can build new commands at runtime by building up new strings and then executing them, a very clever way of creating applications that modify themselves. *Everything is text.* You'll see this mantra throughout this book. The reason is that the source of most beginners' problems with Tcl is the fact that everything is text.

Tcl comes with a graphical toolkit called Tk that allows you to create graphical applications quickly, one of the main focuses of this book.

The Tcl interpreter executes Tcl scripts. This interpreter, called **wish**, short for windowed shell, can run any Tcl command as well as commands you create on your own.

In addition to **wish**, a Tcl interpreter that allows you to execute any Tcl or Tk command, you can also use **tclsh**, short for Tcl shell. Unlike **wish**, **tclsh** supports only the basics of the Tcl language and does not allow you to create any windows or menus as provided by Tk. If your scripts work only with files, then you may want to avoid the overhead of **wish** and use the smaller **tclsh**.

Both interpreters can be used to execute Tcl script files and to run interactively. In interactive mode, you can type in Tcl commands one at a time. This is very useful for testing commands. In batch mode, **tclsh** or **wish** will execute a Tcl script and then automatically quit.

The **tclsh** interpreter is built with just the Tcl language, not the Tk toolkit for graphical applications. This means that if you use **tclsh** to execute your Tcl scripts, you won't get any menus, scrollbars, or other graphical elements. However, **tclsh** is good for commonly run nongraphical tasks, like a backup script.

On the other hand, **wish** is an interpreter with Tk, so you can make graphical widgets to your heart's content. Throughout this book, **wish** will be the interpreter of choice in most circumstances.

Make a Wish

The first step, then, is to find your **wish** interpreter. Normally, **wish** is named simply that, **wish**. On Windows systems, you may find **wish** named **wish.exe** or **wish80.exe**, following Windows conventions. The name **wish80.exe** is based on version 8.0 of **wish**. Your version of **wish** may have a higher or lower version number. You can use the Windows **Explorer** search commands to find **wish.exe** on your system, but you can often just look in the *Start* menu and avoid having to search your hard disk.

Furthermore, when installing **wish** on Windows, you can choose which folder in the *Start* menu the application's icons appear in. Tcl defaults to *Start/Programs/Tcl*.

To get the most from this book, you'll want version 8.0 or later of **wish**, although, if you have an earlier version, you can still get a lot of use out of it. Version 4.1 was the first version that officially supported Windows and the Macintosh, an important point in making cross-platform Tcl scripts. Version 4.2 added standard convenience, color, and file dialog boxes. Version 8.0 took care of many of the details that bedeviled Tcl script writers, especially when creating cross-platform scripts. Version 8.0 added more standardized fonts and colors in addition to native widgets on Windows. This book is written to Tcl/Tk 8.0, but you should still be able to take advantage of most of the book if you use an earlier version. Tcl also remains remarkably compatible, so versions higher than 8.0 should work fine with the examples in this book. The basics of the language have not changed for many versions.

If you are still using an earlier version, you'll need to modify some of the example scripts. For best results, get Tcl 8.0 and Tk 8.0 or higher. If you're running an older version, Tcl 7.6 and Tk 4.2 should work fine for most of the examples. Using the latest version, of course, will get you the best feature set and the most bug fixes.

Checking the Version

To check the version number of **wish**, run the command (**wish**).

WINDOWS

On Windows 95 or NT, you can select the **wish** program icon in the *Start* menu. On Windows NT or 95, you can also launch a DOS shell window and run **wish** from there. On regular Windows 3.1, this won't work because **wish** is a Win32 application that requires Windows. This is one of the differences between Windows NT and regular Windows.

When you run **wish**, you'll see a blank window, as shown in Figure 1.1, and a command prompt, normally a percent (%) character in a terminal or console window.

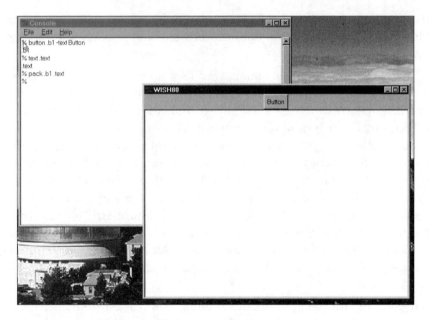

Figure 1.1 The **wish** window.

On Windows, you'll see an extra console window where you can enter Tcl commands at the **wish** prompt, usually %. On UNIX, the console window is the shell window you launched **wish** from.

At the **wish** prompt, enter the following command:

```
puts $tk_version
```

wish will print the response on the next line. Many Tcl commands work like this, especially the `puts` command (short for *put string*), which prints out a text string.

If the response is 8.0 (or higher), then you're in business. If the response is something like 3.6, then you won't be able to run all the programs in this book.

```
% puts $tk_version
8.0
```

CD-ROM

Don't worry, though, the CD-ROM that comes with this book has the latest version of Tcl and Tk as of this writing. For older versions, the **wish** and Tk version number should be at least in the 4s, such as 4.2, and Tcl in the 7s, such as 7.6 to work with most of the examples in this book.

Now, you've just executed your first Tcl command. The next step is to enter your first Tcl program.

A First Tcl Program

You can accuse me of being unoriginal, but the first program is the tried and true "Hello World." Enter the following line at the **wish** prompt:

```
button .b -text "Hello World" -command { exit }
```

Later, we'll go through each element of this command, which creates a pushbutton widget. After you enter it, you see nothing. You've created a widget, but it just isn't visible yet. This brings us to our second command and our second mantra:

The packer, controlled from the pack command, makes things visible.

You'll see this mantra just as often as the first.

You must execute the pack command to make the button widget visible:

```
pack .b
```

The pack command takes the name of the widget or widgets, in this case, the single widget named *.b* (yes, the leading period is part of its name), and places the widget in a window. The key part of the pack command, which you'll see in depth in Chapter 3, is how it places the widgets in the master— or application—widget. (Widgets in Tk appear in a hierarchy, which is described in depth in the section on Widget Names.)

Now you should see a widget in the **wish** window, as shown in Figure 1.2.

Figure 1.2 "Hello World" in Tcl.

NOTE   A **widget** is an item on the screen that users can interact with. Examples include a menu, a menu choice on a menu, a scrollbar and, in this case, a button. Virtually all graphical interfaces follow the idea of widgets. In most circumstances, a widget is a window with some smarts attached to it. Widgets usually know how to draw themselves and how to react to user input. In Tcl, a widget is a very high-level construct, which frees you from most of the low-level details of programming with widgets. This is one the advantages of a high-level scripting language.

The First Commands in Depth

The first example uses two Tk commands, `button` and `pack`. Tcl is most useful when its rather small command set is extended. Tk is one such extension. Tk extends the basic Tcl language with commands to create and manipulate a number of neat widgets (see Chapter 3 for more on widgets). The `button` command creates a button widget. A `button`, as you'd guess, is a pushbutton widget.

That's simple enough. The hard part is in all the options available for buttons and in button—and widget—names.

Widget Names

In Tk, all widgets appear in a hierarchy. The main reason for this is the fact that the underlying windowing systems, X and Win32, both follow this model for creating windows. (Each widget typically has its own window.)

An application must have a top-level window. Widgets, like menu bars and pushbuttons, go inside this top-level window or are nested inside other windows, which are called **containers** because they contain other widgets.

You can nest windows to almost any depth (you'll eventually run out of screen space).

Because of this hierarchy, there must be a top-level widget that encapsulates the whole application. In the case of Tk, this widget is named "." (that's right, a period). A child of the top-level widget (remember there is a hierarchy, so you can go down many levels) is named *.name*, where *name* is the name of the widget. With container widgets, such as the `frame` widget (see Chapter 3), the full widget name becomes something like *.container.name* or *.container.container2.name*. The idea of using a period to separate parts of the name is purely arbitrary. You just have to learn this.

Similar to dealing with files and directories, *.name* is the full path, the full name of the widget. In most Tk commands, you'll need the full path name of any widgets you use.

In this example, the widget is named *b*, and the full path name of the widget is *.b*. Thus, our `button` command creates a button named *.b*.

Button Options

In our example, we created a `button` with two command-line options, `-text` and `-command`. In fact, these are just a few of the options available with the `button` command (see Chapter 3 for more on these options). For now, though, we'll stick to the `-text` and `-command` options.

The `-text` option specifies the text to display in the button. If we change this option to be "This is new text", as in the following commands, we'll see a different widget, as shown in Figure 1.3.

Figure 1.3 A button widget displaying new text.

The following commands create a `button` widget with different text:

```
button .c -text "This is new text" -command { exit }
pack .c
```

10

The -command option specifies the Tcl commands, called a **script**, to execute when the user pushes the button. In most user interface toolkits, the command option is termed a **callback function**, because the toolkit calls you back when the button is activated. Because Tcl is a scripting language, this callback can be any set of Tcl code, such as the code we'll examine throughout this book.

In this example, the Tcl code to execute is { exit }, where { and } are used to mark the beginning and end of the code (there's a more technical definition we'll see later) and the command executed is exit, which, as you'd guess, exits a Tcl program. Throughout this book, you'll learn more and more Tcl commands. In addition, you can write your own commands, in Tcl or C.

In Tcl, most commands, such as the button command, are one line long. This comes from Tcl's roots as a command-line interpreter. Therefore, if we have really long text that we want to divide up among a number of lines, we need to use a \ (backslash) character at the end of one line as a line continuation marker. This continues the current line onto the next line. Whenever the backslash occurs as the last character of a line, it is interpreted as a line continuation marker. The following example shows this.

```
button .d \
   -text "This is longer text" \
   -command { exit }
```

This example shows a single Tcl command that spans a number of lines. To the Tcl interpreter (such as **wish**), this command is simply one line long because of the line continuation markers.

Forgetting or misplacing a \ character is a common problem in Tcl scripts.

Looking Up Information on Tcl and Tk Commands

This book forms a getting-started guide, not an exhaustive reference manual. Because of that, at various times you'll need to see the Tcl reference for a particular command. Tcl comes with documentation in the form of on-line manual pages on UNIX and a Windows Help file on Windows. This documentation covers every Tcl and Tk command.

On UNIX, you can use the **man** program to look up more information on the Tk button command:

```
man button
```

Usually, Tcl manual entries are stored in section n, in a location such as **/usr/local/man/mann**. You can also use the graphical on-line manual browsers **xman**, which comes with the X Window System on most UNIX systems or **TkMan**, a manual browser written in Tcl/Tk. Figure 1.4 shows the UNIX manuals.

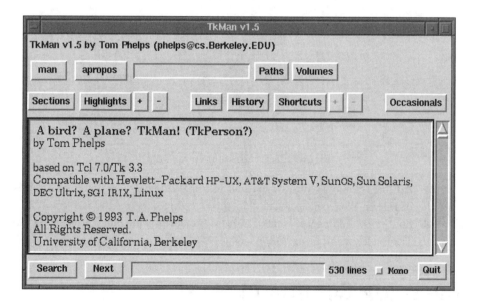

Figure 1.4 Browsing Tk documentation with **TkMan**.

WINDOWS

Windows, too, comes with a graphical help browser, which virtually all Windows applications support; **wish** is no exception. You can launch this help by clicking on the Tcl/Tk Manual icon from the Windows *Start* menu. Once the help system starts up, you'll see a listing of all the pages in one help topic. When you choose a topic, such as the `button` command, you'll see a window like that in Figure 1.5.

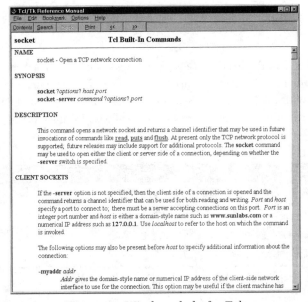

Figure 1.5 Windows help for Tcl.

CD-ROM

All the Tcl and Tk on-line manual information is also available as a series of HTML Web pages, located in the **doc** directory on the CD-ROM. The SunScript Web pages, located at **http://sunscript.sun.com**, also provide the Tcl and Tk manuals as Web pages.

The pack Command

The `pack` command is much harder to explain than the `button` command. The `pack` command places child widgets, such as *.b*, in a window, usually the main **wish** window and makes the widgets appear. This command, with its many options, is very useful for controlling the layout of your Tcl scripts, as shown in Chapter 3.

Up to now, you've had to type in each Tcl command one at a time. Now, you can place these commands in a file and pass the file name to the **wish** interpreter for execution.

13

Making a Tcl Script from Our Commands

A Tcl script is merely an ASCII text file containing Tcl commands. (Remember the mantra that everything is text.) To create Tcl script files, you can use any text editor. On UNIX, this includes popular editors such as **emacs**, **vi**, **dtpad**, and **nedit**. The CD-ROM contains a text editor called **tkedit** which you may like, as shown in Figure 1.6. The program TkDesk, discussed in the Introduction, also edits files.

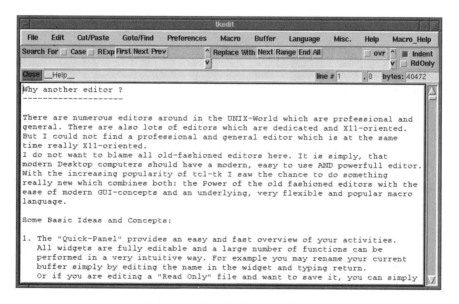

Figure 1.6 The **tkedit** text editor.

On Windows, you can use **WordPad**, **Notepad**, or a host of other text editors. Microsoft Word or other word processors that can save to text work

14

fine, too. I've received e-mail recommending a Windows shareware program called **Homesite** (used mainly for editing Web pages) as a viable text editor on Windows for scripting languages like Tcl or Perl.

WINDOWS

Some of the Windows text editors, like **WordPad**, will append an extra *.txt* to the end of your file names on the naive assumption that you really want all ASCII text files to end with a *.txt* extension when you really want a *.tcl* extension. To make matters worse, by default the Windows **Explorer** doesn't show the file name extensions (you can change this from the *View* menu in Explorer). You may experience this problem when you try to access a file like **hello.tcl** and cannot find it; the real file name may be **hello.tcl.txt**. The best solution for this problem is to pick another text editor.

CD-ROM

If you're at a loss for a text editor, you can try the example editor, **textedit.tcl**, located in the **book** directory on the CD-ROM, and shown in Figure 1.7.

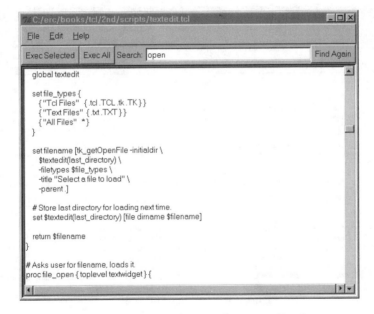

Figure 1.7 The simple text editor **textedit.tcl**.

This simple editor is written entirely in Tcl/Tk, using code from the various chapters in this book (mostly Chapter 5). As a text editor, this needs a lot of work, and you're welcome to practice your Tcl scripting by extending **textedit.tcl**.

Text editors form an integral tool for software development, and all of us have our own preconceived notions about what we like. So, pick the editor that works best for you. After you've chosen a text editor, the next step is to create a Tcl script file.

Enter the following commands into an editor and save the file as **hello.tcl**:

```
#
# Simple Hello world script.
#
button .b -text "Hello World" -command { exit }
pack .b

# hello.tcl
```

In this Tcl code, a # indicates a comment. All text from a # to the end of a line is ignored. (You can play some clever games with the way Tcl determines the end of a line. We'll get into that shortly.)

All the example files for this book are located in the **book** directory on the CD-ROM.

To run the **hello.tcl** file from Tcl, you can use the following commands, depending on your operating system.

On UNIX, the **wish** interpreter will be named **wish8.0** (the *8.0* may be replaced with the version number of your **wish** interpreter, such as *4.2*) or simply **wish**, normally a symbolic link to the latest version. To run the **hello.tcl** script, your command will then be

```
wish8.0 hello.tcl
```

or

```
wish hello.tcl
```

On Windows (except for Windows 3.1), you need to start up an MS-DOS prompt window. From the DOS prompt, typically `C:\>`, you then launch **wish80.exe**. (The *80* may get replaced by your version of **wish**, such as **wish42.exe**.) The Windows command will be

```
wish80 hello.tcl
```

You can also double-click on the **hello.tcl** entry in the Windows Explorer if you have an association between files ending in *.tcl* and the **wish** interpreter. Normally the Tcl installation sets this up for you.

Older versions of **wish**, such as with Tk 3.*x*, require a `-f` flag before the file name, making the command **wish -f hello.tcl**.

When you run the proper command for your system, you should then see a small window with a Hello World push button, as shown in Figure 1.2.

If you get an error that the **wish** program could not be found, check that Tcl is indeed installed (see Appendix B for instructions) and verify that the Tcl **bin** directory is indeed in your PATH. That is, in the list of directories the operating system checks for programs.

Making Your Tcl Scripts Look Like Real Programs

Running **wish** to launch your scripts is OK for testing and development, but we'd all like for Tcl scripts to appear the same as real programs. That is, we'd like to be able to run the program from the UNIX command line or the

Windows Explorer. The means to do this, as you'd suspect, differ between UNIX and Windows. (Don't be discouraged, the vast majority of Tcl/Tk works exactly the same on Windows and UNIX. Only a few areas differ, but unfortunately, many of these differences hit you just as you're getting started with Tcl.)

In the next sections, you'll see how to configure the operating system to launch your Tcl scripts on both Windows and UNIX.

Making Your Tcl Scripts Look Like Real Programs on Windows

Modern versions of Windows, including Windows 95 (and beyond), provide a registry that associates types of files—usually denoted by a file name extension such as *.tcl*—with an executable program, such as **wish80.exe**.

When you installed Tcl/Tk, as described in Appendix B, the installation program should have set up the proper file associations in the registry. To test this, try to double-click on the entry for **hello.tcl** in the Windows Explorer, as show in Figure 1.8. If this properly launches your first Tcl script, then all is OK.

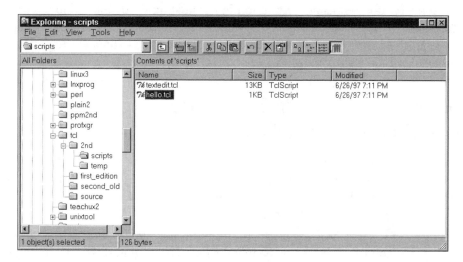

Figure 1.8 Double-click on the entry for **hello.tcl** in the Windows Explorer and see if the script runs.

If not, you can associate files ending in *.tcl* and *.tk*, the two most common file name extensions for Tcl applications, with the wish interpreter—**wish80.exe**—from the registry editor, **REGEDIT.EXE** (called **REGEDT32.EXE** on Windows NT). You can launch this application from the *Run...* choice on the Windows *Start* menu.

WARNING

Registry editors access low-level system information and can mess up your Windows system to a greater degree than you'd think possible, so be careful.

In most cases, installing the binary version of Tcl, as described in Appendix B, will take care of all the necessary associations. So, don't mess with registry editors unless you really have to.

Before changing anything, test to see if Windows already has the proper association, as described previously. In the registry editor, look for **HKEY_CLASSES_ROOT\TclScript\shell\open\command**, which should show something like `C:\tcl\bin\wish80.exe   "%1"` and **HKEY_CLASSES_ROOT \.tcl**, which should have a value of `TclScript`, for the association. See John Woram's excellent *The Windows 95 Registry* for more on the registry.

If everything works according to plan, you should be able to launch any Tcl script by double-clicking in the Windows Explorer. Unless noted otherwise, all the Tcl scripts in this book use a *.tcl* file name extension, to make it easier to launch from Windows.

Making Your Tcl Scripts Look Like Real Programs on UNIX

As you'd expect, UNIX provides different assumptions than Windows. On UNIX, the task is much easier because UNIX uses the concept of file permissions to govern which files can be executed. Any file with execute permission is treated as a program to run.

In most cases, UNIX expects any file with executable permissions to be a program compiled for your system. If not, you'll generally get an error launching the program. UNIX also has a long history of supporting shell scripts, ASCII text files that contain commands in a given scripting language. Sound familiar? It should. Tcl is merely another scripting language, albeit a very useful one.

The problem with shell scripts is that the ASCII script file is not executable in and of itself. Each script requires the proper interpreter, such as **wish8.0**, to run the script. The interpreter is the compiled program that can run. The script is merely data for the interpreter.

To help make shell scripts appear to be executable programs and to make launching these scripts easier, UNIX supports a special syntax. If the very first line of the script file starts with #! and the name of a interpreter program, UNIX will launch the interpreter program and pass that program the script file to execute. For example, UNIX abounds with Bourne shell scripts that start out with the following first line:

```
#!/bin/sh
```

The # starts a comment, so if the system does not support the special syntax, it ignores the whole line.

The UNIX Command Line

On UNIX, virtually all scripting languages (including Tcl), use the # character to mark the start of a comment. (Some scripting languages require that the # must be in the first column.)

This comment tells the command shell that you're running in, usually **csh** or **ksh**, which program to run to execute the script (in this case, **/bin/sh**). This is a handy way to request that a shell script be run under the interpreter for which it was designed. For example, I use the C shell (**csh**) for my daily work, but virtually all UNIX shell scripts are written in the Bourne shell (**sh**) language. This initial comment tells my **csh** to run **sh** for the script (rather than running another copy of **csh**).

This is just a convention, but most UNIX command shells like **sh**, **csh**, and **ksh** follow it. Because this convention is so widely followed, you can take advantage of this to ask the shell (usually **csh** or **ksh**) to run **wish**, the Tcl interpreter, instead. These Tcl scripts require **wish** or **tclsh**, so you'll probably want to use **wish**, because it supports Tk as well as plain old Tcl. In addition, because this first line is a comment, any shell that does not follow the convention will merely ignore the comment, so you're safe either way.

You'll want to place the path to your copy of **wish** in this type of specially formatted comment on the first line of your scripts, provided your script runs on UNIX. The hope is that the UNIX shell will see this and automatically launch the proper interpreter, **wish** in our case. If you put all this together and mark your Tcl scripts as executable files, then you can skip the **wish** part of the command line and merely type in the name of your script as a command, because the **wish** part is in the script, as part of this specially formatted comment. For example,

```
hello.tcl
```

Here's what you need to do. First, insert into the first line of our example script a comment similar to the following one:

```
#!/usr/local/bin/wish8.0
#
# Simple Hello world script.
#
button .b -text "Hello World" -command { exit }
pack .b

# hello.tcl
```

In this example, **/usr/local/bin/wish8.0** is the path to my Tcl interpreter. Your installation may vary, and, in fact, the name of your Tcl interpreter may vary.

To find out where your Tcl interpreter is located, enter the command `which wish8.0` at the shell prompt, as shown here:

```
$ which wish8.0
/usr/local/bin/wish8.0
```

If this command doesn't work, then either you don't have a **which** command, you're using a different version of Tcl/Tk, or you have not installed Tcl/Tk. See Appendix B for installing Tcl/Tk. If you're using a different version of Tcl/Tk, you can look for executables starting with **wish**, normally installed in **/usr/local/bin** (or **/usr/bin** on Linux).

After you've set up the proper starting comment to launch **wish**, you can make your **hello.tcl** file an executable file with the **chmod** command:

```
chmod +x hello.tcl
```

You should now be able to execute your script from the UNIX command line:

```
hello.tcl
```

If you have any problems, chances are your command shell doesn't support this convention. If so, you'll probably have a number of errors, because Tcl commands are not compatible with most UNIX shell commands (some are compatible, which can lead to interesting results if you execute a Tcl script as a Bourne shell script).

There's one main problem with this special first-line comment: some systems, especially Hewlett-Packard's HP-UX, allow only 32 characters in the path. Thus, long paths like **/usr5/local/tcl/Tcl8.0/bin/wish8.0** won't work. In that case, you can use this following trick:

```
#!/bin/sh
# This comment continues on in Tcl,
# but not in sh\
exec /usr5/local/tcl/Tcl8.0/bin/wish8.0 "$0" ${1+"$@"}

# If the above exec doesn't work,
# replace ${1+"$@"} with "$@".

# Place your Tcl code here.
# The file will get re-loaded under wish
# and the above comments will get skipped.
#
puts "argv0 = $argv0"
puts "argv  = $argv"
exit
```

Save this file as **exectest.tcl** and then mark it executable with **chmod**:

```
chmod +x exectest.tcl
```

Then, run it with a different number of command-line parameters to see the Tcl output from the `puts` commands, as shown here:

```
$ exectest.tcl 1 2 3 4 5 6
argv0 = exectest.tcl
argv  = 1 2 3 4 5 6

$ exectest.tcl first second
argv0 = exectest.tcl
argv  = first second
```

In each case, the name of the program to run is **exectest.tcl**. We know that **exectest.tcl** is not a compiled program but rather a Tcl script. The magic of the `#!` construct tells UNIX how to run the script as a program with the proper **wish** interpreter.

The preceding code asks the shell to run **/bin/sh** to execute the script. From **sh**'s perspective, the first thing that happens is to call **exec** and execute **wish** with the same file and command-line arguments. That is, **wish** will get the same file that **sh** is executing. This trick works by cleverly taking advantage of how different scripting languages treat comments and lines and commands.

Tcl allows the backslash character, \, to extend a line. In your script file, the single command extends over one line of text. But to Tcl, this is treated as one single line of text. For example, the following comment extends over two lines of text, but Tcl treats it as one long comment:

```
# This is a long comment\
This is still a comment.
```

Thus, in the following construct, Tcl ignores the `exec` command:

```
#!/bin/sh
# This comment continues on in Tcl,
# but not in sh\
exec /usr/local/bin/wish8.0 "$0" ${1+"$@"}
```

Since **sh** doesn't understand line continuation characters on comments, **sh** tries to execute the exec command, which stops **sh** anyway and launches **wish8.0**.

NOTE Tcl also supports an exec command, covered in Chapter 10. In the preceding example, though, the exec command is a Bourne shell, or **sh**, command and not a Tcl command. Tcl never sees the exec, because to Tcl, that's all part of one long comment.

This convoluted way to run Tcl scripts breaks down because of one main problem: Not everyone installs Tcl in the same location. Although this will work for your testing, your scripts will get defeated by other users who install Tcl in different directories.

To get around this, you can skip the full path for the with interpreter, as follows:

```
#!/bin/sh
# This comment continues on in Tcl,
# but not in sh\
exec wish8.0 "$0" ${1+"$@"}
```

This command tells the Bourne shell, **/bin/sh**, to launch the program named **wish8.0**. **sh** looks for **wish8.0** in all the standard locations defined in the PATH environment variable. So long as **wish8.0** is installed and the directory is in your PATH environment variable, this will work to launch the Tcl script.

With this, our script changes to the following:

```
#!/bin/sh
# This comment continues on in Tcl,
# but not in sh\
exec wish8.0 "$0" ${1+"$@"}

# If the above exec doesn't work,
# replace ${1+"$@"} with "$@".

# Place your Tcl code here.
```

```
# The file will get re-loaded under wish
# and the above comments will get skipped.
#
puts "argv0 = $argv0"
puts "argv  = $argv"
exit

# exectest.tcl
```

The two things that can go wrong are that the directory where **wish8.0** is not in the user's PATH or that the user doesn't have a program named **wish8.0**. (Maybe the user has **wish8.1**, or **wish4.2**, etc.)

If you distribute your Tcl code, you'll need to deal with these two potential problems. You can either tell users to edit the top lines of your Tcl files or provide an automated means to specify which version of Tcl to run. See Chapter 14 on advanced applications for more on this issue.

What Happens If You Try This From tclsh?

In addition to problems with UNIX shells, if you try to run the **hello.tcl** script under **tclsh** instead of **wish**, you'll get an error message like the following:

```
invalid command name "button"
```

Of course, this is because **tclsh** doesn't have the pack or button commands defined. These commands are part of Tk, an add-on to Tcl. (You could add these commands individually to Tcl, but then that is exactly what Tk has done.)

Testing Your Tcl Programs

When you double-click on a Tcl script from Windows or launch a Tcl script from a graphical interface on UNIX, you lose most of the error output by the Tcl interpreter—and during early development, most scripts have a few errors. Because of this, I usually start out working with the **wish** command prompt, so that I can better see any errors that arise. Even though you can enter whole commands, this isn't very convenient.

When I'm starting out with a new script, I usually edit with a text editor, launch **wish** with no arguments, and then load the script into the already-running **wish** with the source command. The source command loads in a Tcl script file and executes the commands in that file. The syntax is simple:

```
source filename
```

If the file is in a separate directory, you also need to type in a path to the file, such as:

```
source /eric/examples/example1.tcl
```

On Windows, you can use either the forward slash favored by UNIX, /, or the backward slash used by DOS, \. But, remember that the backslash is a special character in Tcl, so you'll need two: \\. For example,

```
source \\eric\\examples/example1.tcl
```

You can use source to load most of the example files throughout this book. In fact, I'd recommend that approach to better see any errors from **wish**.

Now you have started the short learning curve of Tcl and Tk scripting. In Chapter 2, you'll find a lot about the basics of the Tcl syntax, including some tricky areas that can mess you up.

Summary

This chapter introduces how to create graphical applications with Tcl and Tk by showing the obligatory "Hello World" program. You should also know how to look up information on Tcl and Tk commands. In this book, you'll find the most important options for Tcl commands. This is not a reference, though, so the on-line manuals will be a big help as you learn Tcl.

By now, you should be able to create a Tcl script file and run this file on your system, be it Windows or UNIX. I hope you're not overwhelmed by the operating system differences. In almost all respects, Tcl scripts work the same on all supported platforms. This chapter covers more system differences than most, as you'll see as you read ahead.

In Chapter 2, you'll see what the curly braces, { and }, really mean, as well as the basics of Tcl syntax, which is necessary for all Tcl programming.

Tcl/Tk Commands Introduced in This Chapter

```
button
pack
puts
source
```

Tcl Basics

This chapter covers:

- Starting to program in Tcl
- Tcl syntax
- Tcl variables
- Controlling the flow of the script
- Built-in procedures in Tcl
- Writing your own procedures
- Math in Tcl and math procedures

Tcl Syntax

This and the next chapter are perhaps the most important in this book. In this chapter, you'll cover the basics of Tcl syntax and learn how to get what you want done with Tcl. It may be hard to plow through a chapter on syntax, but you'll use each topic introduced here over and over again.

Syntax is usually terribly boring. Luckily, the Tcl language itself is exceedingly simple, making for a small interpreter. The Tcl interpreter deals solely with commands and arguments. Each distinct line (remember the line continuation marker, \, from Chapter 1) starts with a command. Anything else on the line is an argument that gets passed to that command. *Everything* is text.

Thus, a Tcl script really looks like the following:

```
command1 arg1 arg2 arg3 ...
command2 arg1 arg2 arg3 ...
command3 arg1 arg2 arg3 ...
command4 arg1 arg2 arg3 ...
...
```

In fact, to help plow through the Tcl syntax, Table 2.1 provides the one-minute introduction to Tcl.

Table 2.1 The one-minute introduction to Tcl syntax.

Syntax	Means
`command arg1 arg2 arg3`	Execute the command, with the given arguments.
`"Text in quotes"`	Pass the text between the braces as one argument, performing command and variable substitution.
`{Text in braces}`	Pass the text between the quotes as one argument; defer substitution until later.
`$variable`	Substitute the value of the given variable.
`[command arg]`	Execute the command; then substitute the return value in place of the entire command between the square brackets.
`command arg1 \` `    arg2`	Extend command over one line.

These are the basics. In the next sections, you'll see all this and more, along with a plethora of Tcl's built-in commands.

Tcl scripts contain a sequence of commands, one after another, with each command on its own line. Tcl stretches the definition of a line a bit, though.

Even though some parts may look like involved syntax (especially for the clever—or deranged—if and while commands shown later in this chapter), a Tcl script is really made up of a set of commands and their arguments, each command on a separate line.

N O T E You can also place two (or more) commands on a line, if you separate them with a semicolon, ;, character, as shown in the following example:

```
set var1 Marley ; set var2 Tosh
```

The set command sets a variable to a value. You'll see more of this in the section on Tcl variables.

Commands and their arguments are separated by spaces. That's how the Tcl interpreter divides one part from another. That's simple enough. Unfortunately, it gets more complex. From these simple roots, you start to see some complexity—and quirks—of the language.

Commands and their arguments are separated by spaces. How then can you get spaces into text you want to display? Here comes the first exception to the rules. If you want to place spaces in an argument, you can enclose the full argument in double quotation marks, " ". This handy piece of syntax appeared in an example in the last chapter:

```
button .c -text "This is new text" -command { exit }
```

The text *This is new text* is treated as one single argument and passed to the button command.

The Tcl interpreter breaks this command into the following elements:

```
button
.c
-text
"This is new text"
-command
{ exit }
```

As you can see, the curly braces, { and }, are a lot like the double quotation marks, in that spaces are preserved inside the braces. These curly braces form the key to Tcl scripting, because they defer execution until later.

Tcl uses the curly braces as a means to group items together. Everything enclosed within curly braces becomes one single argument to a Tcl command. In the preceding example, { exit } is one argument. This means that we can extend the definition of a Tcl command to appear more like the following:

```
command { arg1 }  { arg2 } { arg3 } ...
```

Within the curly braces, each argument may contain many Tcl commands or a list of data. For example,

```
command {set a 1; set b 2} {set c 3; set d 4}
```

This command receives two arguments, {set a 1; set b 2} and {set c 3; set d 4}. How the arguments are used is left to the command. Each command determines how it treats each argument.

In addition, after the start of a curly brace, Tcl treats all data following as part of the argument until it finds the ending brace. For example, the following command sets a variable to hold textual data with a space:

```
set var1 {Bob Marley}
```

All the data from the starting curly brace to the ending curly brace is considered part of the argument, so the set command has two arguments, var1 and {Bob Marley}. This is very important for understanding Tcl syntax.

You can even place new lines within the braces. For example, the Tcl syntax allows for the following to be a single command:

```
command { arg1 } {
    arg2
} {
    arg3
}
```

or

```
command {
    set a 1
    set b 2
} {
    set c 3
    set d 4
}
```

Tcl treats this example as a single command on what it thinks is a single line. The curly braces allow you to align your commands in a more readable fashion.

In fact, Tcl extends this one step farther and treats `if` as an ordinary command, not as part of the syntax of the language. The `if` command looks like

```
if {expression_argument} {action_argument}
```

You'll see more about the `if` command in the section on Controlling the Flow of the Script. For now, take a careful look at how Tcl uses curly braces, { and }.

NOTE

You can also format this command as

```
if {expression_argument} {
    action_argument
}
```

The Tcl interpreter treats this command the same as the previous command, that is, as one "line" of Tcl.

Some people prefer different indenting styles instead of the K&R style, which we have been using. (K&R comes from the C language book, *The C Programming Language*, written by B. W. Kernighan and D. M. Ritchie.) But watch out, Tcl is not a free-form language. The following style will *not* work:

WARNING

```
if {expression_argument}
{
        action_argument
}
```

Can you tell why? The Tcl interpreter will break up these statements into two commands:

```
if {expression_argument }
{ action_argument }
```

This is not likely your intent and generally creates a syntax error—but not always! You will find that your one command is now treated as two separate commands. To keep this as one command, you need to ensure that the curly brace starts the next argument from the first actual line of text, as shown here:

```
if {expression_argument} {
        action_argument
}
```

The line ending in the open brace tells Tcl to continue processing the same command until the interpreter finds the closing brace. This may seem strange, but remember that Tcl is not a free-form language and that, even though other languages such as Java or C++ treat if as a part of the syntax, Tcl treats if as a Tcl command. This will become more apparent as you learn more Tcl commands.

If you work with Java, C, or C++ and you don't like this indenting style, you'll need to pay careful attention to your Tcl code. This problem hits quite a few people learning Tcl.

The curly braces are like double quotation marks except for the following:

- You can nest sets of curly braces, for example, { { } } (not that this particular argument will do much).
- The curly braces delineate code to be executed later. This is very important.

- The interpreter does not make **substitutions** within the curly braces until executed (later). You'll see more on substitutions under the section titled Variables and Substitutions.

One of the most useful features of the Tcl language is the use of variables.

Tcl Variables

Like virtually all programming and scripting languages, Tcl lets you store a value (or a list of values) into something called a variable. A **variable** is a lot like the c = a + b you learned back in algebra. Tcl lets you pick a name and then use that name to represent a value. In computer terms, you set the value into the variable.

To set a value into a variable, you use the set command:

```
set var 6
```

You may want to test out this command, and the others in the chapter, using **wish** (or **tclsh**) in interactive mode. You can also use **tclsh**, but because so much of this book uses graphical commands, which are available in **wish** but not **tclsh**, the examples will stick with **wish**.

Type in **wish** at your DOS or shell command-line prompt. On Windows, you can simply select **wish** from the *Start* menu. After you start **wish**, you should see the **wish** prompt, a percent sign character, % (or something like tcl>, if you started **tclsh** instead of **wish**). At the prompt, you can type in any Tcl command you want.

When you type in set var 6, you'll notice that **wish** prints out the value set into the variable:

```
% set var 6
6
```

(Don't type the % character, **wish** does that.)

Most Tcl commands print out their return values, unless the return value is used for some other command.

N O T E

Variables in Tcl are stored as text strings, even though the preceding example could fool you into thinking it is a number; it's really stored as a string. (A **string** is computerese for a sequence of characters, such as *ABC*.) A nice part about Tcl is that the string can grow as large as necessary, so you don't have to worry about string lengths or allocating memory (like you have to do in C and C++ programs).

You can set any type of value into a variable. For example,

```
set var Marley
```

You can see what's stored in a variable using the `puts` (short for *put string*) command:

```
% puts $var
Marley
```

Notice the dollar sign, $. This is our first experience of variable substitution, one of the trickier parts of Tcl.

Variables and Substitutions

The dollar sign signifies **variable substitution**, which substitutes the value of the variable in place of the variable. That is, if you have `$var`, this tells the Tcl interpreter to substitute the value stored in the variable in place of the string `"$var"`. Remember that everything in Tcl is text, so the interpreter would have no way of knowing whether you wanted the value held in *var* (*Marley*, from our example), or the string `"var"` itself. Hence the $ for variable substitution. There's no particular reason for using a $, you just have to remember this.

Place the $ before the variable name, e.g., `$var`, to have the interpreter substitute in the current value held in the variable *var*. The trick to remember is that the value substituted is the value held in *var* when it is parsed.

You can sometimes get into problems with this, which is why the curly braces, { and }, defer execution (and parsing) until later.

If $var means to substitute the contents of the variable named *var*, how can you display a string in Tcl with the letters "$var"? Well, you use the backslash (familiar to C programmers) with the dollar sign, \$.

Try the following commands:

```
set var 6
set var2 $var
set var3 \$var
```

Before you read ahead, you should already know what values will be stored in each of these variables. If you don't, try out the commands one at a time:

```
% set var 6
6
% set var2 $var
6
% set var3 \$var
$var
```

These examples just use the set command. The same concepts apply to all Tcl commands, such as the expr (expression) command, shown next.

```
set var4 42
expr 2 * $var4
```

You should see the result 84. The expr command takes in most kinds of math or logical operations and returns the result. In addition to variable substitution, there's also command substitution.

Command Substitution

Many times you need to save the result of a command and use that value as an argument for another command. The way to do this is through the magic of **command substitution**.

If you see the square braces, [and], in a command, this means that the contents between the square braces are to be parsed and executed first; then the results should be substituted into the overall command, as shown in the following example:

```
set var5 [expr 2 * $var4]
```

In this code, the [expr 2 * $var4] part gets executed first, and the result, 84, is then substituted to make a new command:

```
set var5 84
```

You can use any valid Tcl command within the square braces command-substitution markers; you aren't limited to the handy expr command. You can also nest the embedded commands. For example,

```
puts [set var6 [expr $var5 + 1] ]
```

If you type in this command, you should see the result, 85, printed out. Also, the variable *var6* gets set to the same value.

The Tcl interpreter works in what is called two-phase execution. In the first phase, the interpreter parses substitutions like the dollar sign and back slash. In the second phase, the commands get executed. If you nest things, such as with the square braces command-substitution markers, then this two-phase process is started again, for the data within the [and] characters. This is really very simple, but it can trip you up if you aren't careful.

Table 2.2 shows the various types of substitution in Tcl.

Table 2.2 Variable and command substitution.

Tcl	Meaning
$*variable*	Substitute variable value.
${*variable*}*text*	Prepend *variable* value onto *text* with no spaces.
[expr 1+1]	Substitute results of command.

`"text $variable"`	Substitute *variable* into quoted text.
`{text $variable}`	Don't substitute *variable* into quoted text; defer to later.

The `${variable}` syntax looks rather odd. It allows you to substitute the value stored in a variable into a text string with no spaces, as you can see in the following example:

```
set time_of_day 4
puts ${time_of_day}pm
```

The result of the last command is

```
4pm
```

There's a much better way to do this using the `format` command; see the section on Built-In Procedures in Tcl. It's important to know how the `${variable}` syntax is an exception to the normal { and } rules.

N O T E

Worrying about the curly braces, along with how and when substitutions apply, is the most difficult part of learning Tcl. If you get frustrated now and then, just keep trying different combinations and try to see how the interpreter will treat your code.

N O T E

You can test out how Tcl substitutes with the handy `subst` command, which uses the following syntax:

```
subst -nobackslashes -nocommands -novariables string
```

All the *no* items are optional: `-nobackslashes` means skip back slashes (for multiline commands), `-nocommands` means skip command substitution, and `-novariables` means skip variable substitution. Look at the following commands and output:

```
% set var5 84
84
```

```
% subst {set var6 $var5 }
set var6 84
% subst -novariables {set var6 $var5 }
set var6 $var5
```

The first `subst` command performs a full substitution and extracts the value of *var5*, 84, replacing that part of the command. The second `subst` command explicitly turns off variable substitution.

Changing Data in Variables

In addition to the `set` command, Tcl provides other means to modify the values stored in variables, as shown in Table 2.3.

Table 2.3 Changing data in variables.

Command	Meaning
append *variable values*...	Append one or more *values* to *variable*.
incr *variable amount*	Increment *variable* by 1 or by *amount*.
set *variable value*	Set *value* into *variable*.
unset *variable1 variable2*...	Unset *variable1, variable2,* and so on.

With the `incr` (short for increment) command, the optional *amount* must be an integer value. Otherwise, `incr` adds 1 to the value stored in the *variable*. This value should be an integer.

You can store individual values into a variable, and you can also store multiple values in an array.

Array Variables

Tcl provides what is called associative arrays. An **associative array** associates a key name with a value. Each value in the array has a key name. You can treat an array as one identifier that represents a set of variables (called **keys**) and values.

N O T E This is a lot different from most programming languages. In most programming languages, an array holds a set of values that are indexed with numbers. In Tcl, an array holds a set of variables and values.

The syntax for naming an element in an array is

arrayname(element_name)

where *arrayname* is the name of the array and *element_name* is the name of one of the elements (keys) in the array. To extract a value of an array element, you use variable substitution the same way as before

$arrayname(element_name)

An example will help:

```
set employee(name) "Eric Foster-Johnson"
set employee(city) "St. Paul"
set employee(state) "Minnesota"
set employee(attitude) "Thinks empowerment is an evil plot"
```

The array *employee* now holds four elements—four separate values tied together with one name. These elements are *name, city, state*, and *attitude*, soon to be on I.D. cards everywhere.

The standard $ syntax for accessing the value of a variable still holds, only now the variable name is a bit more complex, as the next example shows:

```
% puts $employee(name)
Eric Foster-Johnson
% puts $employee(attitude)
Thinks empowerment is an evil plot
% puts $employee(state)
Minnesota
```

40

What you are doing is building the full name of the element within the array.

To help you work with arrays, Tcl offers a number of helper commands. The `parray` command prints all the elements of an array:

```
% parray employee
employee(attitude) = Thinks empowerment is an evil plot
employee(city)     = St. Paul
employee(name)     = Eric Foster-Johnson
employee(state)    = Minnesota
```

NOTE The order of the items in the array is not necessarily the order in which you entered them. Usually the items are alphabetized, but you cannot depend on this. If you need the items in a certain order, you'll need to arrange the output yourself.

The `array` Command

The `array` command offers a multitude of options, all of which pertain to, you guessed it, arrays. Each option controls how the `array` command works and the parameters that are required. You'll see more of these command families with the `string` command in Chapter 5 and the `file` command in Chapter 6. Table 2.4 lists the basic options for the `array` command, while Table 2.5 lists the search-related options.

Table 2.4 The basic options for the `array` command.

Command	Usage
`array exists name`	Returns 1 if *name* is really the name of an array variable.
`array get name`	Returns a list of variable/value pairs of all the items in the array.
`array names name pattern`	Returns all the array item names in the array that match the (optional) *pattern*.

array set *name list*	Sets values in array from list; list should be in the same format as returned by the array get command.
array size *name*	Returns the number of elements in the array.

To try out the array commands, enter the following into **wish** or **tclsh**, after you enter in the *employee* array as shown previously

```
% array exists employee
1
% array get employee
attitude {Thinks empowerment is an evil plot} state Minnesota city {St.
Paul} name {Eric Foster-Johnson}
% array names employee
attitude state city name
% array size employee
4
```

The array set command is a little more complex. It expects a list in the same format as returned by the array get command. You can use array set, then, to copy one array to another, as shown next (and again using the same *employee* array):

```
#
# Tcl array set example.
#

# Set values into test array.
set employee(name) "Eric Foster-Johnson"
set employee(city) "St. Paul"
set employee(state) "Minnesota"
set employee(attitude) "Thinks empowerment is an evil plot"

# Copy this array.
```

```
array set new_emp [array get employee]
parray new_emp
```

```
# arrayset.tcl
```

When you run the **arrayset.tcl** script, you should see output like the following:

```
new_emp(attitude) = Thinks empowerment is an evil plot
new_emp(city)     = St. Paul
new_emp(name)     = Eric Foster-Johnson
new_emp(state)    = Minnesota
```

Searching Through Arrays

There are also a host of options to the `array` command for searching through an array, as shown in Table 2.5.

Table 2.5 Searching arrays with the `array` command.

Command	Use
`array anymore name searchid`	Returns 1 (true) if anymore items are in the array for a given *searchId*; 0 (false) otherwise.
`array donesearch name searchid`	Stops an array search.
`array nextelement name searchid`	Returns the name of the next element in the array for the given search ID.
`array startsearch name`	Returns a search ID for an item-by-item search in the array.

To better see how the array searching options work, the following example shows how you can fill a list and then search through it, item by item, using the `array` command options from Table 2.5.

```
#
# Tcl array search example.
#

# Set values into test array.
set employee(name) "Eric Foster-Johnson"
set employee(city) "St. Paul"
set employee(state) "Minnesota"
set employee(attitude) "Thinks empowerment is an evil plot"

# Search through all elements of the array.
set searchId [array startsearch employee]

# Loop for all items in array from search.
while { [array anymore employee $searchId] } {

    set element [array nextelement employee $searchId]

# Note use of quotes to
        # make one argument to puts.
    puts "$element = $employee($element)"
}

# Terminate the search.
array donesearch employee $searchId

# arsearch.tcl
```

We cheat a bit by using the while command, which is explained later
under the section on Controlling the Flow of the Script.

Emulating Multidimensional Arrays

Tcl allows for single-dimensional arrays only. That is, you can place
only one single element name within the parenthesis. Certain situations
cry out for a multidimensional array, such as describing the squares on
Tic Tac Toe game, which uses a 3 × 3 square board. A two-dimensional
array would allow you to indicate each square on the board by its row

44

and column, the same method used in spreadsheet programs and the Battleship game.

You can fake multidimensional arrays by taking advantage of the fact that the array element names are just text (remember the mantra). So, an element name of *2,3* is perfectly valid:

```
set tic_tac_toe(2,2) X
set tic_tac_toe(3,1) O
```

This makes the *tic_tac_toe* array appear as if it really has two dimensions. But, if you print out the names in the array, with the `array names` command, you'll see the real story:

```
% array names tic_tac_toe
3,1 2,2
```

Special Arrays for Environment Variables

The *env* variable holds the set of environment variables that Windows NT, DOS, and UNIX all support. For example, DOS, NT, and UNIX typically support a `PATH` environment variable. You can access the contents of this environment variable, the same as for any other array. Simply use the name of the environment variable as the element name in the array, as in this example from Linux:

```
% puts $env(PATH)
/usr/local/bin:/bin:/usr/bin:/usr/X11/bin:
/usr/andrew/bin:/usr/openwin/bin:/usr/games:.:
/home/erc/bin:/usr/local/java/bin:
/usr/local/SmallEiffel/bin:
```

Under Windows NT, you'll see a much different list, depending on what is set up in the **System** choice from the **Control Panel** (abbreviated here):

```
% puts $env(PATH)
C:\WINDOWS\system32;C:\WINDOWS;
```

```
C:\DOS;C:\PERL\BIN;C:\TCL\BIN
```

You can use the `parray` command to print out the entire contents of the *env* array, as shown here on a Windows NT system:

```
% parray env

env(COMPUTERNAME)        = YONSEN
env(COMSPEC)             = C:\WINNT\system32\cmd.exe
env(DISPLAY)             = localhost:0
env(GLOB)                = D:\etc\glob.exe
env(HOME)                = .
env(OS)                  = Windows_NT
env(PATH)                = C:\WINNT\system32;
C:\WINDOWS;C:\DOS;C:\PERL\BIN;C:\TCL\BIN
env(PROCESSOR_ARCHITECTURE)   = x86
env(PROCESSOR_LEVEL)     = 5
env(TEMP)                = C:\temp
env(USERNAME)            = erc
env(WINDIR)              = C:\WINNT
```

As you can see, this usually results in a *lot* of output. You can also use the `array startsearch` and `array nextelement` commands to go through the *env* array.

Most environment variables differ greatly between Windows and UNIX. You'll need to be aware of this for cross-platform scripts.

CROSS-PLATFORM

Special Array to Describe Your Computing Platform

The special array *tcl_platform* contains information about your current platform. This array can be useful for determining what kind of system your script executes on. For example,

```
% parray tcl_platform
tcl_platform(machine)    = intel
tcl_platform(os)         = Windows NT
tcl_platform(osVersion)  = 4.0
tcl_platform(platform)   = windows
```

On a UNIX system, this looks more like the following:

```
% parray tcl_platform
tcl_platform(machine)    = 9000/715
tcl_platform(os)         = HP-UX
tcl_platform(osVersion)  = A.10.20
tcl_platform(platform)   = unix
```

CROSS-PLATFORM

I find the *platform* element the most useful for cross-platform Tcl scripts. `$tcl_platform(platform)` holds a value of `unix` on UNIX systems and `windows` on Windows systems. Usually, this is enough to handle most differences, because the UNIX versions of Tcl are very similar to each other. The Windows versions of Tcl are similarly very close, with most of the differences under Win32s on Windows 3.1.

Controlling the Flow of the Script

A Tcl script normally executes from the start to the end, top to bottom. Each command is parsed and then executed in turn, although you can defer execution using syntax elements like the curly braces, { and }.

This situation normally works fine until you want a trifle more complex script. To aid this, Tcl offers a number of commands that allow for branching and decision-making including `if-then` statements, `for`, and `while`. If you've ever used a programming language before, all these statements will be old hat. All you need to learn is the syntax under Tcl, so you'll probably want to just skim the next sections. However, you should pay attention to syntax.

Even though these statements look like real syntax, keep aware that `if`, `while`, `for`, and so on are merely Tcl commands with (usually long) arguments. The most common mistake I make is to think that the Tcl interpreter is smarter than it really is. Tcl is a very simple language. Most of the syntax, such as the `if` statement, is just for the sake of appearances. The `if` command is really just a normal Tcl command, although it is very easy to be fooled into thinking that the Tcl language supports the idea of an `if` statement.

The basic format of an `if` command looks like the following:

```
if {expression} then {action}
```

For example,

```
if {$i < 5} then {
    puts "$i is less than 5"
}
```

If you're used to C programming, you may mistake the curly braces, { and }, for C's parenthesis, (and), which surround the `if` expression. Unlike C, Tcl uses curly braces around the expression *and* the body.

N O T E

As mentioned previously, you must be careful when placing the curly braces. The following syntax is not correct:

WARNING

```
if { $i < 5 }
{
    puts "i is less than 5"
}
```

If you cannot tell why, see the beginning of this chapter. This is very important and a common source of problems.

The `then` part is optional. If the expression result is true, that is, if it generates a nonzero value (usually 1), then the action code gets executed. If the expression result is false (0), then the action code does not get executed.

The `if` command is really getting three arguments (or two, if you omit the optional `then` part), including an expression and the action. The curly braces allow you to place a lot of Tcl commands within one argument to the `if` command.

Expressions

The expression part of the `if` command can come from the result of any Tcl command or by using one of Tcl's built-in expression operators for comparing values, listed in Table 2.6.

Table 2.6 Expression operators for comparing values.

Operator	Meaning
`!v1`	Returns 1 if *v1* is 0; 0 otherwise.
`v1 < v2`	Returns 1 if *v1* is less than *v2*; 0 otherwise.
`v1 > v2`	Returns 1 if *v1* is greater than *v2*; 0 otherwise.
`v1 <= v2`	Returns 1 if *v1* is less than or equal to *v2*; 0 otherwise.
`v1 >= v2`	Returns 1 if *v1* is greater than or equal to *v2*; 0 otherwise.
`v1 == v2`	Returns 1 if *v1* is equal to *v2*; 0 otherwise.
`v1 != v2`	Returns 1 if *v1* is not equal to *v2*; 0 otherwise.
`v1 && v2`	Returns 1 if both *v1* and *v2* are nonzero; 0 otherwise.
`v1 || v2`	Returns 1 if either of *v1* or *v2* is nonzero; 0 otherwise.

In Tcl, true is 1 (or any nonzero value), and false is 0. The expressions in Table 2.6 allow you to check for a specific condition.

N O T E   For comparing text strings, see the `string compare` command in Chapter 5.

In addition to the basic `if` command, you can also provide an `else` part that gets executed if the expression result is false. The syntax follows:

```
if {expression} then {if-action} else {else-action}
```

To get even more complex, there's an `elseif`, which allows you to place multiple expressions in one statement:

```
if {expression1} then {
    if-action
} elseif {expression2} {
    elseif-action
} else {
    else-action
}
```

If the first expression (*expression1*) is false, then the `if` command tests the second expression (*expression2*). If that expression is true, the *elseif-action* gets executed. If all tests result in a false value, then the *else-action* gets executed. You can include more than one `elseif` part. For example,

```
if {expression1} then {
    if-action
} elseif {expression2} {
    elseif-action2
} elseif {expression3} {
    elseif-action3
} elseif {expression4} {
```

```
    elseif-action4
} elseif {expression5} {
    elseif-action5
} elseif {expression6} {
    elseif-action6
} else {
    else-action
}
```

You can go for a lot more levels than this. Sooner or later, though, your code will get too complex to be readable.

Better to Switch Than Fight

If you have a lot of tests, you can use the `switch` command. The basic syntax follows:

```
switch options string {
     pattern1 {action1}
     pattern2 {action2}

     ...
     default {default_action}
}
```

 You can skip the curly braces that surround all the patterns, but then you must use the line continuation marker, \, if your `switch` command extends beyond one line. There are some differences using this alternative format. See the following section Trade-Offs with the `switch` Command.

C programmers should be very familiar with the `switch` statement. `switch` takes a single string and compares it against a number of choices. If it finds a match, it executes the body of Tcl code following the matched choice. For example,

```
set animal cat
switch $animal {
    dog { puts "Dogs make good pets." }
    cat { puts "Cats are better." }
    platypus { puts "Watch out for the Platypus Society" }
    default { puts "Why did you pick a $animal?" }
}
```

If you type in this code into **tclsh** or **wish**, you'll see the following output:

```
Cats are better.
```

This code compares the value held in the variable *animal* against a number of choices: *dog*, *cat*, *platypus*, and *default*. Because the value of the variable *animal* was *cat*, the code after the *cat* choice gets executed.

The `default` section provides an escape clause. If none of the patterns match the initial value, the code body after `default` gets executed. Because users frequently ignore your careful instructions and enter bad values, you should include the `default` section in all `switch` commands.

If you have a number of choices that can use the same code, you can use a shorthand. If you place a minus sign, -, for the body, this means to use the body of the next choice. For example,

```
set animal cat
switch $animal {
    dog -
    cat -
    platypus { puts "A $animal makes a good pet." }
    default { puts "Why did you pick a $animal?" }
}
```

You'll see the following output from these commands:

```
A cat makes a good pet.
```

The *cat* and *dog* choices both execute the same code as the *platypus* choice.

Trade-Offs with the `switch` Command

There are two ways you can use the `switch` command, including the way we've been using so far:

```
switch options string {
    pattern1 {action1}
    pattern2 {action2}
    ...
    default {default_action}
}
```

This method places curly braces around the entire set of patterns and actions. With Tcl's simple syntax, this provides two side effects. First, all the patterns and actions are collected together into one argument to the `switch` command. Second, because all the patterns and actions are placed within curly braces, the Tcl interpreter defers all command and variable substitution until later, when the `switch` command is executed.

The second method for using the `switch` command removes the curly braces around all the patterns and actions:

```
switch options string \
    pattern1 {action1} \
    pattern2 {action2} \
    ... \
    default {default_action} \
```

Each pattern and each action now form a separate argument to the `switch` command. This means that normal command substitution (with square brackets, [and]) and variable substitution (using the dollar sign, $) take place as the command is parsed. Because of this, the second method can act differently from the first. I usually use the first method because it's easier to create multiline `switch` statements using curly braces.

More Expressive Comparisons

Up to now, all the values have exactly matched the initial string. The Tcl `switch` command is more flexible than that, though. You can also allow for partial matches using special options. The `switch` command allows for three types of matching, as described in Table 2.7.

Table 2.7 Switch options.

Option	Meaning
-glob	Use string matching syntax.
-regexp	Use regular expression matching syntax.
-exact	The choice must exactly match the string.

If you're familiar with UNIX shell commands, the -regexp and -glob options should make sense. In addition to the ability to match a text string exactly, such as *Marley*, the -glob option (the default) allows you to use a set of special characters to perform an inexact match based on a pattern. The ability to perform an inexact match allows your Tcl scripts to accept a wide range of input and properly deal with the data. Without special patterns, you'd need to code every single possible combination of input—a very unwieldy task.

So, in the next sections, I'll start with the -glob style of pattern matching and then delve into the more difficult regular expressions.

Starting with the -glob option, you can create inexact patterns using the special characters and combinations listed in Table 2.8.

Table 2.8 Special globbing characters.

Character	Meaning
*	Matches zero or more characters, of any value.
?	Matches one single character, of any value.
\c	Matches only the single character *c*.
[*char*]	Matches the single character, any

continued

Table 2.8 continued.

	single character between the square braces, or a character in a range in the form of `c1-c2`.

NOTE

These globbing characters also work with the `string match` command. See Chapter 5.

These special characters make more sense with a few examples. The square bracket syntax is the toughest. Table 2.9 shows some clearer examples.

Table 2.9 Globbing matches.

Sequence	Matches
`[Cc]`	One character: Uppercase *C* or lowercase *c*.
`[a-z]`	One character: Anything from lowercase *a* to lowercase *z*.

Remember that the square brackets are specifying a single character match, even though you may place more than one character between the brackets. Also, these square brackets do not perform command substitution.

More Example Globs

In the example `switch` command, the user must type in *cat*, *dog*, or *platypus*. Anything else is not understood. But, what if the user types in *Cat*, *DOG*, or *pLaTyPuS*? This example will fail to detect the input and will use the default case. We can fix the `switch` example, though, as shown next:

```
switch -glob $animal {
    [dD][oO][gG]* { puts "Dogs make good pets." }
    [cC][aA][tT]* { puts "Cats are better." }
```

```
    [pP][lL][aA][tT][yY][pP][uU][sS]*
        { puts "Watch out for the Platypus Society" }
    default { puts "Why did you pick a $animal?" }
}
```

N O T E

Because the -glob option is the default, you can omit the text -glob.

With this example, the *cat* part will match *Cat*, *caT*, *CAT*, or *cats*, along with any combination thereof. The extra star at the end allows for any (or no) characters following, which allows *cats*, with an extra *s*, to match. It also allows *catheter* and *catalog* to match, which is not really a good thing.

We can make another refinement that takes care of plurals:

```
switch -glob $animal {
    [dD][oO][gG]s -
    [dD][oO][gG] { puts "Dogs make good pets." }

[cC][aA][tT]s -
    [cC][aA][tT] { puts "Cats are better." }

[pP][lL][aA][tT][yY][pP][uU][sS]es -
    [pP][lL][aA][tT][yY][pP][uU][sS]
        { puts "Watch out for the Platypus Society" }

default { puts "Why did you pick a $animal?" }
}
```

As you can see, handling odd user input requires a lot of code (in any programming language).

Regular Expression or Regex Matches

In addition to the -glob matches, you can also use the -regexp matches (which are also used with the regexp command on its own). This style of pattern matching, called **regular expressions**, is much looser. For example, with regular expressions, a pattern of [a-z] matches any text string with a lowercase letter, rather than a single lowercase letter that the glob style of pattern matching requires.

Regular expressions provide the ability to compare data that may not be in the format you want, using a set of rules to roughly describe the data format.

Table 2.10 shows the special characters for regular expression-style matching.

Table 2.10 Special `regex` matching characters.

Character	Meaning
.	Matches any single character.
\c	Matches only the character *c*.
^	Matches a null string at the start of the value.
$	Matches a null string at the end of the value.
[*chars*]	Matches any single character from *chars*. You can use a range, like a-z, or ^ to match any single character *not* in the remainder of the *chars*.
(*pattern*)	Matches against the *pattern*; this allows for grouping.

As before, what you can put between the square brackets is the toughest to master. [a-z] matches any string with a lowercase letter. With the -glob option, [a-z] matches against a single lowercase character. With -rexgep, [a-z] matches against a string with any lowercase letter, such as *AAAAAAAAAa*. This is an important distinction. Back to the -regexp style, [a-zA-Z] matches any string with a lowercase or uppercase letter, and [a-zA-Z0-9] matches any text string with any alphanumeric character.

Because patterns like [a-z] match any text string with a lowercase letter, a string like *AAAAAAAAAa* matches against [a-z] (because of the lowercase *a*) as well as [A-Z] (because of the uppercase *AAAAAAAAA*).

This brings to light an interesting aspect to the switch command. The switch command finds the first match and then executes the Tcl code associated with that match. To show this, try the following example:

```
# Example of switch -regexp

set var AAAAAAAAAa

# This pattern matches both.
  # switch finds the first match, though.
switch -regexp $animal {
    [a-z] { puts "OK" }
    [A-Z] { puts "Also OK" }
}


# switch1.tcl
```

The ^ character within the square braces acts as a negator as [^a-z] matches any string that does *not* contain a lowercase letter.

So far, the -regexp pattern-matching tools appear to parallel the tools available with the -glob option. So why add the extra confusion? One reason is that with -regexp pattern matching, you can combine patterns to create a much more powerful, if confusing, pattern-matching system. That is, you can match one or more whole patterns rather than just one or more characters. This allows for sophisticated text processing with just a few Tcl commands.

Table 2.11 lists the means to match whole patterns.

Table 2.11 Combining elements in a regex pattern.

Character	**Meaning**
*	Matches a sequence of zero or more matches of the preceding element.
+	Matches a sequence of one or more matches of the preceding element.
?	Matches either a null string or the preceding element.
pattern1|*pattern2*	Matches either *pattern1* or *pattern2*; usually used with parenthesis.

In Table 2.11, the preference is for the first, longest match possible with the given pattern. `[A-Z]` matches any uppercase character. The asterisk adds repetition, so that `[A-Z]*` matches any sequence (including none) of upper-case characters. The `regexp` command, as well as `switch -regexp`, try to find the first match, and then stretch the match as far as it can.

These rules for which parts to match include:

- Everything is considered from left to right.
- If there are possibilities for more than one match, `regexp` matches the earliest valid part of the text string.
- If you use the | character to provide an OR operation to allow more than one subpattern to compare, `regexp` starts at the left and picks the first match.
- With the characters that allow repetition, `*` `+` `?`, the longest match takes precedence over shorter matches.

With this, you can build up complicated patterns of a number of elements. For example, a variable name in many computer languages must start with an alphabetic character. It can then be followed by any alphanumeric characters. That is, *var1*, *v1*, and *variable* are all valid variable names, but *1var* is not (the leading numeral is prohibited).

N O T E   Tcl actually has a looser requirement for variable names, but I find it best to use these rules when creating variables.

Putting this all together in a `regexp` expression, we get the following:

```
^([a-zA-Z])+[a-zA-Z0-9_]*$
```

This is a complex expression. If we go through it element by element, we get:

- `^` matches any null data at the start of the string.

- ([a-zA-Z]) matches any alphabetic character.
- + means that we must have one (or more) alphabetic characters. This takes care of the rule that a variable name must start with an alphabetic character.
- [a-zA-Z0-9_] matches any alphanumeric character or an underscore, _, character.
- * matches zero or more sequences of the preceding rule (any alphanumeric character or an underscore).
- $ matches any null data at the end of the string.

To test this, I'll show the regexp command, which is shorter than the switch command.

The regexp Command

The regexp command takes in a regular expression pattern, like the preceding one, and a value. It returns 1 (true) if the value matches the pattern or 0 (false) if the value does not match the pattern. The syntax is

```
regexp {pattern} value
```

The *pattern* may be any valid regexp pattern described previously.

So, to test this pattern, ^([a-zA-Z])+[a-zA-Z0-9_]*$, place it in curly braces and compare with values. You must place the regexp pattern within curly braces to prevent the Tcl interpreter from performing variable substitutions with the $ character, and so on.

 There are cases where you want to place the regular expression pattern within curly braces and other cases where you want to place the regular expression pattern within double quotes. Each enclosure has its own set of N O T E problems, especially for complicated patterns.

Try the following examples (and compare the results returned):

```
% regexp {^([a-zA-Z])+[a-zA-Z0-9_]*$} var1
```

```
1
% regexp {^([a-zA-Z])+[a-zA-Z0-9_]*$} variable
1
% regexp {^([a-zA-Z])+[a-zA-Z0-9_]*$} 1var
0
% regexp {^([a-zA-Z])+[a-zA-Z0-9_]*$} start_value
1
% regexp {^([a-zA-Z])+[a-zA-Z0-9_]*$} a12345bcdef34565
1
```

You can see that *1var* is an invalid name, while *var1*, *variable*, *start_value*, and *a12345bcdef34565* are OK.

Using -regexp in the switch Command

You can use the regexp patterns with the switch command as well (which is how we got into this mess in the first place), as shown in the following example:

```
# switch -regexp

#
# Procedure returns 1 if a potential
# variable name is valid, 0 otherwise.
# Valid names start with a letter
# and can have letters, numbers or
# underscores for the rest of the Tcl.
# (Tcl is actually looser than this.)
#
proc var_check { varname } {

switch -regexp $varname {
        ^([a-zA-Z])+[a-zA-Z0-9_]*$
            { puts "$varname is OK"; return 1 }
        default
            { puts "$varname is not a valid name"; return 0 }
    }
```

```
}

# switch2.tcl
```

With a value of *a12345bcdef3465*, the var_check procedure will return 1, indicating you have an acceptable variable name:

```
% var_check a12345bcdef3465
a12345bcdef3465 is OK
1
```

With a value of *1var*, var_check will report a bad name:

```
1var is not a valid name
0
```

With a value of *%%%%*, var_check also reports a bad name. Note that Tcl allows both *1var* and even *%%%%* to be variables.

```
% var_check %%%%
%%%% is not a valid name
0
```

All these names are valid Tcl variables, but *%%%%* will cause you grief with the Tcl interpreter.

For a more complicated example, look at the regexp command in the following example:

```
# HTML regexp example.

proc is_http { url } {

    set ret [regexp -nocase \
        {^(http://)?([^/:]+)(:([0-9]+))?(/.*)} \
        $url]

if { $ret == 1 } {
        puts "$url is an HTTP link."
```

```
    } else {
        puts "$url is NOT an HTTP link."
    }
}
```

```
is_http {http://www.pconline.com/~erc}
is_http {http://www.pconline.com:80/~erc}
is_http {mailto:erc@pconline.com}
is_http {www.pconline.com/~erc}
```

```
# regexp1.tcl
```

The regular expression (taken from the handy Http package described in Chapter 11) compares a value to see if it is an HTTP link common in World Wide Web pages. (This is not an exhaustive pattern, though. You need a more complicated expression to truly parse HTTP links.) HTML Web pages make a very good example for cases where complicated regular expressions come in handy, mostly because of the free-form syntax allowed for HTML.

Let's go through the pattern `^(http://)?([^/:]+)(:([0-9]+))?(/.*)` in depth. The `^(http://)` matches *http://*. The `-nocase` option extends this to *HTTP://* (and *Http://* and so on). Adding the question mark, `^(http://)?` matches the pattern or nothing. That is, *http://* or nothing. The nothing part allows *www.pconline.com/~erc* to match, without the *http://*.

`[^/:]` means no / or : can match, as `^`, only when inside square brackets, negates a pattern. So, `[^/:]` means no / or : can match. Adding the + forces the next characters, after an *http://*, to not be / or :.

The `(:([0-9]+))?` allows a match of a colon with a number (e.g., *:80*). This is typically the HTTP network port number, an optional part of a URL, or **Universal Resource Locator**, the addressing scheme of the Web. The ? at the end of this subexpression allows for nothing or a colon-number match.

Finally, `(/.*)` allows for a slash and then any sequence of characters. The period matches one character. The asterisk allows for zero or more matches.

That's a complicated expression. There's even more to the regexp command, though.

Saving the Matched Data

With the `regexp` command, you can place the data that matched a pattern into a variable. This is very useful when processing a text file or textual data with `regexp`. The syntax requires that you add the variable name to the `regexp` command. The syntax is

```
regexp options pattern string variable
```

For example,

```
% regexp (A*)a* AAAaaabaaaaa whole_match
1
% puts $whole_match
AAAaaa
```

In this example, the variable *whole_match* gets the value that `regexp` matched, in this case *AAAaaa*. A few more examples can help:

```
% regexp {([eE]*)} Eric whole_match
1
% puts $whole_match
E
% set url http://www.pconline.com/~erc
http://www.pconline.com/~erc
% regexp -nocase http:// $url whole_match
1
% puts $whole_match
http://
```

Subexpressions with the `regexp` Command

With regular expressions, each pattern within parenthesis in a regular expression is called a **subexpression**. For example, in the pattern `(A*)a*`, `(A*)` is a subexpression. Tcl allows you to extract the value that matches each subexpression and place each value into a separate variable. To do this, simply add variable names to the end of the `regexp` command for all of the subexpression matches you want stored in separate variables, going from left to right with one variable for each subexpression. The syntax follows:

```
regexp options pattern string variable submatch1 submatch2 ...
```

An extremely dense regular expression that separates values is shown next, with the example again coming from the handy Http package discussed in Chapter 11 (I hope these examples encourage you to browse through the Tcl on-line documentation to see the large amount of code already available):

```
if { [regexp -nocase {^(http://)?([^/:]+)(:([0-9]+))?(/.*)} \
    $url x proto host y port srvurl]} {


}
```

In this example, the variables *proto*, *host*, *port*, and *srvurl* end up with the values parsed from the URL passed to the regexp command. The dummy variables *x* and *y* are used as placeholders to deal with the extra subexpressions necessary to parse the URL. The regexp command really shows its value with its subexpressions.

You can try the preceding expression with the following sample script:

```
#
# Example of regexp and sub expressions.
#

proc parse_http { url } {

# Example regexp call from Http package.
  if {
    [regexp -nocase {^(http://)?([^/:]+)(:([0-9]+))?(/.*)} \
    $url x proto host y port srvurl]} {

    puts "For URL=$url:"
    puts "  proto=$proto host=$host port=$port srvurl=$srvurl"
    puts "  Dummies x=$x y=$y"
  }
```

```
}

parse_http {http://www.pconline.com/~erc/tcl.htm}
parse_http {http://www.pconline.com:80/~erc}
parse_http {www.pconline.com/~erc}


# regexp3.tcl
```

When you run this script, you'll see the following values parsed out from the sample URLs by the regexp command:

```
For URL=http://www.pconline.com/~erc/tcl.htm:
  proto=http:// host=www.pconline.com port= srvurl=/~erc/tcl.htm
  Dummies x=http://www.pconline.com/~erc/tcl.htm y=
For URL=http://www.pconline.com:80/~erc:
  proto=http:// host=www.pconline.com port=80 srvurl=/~erc
  Dummies x=http://www.pconline.com:80/~erc y=:80
For URL=www.pconline.com/~erc:
  proto= host=www.pconline.com port= srvurl=/~erc
  Dummies x=www.pconline.com/~erc y=
```

In addition to the regexp and switch commands, these regular expression patterns are used with the regsub command.

The regsub Command

The regsub command allows you to use regular expressions of the type used by the regexp command in replacing values in strings.

The syntax is

```
regsub pattern string_to_match new_value target
```

The regsub command tries to find the *pattern* in the *string_to_match*. If so, then regsub creates a new string by replacing the matched value with the *new_value*. This string is then set into the *target* variable. In addition, if this isn't enough, regsub returns 1 if it found a match and 0 if it did not.

Also, you can use the -all option to replace all matches with the *new_value*, instead of merely the first match. The -nocase option tells regsub to ignore the case in the *string_to_match*. For example, you can use the pattern to find the incorrect element of a string and replace it with a good value. In Minnesota, the native speakers (myself included) often mess up borrow and lend, leading to such phrases as "borrow me a book please."

You can use regsub to fix this:

```
% regsub borrow "borrow me a book please." lend target
1
% puts $target
lend me a book please.
```

The variable *target* gets set to the new string, "lend me a book please."

Although this example just used a normal string for the pattern, you can use the regexp-style patterns as well. For example,

```
% regsub {[cC][aA][tT]*} "The cat in the hat" dog new_value
1
% puts $new_value
The dog in the hat
```

This example replaces the text *cat* (or *Cat* or *CAT* and so on) in the sample phrase with the new value *dog*. The new text string gets written to the variable *new_value*.

This introduction just scratched the surface of Tcl's regular expression matching. There's much more to regexp and regsub, as described in the on-line documentation.

Looping Commands

In addition to the if and switch commands, Tcl sports a number of looping commands, including the familiar for and while commands.

The for command loops for a set amount of iterations. The basic syntax is

```
for {start} {test} {next} {action}
```

The *start* code initializes any data needed for loop control. The *test* determines whether to execute the *action* code. If true, then the *action* gets executed. After each iteration, the *next* code gets executed and the *test* is invoked again, until the *test* returns false (0).

To loop ten times, you can use the following code:

```
# Looping with the for command

for {set i 0} {$i < 10} {incr i} {
    puts "Index is $i."
}


# for1.tcl
```

 The Tcl syntax of the for command looks very odd to C programmers, but Tcl's for is clearly based on that of C. Remember to use Tcl's curly braces, place a dollar sign before the variable, and to use incr to increment the value.

NOTE

See Table 2.3 for more in the incr command, which increments the value by 1. This is a very handy command when working with for loops. You'll see the following output:

```
Index is 0.
Index is 1.
Index is 2.
Index is 3.
Index is 4.
Index is 5.
Index is 6.
Index is 7.
Index is 8.
Index is 9.
```

The `foreach` Command

The `foreach` command is set up to work with lists (see Chapter 6). The basic syntax appears as

```
foreach varname $list {action}
```

The `foreach` command executes the *action* code once for each element in the given *list*. Each time, `foreach` sets the variable (*varname* in this case) to hold the value of the current item from the list. For example,

```
# Example of foreach.

set mylist { 1 2 3 4 5 6 seven }

foreach item $mylist {
    puts "Current item is $item."
}

# foreach1.tcl
```

This example generates the following output:

```
Current item is 1.
Current item is 2.
Current item is 3.
Current item is 4.
Current item is 5.
Current item is 6.
Current item is seven.
```

The `foreach` command is perfect for Tcl lists as well as array elements using the `array names` command, a command that conveniently returns a list of the names in an array. The following example shows an example of `foreach` with the special global array variable *tcl_platform*:

```
# foreach with array names
```

```
puts "tcl_platform holds:"
foreach item [array names tcl_platform] {
    puts "   $item = $tcl_platform($item)"
}
```

```
# foreach2.tcl
```

On a Linux system, you'll see a result like the following:

```
tcl_platform holds:
   osVersion = 2.0.0
   machine = i586
   platform = unix
   os = Linux
```

On a Windows 95 system, you'll see

```
osVersion = 4.0
   machine = intel
   platform = windows
   os = Windows 95
```

The `while` Command

The `while` command loops while an expression returns true. Its syntax is very simple:

```
while {expression} {action}
```

For example,

```
set i 10

while { $i > 0 } {
    puts "Current index is $i."

    incr i -1
```

```
}
```

Executing this example will generate the following output:

```
Current index is 10.
Current index is 9.
Current index is 8.
Current index is 7.
Current index is 6.
Current index is 5.
Current index is 4.
Current index is 3.
Current index is 2.
Current index is 1.
```

The real difference between the while and for commands is that for the while command, you must modify the value tested against (*i* in the preceding example) in the body of the loop. Forgetting to do this is a common error.

Jumping Out of Things

If things get too hairy, Tcl provides a number of commands to jump out of a loop, or even out of the Tcl interpreter entirely.

The break command jumps out of current looping command, instead of jumping back to the top of the loop.

```
# Example of break.

set i 10

while { $i > 0 } {

if { $i == 5 } {
        break
    }
```

```
puts "Current index is $i."

    incr i -1
}
```

```
# break1.tcl
```

These commands will stop the loop when the variable *i* equals 5.

N O T E The break command jumps out of the innermost loop. In the following example, the break command will jump out of the inner loop (the while command using the variable *k*) not the outer loop (the while command using the variable *i*).

```
# Breaks out of innermost loop, not outermost.

set i 10

while { $i > 0 } {

    set k 10

    while { $k > 0 } {

        if { $k == 5 } {
            # Inner loop break, only.
            break
        }
        puts "   Inner loop index is $k."

        incr k -1
    }

    puts "Outer loop index is $i."

    incr i -1
}
```

```
# break2.tcl
```

The `continue` command jumps from the current position to the top of the loop, continuing on with the next iteration of the loop, as shown in the following example:

```
# Example of continue.

set i 10

while { $i > 0 } {

    incr i -1

    if { $i == 5 } {
        continue
    }

    puts "Current index is $i."
}
```

```
# cont.tcl
```

These commands will generate the following output:

```
Current index is 9.
Current index is 8.
Current index is 7.
Current index is 6.
Current index is 4.
Current index is 3.
Current index is 2.
Current index is 1.
Current index is 0.
```

Note that 5 is missing in this output. That's what `continue` did for us.

NOTE Be careful with `continue`. If you had replaced the `break` in the original example with `continue`, the loop would never terminate. That's because the `incr` command appeared after the `break`. In this example, the continue appears after the `incr` command (which decrements the value).

To jump out of everything and end the execution of **wish** or **tclsh**, use the `exit` command, which has the following syntax:

```
exit optional_return_code
```

For `exit` (mentioned in Chapter 1), if you skip the optional return code, the default value returned is 0. This follows UNIX conventions whereby a program terminating successfully returns 0, and programs terminating because of errors return some other value. (Tcl was created in the UNIX environment first, and so follows more UNIX conventions than those for Windows.)

As a handy reference guide, Table 2.12 lists the Tcl commands for controlling the flow of execution.

Table 2.12 Controlling the flow of execution in Tcl scripts.

Command

```
break
continue
exit optional_return_code
for {start} {test} {next} {
      action
}
foreach varname $list {
      action
}
if {expression} then {
      action
```

continued

Table 2.12 continued

```
}
if {expression} then {
      if-action
} else {
      else-action
}
if {expression1} then {
      if-action
} elseif {expression2} {
      elseif-action
} else {
      else-action
}
switch options string {
      pattern1 {action1}
      pattern2 {action2}
      . . .
      default {default_action}
}
while {expression} {
      action
}
```

Built-In Procedures in Tcl

Tcl provides a good number of built-in procedures, some of which you've seen, and others which are mentioned only in passing. In the next few paragraphs, you'll see some of the most useful built-in Tcl commands.

The `puts` command, short for put string, prints out its argument, a text string:

```
puts string
```

In Chapter 6 in the section on files, you'll see that `puts` can be used to write a text string to a file, as well as print to the screen.

N O T E

The `puts` command is very useful for debugging your Tcl scripts. If something seems to be wrong, put in a few `puts` commands to print out values of variables at particular places in the script. You'll find this a great aid to figuring out what is going on.

N O T E

As with all strings, you can take advantage of command and variable substitution, as shown next:

```
set val 1
puts "The value is $val."
puts [set val 1]
```

The first `puts` will print out:

```
The value is 1.
```

The second `puts` will merely print 1.

By itself, the `puts` command is extremely limited. But, you'll use it most often in conjunction with the `format` command. The `format` command allows you to build up a text string from variable values. The advantage provided by the `format` command is that you can specify exactly how to format the resulting text string.

The `format` command works a lot like the `sprintf` function in C. `format` returns a string that is built from a number of arguments. You can insert values into the string and also use expressions to generate the values.

The syntax is

```
format format_string arg1 arg2...
```

The *args* are optional, depending on what you put in the *format_string*.

The following command takes two extra arguments and inserts them in the *format_string*, replacing the *%s* values:

```
#
# Example of format.
#

puts [format "My name is %s" Eric]

# format1.tcl
```

This example is not any better than placing a variable within a `puts` command directly—skipping the extraneous `format` command. The `format` command shines in its ability to specify exactly how the output should look, especially the number of characters allotted for output.

You can also insert other values, such as integers, floating-point numbers, and individual characters. Because everything in Tcl is really a text string anyway, all you're doing is specifying how you want the value interpreted.

With the complementary ability of using the $ variable substitution, the `format` command is not as essential as it is in C or C++.

Table 2.13 lists the `format` values for various types of data.

Table 2.13 Using the `format` command.

Format	Meaning
%c	Insert a single character.
%d	Insert an integer value.
%e	Insert a floating-point value, in scientific notation format.
%f	Insert a floating-point value.
%g	Insert a floating-point value, in scientific notation format.

`%i`	Insert a signed integer value.
`%o`	Insert an integer in octal (base 8) format.
`%s`	Insert a text string value.
`%u`	Insert an unsigned integer value.
`%x`	Insert an integer and display in hexadecimal (base 16) format. (`%X` forces the hexadecimal digits to appear uppercase.)

If you place a number before the *s* (*s* being short for string), then you can control the number of spaces allotted for the text. The syntax is *n.m*, where *n* is the minimal field width and *m* is the maximum width, in characters. For example,

```
% format "My name is %3.3s" Eric
My name is Eri
```

The special `%3.3s` syntax specifies a three-character string. The first *3* indicates a minimum width of three characters. If the text string is shorter than three characters, it will get expanded out. The *.3* part limits it to exactly three characters. If you just use `%3s`, you'll see the following output:

```
% format "My name is %3s" Eric
My name is Eric
```

(You just specified the minimum field width, not the maximum.)

For floating-point numbers, the values are interpreted differently. In the *n.m* format, the value in *m* determines the number of decimal places. For example,

```
#
# format with decimal values.
#

set v 123.456789

puts "Value from puts   is $v"
```

```
puts [format "Value from format is %3.3f" $v]
```

```
# format2.tcl
```

In this example, you can compare the straight output from the `puts` command with the formatted output from `format`:

```
Value from puts    is 123.456789
Value from format is 123.457
```

You can format numbers in hexadecimal or octal as well, as shown here:

```
# format with hexadecimal and octal values.
```

```
set i 123
```

```
puts [format \
    "hex=%x octal=%o decimal=%d" \
    $i $i $i]
```

```
# format3.tcl
```

When you run this script, you'll see the following output, all using the same variable, *i*, repeated three times in different numeric formats:

```
hex=7b octal=173 decimal=123
```

Although the `format` command acts like the ANSI C `sprintf` function, the `scan` command acts like the ANSI C `sscanf` function. The purpose of `scan` is to scan out, or extract, values stored in a string. For example, the following string holds three numbers:

```
"105 42 36"
```

With `scan`, you can pull out these numbers into three variables:

```
# The scan command.
```

```
set result [scan \
    "105 42 36" "%d %d %d" var1 var2 var3]

puts "$var1 $var2 $var3"
puts "Result of scan is $result"
```

```
# scan.tcl
```

When you execute this, you'll see

```
105 42 36
Result of scan is 3
```

The syntax for `scan` is

```
scan string format_string variable1 variable2 ...
```

The `%` options used in the *format_string* use the same syntax as the `format` command does and come from ANSI C. These options were listed in Table 2.13.

You must ensure that you have enough variables for all the values you're trying to extract. Generally, each `%` item represents a value and requires a separate variable.

WARNING

The `scan` command returns the number of values it extracted, or -1 on failure. If you save this value, you can check the input string for errors.

In addition to all the built-in procedures in Tcl, you can easily write your own. This is where Tcl really becomes useful.

Writing Your Own Procedures

There are two ways you can extend Tcl. You can write procedures strictly within the Tcl language, or you can create new Tcl procedures by writing functions in the C programming language that follow special conventions, which are most useful for application-specific behavior (such as recalculating a spreadsheet). You'll see the latter in Chapter 16. For now, there's a lot you can do by staying strictly within the Tcl language, using the `proc` command.

The `proc` command registers a procedure by name and allows you to execute it like any other command in Tcl. The syntax is

```
proc name {arguments} {body}
```

For example, you can help your employer's Human Resource Department with the following procedure:

```
# Defining a procedure.

proc stroke { name } {

    set str [format "%s is a wonderful person!" $name ]

    puts $str

}

stroke Amanda


# stroke.tcl
```

After you call `proc`, then that procedure is ready to be used at any time in the future, as in

```
% stroke Amanda
Amanda is a wonderful person!
```

In this case, *Amanda* is the argument passed to the procedure `stroke`. When invoked, the variable *name* will get set to the argument's value (*Amanda*). Each time you invoke the `stroke` procedure, the *name* variable will get set with a new value, the value passed to the `stroke` procedure as an argument.

The values passed to the procedure as arguments are set into local variables, such as *name* in the `stroke` procedure. See the section on covering Global Variables for more on this topic.

Inside a procedure, you can place any number of Tcl commands. You can also use variables and set values.

Using the `button` command shown in Chapter 1, you can create a procedure to make new buttons:

```
#
# Simple procedure to create a button.
#

proc make_button { name text } {

    button $name -text $text -command { exit }

    pack $name
}


# makeb.tcl
```

This procedure creates a new `button` widget and packs it (more on both of these subjects in the next chapter). Note the use of more than one variable (*name* and *text*). To invoke this procedure, you can use the following example:

```
% make_button .b1 "First Button"
```

After this first button is created, you'll see a window as shown in Figure 2.1.

Figure 2.1 The first button.

82

You can run the `make_button` procedure again, with

```
% make_button .b2 "Second Button"
```

Now, you'll see a larger window, as shown in Figure 2.2.

Figure 2.2 The first two buttons.

You'll need to run these commands from the **wish** interpreter, because the `button` command requires Tk, not just Tcl.

N O T E

You can do a lot of work with procedures. In fact, smart use of procedures can make your Tcl scripts much easier to read. You can also reuse Tcl code in new situations.

The two main reasons to create procedures are to divide up your scripts into smaller, more manageable chunks and to allow you to reuse procedures in other scripts or later in the same script.

You can start writing all your Tcl scripts as one large file starting from the top and going to the bottom. Sooner or later, though, this tends to get too large and unwieldy for normal usage. It will become harder and harder to add new features to the script and to fix the inevitable bugs that are discovered.

The `proc` command comes in very handy. You can break up the large, unwieldy script into smaller pieces, where each piece is a Tcl procedure. You'll soon find that tasks you perform repeatedly become procedures you can write once and reuse many times, saving effort on your part.

Returning Values from Procedures

In conjunction with the `proc` command, you may need to create a procedure that does more than create widgets or print results. You can use the `return` statement to return a value from the procedure.

For example, I am relatively bad at estimating how long a software project will take. So, I may need a procedure to multiply my estimate (usually far too optimistic) by some constant amount:

```
#
# Procedure to estimate software projects.
#
proc estimate { first_guess } {

    return [expr $first_guess * 2.5]
}
```

So now, when I estimate the time it takes to complete a project, I can get a more valid value as I rampage over 30 years of software estimation theory:

```
% estimate 10
25.0
```

In this example, **wish** or **tclsh** will merely print the value. You can instead set a variable to hold the result:

```
set result [estimate 10]
% puts $result
25.0
```

This should look familiar, especially when you look back at the `expr` and `format` commands, both of which return a value.

With `return`, you can optionally pass back error information as well. The full syntax is

```
return -code code -errorinfo info -errorcode code value_string
```

All the arguments are optional. The *value_string* is the value that gets returned. The other arguments are for dealing with error conditions. See Chapter 9 for more on this.

Global and Local Variables

When you start working with procedures, which you'll need to do for any sophisticated Tcl script, you'll soon discover that variables in the main part of the script are not available within your procedures. You can pass variables into procedures as arguments, but you cannot modify or access variables that exist outside of the procedure.

With the global command, though, you can. global marks a variable as having global scope:

```
#
# Use of global in procedures.
#

proc offset { xoffset yoffset } {
    global x y

incr x $xoffset
    incr y $yoffset

# Return an empty string
    return
}

set x 10
set y 20

offset 5 2

puts "X = $x Y = $y"
```

```
# global.tcl
```

You'll see the following output:

```
X = 15 Y = 22
```

Without the `global` statement, the procedure offset can't access the values of *x* and *y*, which will result in an error such as the following:

```
can't read "x": no such variable
```

When you see such an error, and know that you have indeed defined a variable named *x*, you should suspect that you didn't mark the variable as `global` in a procedure.

More on Global Variables

A global variable implies that the variable can be used anywhere—globally—within your Tcl script. A local variable remains in scope only inside a procedure.

This means that you can reuse variable names, like *x* and *y*, within multiple procedures without worry about overlap (unless you mark these variables as global).

This is very useful because common names like *x*, *y*, *width*, *height*, *name*, *widget*, and so on get used again and again inside Tcl procedures.

Call by Reference

If you've ever used the Pascal or Modula programming languages, you'll be used to the concept of calling by value or calling by reference (the C language hides the issue: everything is passed by value and you pass a pointer to simulate passing by reference).

Tcl provides the odd command `upvar` to allow you to simulate calling by reference. `upvar` allows you to access a variable up one level. (You can also pass the level number, but this is virtually impossible to use generally; it results in a very specific solution to a very specific problem.)

upvar links a local variable with another—usually global—variable. This link most often goes up one level, to the procedure that called the current procedure. Any change to the local variable gets reflected in the target variable. And, in most cases, you use upvar to link to an array.

The syntax for upvar follows:

```
upvar level $target_variable link_variable
```

The optional level argument defaults to 1, and in virtually all cases, you should skip this argument. After calling the upvar command, the local *link_variable* now refers to the *target_variable*.

NOTE Notice how the *target_variable* has its value referenced with the dollar sign, whereas the *link_variable* does not. This is an easy part to get mixed up.

upvar exists mainly to allow you to pass arrays to a procedure. Because an array has no value as is (you must access an element in the array to get a value), you cannot readily pass an array to a procedure.

Because of its widespread use with Tcl arrays, the following example shows how to pass an array and access values in the array from a procedure:

```
#
# Use of upvar.
#
proc print_name { emp } {
    # Associate link_var with the actual array.
    upvar $emp link_var

puts "Employee $link_var(name) lives in $link_var(city)."

return
}


# Store some employee data.
set employee(name) "Eric Foster-Johnson"
set employee(city) "St. Paul"
set employee(state) "Minnesota"
```

```
set employee(attitude) "Thinks empowerment is a joke"

# Print name and city values using upvar.
print_name employee


# upvar.tcl
```

Note how we call this procedure, `print_name`, with the array variable, *employee*, and not the normal value (which would be `$employee`). When you run the **upvar.tcl** script, you'll see the following data printed:

```
Employee Eric Foster-Johnson lives in St. Paul.
```

The `upvar` command is most useful for allowing you to pass the name of a variable to a procedure that then operates on that variable. The `parray` command, which prints out the keys and values held in an array, is one such command that uses `upvar`. (In fact, the `parray` command is actually a procedure written in Tcl.)

We can write a simple version of `parray` using the `upvar` command, as shown next:

```
#
# A simple version of parray.
#

# Procedure prints out the values in an array.
# Usage:
#  myparray array_name
#
proc myparray { arrayname } {

# Link array to link_var.
    upvar $arrayname link_var

# Check for errors.
    if { ![array exists link_var] } {
        puts "$arrayname is not an array."
        return
```

```
    }

foreach key [lsort [array names link_var] ] {
        set name [format "%s(%s)" $arrayname $key]
        puts "$name = $link_var($key)"
    }
}


# Store some employee data.
set employee(name) "Eric Foster-Johnson"
set employee(city) "St. Paul"
set employee(state) "Minnesota"
set employee(attitude) "Thinks empowerment is a joke"

puts "\t My parray:"
myparray employee

puts "\t Standard parray:"
parray employee


# myparray.tcl
```

When you run the **myparray.tcl** script, you should see all the values in the array printed twice, once by the `myparray` procedure and once by the built-in Tcl `parray` procedure, which is described in the section on arrays.

You can find the real `parray` command in the file named **parray.tcl** located in the Tcl library directory, usually **C:\Tcl\Lib\tcl8.0** on Windows or **/usr/local/lib/tcl8.0** on UNIX or something like these locations, based on the version number of Tcl that you have installed. The real `parray` command makes use of some special options to the `format` command.

In addition to `upvar`, there's also `uplevel`, sort of a hybrid cross of `eval` (covered in Chapter 5) and `upvar`. You'll usually need this only if you want to create new control statements, such as your own `while` or `for` commands. See the on-line manuals for more on `uplevel`.

Renaming Procedures

The `rename` command allows you to rename a procedure:

```
rename original_name new_name
```

This command allows you to keep old commands while redefining them.

In Tcl, you can simply execute `proc` again with the same name as an existing command to redefine that command. The problem is that the old command is now lost. With `rename`, you can save the old command, in case you need it later, and then redefine a command. So, before you redefine a procedure, its a good idea to rename the old procedure, so that you don't lose the old procedure.

Procedures with a Variable Number of Arguments

Up to now, you've seen procedures that handle a fixed number of arguments. Even so, the `format` command seems to break this rule, in that it can take any number of arguments. As you'd suspect, you can make procedures like this, too.

The special value `args` allows you to use a variable number of arguments in a procedure. The `print_args` procedure, which follows, takes any number of arguments and prints them out:

```
# Variable number of arguments.

proc print_args { args } {

    foreach value $args {
        puts $value
    }
}

print_args 1 2 3 4
print_args 1 two three 4 5 6 7


# printarg.tcl
```

The `args` value is a list (see Chapter 6 for more on lists) that contains all the remaining (in this case, all) arguments to the procedure.

In some procedures, you may want to have one or two named arguments and then allow for any number of following arguments. The `format` command does this for example. It requires a format string. You can follow this with a number of arguments as well. To do this, you place the special word `args` after any arguments you want to name. For example,

```
#
# One required argument plus args.
#

proc one_arg_plus { first args } {

    puts "The first argument is $first. The rest follow:"
    print_args $args
}

proc print_args { args } {

    foreach value $args {
        puts $value
    }
}

one_arg_plus 1 2 3 4 5 6 7


# onearg.tcl
```

The output is

```
% one_arg_plus 1 2 3 4 5 6 7
The first argument is 1. The rest follow:
2 3 4 5 6 7
```

Note that in this example, you see some of the simplicity of the Tcl interpreter. The `one_arg_plus` procedure gets the following values. The variable *first* is set to 1. The special variable `args` is set to the list of 2 3 4 5 6 7. But, when `print_args` gets called from within the procedure `one_arg_plus`, all these values, 2 3 4 5 6 7 get passed as a single argument to the procedure `print_args`. The use of the special variable args hasn't changed. It's just that when you pass a list to a procedure like this, you get the value of the list passed as one argument.

If you don't want this behavior, you can use the `foreach` command shown earlier, or a number of list commands described in Chapter 6 to extract each item from the list.

Procedure Families

Because each procedure requires a new entry in Tcl's name space, and because each new procedure adds complexity to the Tcl language, you may want to group like procedures together into a procedure family.

A common way to make a procedure family is to reuse the procedure name and then use the arguments to differentiate the functions. For example, the `array` command described previously is really a family of commands, all starting with *array*. The `array names` command returns the names of the keys within an array. The `array exists` command tells whether or not a given variable is an array, and so on.

In each case, there is one command, `array`, with subcommands, such as `names` and `exists`, to provide a lot of functionality under one simple name. Other Tcl procedure families include the `string` and `file` commands discussed in Chapters 5 and 6.

You can use the special value `args` to help you write a procedure family and then separate each argument when called, using the first argument to determine what action to take. (You can use a `switch` command to help differentiate.)

Another way to write a procedure family is to use default values.

Default Values in Procedures

With the normal procedure syntax, you provide a list of arguments to the procedure. For example,

```
proc my_proc { first second third } {
    # Body of procedure...
}
```

With default parameters, you replace each argument with a list in the format of { *argument_name default_value* }. For example,

```
proc my_proc { first {second 2} {third 3} } {
    # Body of procedure...
}
```

NOTE You can provide defaults for as many arguments as you want, including all. But, when providing default values, you must start with the last argument and work your way back to the beginning of the list of arguments.

You can use the default values for many purposes. One of the main uses, though, is to create the procedure families already discussed. For example, you can use a Tcl procedure family to hide a global variable. This is often useful if you may later need to change the global variable. Instead of making the global variable available to all users, you hide the global inside a procedure. The following example hides a minimum tolerance value inside a procedure family:

```
# Use of default arguments for procedures.

    #
    # Hidden global holds the tolerance value.
    #
set tolerance 10e-9
global tolerance

# Stores a minimum tolerance value.
# Usage:
#
# min_tolerance get
# min_tolerance    (same as min_tolerance get)
# min_tolerance set value
# min_tolerance init
#
proc min_tolerance { {cmd get} {value 0.0} } {
    global tolerance

    #
    # Do nothing for get case, because value
    # is always returned by this command.
```

```
    #
    switch $cmd {
        get   { }
        set   { set tolerance $value }
        init  { set tolerance 10e-9 }
    }

return $tolerance
}


# mintol.tcl
```

The `min_tolerance` procedure hides the global variable *tolerance*. (Note that *tolerance* is a not a good name for a variable you want to hide; *pkg_knot_tolerance* or something like that may be a better name). The `min_tolerance` procedure also shows an example of default values for the arguments. Using default values allows you to call the `min_tolerance` procedure the following ways:

```
min_tolerance
min_tolerance get
min_tolerance init
min_tolerance set value
```

You can pass zero, one, or two arguments. To determine what to do, the `min_tolerance` procedure uses the `switch` command to switch off the value of the *cmd* argument. The *cmd* argument defaults to *get*, which allows you to call the `min_tolerance` procedure without any arguments.

The *get* argument returns the current value. The *set* argument sets a new value, which should be included (but isn't necessary), and the *init* argument resets the tolerance to its initial value.

The **mintol.tcl** script also has a few other quirks. First off, it uses scientific notation for the numeric values to better approach true mathematical tolerances. Second, the *get* case does nothing, which may look weird. Because the `min_tolerance` procedure always returns the current value of the global variable *tolerance*, there's no reason for the *get* case to do anything special (the value will be returned anyway).

Defining Procedures Within Procedures

It may seem odd, but there's nothing to stop you from defining a procedure within a procedure, as shown here:

```
# Defining procedures within procedures.

proc add { number1 number2 } {

    proc subtract { number1 number2 } {

        proc multiply { number1 number2 } {
            return [expr $number1 * $number2]
        }

        return [expr $number1 - $number2]
    }

    return [expr $number1 + $number2]
}

# add.tcl
```

In the **add.tcl** script, the add procedure—when run—defines a new procedure, subtract. The subtract procedure—when run—defines a new procedure, multiply. When add and subtract are run, all three procedures are available for you to call. The important thing to note is that until the add procedures gets executed, the subtract procedure will not exist. Why? Because the curly braces defer execution until later.

So, if you use the source command to load in the **add.tcl** script, you will not be able to use the subtract procedure until after you have executed the add procedure:

```
source add.tcl
% subtract 5 1
invalid command name "subtract"
% add 5 1
6
```

```
% subtract 5 1
4
```

After you have called the `subtract` procedure, you can call the `multi-ply` procedure:

```
% multiply 4 3
12
```

While you can write your own procedures in Tcl, it's best to first check if a procedure already exists, so that you don't have to spend the time to write and debug a new one. Tcl comes with a lot of built-in procedures. We've seen some in this chapter. For text string procedures, see Chapter 5. For file and list procedures, see Chapter 6. There's also a whole set of math procedures, which are covered next.

Math in Tcl

Tcl provides a number of built-in math procedures. The workhorse is the `expr` command. The syntax is

```
expr expression
```

`expr` evaluates the expression and returns its value. Such an expression can be a mathematical one, resulting in some value, or a logical one, which results in a true (1 or any nonzero value) or false (0), using the logical expressions from Table 2.5.

For example,

```
% expr 2 + 2
4
% expr 2+2
4
% expr (2 + 2) + 5
9
% expr 1 < 2
```

```
1
% expr 1<2
1
% expr 2==2
1
% expr 2 == 3
0
% expr 2==3
0
```

Notice how you can expand the arguments with spaces or crunch the arguments together into one. Both 2 + 2 and 2+2 work with expr.

You can, of course, use variables within expressions:

```
set value 10
expr ($value+2)*2
```

You can use parenthesis to control how the expression gets evaluated. Table 2.13 shows the mathematical expressions that complement the logical expressions in Table 2.6. Some expressions work with both integer values (whole numbers) and floating-point (decimal) values. Table 2.13 shows the expressions that work with both types of numbers. Table 2.14 shows expressions that work only with integer values.

Table 2.13 Math expressions in Tcl that work with floating-point and integer values.

Expression	Meaning
-v1	Negative of *v1*.
v1*v2	Multiply *v1* and *v2*.
v1/v2	Divide *v1* by *v2*.
v1+v2	Add *v1* and *v2*.
v1-v2	Subtract *v2* from *v1*.

This is somewhat misleading, in that everything in Tcl is a text string. Even so, these rules still apply, based on the type of the data you store in the string. If you store a value of 44.5 (with a decimal point), then Tcl treats it as a float-point number (for these purposes, it is still a string). If you store a value of 44, then Tcl treats it as an integer.

Table 2.14 Math expressions in Tcl that work only with integer values.

Expression	Meaning
~v1	Bitwise complement of *v1*.
v1%v2	Remainder after dividing *v1* by *v2*.
v1<<v2	Left-shift *v1* by *v2* number of bits.
v1>>v2	Right-shift *v1* by *v2* number of bits.
v1&v12	Bitwise AND of *v1* and *v2*.
v1^v2	Bitwise exclusive or (XOR) of *v1* and *v2*.
v1|v2	Bitwise OR of *v1* and *v2*.
v1?v2:v3	Returns v2 if v1 is nonzero; otherwise returns v3.

The expressions in Table 2.13 are in the order of precedence, although some, like * and /, have the same precedence. The idea of precedence is mainly to deal with statements like

```
expr $a*$b+$c-$d/$e
```

Because it is always confusing which order the operators will be applied, it is much better to use parenthesis to show clearly the order you intend the operators to be applied, as in the following example:

```
expr ($a*$b)+(($c-$d)/$e)
```

Comparing these two notations, you'll see different results:

```
% set a 1
1
```

```
% set b 2
2
% set c 3
3
% set d 4
4
% set e 5
5
% expr ($a*$b)+(($c-$d)/$e)
1
% expr $a*$b+$c-$d/$e
5
```

If you're familiar with C programming, the expressions in Tables 2.13 and 2.14 should be old hat.

Numeric Notation

Integer values may be defined in decimal, hexadecimal, or octal notation, using standard C conventions (a leading *0x* for hexadecimal and a leading *0* for octal).

WARNING

The leading zero is tricky if you're not used to programming in C. The number 010 is not 10 (decimal) but 8 (decimal). And, 0x010 is really 16:

```
% set a 010
010
% puts $a
010
% format "%d" $a
8
% set b 0x010
0x010
% format "%d" $b
16
```

Usually the leading *0x* alerts you that the number is not a normal decimal number, but many new Tcl scripters get tripped up by the leading *0* for octal numbers.

Floating-point numbers also follow C language conventions, allowing values such as 4.6, 4.6e+16, 4e6, and so on. The **mintol.tcl** script shows an example of scientific notation.

Math Procedures

Tcl's `expr` command supports a range of math functions, most from, you guessed it, standard C. (Did you ever get the feeling that Tcl was written in the C language?)

Unlike most Tcl procedures, you call the Tcl math functions using standard function notation, such as

```
% set a 1
1
% set b 2
2
% set c [expr hypot($a,$b)]
2.2360679774997898
```

Table 2.15 lists the major math functions in Tcl.

Table 2.15 Tcl math functions used with the `expr` command.

Function	Meaning
`acos(a)`	Arc cosine.
`asin(a)`	Arc sine.
`atan(a)`	Arc tangent.
`atan2(a, b)`	Arc tangent of *a/b*.
`cos(a)`	Cosine, using radians.
`cosh(a)`	Hyperbolic cosine.
`double(integer)`	Floating-point value equal to *integer*.
`exp(a)`	Constant *e* raised to power *a*.

continued

Table 2.15 continued

`fmod(a,b)`	Floating-point remainder of a/b.
`hypot(a,b)`	Square root of (a squared plus b squared).
`log(a)`	Natural logarithm of a.
`log10(a)`	Base 10 logarithm of a.
`pow(a,b)`	a raised to power b.
`rand()`	Returns pseudorandom number between 0.0 and 1.0.
`sin(a)`	Sine, using radians.
`sinh(a)`	Hyperbolic sine.
`sqrt(a)`	Square root of a.
`srand(a)`	Sets seed for random number generation to integer value a.
`tan(a)`	Tangent, using radians.
`tanh(a)`	Hyperbolic tangent.

The `expr` command also provides a number of functions to convert from floating-point values to integers, get the absolute value, and so on, as listed in Table 2.16.

Table 2.16 Tcl math conversion functions.

Function	**Meaning**
`abs(a)`	Absolute value of a.
`ceil(a)`	Smallest integer not less than a.
`floor(a)`	Largest integer not greater than a.
`int(a)`	Integer value of a.
`round(a)`	Integer value of rounded a.

NOTE In older versions of Tcl, you could control the precision used when converting floating-point values to strings. The global variable *tcl_precision* handled this. It is usually set to 6, and you can increase or decrease it if necessary. Starting with Tcl 8.0, global variable *tcl_precision* is slated to eventually go away, and you are no longer supposed to use it. The main reason is that the Tcl byte-code compiler in Tcl 8.0 already uses the maximum precision of 17 anyway.

Internally, floating-point values are stored as the C type `double`, using a 64-bit (or greater) double-precision IEEE floating-point value. Integer values are stored as the C type `int`, normally 32 bits.

Summary

There's probably more syntax in this chapter than you'd like, but each bit will be essential for creating useful Tcl scripts.

Tcl scripts are a set of textual commands. Each command has a number of arguments that are passed to the command for execution. Even statements like `if` and `while`, which used to control the flow of a Tcl script, are really just commands with arguments. This is why the curly braces, { and }, are so important; they defer execution and substitution within the braces until later. What you want, especially for variables, are the values at the *time of execution*, not the values at the time of parsing.

Square braces, [and], are used to substitute the return value of a command. The dollar sign, $, is used to substitute the value of a variable.

You can control the flow of a Tcl script with the `if`, `while`, `for`, and `foreach` commands. `break` and `continue` jump out of loops, while `exit` terminates the Tcl script.

You can write your own procedures in Tcl using the `proc` command to register the procedure. And, you can use Tcl's extensive list of built-in math commands, such as `expr`, to perform mathematical operations. These math functions become very important in an interpreted language, so that you can take advantage of compiled code (the built-in math functions) when executing numeric-intensive scripts.

In the next chapter, you'll see a lot more fun graphical applications and meet many of the widgets provided by Tk.

Tcl/Tk Commands Introduced in This Chapter

```
append
array
break
continue
exit
expr
for
foreach
format
if
incr
parray
proc
regexp
regsub
rename
return
scan
set
subst
switch
unset
upvar
while
```

# CHAPTER 3

Interacting with the User

This chapter covers:

- The Tk toolkit
- The `button` widget, making a return appearance from Chapter 1
- Common widget options
- The `label` widget for displaying text
- The `message` widget, a multiline label
- The `frame` widget for containing other widgets
- The `radiobutton` and `checkbutton` widgets for on/off values
- The `scale` widget for sliding values
- How the widget packer works
- Destroying widgets

The Tk Toolkit

One of the greatest strengths of Tcl lies in the ability to create graphical user interfaces for your scripts. With just a bit of forethought, these scripts—like most Tcl scripts—will run the same on Windows 95, Windows NT, UNIX, and MacOS systems. Tcl provides this feature through the Tk toolkit.

How Tk relates to Tcl can be confusing. Determining what Tcl is, what Tk is and how the two relate isn't the easiest task if you're new to Tcl.

Tcl is the cross-platform scripting language. Tcl comes with a number of built-in commands, many of which you've seen in Chapter 2. Tk is an add-on extension to Tcl, which merely provides extra Tcl commands, commands related to creating user interfaces. To use these commands, you need to run a Tcl interpreter that understands and supports the Tk commands. This is the **wish** interpreter that you've probably been using all along. The other Tcl interpreter, **tclsh**, doesn't support any of the Tk commands. So, to run the examples in this chapter—and most of the rest of the book—you'll need to switch to the **wish** interpreter if you're not using **wish** already.

To differentiate between versions of Tcl, the **wish** program usually includes a version number in its name, such as **wish80.exe** on Win32 systems and **wish8.0** on UNIX. For simplicity, I'll refer to **wish** as the name of the program.

Widgets

The main purpose of Tk is to provide a set of Tcl commands to create and manipulate widgets. Commonly used in most user interface software, a **widget** is a single component of the interface. Each widget forms a self-contained unit that knows how to display itself and handle input, making each widget semi-independent. A menu is a widget, as is a menu bar. Each push-button, data-entry field, and check box is also a widget. As you can see, Tk gets pretty detailed. If you look at any user interface, you can pick out the widgets fairly easily. (This is a good exercise to see what widgets other programs present.) Other toolkits, such as Motif or Microsoft Foundation Classes, use slightly different terminology than Tk, but the basic concepts are the same.

Tk provides a number of commands to create widgets, which you'll see in the next sections. After they are created, you can manipulate widgets with even more Tk commands. You can control font styles and sizes, colors, cursors, and how to arrange widgets into a pleasing layout that helps the user figure out your programs.

The Tour de Widgets

In this chapter, you'll get a taste of most of the Tk widgets. Some of the more advanced widgets appear in separate chapters, along with the Tcl commands that make the most sense in conjunction with the widgets. For example, the `listbox` widget makes extensive use of Tcl list commands, so both topics appear in Chapter 6. Even so, this chapter covers a plethora of Tk widgets necessary for building graphical applications. Table 3.1 lists the available widgets in Tk.

Table 3.1 Tk widgets.

Widget	Use
button	Pushbutton, calls Tcl code when clicked on.
canvas	Drawing area widget. You can draw into this widget.
checkbutton	On-off button.
entry	Text-entry widget.
frame	Frames widgets inside 3D bevel.
label	Displays a text message.
listbox	Scrolled list.
menu	Menu.
menubutton	Pulls down menu from menu bar.
message	Multiline label.
radiobutton	On-off button; only one can be on at a time.
scale	Analog value from min to max.
scrollbar	Scrollbar.
text	Text-entry widget.
toplevel	Dialog or application window.

Some of these terms, like `radiobutton`, may be confusing. It's often hard to determine what a widget does and which widget type is most appropriate to use in a given situation.

For right now, don't worry. In the sections that follow, I'll cover the situations where each widget is appropriate. Furthermore, don't hesitate to experiment. Tcl excels for prototyping because you can create a test script in a few minutes. Test out the alternatives and pick the one that works best for your needs. There's no one true answer in user interface design. There is a lot of good advice though. See Appendix A for a list of some excellent user interface books.

Where Widgets Appear

Widgets appear in only one of three places: in a menu, in a top-level—also called a main—window, or in a dialog box. For now, we'll concentrate on placing widgets inside the main window, such as the one shown in Figure 3.1, because you can get started much more quickly using the default main window.

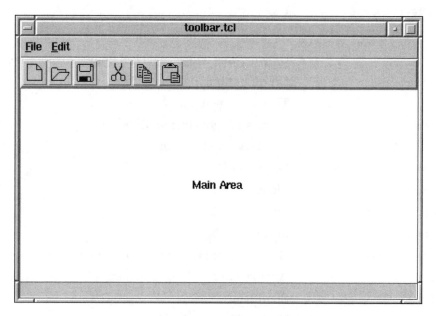

Figure 3.1 The main window of an application.

In this chapter, we'll stick to simpler examples than Figure 3.1, exploring each widget type one at a time. This chapter covers button, checkbutton, frame, label, message, radiobutton, and scale widgets.

Chapter 4 covers menu and menubutton widgets. Chapter 5 covers entry, scrollbar, and text widgets, while Chapter 6 delves into the listbox. Chapter 7 tackles toplevel widgets along with dialogs of all kinds, and Chapter 8 paints on the canvas, as well as covers how to place images and bitmaps into widgets.

Pushing Buttons

One of the simplest widgets, and most illustrative, is the not-so-lowly `button` widget. The simple two-line **hello.tcl** script from Chapter 1 created a `button` widget. Although this widget is simple, you can do a lot with a `button`, for it is the `button` widget that makes most things happen in a graphical user interface.

When to Use a `button`

A `button` widget displays a raised 3D bevel (this is configurable, though), as shown in Figure 3.2. When you press and release the leftmost mouse button with the mouse cursor over a button, a set of Tcl code—set up by you—gets executed. The `button` widget exists to execute commands on demand. So, you'll find `button` widgets most appropriate when the user wants the program to perform some action, such as searching the Internet, formatting a hard disk, or saving a file.

Figure 3.2 A `button` widget.

Creating Widgets

All Tk widgets are created in nearly the same manner. The basic syntax is

```
widget name arguments
```

In this case, *widget* is the type of widget to create, such as `button` or `scrollbar`. The widget types, like `button` and `scrollbar`, are actual Tcl commands provided by the Tk add-on to Tcl. *Name* is the widget name, and *arguments* are any options. The most common options appear in Table 3.2. So, to create a `button`, you only need the following command:

```
button .name
```

where *.name* is the name of the `button`. Of course, this leads to a very uninteresting `button` that has no text displayed and that does nothing when pushed (once packed—you must pack a widget to make it visible). Each widget must have a unique name. All widget names start with a period, ., because all are children of the main window, which has the odd name of the period.

In order to refer to a widget, you need some identifier. In Tcl/Tk, this is the widget name. That's why these names are so important. You'll find more about widget names in the section on Framing Widgets. For now, just make each name be unique and start with a period.

In Chapter 1, the `-text` and `-command` options specified what text the `button` should display and the command it should execute when pushed. There are even more options listed in Table 3.2.

Common Widget Options

Most widgets support a common set of options, as listed in Table 3.2. This is a huge set and not every widget supports every option.

Table 3.2 Common widget options.

Option	Meaning
-activebackground *color*	Active background color.
-activeborderwidth *width*	Border width, in pixels, when active.
-activeforeground *color*	Active foreground color.
-anchor *anchor_pos*	Positions information within the widget, to n, ne, nw, s, se, sw, e, w, and center.
-background *color*	Sets normal widget background color.
-bg *color*	Sets normal widget background color, same as background

`-bitmap bitmap`	Display bitmap in widget, one of `error`, `gray12`, `gray25`, `gray50`, `gray75`, `hourglass`, `info`, `questhead`, `question`, `warning`, or @*filename*.
`-borderwidth width`	Sets border width, in pixels.
`-bd width`	Sets border width, in pixels, same as `-borderwidth`.
`-command tcl_script`	Executes *tcl_script* when invoked.
`-cursor cursor`	Cursor to display when mouse is in widget.
`-disabledforeground color`	Disabled foreground color.
`-exportselection state`	True/false value whether selection in widget should be X (UNIX) selection.
`-font fontname`	Use *fontname* for widget's text.
`-foreground color`	Sets normal widget foreground color.
`-fg color`	Sets normal widget foreground color, same as `-foreground`.
`-geometry widthxheight`	Sets size of widget, normally in pixels, but you may use other units. The `x` part is required.
`-height value`	Sets height, normally in pixels, but you can use different units.
`-highlightcolor color`	Color of highlight rectangle that signifies keyboard focus.
`-highlighthickness size`	Sets size of highlight area, in pixels, that signifies keyboard focus.
`-image image`	Image to display in widget.
`-insertbackground color`	Background color of insertion cursor.
`-insertofftime milliseconds`	Sets time gap between cursor blinks.
`-insertontime milliseconds`	Sets duration of cursor blink "on".
`-insertwidth size`	Sets width, in pixels, of insertion cursor.
`-jump on_or_off`	If true, scrollbars delay updating until mouse button is released.

continued

Table 3.2 continued

-justify *justification*	Sets multiline justification to left, center, or right.
-orient *orientation*	Sets orientation to horizontal or vertical.
-padx *pad*	Pads extra pixels in X direction.
-pady *pad*	Pads extra pixels in Y direction.
-relief *relief*	Sets 3D bevel to flat (no bevel), groove, raised, ridge, solid, or sunken.
-repeatdeley *milliseconds*	Time threshold before auto repeat starts.
-repeatinterval *milliseconds*	Time between autorepeats once begun.
-selectbackground *color*	Selected background color.
-selectborderwidth width	Sets size, in pixels, of border when selected.
-setgrid *on_or_off*	If true, sets resizing grid on; otherwise off.
-state *state*	Sets state to normal, disabled, or active (only for buttons and the like).
-text *string*	Sets text to display.
-textvariable *varname*	Sets variable to use to get text string to display.
-troughcolor *color*	Sets color for rectangular troughs in widget.
-underline *which_char*	Underlines character (by position in string).
-width *width*	Sets width, normally in pixels, but you can use different units.
-wraplength *length*	Maximum length of text string for word-wrapping.
-xscrollcommand *prefix*	Prefix for command used to communcation with horizontal scrollbars.
-yscrollcommand *prefix*	Prefix for command used to communcation with vertical scrollbars.

Widget Examples

Continuing with the lowly `button` widget, you can get a good sense of what the available options do by trying the following examples.

After each set of examples, you should `exit` and restart **wish**, so that none of the previous settings influence the new example.

N O T E

To create a `button` with a text string of "Push me" and a command that puts the string "ouch" when pressed, try the following commands:

```
# .b1 widget example from Chapter 3.
#
button .b1 -text "Push me" -command { puts ouch }
pack .b1

# b1.tcl
```

The `puts` command is described in Chapter 1.

Remember that widgets are created invisible. You must `pack` them to make them visible.

N O T E

These commands create a button widget as shown in Figure 3.3.

Figure 3.3 A simple button widget.

To quit this script, you must close the program from the window menu (located at the upper-left corner of the title bar on most Windows and UNIX systems). In real Tcl/Tk scripts, you should provide a means to exit the application gracefully, usually from an Exit menu choice. See Chapter 4 for more on menus.

Colored Buttons

To create a `button` with some garish colors, try

```
# .b2 widget example from Chapter 3.
#
button .b2 -text "Blue Button" \
        -foreground green -background blue
pack .b2

# b2.tcl
```

If you run these commands alone, you should see a garish button like that shown in Figure 3.4.

Figure 3.4 A garish color combination.

You can also run both of these examples, for buttons named *.b1* and *.b2*, together. Enter both sets of commands into **wish**, as shown here:

```
# .b1 widget example from Chapter 3.
#
button .b1 -text "Push me" -command { puts ouch }
pack .b1

# And, .b2 widget example from Chapter 3.
#
button .b2 -text "Blue Button" \
        -foreground green -background blue
pack .b2

# b1_b2.tcl
```

As shown in Figure 3.5, you'll see both buttons.

Figure 3.5 Both buttons in **wish**.

 Each widget requires a unique name.

NOTE

By using the `pack` command to pack both buttons, you've just seen how you can combine more than one widget in a window. See the section on How the Widget Packer Works for more on controlling the way widgets get packed. For now, just try out the options and experiment away.

The preceding example set the foreground color and background color. Unless you have a monochrome display, the colors should be readily obvious. If you move the mouse into the widget, the colors change to the active colors, which the preceding example didn't change. To modify these colors, try

```
# .b3 widget example from Chapter 3.
#
button .b3 \
    -text "Active color test" \
    -foreground green \
    -background blue \
    -activebackground red \
    -activeforeground orange
pack .b3

# b3.tcl
```

NOTE With different versions of Tcl, the active colors may behave differently. On UNIX, if you move the mouse into this widget, you should see an active foreground color of orange and an active background color of orange. On Windows, starting with Tcl 8.0, the active color only applies when the button is pressed in.

Color Names

The color names like *red*, *orange*, *green*, and *blue* come from the X Window color names used commonly on UNIX.

UNIX On most UNIX systems, you can type in the **showrgb** command (in **wish** or in your command shell), and you'll see zillions and zillions of color names matched with RGB (red, green, blue) color definitions, such as the following:

```
255 250 250    snow
248 248 255    ghost white
248 248 255    GhostWhite
245 245 245    white smoke
245 245 245    WhiteSmoke
220 220 220    gainsboro
255 239 213    PapayaWhip
255 240 245    LavenderBlush
255 228 225    MistyRose
211 211 211    LightGrey
119 136 153    LightSlateGray
119 136 153    LightSlateGrey
  0 191 255    DeepSkyBlue
 65 105 225    RoyalBlue
 30 144 255    DodgerBlue
```

You can use any of these color names in Tcl. The color names are quite forgiving and you can mix upper- and lowercase letters, use *gray* or *grey*, and put in or remove spaces (e.g., *DeepSkyBlue* or *"dEEp SKY blue"* should both work)—remember to put multiword names inside of quotation marks or curly braces.

On Windows, Tcl emulates these colors, usually quite well, so you use the same color names as UNIX. Unfortunately, there's no way of knowing the full set of colors unless you delve into the Tk source code in **xlib\xcolors.c**. Some good colors to start with include the primary colors of blue, red, white, black and so on, as well as lightblue, slateblue, and bisque. Windows also supports a special set of colors that come from the Windows Control Panel, including those listed in Table 3.3.

Table 3.3 Special Windows colors.

Color	Usage
System3dDarkShadow	Bottom shadow for 3D bevels.
System3dLight	Top shadow for 3D bevels.
SystemActiveBorder	Active window border.
SystemActiveCaption	Active caption color.
SystemAppWorkspace	Application workspace color.
SystemBackground	System background color.
SystemButtonFace	Default button background color.
SystemButtonHighlight	Button highlight color.
SystemButtonShadow	Button shadow color.
SystemButtonText	Default button text (foreground) color.
SystemCaptionText	Text color for captions.
SystemDisabledText	Disabled text color.
SystemGrayText	Grayed out text color.
SystemHighlight	Default selected color.
SystemHighlightText	Default selected text color.
SystemInactiveBorder	Inactive border color.
SystemInactiveCaption	Inactive caption color.
SystemInactiveCaptionText	Inactive caption text color.
SystemInfoBackground	Info background color.
SystemInfoText	Info text color.
SystemMenu	Default menu background color.

continued

Table 3.3 continued

SystemMenuText	Default menu text (foreground) color.
SystemScrollbar	Default scrollbar trough color.
SystemWindow	Default indicator color.
SystemWindowFrame	Default highlight color.
SystemWindowText	Default text color.

These values come from the Tk source code file **win\tkWinDefault.h**.

RGB Colors

You can also define colors in terms of their RGB values, using hexadecimal numbers and an equal number of digits for the red, green, and blue components. Start such a color with a #, as in the following examples: #FF0000 (red), #0000FF (blue), #FFF (white), #FFFFFF (white) and even #FFFFFFFFF (also white). You must always use the same number of digits for the red, green, and blue components.

The following example works on the widget named *.b3* created in the file **b3.tcl**:

```
  # Red
.b3 configure -foreground #FF0000
  # Blue
.b3 configure -background #0000FF
```

The # character is supposed to start a Tcl comment. But, for colors, Tk uses the X Window convention from UNIX, which leads to a more complicated syntax where the # sometimes starts a comment and sometimes indicates an RGB color value. Because of this, you'll often need to use \# in place of # to prevent the Tcl interpreter from treating the # as the start of a comment.

Fonts

In addition to colors, you can also specify fonts with the -font option. The -font option expects a font name, which you can specify one of these ways:

- The name of a font you created with the `font` command,
- The options necessary to create a font with the `font` command,
- Special system font names for a given platform (Windows, UNIX, or MacOS),
- An X Window font name common on UNIX, or
- A three-item list that describes the font.

In the next sections, you'll see all methods at work. To make your scripts portable across UNIX and Windows, it's best to stick to the `font` command introduced in Tk 8.0.

NOTE This section requires Tcl/Tk 8.0 or higher. If you're running an older version of Tcl/Tk, you cannot use the `font` command. That's unfortunate, because starting with Tcl/Tk 8.0, we finally have the means to specify fonts in a manner that is not dependent on the operating system. This is a great reason to update if you haven't.

The `font` Command

The `font` command doesn't really create fonts. Instead, it creates a Tk handle to a font available on your current system. The best part about this, especially for long-time users of Tcl, is that you can specify fonts generically without worrying about platform-specific issues.

To use the `font` command, you need to invoke one of many subcommands, such as `font create` to create a font. Many Tcl commands are packaged as a family of related commands, all using the same first word—the actual command—and using the second word to differentiate `font create` from `font configure`, for example.

Creating Fonts with the `font` Command

The `font` command creates a named font you can use with Tk widgets. You're not actually creating the font itself but rather a name that represents a font that is available on your system.

To create a named font, use the `font create` command:

```
font create font_name options
```

The *font_name* provides the name you want to refer to the font in the future. The *options* control the look of the font. If you don't specify options, you get the defaults. For example,

```
font create defaultfont
```

This command creates a new Tcl font, with all the platform-dependent defaults, named *defaultfont*.

Using Newly Created Fonts with Widgets

The whole point of creating fonts with the `font` command is to use them in widgets. To do that is exceedingly easy. All you need to do is pass the newly created font name with the `-font` option, as shown here:

```
#
# Font creation test. This example creates
# a font and then uses that font in a widget.
#

  # Create a font named defaultfont.
font create defaultfont

  # Use that font in a button widget.
button .b4 -text "Default Font" \
    -font defaultfont

pack .b4

# b4.tcl
```

This script creates a font and then uses that named font with a widget. The font that gets created depends on the system. On Windows 95, I saw a Times font. On UNIX a fixed-width (Courier) font. Because the font defaults vary by system, it's best to specify more of the font options, especially the font family.

Font Families

The most important feature distinguishing fonts are called font families in Tcl/Tk. A **font family** determines the basic look of a font. This text, for example, is in a Times font. **Helvetica** is another font family, one that does not have the small serifs used in Times. For data entry, you'll often want a fixed-width font, such as `Courier`.

Each platform supports its own set of fonts and font families. And, depending on what software you have installed, there's no guarantee that two Windows 95 systems, or two X Window systems, for example, will have the same fonts.

To help with this, Tk guarantees that at least three font families are always available: `Times`, a serif font; `Helvetica`, a sans-serif font; and `Courier`, a fixed width font. Case does not matter in font family names, so *Times* and *times* are equivalent.

N O T E

Tk guarantees that these font families will exist, but not the actual fonts themselves. For example, on most Windows systems, the font family called Helvetica really maps to the Windows font called Arial. Tk is not providing you with true exact typography. Instead, you just get the ability to specify similar-looking fonts on multiple platforms so that your Tcl scripts work on multiple systems

To use a particular font family, include the `-family` option when creating a font. For example, to use the `Times` family, you can create a font with the following command:

```
font create timesfont -family Times
```

This command creates a font named *timesfont* using the `Times` font family. For example,

```
#
# Another Font creation test.
#

  # Create a Times font.
font create timesfont -family Times

  # Use that font in a button widget.
button .b5 -text "Times Font" \
    -font timesfont
```

```
pack .b5

# b5.tcl
```

Determining Which Font Families Are Available

To determine which font families are available on your system, you can use the `font families` command, which returns a list of the font families available, as shown here:

```
# Lists available font families using Tk 8.0 font command.
#
set families [font families]

puts "Font families:"

foreach i $families {
        puts $i
}

# fontfam.tcl
```

On a UNIX (X Window) system, you'll see a set of fonts like the following:

```
Font families:
fangsong ti
fixed
lucidatypewriter
charter
lucidabright
times
open look glyph
song ti
helvetica
open look cursor
mincho
courier
lucida
utopia
```

```
nil
clean
terminal
symbol
gothic
new century schoolbook
```

UNIX

Not all these font families are useful for Tcl/Tk scripts. The `nil` font family just shows dashes for each character. The `cursor` family contains bitmap icons, as does the `open look cursor` and `open look glyph` font families. Furthermore, many of the fonts contain non-English characters. If you want to create an interface in another language, this can be very useful, but will look odd for English software. Asian language fonts, such as `fangsong ti`, `song ti`, `gothic`, and `mincho`, tend to work poorly with Tcl/Tk. A future version of Tcl should better support Asian languages, but as of version 8.0, Tcl does not properly support Asian text. Of the Asian fonts, `gothic` is the most surprising, because the name doesn't sound foreign.

On a Windows 95 system, you'll see a list more like the following one:

```
Font families:
System
Fixedsys
Terminal
MS Serif
MS Sans Serif
Courier
Symbol
Small Fonts
Roman
Script
Modern
MS Dialog
MS Dialog Light
MS SystemEx
Marlett
Arial
Courier New
```

Times New Roman

Wingdings

Symbol

Arial Narrow

Arial Black

Arial Rounded MT Bold

Book Antiqua

Bookman Old Style

Century Gothic

Century Schoolbook

Haettenschweiler

Algerian

Braggadocio

Britannic Bold

Brush Script MT

Colonna MT

Desdemona

Footlight MT Light

Garamond

Impact

Kino MT

Wide Latin

Matura MT Script Capitals

Playbill

MS LineDraw

Comic Sans MS

Albertus Medium

Albertus Extra Bold

Antique Olive

CG Omega

CG Times

Clarendon Condensed

Coronet

Letter Gothic

Marigold

Univers

Univers Condensed

Font Options

In addition to the family, you can control a lot more about the fonts you create. Table 3.4 lists the font options.

Table 3.4 Options for creating fonts.

Option	Controls
-family *family_name*	Basic look of the font.
-size *point_size*	Size of font in points (1/72 of an inch).
-weight *thickness*	Thickness of font, either bold or normal.
-slant *slant*	Whether font is roman (normal) or italic (slanted).
-underline *boolean*	True if font should be underlined.
-overstrike *boolean*	True if font should have a line through the text.

To get a handle of these options, it's best to try a few examples and experiment. You can use the following example script as a guide for your explorations:

```
#
# Examples of font options.
#
  # Create a Times font.
font create timesfont -family Times \
    -size 12 \
    -weight bold \
    -slant italic

  # Create an Helvetica font.
font create helvfont -family Helvetica \
    -size 16 \
    -weight normal \
```

```
        -slant roman \
        -underline true

    # Create a Courier font.
font create courierfont -family Courier \
        -size 20 \
        -weight bold \
        -slant italic \
        -overstrike true

    # Use fonts in button widgets.
button .times -text "Times Font" \
        -font timesfont

button .helv -text "Helvetica Font" \
        -font helvfont

button .cour -text "Courier Font" \
        -font courierfont

pack .times
pack .helv
pack .cour

# fontopts.tcl
```

This script tests out the available options and creates three buttons like the ones in Figure 3.6.

Figure 3.6 Testing fonts with the **fontopts.tcl** script.

Changing Fonts Once Created

The `font configure` command allows you to change an existing named font.
The syntax is very similar to the `font create` command, which follows:

```
font configure font_name option value option value ...
```

For example,

```
font configure timesfont \
    -size 18 \
    -family Helvetica \
    -slant roman \
    -weight normal \
    -underline true
```

Any widgets using the font you configured, *timesfont* in this example, will
now display using the new configuration.

To try out `font configure`, you can set up a `button` widget to change
its font when you click on the `button`, as shown next:

```
#
# Changing a font using font configure
# when you click on the button widget.
#

  # Create a Times font.
font create timesfont -family Times \
    -size 12 \
    -weight bold \
    -slant italic

  # Use font in button widget.
button .times -text "Click to Change Font" \
    -font timesfont \
    -command {
        font configure timesfont \
```

```
            -size 18 \
            -family Helvetica \
            -slant roman \
            -weight normal \
            -underline true
    }

pack .times

# fontconf.tcl
```

When you start up this script, you'll see a `button` like the one shown in Figure 3.7.

Figure 3.7 The initial font.

After you click on the `button`, the font should change to something more like that shown in Figure 3.8.

Figure 3.8 The changed font.

To help determine what fonts are available to configure, you can use the `font names` command:

```
set names [font names]
```

The `font names` command returns the names of all the fonts created with the `font create` command. For example, using the **fontopts.tcl** script shown in the section on Font Options, the following font names are defined:

```
% font names
courierfont helvfont timesfont
```

Deleting Fonts

Fonts can take up a lot of memory, so you may want to delete fonts that are no longer of use. To do this, call the `font delete` command:

```
font delete font_name
font delete font_name1 font_name2 ...
```

Any widget using a deleted font will still appear using the last values for the deleted font. If you recreate a deleted font, then widgets using that font will change to the new values.

WARNING

You'll get an error if you try to create a font that already exists.

Here's an example of `font delete` in action:

```
#
# Test for deleting a font.
#

  # Create a Times font.
font create timesfont -family Times \
    -size 12 \
    -weight bold \
    -slant italic

  # Use font in button widget.
button .times -text "Click to Delete Font" \
    -font timesfont \
    -command { font delete timesfont }

  # Button to recreate font.
button .recreate -text "Recreate font" \
```

```
    -command {
        font create timesfont \
            -size 18 \
            -family Helvetica \
            -slant roman \
            -weight normal \
            -underline true
    }

pack .times .recreate

# fontdel.tcl
```

Platform Issues with Fonts

Because each computer supports a different set of fonts, you will always have to battle to get the fonts you want displayed. The `font create` and `font configure` commands try the best they can, but nothing is guaranteed. Because of this, you may want to try the `font actual` command, which returns the actual values for a given font. These values may differ from the values you passed to `font create` or `font configure` because of platform limitations. The syntax follows:

```
font actual font_name
```

This command returns a list of all the attributes of the given font. You can also query for a specific value, using the following syntax:

```
font actual font_name option
```

For example:

```
font actual helvfont -family
```

To try `font actual`, you can use the following script:

```
#
# Examples of font actual.
```

```
#

   # Create an Helvetica font.
font create helvfont -family Helvetica \
    -size 16 \
    -weight normal \
    -slant roman \
    -underline true

   # Create a default font.
font create defaultfont

   # Determine font sizes.
set def_act  [font actual defaultfont]
set helv_act [font actual helvfont]

puts "Default font actual values:"
puts $def_act
puts "helvetica font actual values:"
puts $helv_act

# fontact.tcl
```

Note how the results appear in a format you can use with font configure or font create.

Note also how the default font differs between operating systems. On UNIX, you'll see results like the following:

```
Default font actual values:
-family courier -size 12 -weight normal
-slant roman -underline 0 -overstrike 0
helvetica font actual values:
-family helvetica -size 16 -weight normal
-slant roman -underline 1 -overstrike 0
```

On Windows 95, this is more like the following:

```
Default font actual values:
```

```
-family {MS Serif} -size 12 -weight normal
-slant roman -underline 0 -overstrike 0
helvetica font actual values:
-family Arial -size 16 -weight normal
-slant roman -underline 1 -overstrike 0
```

The `font actual` command returns the options as they really exist for a font. You can also get font metrics to help you get a handle on the exact size for a given font.

Font Metrics

The `font metrics` command returns information about the size of the character cells used for the font, as listed in Table 3.5.

Table 3.5 Tk font metrics.

Metric	Usage
-ascent	Number of pixels tallest letter extends above the baseline.
-descent	Number of pixels deepest letter extends below the baseline.
-linespace	Number of pixels that should be used to separate two lines of text vertically.
-fixed	0 for a proportional-width font, 1 for a fixed-width font.

Most windowing systems draw text from a baseline, which is an imaginary line right underneath most characters. Some characters, such as *j*, *p*, and *q*, extend below the baseline. The distance below the baseline is called the **descent**. The distance above the baseline is called the **ascent**. Uppercase letters like *M* have greater ascent than lowercase letters like *m*. The -ascent font metric returns the ascent of the tallest character in the font.

The `font metrics` command is useful for cases where you need to get the exact spacing for lines of text, such as working with the `canvas` widget (see Chapter 8). To get the font metrics, use the following syntax:

```
font metrics font_name
```

If you're interested in a single metric only, you can pass that metric, from Table 3.5, as well, such as

```
font metrics font_name -linespace
```

You can try out the `font metrics` command with the following script:

```
#
# Example of font metrics.
#

  # Create an Helvetica font.
font create helvfont -family Helvetica \
    -size 16 \
    -weight normal \
    -slant roman \
    -underline true

  # Determine font sizes.
set helv_act [font metrics helvfont]

puts "helvetica font metrics:"
puts $helv_act

# fontmet.tcl
```

When you run this script, you'll see output like the following:

```
helvetica font metrics:
-ascent 14 -descent 4 -linespace 18 -fixed 0
```

The `font metrics` command is mostly useful for determining the vertical space text in a given font requires. You can use the `font measure` command to determine the width of text in a given font, as follows:

```
font measure font_name text
```

The `font measure` command returns the number of pixels wide the given text requires in the given font. For fixed-width fonts, each character has the same width, so you can easily calculate the width of a text string from the width of one character. Proportional-width fonts, though, make this calculation troublesome. For both kinds of fonts, you can use the `font measure` command, as shown here:

```
#
# Measuring the number of pixels wide
# a text string requires in a given font.
#

  # Create an Helvetica font.
font create helvfont -family Helvetica \
    -size 24 \
    -weight bold \
    -slant roman

  # Determine font sizes.
set text "Analysis, Mr. Spock?"

set width [font measure helvfont $text]

puts "$text requires $width pixels wide."

# fontmeas.tcl
```

When you run this script, you'll see output like the following:

```
Analysis, Mr. Spock? requires 396 pixels wide.
```

In summary, the `font` command supports the subcommands listed in Table 3.6.

Table 3.6 The font command:

Command	Usage
font actual *font_name*	Returns actual attributes of font.

`font actual` *`font_name option`*	Returns actual value of option for font.
`font configure` *`font_name`* `options`	Changes fonts options.
`font create` *`font_name options`*	Creates a font.
`font delete` *`font_name`*	Deletes a font or fonts.
`font families`	Returns list of font families.
`font measure` *`font_name text`*	Returns width of text in given font in pixels.
`font metrics` *`font_name`*	Returns all metrics of font.
`font metrics` *`font_name option`*	Returns given metric of font.
`font names`	Returns list of all created fonts.

Other Ways to Name Fonts

When you create a font with the `font create` command, you specify a name that you can then use with the `-font` option when creating widgets as well as with the other `font` commands. In addition to creating fonts with `font create`, Tcl provides a number of other means to specify the fonts you want to use. I prefer the `font create` method because it allows for the most options and is the most portable between operating systems.

If you use older Tcl code, you'll probably see one of the alternative naming methods. I'll quickly introduce these methods and then go into the hardest ones in detail. The first alternative method is to use an X Window long font name, of the format shown here:

```
-*-courier-medium-r-normal--34-*-*-*-m-*-*
```

X Window font names come from UNIX and were originally the only way to specify fonts for Tk widgets. Most older Tcl applications use this method for specifying fonts.

Another method originally worked only on Windows. With this method, you specify a font by a three-element list of family, point size and style. For example,

```
{ Times 12 bold }
```

134

Another, although problematic, method is that you can use the options listed in Table 3.4 to create a set of options that define what you want in a font. For example,

```
#
# Example of specifying a font
# by using the font options.
#
button .b8 -text "Font From List" \
    -font { -size 32 }
pack .b8

# b8.tcl
```

WARNING

I got errors every time I tried to use anything except the -overstrike, -size, or -underline options. In addition, only one option was accepted, severely limiting the usefulness of this method. As they say in the automobile advertisements, your mileage may vary.

There's also a number of predefined system-specific fonts you can use on a given platform. (They are listed in Table 3.8 in the section on System-Specific Fonts.)

The most important of these alternative methods is the X Window long font name method. Again, the reason for this is that most available Tcl scripts use this method for specifying fonts.

X Window Long Font Names

Because Tcl was originally written on UNIX, Tk has always supported the X Window font-naming convention. Most UNIX font names (really X Window System font names) tend to be very long. The UNIX command **xlsfonts** will list out zillions of available fonts. Here are a few:

```
-adobe-courier-bold-r-normal--17-120-100-100-m-100-iso8859-1
-adobe-helvetica-bold-o-normal--0-0-75-75-p-0-iso8859-1
-b&h-lucida-medium-i-normal-sans-34-240-100-100-p-192-iso8859-1
-bitstream-charter-medium-r-normal--33-240-100-100-p-183-iso8859-1
-daewoo-mincho-medium-r-normal--0-0-100-100-c-0-ksc5601.1987-0
-jis-fixed-medium-r-normal--24-170-100-100-c-240-jisx0208.1983-0
```

```
-sun-open look glyph--10-100-75-75-p-101-sunolglyph-1
lucidasanstypewriter-24
```

The font format used by UNIX is called the X (short for X Window System) Logical Font Description, or XLFD. Few users know about XLFD, but it is responsible for the long font names used on UNIX and supported by Tk on all platforms.

Coming Up with X Window Font Names

XLFD font names include a number of fields, all separated by a hyphen. The hyphen is important because this means you'll normally need to place font names in quotation marks so that Tcl doesn't interpret the leading hyphen incorrectly (as an option perchance). Table 3.7 lists the fields in an XLFD font name used by Tk.

Table 3.7 Decoding XLFD font names.

Field	Example	Description
foundry	adobe, b&h	The company that created the font.
font family	times, courier	Basic font, usually same as font name on Windows.
weight	bold, medium	How thick the letters are.
slant	i, r	Italic, roman, oblique, etc.
set-width name	normal, condensed	Width of characters.
additional style	sans	Extra info to describe font.
pixel size	26, 20	Height of characters, in pixels.
point size	190, 140	Height of characters, in points * 10.
dots-per-inch	100-100, 75-75	Dots per inch in X and Y directions.
spacing	m, p	Spacing (e.g., fixed-width or proportional).
average width	94, 159	Average width, in pixels * 10.
charset registry	iso885-1	Character set encoded in the font.

Some fields in XLFD font names may have spaces, such as a font family of *Times New Roman.*

N O T E

The *slant* field uses one or two letters to describe the slant of the font. Most fonts use *r* for roman (normal) or *i* for italic. Other choices include *o* (oblique), *ri* (reverse italic), *ro* (reverse oblique), and *ot* (other).

The oddly named *set-width* name field describes the width of the characters. Examples include *condensed, semicondensed, narrow, normal,* and *double wide.* Most are *normal,* though.

The additional *style* field allows the font designer to place any extra information needed to describe the font's style, usually something like *sans* for a sans-serif font. Most font names leave this space blank (where you'll see two hyphens in a row).

A *pixel size* of 0 usually indicates a scalable font.

The *point size* field holds a value 10 times the real size in terms of **points** (1/72nd of an inch). Thus, a point size of 190 means a 19-point font.

The *spacing* field tells you if the font has a fixed width (*m*, *c*) or proportional (*p*). Generally, proportional fonts look better.

Like the point size, the *average width* is also inflated. This value is ten times the average width in terms of pixels. The inflation allows for floating-point numbers to be incoded as integers (e.g., 9.4 becomes 94).

The *charset registry* tells what encoding is used for the characters in the font. The vast majority of X fonts (typically used on UNIX) are encoded using ISO 8859-1 (often called Latin-1), which is a superset of US ASCII. Other character sets include ISO 8859-2 for other European languages such as Czech and Hungarian, JIS 0208-1983 for Japanese Kanji, and a number of Windows code pages. Because of this, I usually use a wildcard (see the discussion in the next section) for this field. Some vendors, like Hewlett-Packard, support their own supersets of ASCII. In HP's case, this superset is called HP-Roman-8 and Hewlett-Packard provides a number of Roman-8-encoded fonts with their systems. You typically won't find these fonts on systems from other vendors.

Wildcards in Font Names

You can use an asterisk, *, in place of most fields. Tk (on Windows) or the X server (on UNIX) will convert the asterisk to a valid value, providing a match can be found. This allows you to know only part of a font name and still use it. It also shortens the very long XLFD font names.

WINDOWS

Tk on Windows supports the X Window font names. Even so, the fonts available on a Windows system differ from UNIX. Furthermore, it is almost impossible to determine the full XLFD font names on Windows, without a program like **xlfsonts**, that exists only under the X Window System. What I usually do is load a word processor program, such as Microsoft Word, and look at a listing of the fonts available. I then use that font name to develop an XLFD name for Tk. For example, with a font name of Arial on Windows (which is typically very close to the Windows default system font), you can generate the following font name:

```
"-*-arial-medium-r-normal--*-*-*-*-*-*"
```

The *medium-r-normal* part is used to get a normal (not bold) font. Note that after the double dash come six asterisks.

Try the following examples, generated from the Courier, Symbol, and Times New Roman fonts, available on most versions of Windows:

```
#
# Using X Window XLFD font naming on Windows.
# (This may actually work on your UNIX system,
# as well. Arial is the only Windows-specific
# font mentioned and Tk maps Arial to and from
# Helvetica.)
#

button .arial -text "Arial" \
        -font "-*-arial-bold-r-normal--*-*-*-*-*-*"

button .courier -text "Courier" \
        -font "-*-courier-medium-r-normal--*-*-*-*-*-*"
```

```
button .symbol -text "Symbol" \
        -font "-*-symbol-medium-i-normal--*-240-*-*-*-*"

pack .arial .courier .symbol

# winxlfd.tcl
```

This script should also run on most versions of UNIX. The Courier and Symbol fonts are common on X Window systems and the Arial font seems to get mapped to Helvetica.

The first example uses a bold font in the default size. The second uses a normal font (Courier is also usually a monospaced font). The third example uses the Symbol font, usually filled with mathematical (mostly Greek) symbols, in a 24-point italic font.

The Three-Element List Method

The three-element list method is very similar to creating fonts with the `font create` command. With this method, though, you need to specify two or three options for the font you want: family, point size, and optionally a list of styles in a three-element list. For example,

```
{ Times 12 bold }
```

WINDOWS

This method originally comes from the Windows port of Tcl/Tk. This should look familiar to Win32 programmers.

If the font name has spaces in it, for example, *Times New Roman*, then you need to delimit the name with either quotes or curly braces:

```
{ {Times New Roman} 12 bold }
{ "Times New Roman" 12 bold }
```

U N I X

Times New Roman is a Windows font. You're unlikely to have this font on UNIX.

The font families command lists the available font families on a given system.

In using this method, you can skip the list of styles. For example,

```
{ Helvetica 18 }
```

Or, you can include a list of styles within the list that specifies the font, as shown next:

```
{ Times 12 { bold italic underline } }
```

Note the list embedded within the list. The available styles include: bold, italic, normal, overstrike, roman, and underline.

To try out this method, you can use the following script:

```
#
# Example of specifying a font
# by using the font options.
#
button .b9a -text "Font From List" \
    -font { Times 12 bold }

button .b9b -text "Shorter List" \
    -font { Helvetica 18 }

button .b9c -text "Style List" \
    -font { Times 12 { bold italic underline } }

pack .b9a .b9b .b9c

# b9.tcl
```

System-Specific Fonts

Each operating system supports a number of system fonts that you can use in your applications, as shown in Table 3.8.

Table 3.8 Available system-specific fonts.

Platform	Available System Fonts
Macintosh	`application`, `system`
Windows	`ansi`, `ansifixed`, `device`, `oemfixed`, `system`, and `systemfixed`.
X Window (UNIX)	All font names supported by **xlsfonts**.

X Window Fonts on UNIX

While the X Window System runs on many more platforms than just UNIX, X provides the de facto graphics system for virtually all versions of UNIX. For better or worse (better and worse, actually), X is closely tied to UNIX. Because of this, you can use X Window commands on UNIX. For example, the **xlsfonts** command prints a complete list of all available font names and was discussed in the section on X Window Long Font Names.

When you have a full font name, such as `-*-courier-medium-r-normal--*-*-*-*-*-*`, you can use the **xfd** command to view the font, using a command like the one following:

```
xfd -fn "font_name"
```

It's best to enclose the font name in quotes, so that the dashes so common in X Window Font names are not interpreted as command-line parameters.

To help select fonts, you can also use the **xfontsel** command, which displays a sample of a font and allows you to experiment with fonts and font sizes. Figure 3.9 shows the **xfontsel** program.

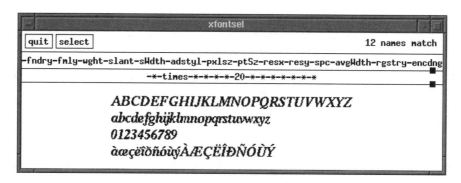

Figure 3.9 Selecting fonts with **xfontsel**.

Fonts on Windows

Windows 95 and NT versions of Tcl/Tk support the following predefined font names: ansi, ansifixed, device, oemfixed, system, and system-fixed. You can use these fonts, as shown here:

```
#
# Using Windows system-specific fonts.
# THIS EXAMPLE ONLY WORKS ON WIN32 SYSTEMS!
#
# Tcl/Tk on Windows supports the following
# predefined fonts: ansi, ansifixed, device,
# oemfixed, system, and systemfixed.
#

button .ansi -text "ansi" -font ansi
button .ansifixed -text "ansifixed" -font ansifixed
```

```
button .device -text "device" -font device
button .oemfixed -text "oemfixed" -font oemfixed
button .system -text "system" -font system
button .systemfixed -text "systemfixed" \
    -font systemfixed

pack .ansi .ansifixed .device .oemfixed \
    .system .systemfixed

# winfont.tcl
```

The **winfont.tcl** example will not work on UNIX, because these Windows-specific fonts are not defined on the UNIX version of Tcl/Tk. You will get an error something like the following:

```
Error in startup script: font "ansi" doesn't exist
    (processing "-font" option)
```

Viewing Windows Fonts

One of the best ways to try out fonts in Windows is with the **WordPad** application (or any word processor such as MS Word), which should be available from the *Start* menu. You can select different fonts and type in sample text. You can use the **Character Map** application, usually under the *Start/Programs/Accessories* menu, to show all the characters in a font.

If you need to create cross-platform applications, you should either stick to the `font create` command or use the X Window-style XLFD names. Even though the long font names are tedious to type in, they do work on both Windows and UNIX.

That may seem like a lot on fonts for the simple `-font` option used when creating widgets. But, a great part of what your application looks like is controlled by fonts, so this is a rather important option. Luckily, most of the other options are easier to use.

Calling Code from Widgets

Continuing on with the button widget, one of the most common tasks is to execute a Tcl procedure from the -command option to the button. The -command option tells the Tcl interpreter what code to execute when the button gets activated. Up to now, all the examples use simple Tcl commands placed directly with the -command option, as shown here:

```
#
# Exploring the -command option for buttons.
#

button .bcmd1 -text "Click to Exit" \
    -command exit
pack .bcmd1

# b_cmd1.tcl
```

This simple example just calls a built-in command, exit.

You can extend this to use any procedure whether built-in or written by you, as shown next:

```
#
# Exploring the -command option for buttons.
#

button .bcmd2 -text "Click to Exec Procedure" \
    -command myproc
pack .bcmd2

proc myproc { } {
    puts "You clicked the button!"
}

# b_cmd2.tcl
```

When you click on the `button`, you'll see the message printed in the console window.

In many cases, though, you don't just want to call a procedure, but to pass data to the procedure as well. The following example shows three ways to pass data: as static values, with a variable that gets evaluated once, and with a variable that gets evaluated each time it gets called. Here is the example:

```
#
# Exploring the -command option for buttons.
#

button .bcmd3a -text "Click to Exec Procedure" \
    -command { myproc 1 2 3 }
pack .bcmd3a

set var 1
button .bcmd3b -text "Click to Use New Value" \
    -command { myproc $var 2 3 }
pack .bcmd3b

button .bcmd3c -text "Click For Old Value" \
    -command "myproc $var 2 3"
pack .bcmd3c

proc myproc { a b c } {
    puts "You passed $a $b $c"
}

#
# Notice the value is changed after
# all widgets were created.
#
set var 2

# b_cmd3.tcl
```

The `button` *.bcmd3a* just gets three values to the `myproc` procedure. In this case, curly braces or quotes are necessary to pass an argument that has spaces in it. The value after the `-command` option is one single argument. You need to convert the multiple values—the procedure to call and its data—into one argument—hence the curly braces.

Button *.bcmd3b* passes the Tcl code to execute to the `-command` option with curly braces. From Chapter 2, curly braces defer execution and variable substitution until later. When you click on the *.bcmd3b* `button`, the variable *var* gets evaluated with whatever value it holds at the time you click.

The `button` *.bcmd3c* differs. This `button` uses double quotes for the `-command` option. With double quotes, variable substitution gets performed right away, before you ever click on the `button`. The substituted code then gets passed to the `-command` option.

This is very important and the cause of many problems when learning Tcl. Remember:

- When you want to lock in a value as it was when the widget was created, use double quotes.
- When you want to use the current value for a variable that may change, use curly braces.

If this doesn't make sense, keep working with the **b_cmd3.tcl** example until it does. I tend to use the double quotes more than curly braces, especially for Tcl code that automatically creates widgets from inside a Tcl procedure. The differences between curly braces and double quotes are covered in Chapter 2. It is very important that you understand the difference.

Text Options

Most widgets support two main options for text, `-text` and `-textvariable`. The `-text` option sets the widget to display the given text.

The `-textvariable` option sets the widget to display the value held in a variable. For example,

```
#
# Using the -textvariable widget option.
#
#
set count 0
global count

    # Create a button that uses a text variable.
set widget_text "Click to Reset"
global widget_text
button .textvar -textvariable widget_text \
    -command {
        global count
        set count 0
    }

pack .textvar

    #
    # The second button increments its
    # variable when clicked.
    #
button .count -textvariable count \
    -command incr_count
pack .count

proc incr_count { } {
    global count

    set count [expr $count + 1]
}

# textvar.tcl
```

The **textvar.tcl** script creates two buttons, as shown in Figure 3.10. Both buttons use the -textvariable widget option, so both buttons get the text to display from the contents of the *widget_text* and *count* variables, respectively.

Figure 3.10 The **textvar.tcl** script showing variables as widget text.

The first button resets the *count* variable to 0 when pressed. The second button increments the *count* variable. Notice that, in all cases, the -command Tcl code lists the variable as global. This is because we want to change the *count* variable in global scope.

As the value changes, the widget gets updated. This is a very handy way to display data in widgets.

Technically, all the global statements are not necessary in this context because -textvariable makes the variable global anyway. You only need to mark the variable global inside the incr_count procedure. Even so, it's a good practice to follow because your procedures will not see the variable unless its marked as global. The following script removes the unnecessary global statements:

```
#
# Using the -textvariable widget option,
# this time skipping the global statements
# where not necessary.
#
#
set count 0

    # Create a button that uses a text variable.
set widget_text "Click to Reset"
button .textvar -textvariable widget_text \
    -command {
        set count 0
    }
```

```
pack .textvar

    #
    # The second button increments its
    # variable when clicked.
    #
button .count -textvariable count \
    -command incr_count
pack .count

proc incr_count { } {
    global count

    set count [expr $count + 1]
}
# textvar2.tcl
```

NOTE You still need a global statement inside the incr_count procedure.

Changing Widgets Once Created

After you create a widget, you can change most values stored with a widget. The -textvariable option lets you do this by changing a single text variable. You can also change any option passed at widget creation, using the configure option with each widget.

This gets a bit complicated, but Tk automatically registers a new command for each widget you create. Tcl allows you to extend the language with new commands, and Tk takes advantage of this capability. This new command is the widget name, such as *.b5*, which has now entered the Tcl interpreter as a new command. This is one reason why each widget must have a unique name, because each Tcl command must be unique.

The configure option changes values in the widget. The cget option retrieves a value from the widget. The syntax for configure is

widgetname configure *arguments*

The *arguments* allowed are the same as when you created the widget, such as -text, -foreground, and so on. For example,

```
#
# Using configure.
#
button .conf -text "Before Configure" \
    -command change_conf
pack .conf

proc change_conf { } {

    .conf configure \
        -foreground white \
        -activeforeground white \
        -background black \
        -activebackground black \
        -text "After Configure"
}
# config1.tcl
```

After clicking on the button, you should see it change color.

NOTE If you doubt that a widget is reflecting a new value, then try something really garish. For example, set the colors to *pink*, *maroon*, and *limegreen*. This should give you an immediate visual cue as to whether the config-ure option is working.

The cget option retrieves one value from the widget, as shown here:

```
#
# Using cget.
#
button .cget -text "This is the text" \
    -command get_value
pack .cget
```

```
proc get_value { } {

    set txt [.cget cget -text]
    set fore [.cget cget -foreground]
    set back [.cget cget -background]

    puts "For widget .cget, text is <$txt>"
    puts "\t Foreground color=$fore, Background=$back"
}

# cget.tcl
```

When you click on the button, the script prints out the value of the text, foreground, and background options for the widget.

Now that you've seen the basic ways to create a widget, control its options, and change a widget once created, the next step is to delve into more Tk widgets than we have for the button we've been using so far. The next sections cover the basic Tk widgets.

Displaying Text Messages with Labels

A label widget is even simpler than a button, because it displays text (or a bitmap, covered in Chapter 8). As show in Figure 3.11, a label widget is a simple beast.

Figure 3.11 A label widget.

Use the label command to create label widget:

```
#
# The label widget.
#
```

```
label .l -text "This is a label"
pack .l

# label.tcl
```

Even though it may appear lowly, you'll need a lot of `label` widgets to place text that explains the interface. For example, an error dialog box displays a `label` widget (amongst other widgets) that contains an important error message.

Even though labels may just seem like glitz in the interface, don't doubt their importance. What good is a user interface that users can't figure out? Furthermore, you can use the `-textvariable` option with labels to display the value of a variable in the `label`.

Multiline Labels

A `message` widget holds a multiline label, such as this one:

```
#
# message widget.
#

message .m -text \
  "This is a test of the Emergency\
  Tcl system. Had this been a real\
  emergency, your widgets would blink."

pack .m

# message.tcl
```

The `message` widget supports the `-width` option, which allows you to control how much space appears before the `message` widget wraps to the next line.

The default for units is pixels, but you can also try units such as c (for centimeters), i (for inches), m (for millimeters), and p (for points, each 1/72 of an inch). Try the following `configure` options for the `message` widget .*m*:

```
source message.tcl
.m configure -width 2c
.m configure -width 5i
.m configure -width 20m
.m configure -width 20p
.m configure -width 25
.m configure -width 100
```

The sizes aren't exact, because many systems cannot accurately calculate exact dimensions when the screen size isn't known. (If you replace a 15 inch monitor with a 17 inch monitor, you typically don't have to perform any configuration, but every dimension will now be off.)

At 2 cm, the widget appears as shown in Figure 3.12.

Figure 3.12 A narrow message widget.

At 5 inches, the widget appears as shown in Figure 3.13.

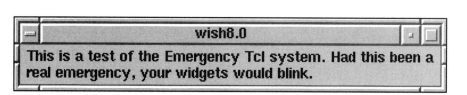

Figure 3.13 A wide message widget.

Radio- and Checkbuttons

Radiobuttons and checkbuttons allow you to provide the user with a set of on/off or true/false choices. The user can turn on or off each widget. With radiobuttons, the user is further limited to having only one radiobutton, within a given frame or **wish** window, on. (A frame widget groups other widgets and is covered in the section on Framing Widgets.) This is another reason why you'll use frame widgets for grouping.

When To Use Radio- and Checkbuttons

Use a checkbutton to control a mode, for example, to control whether the printing is draft or full quality. Use a radiobutton to select between one of many options, where only one option is permissible at a time. In both cases, checkbuttons and radiobuttons should merely set variable values. If you want checkbutton or radiobutton to execute Tcl code when clicked, you should be very careful about that code. Users do not expect checkbuttons and radiobuttons to initiate actions.

Working with Radio- and Checkbuttons

Create a radiobutton with the radiobutton command, and a checkbutton with, you guessed it, the checkbutton command. Try the checkbutton first, because it's easier to understand.

Create the following checkbutton:

```
# checkbutton.
```

```
checkbutton .check1 -text "Check" \
    -variable check \
    -command { puts ".check1 holds $check." }
pack .check1

# check1.tcl
```

The **check1.tcl** script creates a platform-specific checkbutton. On Windows, you'll see a checkbutton like that in Figure 3.14.

Figure 3.14 The checkbutton on Windows.

On UNIX, you'll see a widget more like Figure 3.15.

Figure 3.15 The checkbutton on UNIX.

The -variable option names the variable that the checkbutton will use to hold its value. The default -variable is the widget name. Usually, you'll want to specify your own variable.

 A checkbutton typically has its own variable, whereas a radiobutton usually shares a variable with all other radiobuttons in the same frame.

NOTE

Now, click the checkbutton on and off. When on, you'll see that the variable *check* holds a value of 1. When off, you'll see a value of 0. This is the default. You can also specify a value for when a checkbutton is on (-onvalue) and when it is off (-offvalue), as shown here:

```
# checkbutton with on and off values.
```

```
checkbutton .check2 -text "Check with Value" \
    -variable check \
    -onvalue "Print all" \
    -offvalue "Do not print" \
    -command { puts ".check2 holds $check." }
pack .check2

# check2.tcl
```

The -onvalue gives a value for the variable when the checkbutton is on, and the -offvalue gives a value for when the checkbutton is off. In both cases, the -variable option names the variable that gets the value. The -onvalue and -offvalue options just change the possible values from the default 1 and 0.

Of course, you can skip these options and simply control the activity with the -command option and the Tcl code you give for the -command option. Watch out, though, because the Tcl code gets called when the widget turns on as well as when it turns off. This is the purpose of the on and off values, to allow you to control the value set when widget gets turned on or off.

The -indicatoron option allows you to turn the display of the indicator on or off. Load the example file, **check2.tcl**, with the source command and then try the following commands:

```
.check2 configure -indicatoron 0
```

This command turns off (0 is false in Tcl) the display of the indicator. You can turn it back on with the following command:

```
.check2 configure -indicatoron 1
```

With the indicator off, the checkbutton looks more like a button that keeps its state by remaining on.

Radiobuttons

Radiobuttons are like checkbuttons, but only one radiobutton may be on inside a given **parent widget** (usually a dialog box, the main window, or a `frame` widget, covered under the section on Framing Widgets). This makes `radiobuttons` harder to work with—at least for testing—because you always need at least two.

The following slightly more complicated code creates a small print options display that controls whether to print all pages or just the current page. Such a set of options is very common in a *Print* dialog box in most applications.

To build this, we'll start with a variable to hold the state of how many pages to print: *All* or the *Current Page*. We'll call this variable *print_pages*. One `radiobutton` will set the variable *print_pages* to *All*; the other will set it to *Current Page*. The `radiobuttons` won't cause anything to happen, just to change the mode of how much to print. In general, you do not want a `radiobutton` to initiate an action. That's the purview of the `button` widget.

In most cases, all radiobuttons in a single parent widget will share the same variable name. That's because all are setting different values for the same option.

To actually print a document (or in our case, just display a text message), the user will click on a `button` widget (labeled *Print*). All together, this makes for one of the most real, and complex, examples so far. You'll want to look at this one closely:

```
# radiobutton example.

    # Print procedure.
proc print { } {
    global  print_pages

    puts "Printing $print_pages."
}

label .print_options -text "Print Options"

radiobutton .all -text "All" \
```

```
    -variable print_pages \
    -value all \
    -anchor w

radiobutton .current -text "Current Page Only" \
    -variable print_pages \
    -value "current page only" \
    -anchor w

button .print -text "Print" -command { print }

pack .print_options .all .current .print -fill x

    # Turn on radiobutton, as a default.
.all invoke

# radio.tcl
```

Figure 3.16 shows this example on the screen on Windows.

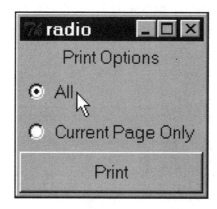

Figure 3.16 A print options window using radiobuttons.

Figure 3.17 shows this same example on UNIX.

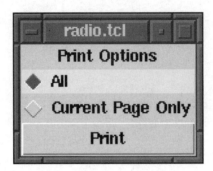

Figure 3.17 A print options window using radiobuttons.

This Tcl example introduces some new concepts, including:

- The -anchor w option anchors the radiobuttons to the Western side (left) of the widget, within the available space used by the widget.

- Neither radiobutton uses the -command option, but the *Print* button does. The radiobuttons are merely setting a value into a variable.

- The *Print* button calls a Tcl proc for its -command option. Remember you can call any set of Tcl code from the -command option.

- The proc *print* is forced to use the global statement so that it can access the variable *print_pages*. Inside a procedure, you can only access variables that are local to the procedure. If you need to access a variable outside of the procedure, you must declare it as being global.

- Even though checkbutton widgets have -onvalue and -off-value options, radio buttons have only a -value option. This tends to confuse and so is an easy mistake to make.

- The -fill x option to the pack command tells the packer to fill widgets in the x (horizontal) direction. See the section on the packer for more on this.

- The invoke option on the last line of the example turns one of the radiobuttons on. It is always a good idea to start with one button being on, rather than in an undetermined state.

Flashing Radiobuttons

You can control radio- and checkbuttons from your Tcl scripts using a number of options such as `flash`, `invoke`, `select`, and `deselect`. All these options work off the command created for the name of the widget. That is, Tk registers a new command for each widget created. So, when it creates a widget named *.all*, Tk also registers a command named `.all`. (We've already used this command with the `configure` and `cget` options.)

Radio- and checkbuttons add in some new options to this widget command.

The `flash` option causes the widget to flash briefly. You can try this with the **radio.tcl** script. To use `flash`, try

```
.all flash
```

(Remember to replace *.all* with the name of your widget.)

The `select` option turns a widget on, as shown here:

```
.current select
```

The `select` option just turns the widget on, it does not invoke the Tcl code associated with the widget's `-command` option (if set).

The `deselect` option, as you'd guess, turns a widget off:

```
.current deselect
```

To turn a widget on and invoke the Tcl code associated with the `-command` option (if any Tcl code was set up), use `invoke`:

```
.current invoke
```

To toggle a `checkbutton` (but not a `radiobutton`) widget (from on to off or off to on), use

```
.check1 toggle
```

The `toggle` option generates an error on `radiobuttons`.

WARNING

The Scale Widget

Use the `scale` widget for sliding values (what a comment on our times). A `scale` widget is a lot like a `scrollbar` (covered in Chapter 6) in that it goes from a start position to an end position.

The basic `scale` goes from 0 to 100 and is aligned vertically, as shown in Figure 3.18. The commands to create a `scale` follow:

```
#
# Simple scale widget.
#
scale .scale1
pack .scale1

# scale1.tcl
```

Figure 3.18 A basic `scale` widget.

When To Use a `scale` Widget

Scale widgets work best for values that go from a minimum to a maximum and don't require a great degree of accuracy. Setting a decimal value from

0.00001 to 0.00010 is probably not a good idea. Scales are often used to select color values (typically going from 0 to 255 for 256 colors), screen resolutions (usually with a limited number of values such as 800 × 600 to 1024 × 768) and the length of time for a meeting in a calendar program. Scales are not highly exact, because there aren't many pixels on the display and few users have the exacting hand-eye coordination to set values accurately with very small increments.

With the `scale` widget, you can adjust the starting value with the -`from` option and then ending value with the -`to` option:

```
#
# scale widget with -from and -to.
#
scale .red -from 0 -to 255
pack .red

# scale2.tcl
```

You can add a label to explain the `scale` (a recommended option):

```
#
# scale widget with a -label.
#
scale .blue -from 0 -to 255 -label "Blue"
pack .blue

# scale3.tcl
```

For scales, the text is stored with the -`label` option, not the more common -`text` option.

NOTE

Controlling the Scale

A `scale` widget is oriented as either `horizontal` or `vertical`, defaulting to `vertical`. You can control this with the -`orient` option.

You can set up tic marks (really tic numeric labels) at an interval with the -tickinterval option. If the -tickinterval is too low, you'll see the numbers mashed together, so I usually start out with a -tickinterval of 50. See the section on Making Scales Bigger for an example of the -tickinterval option.

The -showvalue option lets you turn on (1) or off (0) the numeric display of the current value of the scale.

Try the following commands to turn the value off, using the **scale3.tcl** example file:

```
.blue configure -showvalue 0
```

and turn the display back on

```
.blue configure -showvalue 1
```

A number of user actions cause a scale to jump. The -bigincrement option controls how far to jump in such a case:

```
.blue configure -bigincrement 10
```

Controlling Floating-Point Conversions

Because all Tcl values are really stored as strings, the scale widget gives you some control over the conversion process. This really only applies for scales involving highly accurate numbers.

The -digits option controls the number of significant digits to retain when converting the value.

You normally use the -digits option with the -resolution option, which controls the resolution of the scale, a term that requires some explanation. If you want to set the scale to increment by 0.01 each time, then set the -resolution option to 0.01. If you do so, you'll note that the scale value (if -showvalue is set to 1) will all of a sudden appear as a floating-point number.

The default for the -resolution is 1, so it increments by whole numbers. To change this, use something like the following:

```
.blue configure -resolution .01
```

When you do this, you'll see the `scale` go from 0.00 to 255.00 in .01 incre-ments, a tiny amount for each step.

```
.blue configure -digits 4
```

If you set the `-digits` options to 4, (with the `-resolution` of .01 shown earlier) then you lose a decimal point. Why? Because 255.0, the maximum value, requires 4 digits to display. Thus, 255.00 becomes 255.0 with this option. You need to set the `-digits` options to 5 to get back the two deci-mal digits. Note how this is dependent on the minimum and maximum val-ues of the `scale`, set with the `-from` and `-to` options, respectively.

Executing Tcl Code When the Scale Changes

You can set up a variable to hold the value of a `scale`, and, of course, this variable will track changes in the `scale`. Use the familiar `-variable` option.

This is not `-textvariable` but `-variable`.

You can also use the equally familiar `-command` option to set up Tcl code to call when the `scale` changes.

When the user slides the `scale` thumb, this code can get called many times in a short interval. To maintain performance, you should stick to a short set of Tcl code for the `-command` option.

One tricky part of the `scale's` `-command` option is that the value of the `scale` will be appended to the code. Thus, if you write a procedure for this case, you should include a variable parameter, as shown next:

```
#
# scale widget with -command Tcl code.
#
```

```
   # Scale's value gets appended to call.
proc scale_value { value } {
    puts "New scale value: $value"
}

scale .scale4 -label "Scale Test" \
    -command scale_value

pack .scale4

# scale4.tcl
```

As you move the scale, you'll see the new value printed. Note how the -command Tcl script, the scale_value procedure, assumes it gets a value, even though we don't explicitly pass that value. The scale widget appends this value to the call. So, how do you pass parameters of your own to such a procedure? Pass your parameters at the beginning and assume the scale widget adds the current value at the end, as shown here:

```
#
# scale widget with -command Tcl code
# and extra parameters.
#

   # Scale's value gets appended to call.
proc scale_value { p1 p2 p3 value } {
    puts "$p1 $p2 $p3 and new scale value: $value"
}

scale .scale5 -label "Scale Test" \
    -command "scale_value One Two Three"

pack .scale5

# scale5.tcl
```

The scale shown in **scale5.tcl** passes three parameters of its own to the scale_value procedure. The scale widget adds a fourth parameter—the current value of the scale—at the end.

Making Scales Bigger

Frequently, you'll want the `scale` to extend wider than it normally would. To expand a `scale`, you can use the `-length` option and specify how wide to make a horizontal scale or how tall to make a vertical `scale`:

```
#
# scale widget with -length.
#

scale .green -label "Green" -from 0 -to 255 \
    -length 300 \
    -orient horizontal \
    -tickinterval 50

pack .green

# scale6.tcl
```

The `scale` widget in **scale6.tcl** uses the `-length` option to extend the length of the `scale`, the `-orient` option to make it `horizontal`, and the `-tickinterval` to display a numbers along the `scale`, as shown in Figure 3.19.

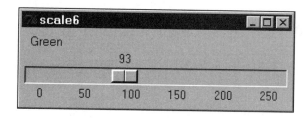

Figure 3.19 A horizontal scale.

Special Scale Widget Commands

The `scale` widget provides two main special commands, `get` and `set`. To use these commands, you need the name of the `scale`, as in the following example (which assumes you've entered in the **scale6.tcl** file):

```
% .green get
79
```

This returns the value of the `scale` widget named *.green*, again using the command that Tk registers that is the name of the widget (just like the `configure` option does).

To set a value into the `scale`, use the `set` option:

```
% .green set 42
```

Use the `set` option to ensure that all scales start at a default value you choose.

RGB Scales

You can use the following example to show more about how `scale` widgets work. The following Tcl code creates three `scale` widgets and a `button` for testing the color. An *Exit* button quits the script. The scales control the familiar red, green, and blue components of a color value, in this case, the background color of the `button` widget. The border of the `button` widget appears very wide, so you can see not only the background color selected but also how Tcl creates the top and button 3D shadow colors, as you move the scales.

The example code follows:

```
#
# RGB color-setting scale.
#

  # Changes background color used by button.
proc modify_color { which_color value } {
    global color red green blue

    switch $which_color {
        red   { set red   $value }
        green { set green $value }
        blue  { set blue  $value }
```

```
    }

    set color [format "#%2.2x%2.2x%2.2x" \
        $red $green $blue]

        # Change background color of button.
    .color configure -background $color
}

global color red green blue
set color "Select a color"
set red    75
set green 75
set blue   75

button .color -textvariable color -anchor w \
    -borderwidth 10 \
    -command { puts "Color is: [.color cget -text]" }

scale .red -from 0 -to 255 -label "Red" \
    -length 300 -orient horizontal \
    -command "modify_color red" \
    -tickinterval 50
.red set $red

scale .green -from 0 -to 255 -label "Green" \
    -length 300 -orient horizontal \
    -command "modify_color green" \
    -tickinterval 50
.green set $green

scale .blue -from 0 -to 255 -label "Blue" \
    -length 300 -orient horizontal \
    -command "modify_color blue" \
    -tickinterval 50
.blue set $blue
button .exit -text "Exit" -command {
    puts "Color is: [.color cget -text]" ; exit }
```

```
pack .color .red .green .blue .exit

# rgbscale.tcl
```

This script file creates a window like that shown in Figure 3.20.

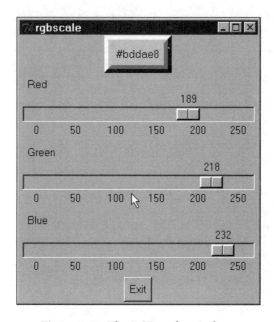

Figure 3.20 The RGB scale window.

You can use the **rgbscale.tcl** script to help you select colors for your widgets. Tcl also offers a color selection dialog box, described in Chapter 7.

Note the lines with the set options. These commands provide an initial value for the scale.

How the Widget Packer Works

After a whirlwind tour of many of Tk's widgets, now we'll get into real widget applications. Even though single-widget tests illustrate individual widgets, the hardest part is putting widgets together in a pleasing easy-to-understand layout.

In Tk, the **pack geometry manager** is the main way you have to control how multiple widgets get placed together, run from the `pack` command. In most uses, the `pack` command provides you with one strip of widgets, going either horizontal or vertical. All widgets inside that packer then appear one after another going either from top to bottom or left to right. Of course, there are a lot more options, but this is the basic idea.

The `pack` command deals best with a single horizontal or vertical row or column. For anything else, `pack` typically proves too difficult to use. (In this situation, you can use the `grid` geometry manager discussed in the section on Using a Grid Layout.)

Because `pack` deals best with a single row or column (and because `pack` requires less configuration than `grid`), you need to start thinking in terms of a single row or column. Few real world widget layouts match this pattern, so you need to start thinking about widgets within widgets. To do this, you'll often use a `frame` widget (discussed in the section on Framing Widgets), which can hold a set of child widgets within the `frame`. By placing `frames` within `frames`, you can create the single row or column that works best with the `pack` command.

Although this may sound convoluted, every real Tcl/Tk application requires nested widgets, in other words, `frames` within `frames`. For example, consider the main application window for a typical application, shown in Figure 3.21.

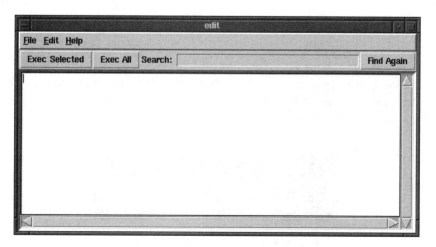

Figure 3.21 A typical main application window.

There are quite a few widgets shown in Figure 3.21, but there is really only one column. Taking a look at the overall structure, the menu bar spans the entire window across the top. Below the menu bar, a toolbar also spans the main window. Following the toolbar comes the main area and then a status area. In all, the application shown in Figure 3.21 really has just one column. Each widget within the column, the toolbar for example, holds other widgets, but the overall structure is one simple column. This type of layout works well with the pack command.

In the next sections, you'll see examples of the pack command's many options, devised to be as simple as possible to better show the differences in packing styles. After that, you'll see the grid method for widget layout and then read about frame widgets, integral to either layout method.

The pack command defaults to placing widgets one after another, from the top to the bottom. To pack widgets horizontally, use the -side left option, as shown in the following code example:

```
#
# pack -side left
#
button .widget1 -text "Widget 1"
button .widget2 -text "Widget 2"
button .widget3 -text "Widget 3"

pack .widget1 .widget2 .widget3 -side left

# pack1.tcl
```

With this option, as shown in Figure 3.22, the **wish** window contracts to fit exactly the space needed to hold the widgets. You can add (and pack) more widgets, and the window will enlarge.

Figure 3.22 Packing from the left side.

You can reverse this order and `pack` from the `right`, although this is not used as much as packing from the `left`:

```
#
# pack -side right
#
button .widget1 -text "Widget 1"
button .widget2 -text "Widget 2"
button .widget3 -text "Widget 3"

pack .widget1 .widget2 .widget3 -side right

# pack2.tcl
```

When you do this, the widgets will reverse positions, but still remain horizontal.

When you want a vertical stripe, you can pack from the `top` or `bottom`:

```
#
# pack -side top
#
button .widget1 -text "Widget 1"
button .widget2 -text "Widget 2"
button .widget3 -text "Widget 3"

pack .widget1 .widget2 .widget3 -side top

# pack3.tcl
```

This configuration is shown in Figure 3.23.

Figure 3.23 Packing from the top.

Inserting Widgets into the Layout

You can insert new widgets into a layout by using the `-after` and `-before` options. Try the following code and compare the result shown in Figure 3.23 with those in Figure 3.24:

```
#
# pack -side top inserting a widget.
#
button .widget1 -text "Widget 1"
button .widget2 -text "Widget 2"
button .widget3 -text "Widget 3"

pack .widget1 .widget2 .widget3 -side top

 # This widget gets inserted into the packing order.
button .widget4 -text "Widget 4"

pack configure .widget4 -after .widget1

# pack4.tcl
```

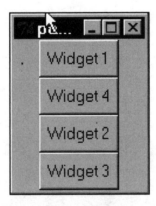

Figure 3.24 Inserting a widget after another.

N O T E The new `pack` syntax uses the `configure` option for all the preceding examples. You can use it or not. Because Tk is moving in the direction of the `configure` option, you may want to start using it, as shown in the following examples.

You can also `pack` a widget before another:

```
#
# pack -side top inserting a widget.
#
button .widget1 -text "Widget 1"
button .widget2 -text "Widget 2"
button .widget3 -text "Widget 3"

pack .widget1 .widget2 .widget3 -side top

 # This widget gets inserted into the packing order.
button .widget4 -text "Widget 4"

pack configure .widget4 -before .widget1

# pack5.tcl
```

This result is shown in Figure 3.25.

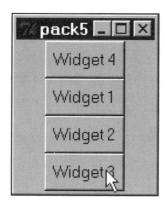

Figure 3.25 Packing before another widget.

The same options work horizontally, too.

Filler Up

You can ask that the packer fill widgets out to the available space. This is useful when trying to align small widgets with large.

The -fill option takes x, y, both, or none (the default) for the value. If you specify to fill x, then you're asking that the widgets be expanded horizontally, if necessary.

Try the following commands:

```
#
# pack example using -fill x.
#
button .w1 -text "Widget———-1"
button .w2 -text "Widget2"
button .w3 -text "Widget3"

# Try this with -fill x and without.
pack .w1 .w2 .w3 -fill x -side top

 # Uncomment this line to pack without -fill.
#pack .w1 .w2 .w3 -side top

# packfill.tcl
```

The pack command uses the -fill option to ensure that all widgets get filled out horizontally, as shown in Figure 3.26. The first widget clearly requires more width than the others. With the -fill option, all the widgets get stretched as necessary to make all the same width.

Figure 3.26 Using -fill x with pack.

Try the **packfill.tcl** script without the -fill option, by commenting the first pack command and uncommenting the pack command without -fill:

```
pack .w1 .w2 .w3 -side top
```

Without the -fill option, the last two widgets do not stretch to fit, as shown in Figure 3.27.

Figure 3.27 The **packfill.tcl** script without the -fill option.

You can also use -fill y (useful when packing horizontally), -fill both, or the default of -fill none.

Padding

In addition to filling, you can also pad. **Padding** is placing extra space between widgets. In Tk, there are two kinds of padding, **external** (outside of the widget) and **internal** (within the widget).

External padding goes between widgets. Internal padding makes widgets larger. For external padding, use the -padx and -pady options. For internal padding, use the -ipadx and -ipady options, as shown in the following example, which builds on the **packfill.tcl** script:

```
pack configure .w1 .w2 .w3 -pady 10 -ipady 5
```

The -expand option to the packer allows widgets to enlarge, such as when the window gets resized. You can also use the -anchor option, as shown in the section on radiobuttons, to place the widget if there is more available space than the widget will use.

The -expand option proves very important for making the full main window of your application and is covered in Chapter 4.

Finding Out About the Packer

The pack info command gives you information about the widgets:

```
% pack info .widget5
-in . -anchor center -expand 0
-fill none -ipadx 0 -ipady 0
-padx 0 -pady 0 -side top
%
```

Finally, to wrap up our discussion of the packer, you can use the pack forget command to undo a packing job:

```
pack forget .widget5
```

This will make the widget named *.widget5* disappear.

Placing Widgets

In addition to the `pack` command, there's also a command called `place`. The placer is fairly simple-minded compared to the packer. With the `place` command, you specify the exact position of the widget. Or, you can use **rubber-band positioning** where you place a widget in relation to another widget. When that other widget moves or changes size, the rubber-band positioning modifies the first widget's placement as well.

To locate a widget exactly, use the `place configure -x` and `-y` options:

```
#
# Example with place geometry layout.
#

button .b1 -text "Placed at 50, 40"
place configure .b1 -x 50 -y 40

#
# Try these other commands:
#
#place configure .b1 -anchor ne
#place configure .b1 -anchor se
#place configure .b1 -anchor w
#place configure .b1 -anchor center
#place configure .b1 -anchor n
#place configure .b1 -anchor s
#place configure .b1 -anchor sw

#place configure .b1 -width 10c -height 1c
#place configure .b1 -width 2i -height 30
#place configure .b1 -width 100 -height 5

# place.tcl
```

The `-anchor` option allows you to control which side of the widget is locked in place. Try the following (after you enter the preceding example):

```
place configure .b1 -anchor ne
```

```
place configure .b1 -anchor se
place configure .b1 -anchor w
place configure .b1 -anchor center
place configure .b1 -anchor n
place configure .b1 -anchor s
place configure .b1 -anchor sw
```

You should see the widget move about.

To control the size of the widget, you can use the -width and -height options. These can be in pixels or other screen units (e.g., m for millimeters and i for inches), as shown here:

```
place configure .b1 -width 10c -height 1c
place configure .b1 -width 2i -height 30
place configure .b1 -width 100 -height 5
```

The last example should make the widget really short.

You can also place widgets relatively with the -relx, -rely, -relwidth, and -relheight options. The -relx and -rely use the positions going from 0.0 to 1.0 in the parent window. You pick a relative position from 0 to 1, and the place command will keep the widget in its relative location, even if the parent widget moves or gets resized.

For the -relwidth and -relheight, the values are similar. For example, 0.5 means half the size of the parent.

The grid Layout Manager

Starting with the Tk 4.1, the grid command dramatically simplifies a lot of layout problems inherent in the older pack command. For example, common layouts, like data-entry forms, become a lot easier than with the pack command.

The main use of the grid command is to control the layout of such data-entry forms. These forms are the hardest things to get to line up properly if you use the pack command. The reason is that you need a two-dimensional gridded layout with the cells maintaining the proper height;

the `pack` command works much better with a single row or column, not the multiple rows and columns you need for a data-entry form.

When to Use the `grid` Command for Layout

The `grid` works best for data-entry forms, where you have `label` and `entry` widgets that need to line up. (The `entry` widget is described at the beginning of Chapter 5.)

Creating Data-Entry Forms

In a data-entry form, you typically want to have a set of rows and columns, with everything lining up. One of the first things you notice is that some widgets, like the `button`, require more height than others, like the `label`. Because you need `label` widgets in every form, this makes layout harder, because the `label` and the `button` (and most other widgets, in fact) just don't want to line up. This is where the `grid` command comes in handy.

To start with, you create widgets the same, only you don't `pack` them. Instead, you use the `grid` command, as shown in this **grid1.tcl** example:

```
#
# grid1.tcl
# Test of grid command for placing widgets.
#

  # Label and button.
label .l1 -text "Print Control"
button .b1 -text "Advanced..."

checkbutton .c2 -text "Draft mode"
button .b2 -text "Draft Options..."

grid config .l1 -column 0 -row 0 -sticky e
grid config .b1 -column 1 -row 0 -sticky snew

grid config .c2 -column 0 -row 1 -sticky w
grid config .b2 -column 1 -row 1 -sticky snew
```

```
# grid1.tcl
```

The `grid config` (or `grid configure`) command takes the name of a widget and any options. The chief options are the row and column the widget should occupy. The `grid` command lays out all the child widgets in a grid, with column 0 starting at the far left and row 0 starting at the top. Each widget gets placed within a grid cell.

The size of each grid cell is mostly determined by the minimum width and height needed by the widgets in a given column or row. For example, the widest widget in a given column determines the width of that column. The tallest widget in a given row determines the height of that row, and so on.

For each widget, you can specify the column and row it occupies, as well as the number of columns and rows it spans. The default span is one column and one row. You may want to increase the spans for some widgets to better control the layout. A `message` widget, for example, typically occupies more space than a `label`.

Because each column is as wide as the widest element, some widgets are likely to have extra space in their cells. You can use the `-sticky` option to control whether or not to stretch a widget to the North (n), South (s), East (e), or West (w) side of the cell. I typically use all four, `snew`, for the widgets on the right side of a `label` and either `e` or `w` for `label` widgets.

You can test this by loading the **grid1.tcl** script (with `source`) and then entering the following command:

```
grid config .l1 -column 0 -row 0 -sticky w
```

This command changes the *Print Control* `label` from being sticky on the East edge to the West edge. This should move the `label`.

Table 3.9 lists the options to the `grid configure` command.

Table 3.9 `grid configure` options.

Option	Usage
`-column` *col_num*	Place widget in column *col_num*.
`-columnspan` *num*	Widget spans *num* columns.

-in *parent*	Insert widget inside *parent*. Default is widget's parent.
-ipadx *pad*	Set internal horizontal padding to *pad*.
-ipady *pad*	Set internal vertical padding to *pad*.
-padx *pad*	Set external horizontal padding to *pad*.
-pady *pad*	Set external vertical padding to *pad*.
-row *row_num*	Place widget in row *row_num*.
-rowspan *num*	Widget spans *num* rows.
-sticky *boundary*	Stretch widget within cell to given bounaries, one or more of n, s, e, w.

Relative `grid` Placement and `grid` Shortcuts

To deal with the rows and columns in a grid, especially the rows, I often use a variable as the row counter, incrementing this variable to add a new row. This allows you to move a row up and down to adjust the layout much more easily than having to edit all the hard-coded values. For example,

```
set row 0
grid config .l1 -column 0 -row $row -sticky e
```

The `grid` command also supports a relative mode where you can base a layout on the previous widgets. For a shorthand method, this gets a little tricky.

If you just use the defaults, each `grid` command will increment the row by one. The column number remains 0 unless you provide more than one widget name. For example, to provide the same basic layout as shown in the **grid1.tcl** script, you could use the following `grid` commands:

```
grid config .l1 .b1
grid config .c2 .b2
```

These commands place widget *.l1* at column 0 and row 0. Widget *.b1* gets column 1, still on row 0, because this is part of the same command. Widget *.c2* starts on row 1 (the second row) because each call to `grid` automatically increases the row by 1 unless you use the -row option. The widget *.b2* gets column 1, row 1.

Using this default logic, you can place special characters to further control the layout. An x character makes a blank column. Try the following commands:

```
#
# Test of relative grid placement
#

  # Label and button.
label .l1 -text "Print Control"
button .b1 -text "Advanced..."

checkbutton .c2 -text "Draft mode"
button .b2 -text "Draft Options..."

grid config .l1 x .b1
grid config .c2 .b2

# gridrel.tcl
```

You should see a blank area on the first row.

This shorthand method also allows for dashes and hat characters (^) to further extend the column and row spans, respectively. See the on-line manual information on the grid command for more on this. (Realistically, this is too complicated to be useful. I never bother with these special characters.)

Other grid Options

When a grid gets sized larger, it needs to decide how to apportion the extra space. You can control this by using the grid columnconfigure and grid rowconfigure commands. The syntax follows:

```
grid columnconfigure parent_widget column -weight value
grid rowconfigure parent_widget row -weight value
```

The -weight option specifies a relative weighting factor for apportioning extra space. A weight of 0 means that you shouldn't add any extra space to the column or row. A weight of 2 means that you should give twice as much space as a column or row with a weight of 1, and so on, for whatever values you choose to use. I usually use a 0 for no extra space or 1 to get the extra space. This alone usually provides all the control I need.

For example, we can extend the earlier **grid1.tcl** script to give the second column and first row all the extra space, as shown here:

```
#
# Test of grid command for placing widgets.
#

  # Label and button.
label .l1 -text "Print Control"
button .b1 -text "Advanced..."

checkbutton .c2 -text "Draft mode"
button .b2 -text "Draft Options..."

grid config .l1 -column 0 -row 0 -sticky e
grid config .b1 -column 1 -row 0 -sticky snew

grid config .c2 -column 0 -row 1 -sticky w
grid config .b2 -column 1 -row 1 -sticky snew

grid columnconfigure . 0 -weight 0
grid columnconfigure . 1 -weight 1

grid rowconfigure . 0 -weight 1
grid rowconfigure . 1 -weight 0

# grid2.tcl
```

Once you enter the **grid2.tcl** script, resize the window. You'll see that the second column and the first row capture all the extra space. This is very useful for ensuring that the columns and rows you want to enlarge gain the extra space when the window grows.

To remove a widget from a grid layout, use grid forget:

```
grid forget widgetname
```

To retrieve the number of columns and rows, respectively, in a parent widget, use the `grid size` command:

```
grid size parent_widget
```

For example,

```
% grid size .
2 2
```

These results show two columns and two rows in the top-level widget named with a period (.).

The `grid location` command converts an X Y value into a column and row index in the `grid`. The syntax follows:

```
grid location parent_widget x y
```

For example,

```
% grid location . 10 10
0 0
% grid location . 200 10
1 0
% grid location . 10 200
0 1
```

The first number to return is the column; the second number, the row.

There's even more to the `grid` command. You'll see `grid` used with `entry` widgets in Chapter 5. The on-line manual information for `grid` shows the many options available. I almost never use anything other than `grid configure`.

Framing Widgets

The `frame` widget organizes other widgets—called **child widgets**—into a group. You can configure the `frame` to display a border, lending a clear grouping, or use no border (a zero-width border), making the `frame` invisible. In either case, you'll find the `frame` essential for laying out widgets.

When To Use a `frame` Widget

Anytime you need to impose a layout on a group of widgets, you'll probably need a `frame` widget. After reading the section on the `pack` command, it should be clear that widget layouts in Tk work best with a single row or column of widgets. But, few real applications are this easy to lay out. Because of this, you'll need the `frame` to help divide the widgets into single rows and columns. A `frame` can hold a single row or column, and combining frames you can make the whole layout work better with `pack`. Even if you use the `grid` placement, `frames` help divide the widget layout into smaller, easier to handle, parts.

The `frame` widget places a frame, a 3D bevel, around other widgets. This is important for grouping items. Also, due to limitations in the Tk packer, you'll need to group widgets inside frames to properly position them in relation to other frames and other widgets.

The idea of a hierarchy of widgets is hard to get used to, but once you've got the hang of it, you'll be making very complicated hierarchies. Think of the **wish** window as a top-level container widget. Inside this **wish** window, you can place `button`, `label`, `message`, and other widgets. All these widgets are contained within the **wish** window.

Inside the **wish** window you can also embed other container widgets, such as the `frame` widget. Inside this `frame` widget, you can place widgets such as `button`, `label`, `message`, and even `frame`. If you compare this to files, directories, and subdirectories, it should make sense. In this analogy, treat the `frame` widget as a subdirectory and files like the `label`.

Try the following example to see widgets inside of and outside of a `frame` widget:

```
#
# Use of the frame widget.
#

frame .f1 -relief groove -borderwidth 10 \
  -background orange
```

```
# Create buttons inside frame.
button .f1.b1 -text "Inside frame f1"
button .f1.b2 -text "Also inside frame f1"

pack .f1.b1 .f1.b2 -side left

# pack frames after child widgets.
pack .f1

# Create buttons outside frame.
button .b1 -text "Outside frame"
button .b2 -text "Also outside frame"

pack .b1 .b2

# frame1.tcl
```

Figure 3.28 shows the `frame` widget.

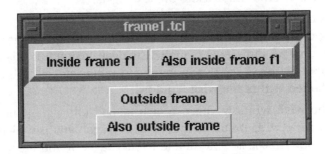

Figure 3.28 A `frame` widget.

This example shows two key concepts: widgets inside a `frame` and how you can use `frame` widgets to allow for more than one row or column that the `pack` command works best with.

In this example, the `frame` widget *.f1* encloses two buttons, *.f1.b1* and *.f1.b2*. Note the use of the long names for these `button` widgets. The naming clearly indicates that *.f1.b1* and *.f1*.b2 are embedded within *.f1*. The `frame` sports an orange background color to better show its outline.

The two buttons outside the frame have names *.b1* and *.b2*. All widget names must be unique, and *.b1* is not the same to Tcl as *.f1.b1*.

Widget Names

In Tk, widget names indicate a hierarchy. In the preceding example, the widgets *.f1.b1* and *.f1.b2* are said to be children of the frame widget *.f1*. The naming shows this. The widget *.f1* is in turn a child of the root widget, named with a period (.).

You can nest widgets as deep as you like. The convention though is to name widgets based on the parent hierarchy. The widget *.b1* is a child of . , whereas *.f1.b1* is a child of *.f1*.

Each `frame` widget provides a separate layout area. That is, you can use `pack` within one `frame` and `grid` within another. Or, you can use `grid` within all frames, or `pack` the same way. Each `frame`, though, starts out as a blank slate where layout is concerned. That way, you can `pack` widgets as a row in one frame and as a column in another.

With the `grid` command, the cells in one `frame` are independent of the cells in other frames. The following example shows some of these concepts. In addition, I often use a variable, such as *fr* or *frm* (both short for `frame`) to indicate the current widget name up to and including the `frame` widget. For example,

```
set fr .top.next.further_in
button $fr.b1 -text "Inside $fr"
```

This often helps with long widget names. With that in mind, try the following example. The **frame2.tcl** example shows the `pack` command with multiple frames:

```
#
# Multiple frames with pack.
#

  # First frame
set fr .frm1
frame $fr -relief ridge -bd 4

button $fr.b1 -text "Inside $fr-1"
button $fr.b2 -text "Inside $fr-2"
button $fr.b3 -text "Inside $fr-3"
```

```
pack $fr.b1 $fr.b2 $fr.b3 -side left -fill x
pack $fr -side top -fill both

# Second frame
set fr .frm2
frame $fr -relief ridge -bd 4

button $fr.b1 -text "Inside $fr-1"
button $fr.b2 -text "Inside $fr-2"
button $fr.b3 -text "Inside $fr-3"

pack $fr.b1 $fr.b2 $fr.b3 -side top -fill x
pack $fr -side top -fill both

  # Third frame
set fr .frm3
frame $fr -relief ridge -bd 4

button $fr.b1 -text "Inside $fr-1"
button $fr.b2 -text "Inside $fr-2"
button $fr.b3 -text "Inside $fr-3"

pack $fr.b1 $fr.b2 $fr.b3 -side left -fill x
pack $fr -side top -fill both

# frame2.tcl
```

The grid command acts similarly. You'll see more examples of multiple frames in Chapter 7 on dialog boxes.

 Always pack the innermost widgets first, then pack the enclosing frame widget. If you use the grid command, follow the same logic: set up the inner widgets first and then the containing frame widgets.

The preceding frame uses a groove style of relief. You can also use raised (the default for buttons), sunken, flat, solid, or ridge for the relief.

NOTE You can use the -relief option with most widgets; however, it's most commonly used with the frame widget.

To test the -relief option, try creating the following buttons:

```
#
# Use of the -relief option.
#

button .flat -text "flat" -relief flat \
  -borderwidth 5

button .groove -text "groove" -relief groove \
  -borderwidth 5

button .raised -text "raised" -relief raised \
  -borderwidth 5

button .ridge -text "ridge" -relief ridge \
  -borderwidth 5

button .sunken -text "sunken" -relief sunken \
  -borderwidth 5

pack .flat .groove .raised .ridge .sunken

# relief.tcl
```

These examples are shown in Figure 3.29. The **relief.tcl** script shows all but the solid style, because solid is mostly intended to meet the MacOS user interface guidelines. You can also try setting the -relief option to solid.

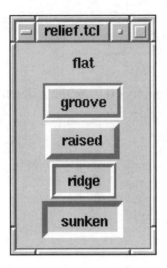

Figure 3.29 The relief options.

In this example, the border width was set to a larger value to better show the relief options. For buttons, you can normally use the default border width.

For frame widgets, though, if you want any -relief option other than flat, you'll want to set a -borderwidth to 2 or 3 pixels.

Now that we have the frame widget under our belts, you'll see much better looking examples of the Tk widgets.

Destroying Widgets

After spending all this effort creating widgets, you can destroy widgets with the destroy command:

```
destroy widgetname
```

If you destroy a widget with embedded children, such as a frame widget, then all child widgets get destroyed, too.

Finally, there's the Tk bell command, which rings the bell, or more likely, beeps the beeper:

```
bell
```

Summary

Tk comes with a plethora of widgets, including `button`, `label`, `frame`, `radiobutton`, and `scale`. Most widgets accept a set of common options for controlling the look and feel of the widget.

The `frame` widget allows you to embed a set of child widgets within a 3D bevel frame. Using frames allows you to group widgets better, and also to better place widgets with the `pack` command.

The `pack` command controls how widgets are placed. It supports a lot of options, but the most common ones are `-side left` for horizontal packing; `-side top`, for vertical packing; and `-fill x` for filling widgets out when placed in columns. The `grid` command helps you to lay out data-entry forms.

You can destroy widgets with the `destroy` command.

In Chapter 4, you'll see how to create menus, menu bars, and cascading pullright menus.

Tcl/Tk Commands Introduced in This Chapter

```
bell
button
checkbutton
destroy
font
frame
grid
label
message
pack
place
radiobutton
scale
```

Menus

This chapter covers:

- Creating menus
- Menu choices
- Cascading submenus
- Tear-off menus
- Menu bars
- Keyboard shortcuts and accelerators
- Standard menus
- The main window
- Option menus
- Pop-up menus

Creating Menus

Just about every windowed application sports a menu bar with pull-down menus. In this chapter, you'll get a close look at how to create Tk menus, cascading submenus, and pop-up menus, and at almost everything to do with menus.

Menus form an integral part of virtually all windowed applications and with good reason, because menus—if properly designed—can help users pick up an application with little fuss. Each operating system provides user interface guidelines that drive menu design. If you follow these guidelines, users should be able to learn and use your applications with less training and less frustration. The whole idea behind interface standards is that the time users spend and the skills they develop learning one application can transfer to another application. If your applications don't fit in with the standards, you make life harder on the user, no matter how poor you think the current standards are.

To better fit with the operating system guidelines—especially for the Macintosh, which sports a menu bar across the top of the screen, not on top of an application window—Tk's menu commands changed starting with version 8.0.

Using the 8.0 menu commands, especially for the menu bar, allow your application to better fit within the operating system interface guidelines. This doesn't matter so much on UNIX, which follows a Motif-like style, but the new commands make Windows native menus on the Windows platform, which helps to better make your Tcl scripts look like real applications. If you use a Macintosh (generally beyond the scope of this book), the new commands are essential for making a menu bar that traverses the top of the screen, not the top of the application window.

These new menu commands don't exist prior to Tcl/Tk 8.0. Consequently, this chapter covers both the old and new methods. We'll start with the older method, which works on newer as well as older versions and lays the groundwork for the newer method. The newer method builds on techniques used with the older method. To help deal with these version differences in your code, I'll provide two routines, to create a menu bar and a menu, respectively, that call the new method if available or the old method if not. Using these routines should free you from having to deal with the supporting different versions.

Briefly, to create a menu with Tk, use the `menu` command. You then fill in the `menu` with menu choices. A separate command creates each menu choice. Menus are normally hidden until pulled down from a menu bar. This means that you don't have to pack a `menu`; something else handles this task. The task of handling this changed with Tk 8.0. In Tk 8.0, you treat the menu bar as a sort of sideways menu. Then, you effectively create a submenu or a cascading menu from the menu bar for all your real menus like *File*, *Edit*, and *Help*. With older versions of Tk, you create a `menubutton`, which takes over the task of pulling down a menu.

In the next sections, you'll see how to create menu bars, menus, and menu choices. This chapter also covers the important user interface guidelines for creating menus, as well as pop-up and option menus, two handy menu variants.

Menubuttons Display Menus

Starting with the older, pre-Tk 8.0 method, the first thing you need to do is create a `menubutton` widget:

```
menubutton .file -text "File" -menu .file.menu
pack .file -side left
```

The `menubutton` is not used in the new method, but it is required for the old method for creating menus.

The most important part of the `menubutton` is the `-menu` option, which lists the name of the menu to pull down when the `menubutton` is activated. This menu must be a child of the `menubutton`, as you can see from the name *.file.menu* used in the preceding example. This name is purely arbitrary. I find it useful to include the word *menu* in a menu's name, but you don't have to.

When you have a `menubutton`, the next step is to create a menu, for which you use the `menu` command:

```
menu .file.menu
```

After you create the `menu`, the next step is to populate it with menu choices.

Populating Menus with Menu Choices

You create menu choices from the `menu` widget itself, not from any widget command like `button` or `checkbutton`. Instead, you use the name of the menu, with the `add` option. You can add a

- `command`, a normal menu choice.
- `separator`, a horizontal line to help group and separate menu choices.

- checkbutton, much like the widget of that name.
- radiobutton, again, a lot like the widget of that name.
- cascade, for cascading submenus. A cascade is a lot like a menubutton placed on a menu.

The widgets you add to a menu will appear when the user clicks on the menubutton. For example, to create a standard *File* menu, you'd use the following commands:

```
#
# Example File menu.
#

menubutton .file -text "File" -menu .file.menu
pack .file -side left

menu .file.menu

.file.menu add command -label "New" \
  -command { puts "New" }
.file.menu add command -label "Open..." \
  -command { puts "Open" }

   # Add a line separating choices.
.file.menu add separator

.file.menu add command -label "Save" \
  -command { puts "Save" }
.file.menu add command -label "Save As..." \
  -command { puts "Save As..." }
.file.menu add separator

.file.menu add command -label "Print" \
  -command { puts "Print" }
.file.menu add separator

.file.menu add command -label "Exit" \
  -command { exit }
```

```
# filemenu.tcl
```

The section on Standard Menus covers the function of each of these menu choices.

 You don't `pack` menus. The `menubutton` will handle this task. You don't pack menu choices either.

N O T E

You can see this menu in Figure 4.1.

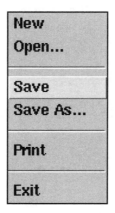

Figure 4.1 A File menu.

For each menu choice, the `-command` option (which is somewhat hard to keep apart from the `command` type of menu choice) identifies the Tcl script that gets executed when the user chooses this menu choice.

You can also use radio- and checkbuttons in menus:

```
#
# Menu using radio- and checkbuttons.
#
proc print_opts { } {
    global file_opts show_hidden

    puts "$file_opts file options"
    puts "$show_hidden hidden."
```

```
}

menubutton .view -text "View" -menu .view.menu
pack .view -side left

menu .view.menu

.view.menu add radiobutton -variable file_opts \
    -value full -label "Full File Options"
.view.menu add radiobutton -variable file_opts \
    -value partial -label "Partial File Options"
.view.menu add radiobutton -variable file_opts \
    -value filename -label "File Name Only"
.view.menu add separator

.view.menu add checkbutton -variable show_hidden \
    -label "Show Hidden Files" \
    -onvalue show -offvalue hide

.view.menu add separator
.view.menu add command -label "Print Choices" \
  -command { print_opts }

.view.menu add separator
.view.menu add command -label "Exit" \
  -command { exit }

# Set default values.
set file_opts partial
set show_hidden hide

# viewmenu.tcl
```

This script creates a typical *View* menu for an application, except for the *Exit* choice—added for convenience to this test script. The *View* menu appears in Figure 4.2.

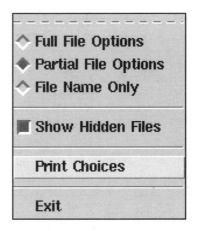

Figure 4.2 A *View* menu with radio- and checkbuttons.

The `radiobutton` choices share a variable, whereas the `checkbutton` has its own variable. Note also that you can set up initial values by setting a value into these variables. This way, there always is a valid initial state. *Print Choices* prints out the current state of the variables.

Cascading Submenus

Up to now, each menu choice has provided a simple action when invoked. The `cascade` menu choice complicates this a bit, by allowing a menu choice to pull right a cascading menu.

Even so, the form to create a cascade is very similar to that used by the `menubutton` and `menu` commands. First, you create the `cascade` choice on a menu, using the `add cascade` option. Then, you create the cascaded menu itself. A cascaded menu is simply a `menu` widget. That's all you have to do. You can then extend this example and create cascades that cascade themselves, as shown here:

```
#
# Cascaded submenus.
#
```

```
menubutton .cascd -text "Cascade" -menu .cascd.menu
pack .cascd -side left

  # Main menu.
menu .cascd.menu

.cascd.menu add cascade -label "Cascade Test" \
  -menu .cascd.menu.cas
.cascd.menu add command -label "Exit" \
  -command exit

  # First submenu.
menu .cascd.menu.cas

.cascd.menu.cas add command -label "Cascade Choice 1"
.cascd.menu.cas add command -label "Cascade Choice 2"

  # Second cascade.
.cascd.menu.cas add cascade -label "Second Cascade" \
  -menu .cascd.menu.cas.cas2

  # Second submenu.
menu .cascd.menu.cas.cas2

.cascd.menu.cas.cas2 add command -label "Second Cascade 1"
.cascd.menu.cas.cas2 add command -label "Second Cascade 2"

# cascade.tcl
```

Remember that each cascade menu must be a child of the parent menu it pulls-right from.

When we're all done, the multicascading menu appears in Figure 4.3.

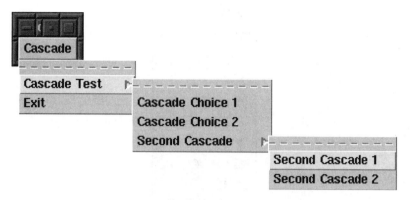

Figure 4.3 Cascaded, or pull-right, menus.

Tear-Off Menus

You can turn any menu into a tear-off menu by using the `-tearoff` option when you create the menu:

```
menu .file.menu -tearoff yes
```

By default, the `-tearoff` option is turned on. To turn it off, use a command like the following:

```
menu .file.menu -tearoff no
```

A tear-off menu displays a small perforated line as the first menu choice, as shown in Figure 4.4.

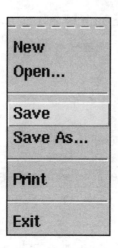

Figure 4.4 A tear-off menu.

If you click on this line, the menu is "torn off" and appears as a small dialog box, as shown in Figure 4.5.

Figure 4.5 A torn-off menu.

The -tearoff option is all that you need to convert a menu into a tear-off menu. Long familiar on UNIX from Motif applications, in Tk, tear-off menus automatically work on Windows, too.

Because this is such a neat option, you'll probably want to use it, at least for all menus on the menu bar. For really complicated applications, especially with cascaded submenus, the ability to tear off a menu means that you can access frequently used menu choices much more easily than calling up the given cascaded sub menu.

Up to now, all the examples merely placed the menubuttons horizontally using the `pack -side left` option discussed in Chapter 3. What's really needed, though, is a menu bar.

Making Menu Bars

The old way to create a menu bar is simply to create a `frame` widget and place it at the top of your window. The new way uses a sideways `menu` widget. Starting with the old way, I usually create a `frame` widget with a `-borderwidth` of 1 and a `-relief` of `raised`, as shown here:

```
#
# Old way to create a menubar.
#
frame .menubar -relief raised -borderwidth 1

 # File menu.
menubutton .menubar.file -text "File" -menu .menubar.file.menu
pack .menubar.file -side left

menu .menubar.file.menu

.menubar.file.menu add command -label "Exit" \
  -command { exit }

 # Edit menu.
menubutton .menubar.edit -text "Edit" -menu .menubar.edit.menu
pack .menubar.edit -side left

menu .menubar.edit.menu
```

```
.menubar.edit.menu add command -label "Undo"

  # Create a faked main area.
label .main -text "Main Area"

pack .menubar -side top -fill x -expand true

pack .main -pady 100 -padx 200

# framebar.tcl
```

This example, as shown in Figure 4.6, uses a `label` widget as a faked main area. Most windowed applications have some sort of main area, and the menu bar is expected to span the top of this main area. In your applications, you're likely to fill this in with whatever widgets are necessary for your programs.

The `-fill x` option to the `pack` command for the menu bar ensures that the menu bar will stretch to fit. (See the section on the Main Window for more on this topic.)

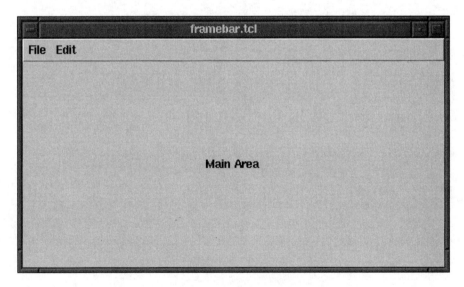

Figure 4.6 Creating a menu bar from a frame widget.

Creating Menus and Menu Bars the New Way

Because of the changes starting in Tk 8.0, the whole process for creating menus and menu bars gets more complex, but you'll see that it follows the model introduced so far.

In the new method, the menu bar is really a menu widget turned sideways, going across the top of the window. To create a new menu bar, you use the menu command with a -type option of menubar:

```
menu .menubar -type menubar
```

(Other values for the -type option are normal and tearoff.)

The -type option is new with Tk 8.0.

NOTE

There's one extra step, you must tell the parent window ("." in this case) that there is a menu bar. This is to allow for the Windows native menu bar, as well as the special processing on the Macintosh. To perform this step, you need to use the configure command with the top-level widget. For example, if your menu bar resides in the main application window (named "."), you can use the following commands to create a menu bar:

```
menu .menubar -type menubar
. configure -menu .menubar
```

To combine both the old and new code, you can use the global variable *tk_version* (introduced in Chapter 1) to determine whether or not the new version is supported. I'm assuming that you'll want to use the new method if possible because it uses native widgets. The following handy utility function allows you to create menu bars without worrying about the version differences:

```
#
# Procedure used to create a menu bar using the
# new and old Tk methods.
#
# toplevel = name of toplevel window, e.g., "." to
# create menubar in.
# menubar = name of menubar to create.
#
proc CreateMenubar { toplevel menubar } {
    global tk_version

    if { $tk_version >= 8.0 } {
        menu $menubar -type menubar

        $toplevel configure -menu $menubar
    } else {
        # Old method
        frame $menubar -borderwidth 1 -relief raised

        pack $menubar -side top -fill x -expand true
    }

}

# menubar.tcl
```

We'll call this handy procedure in a number of examples in this chapter, so you'll need to use the `source` command to source in **menubar.tcl**.

With the `CreateMenubar` procedure, you can create a menu bar as follows:

```
CreateMenubar . .menubar
```

This command creates a menu bar in the main window "." with a name of *.menubar*. (I usually give my menu bars the highly original name *.menubar*.)

For menus, the version differences barge to the forefront, unfortunately.

Creating Menus the New Way

The new way to create a menu on the menu bar is to create a cascade button—as we did in the previous section on Cascading Submenus. Viewing the menu bar as a sideways menu means that real menus are treated as cascaded submenus in Tk. That may sound weird, but it's actually harder to explain than use.

The following code calls the new method if available and otherwise creates the menu the old way:

```
#
# Utility to create menus.
#
  # Used to hide menubutton names for old Tk.
set menu_count 0
global menu_count


#
# Procedure creates a menu on a menubar, using the
# new and old Tk methods.
#
# menubar = name of parent menubar.
# basename = base name of menu, e.g., "file"
# text = text to display.
# mnemonic = which letter to underline in $text
# tearoff = "tearoff" to create a tearoff menu. Anything
# else creates a normal menu.
#
# Returns the menu name, so you can use this in your
# code to create menu choices. YOU MUST USE THIS NAME!
#
proc CreateMenu { menubar basename text mnemonic } {
    global tk_version menu_count

    if { $tk_version >= 8.0 } {
        # Set up menu name.
        set menu_name "$menubar.$basename"
```

```
        $menubar add cascade -label $text -menu $menu_name \
            -underline $mnemonic
    } else {
        # Old method

# Set up menu name.
        set menu_name "$menubar.menu$menu_count.$basename"

        menubutton $menubar.$menu_count -text $text \
            -menu $menu_name -underline $mnemonic

        pack $menubar.$menu_count -side left

        # Increment count of menubuttons.
        set menu_count [expr $menu_count + 1]

    }

    menu $menu_name

    return $menu_name
}

# menu.tcl
```

The `CreateMenu` procedure creates a menu from the following parameters: the name of the parent menu bar, the base name for the menu, the text to display, and which letter to underline, called a **mnemonic**. For example,

```
set menu_name [CreateMenu .menubar \
    filemenu "File" 0]
```

This code calls the `CreateMenu` procedure with a menu bar name of *.menubar*, a base name of *filemenu*, and text of *File*, with the *F* in *File* underlined as a mnemonic.

WARNING

There is one major difference between the two approaches. With the old method, each `menu` must be created as a child of the associated `menubutton`. With the new method, menus are children of the menu bar. This does make a difference in the naming of the menus. This is why the `CreateMenu` procedure returns the name of the created `menu`.

You must use the name of the menu returned by CreateMenu. If the new method is in use, this name will be something like *.menubar.filemenu*, that is, the name of the menu bar with the base name. If the old method is in use, then the name of the menu will be more like *.menubar.menu0.filemenu*. The extra name is the name of the menubutton, created for you—transparently—inside the CreateMenu routine. This is why it's so important to use the returned menu name.

To try out the CreateMenu and CreateMenubar procedures, you can use the following code:

```
#
# Using menus and menu bars.
#
CreateMenubar . .menubar

    #
    # You must use the name returned from
    # CreateMenu as the menu name.
    #
set menu_name [CreateMenu .menubar \
    filemenu "File" 0]

$menu_name add command -label "Open" \
    -command { puts "Open" } -underline 0
$menu_name add command -label "Exit" \
    -command { exit   } -underline 1

set menu_name [CreateMenu .menubar \
    editmenu "Edit" 0]

$menu_name add command -label "Undo" \
    -underline 0

# menu1.tcl
```

To use this new code, you'll need to source in both **menu.tcl** and **menubar.tcl**. For example,

```
% source menubar.tcl
```

```
% source menu.tcl
% source menu1.tcl
```

One new item cropped up in the CreateMenu procedure: the -underline option. The -underline option specifies a keyboard shortcut, or mnemonic.

Keyboard Shortcuts and Accelerators

The Windows and Motif style guides both specify a set of **keyboard short-cuts** (also called **mnemonics**) and **accelerator keys** for the standard menus. Both are means to choose menu choices by using the keyboard instead of the mouse.

A keyboard shortcut is an underlined part of the menu choice or menubut-ton text, such as the *F* in *File*. Normally, you press **Alt-F** to invoke this choice, the same as if you clicked on the word *File* with the mouse. The keyboard short-cut is always part of the text displayed, for example, the *F* in *File*.

An accelerator is an alternate keyboard combination, usually a **Control-** or **Shift-**key combination, that also invokes the same action as the menu choice. For example, **Ctrl-C** usually invokes the Copy action, and **Ctrl-V**, the Paste action. (*X* is cut, *C* is copy, and *V* is paste; all three keys are right next to each other on the standard QWERTY keyboard.) Typically, the accelera-tor is not part of the text for the menu choice.

For keyboard shortcuts, to get an underline in the menubutton or on a menu choice, use the -underline option. Specify the index of the charac-ter to underline, starting from 0, as shown in the **menu1.tcl** script. This option just makes an underline appear below the text. But, if you do this on a menu, Tk will automatically set up the keyboard binding as well.

For the accelerator, use the -accelerator option to display text for the accelerator on the right side of the menu choice. Both appear in the follow-ing code:

```
#
# Example Edit menu.
#

  # Old way to create a menubar.
frame .menubar -relief raised -borderwidth 1

  # Edit menu.
menubutton .menubar.edit -text "Edit" \
  -menu .menubar.edit.menu -underline 0
pack .menubar.edit -side left

menu .menubar.edit.menu

.menubar.edit.menu add command -label "Cut" \
  -underline 2 -accelerator "Ctrl+X"

.menubar.edit.menu add command -label "Copy" \
  -underline 0 -accelerator "Ctrl+C"

.menubar.edit.menu add command -label "Paste" \
  -underline 0 -accelerator "Ctrl+V"

  # Create a faked main area.
label .main -text "Main Area"

pack .menubar -side top -fill x -expand true

pack .main -pady 100 -padx 200

# editmenu.tcl
```

You can see this menu in Figure 4.7.

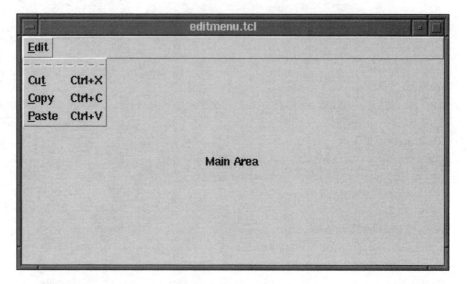

Figure 4.7 Keyboard shortcuts and accelerators on the Edit menu.

The -accelerator option just stores a string for display only. No accelerator is really set up by this option. Unlike the keyboard shortcut that Tk will set up for menu choices, you must add a binding for the key combination.

Binding Events to Call Tcl Scripts

A **binding** is a sort of Tcl procedure that get executed when a certain keyboard, mouse, or other event occurs, such as when the user presses the **Return** key in a widget.

Tk provides a powerful ability to bind a keyboard or mouse event to some action, for example **Control-V** to a paste action. The original bindings in Tk come directly from X Window System keyboard and mouse events. Even so, the same bindings work on Windows.

You can bind the following event types in widgets to Tcl scripts, as shown in Table 4.1.

Table 4.1 Types of events you can bind.

Event Type	Meaning
Button	Mouse button press.
ButtonPress	Mouse button press.
ButtonRelease	Mouse button was pressed, now released.
Key	Key on keyboard pressed.
KeyPress	Key on keyboard pressed.
KeyRelease	Key on keyboard pressed, now released.
Enter	Mouse pointer enters window.
Leave	Mouse pointer leaves window.
Motion	Mouse moves through window.
Expose	Redraw event on a window.
Map	Window is mapped (packed) to the screen.
Unmap	Window is unmapped (hidden).
FocusIn	Keyboard focus enters window.
FocusOut	Keyboard focus leaves window.
Gravity	Window "gravity" changes (UNIX-only).
Circulate	Window stacking order changes.
Configure	Window position or size changes.
Destroy	Window is destroyed.
Property	An X Window property data is written to window (UNIX -only).
Visibility	Window visibility changes.
Reparent	Window's parent is changed by window manager (UNIX -only).
Colormap	Window's colormap is mapped in or out.

The `Configure` event indicates a change in a window's configuration. The only real change that's useful is a change in the window's size. Few of these events are ever used in bindings, except for the mouse and keyboard events.

When you use the `bind` command, you can bind a particular event in a widget to a Tcl script. That is, you can bind a click on the leftmost mouse button inside a `label` to execute a particular Tcl script. (Not that this is desirable, because labels should not invoke actions.)

You can also make more general bindings. For example, anytime **Control-V** is pressed, the Tcl paste procedure (presuming you write such a procedure) is executed. To do this in Tcl, you can use the following as a template:

```
bind . <Control-v> { puts "paste" }
```

Note the use of a period (.) for the widget name. This binds the highest-level widget (and all its descendants). It also allows us to bind all occurrences of **Control-V**, anywhere in the program. An alternative way is to use the special name `all` to bind the event to all widgets in the program:

```
bind all <Control-v> { puts "paste" }
```

The `Control` key is a modifier. Tk recognizes a number of modifiers, shown in Table 4.2.

Table 4.2 Event modifiers for binding.

Modifier	Meaning
Alt	Alt key.
Control	Control key.
Shift	Shift key.
Lock	Caps Lock key.
Meta	Usually Alt key.
M	Same as meta.
Button1	Mouse button one (normally leftmost).

B1	Same as *Button1*.
Button2	Mouse button two.
B2	Same as *Button2*.
Button3	Mouse button three.
B3	Same as *Button3*.
Button4	Mouse button four.
B4	Same as *Button4*.
Button5	Mouse button five.
B5	Same as *Button5*.
Mod1	Modifier 1.
M1	Same as *Mod1*.
Mod2	Modifier 2.
M2	Same as *Mod2*.
Mod3	Modifier 3.
M3	Same as *Mod3*.
Mod4	Modifier 4.
M4	Same as *Mod4*.
Mod5	Modifier 5.
M5	Same as *Mod5*.
Double	Used for double-clicks of mouse events.
Triple	Used for triple-clicks of mouse events.

If you don't understand what a modifier or event is really for, don't worry. Many of these events are obscure X Window events and are rarely, if ever, used. See Appendix A for a listing of X Window programming books if you're interested in finding out more about how the X Window System deals with events.

You can use these modifiers to control the exact event you are looking for, such as the following infamous binding:

```
bind all <Control-Alt-Key-Delete> \
    { puts "DOS is over!" }
```

NOTE

On Windows machines, your application will never see a **Ctrl-Alt-Delete** event, because DOS or Windows will grab the event.

The basic syntax of bind is

```
bind all/widget/tag <event> tcl_script
```

The *widget* is the name of the widget for which you want to bind an event. The keyword all applies to all widgets. Alternatively, you can bind an event for a tag in a text or canvas widget, instead of an entire widget itself. See Chapters 5 and 8.

The *event* part appears between angle brackets, < and >. You can use a lot of detail if necessary. For example, holding down the **Shift** key and mouse button 1 would have an event syntax of <Shift-Button-1>. The number is the number of the button. For buttons, you can abbreviate even further. For example, you can signify **Button-1** with just <1>.

For keys, use the actual key value, such as **x** or **v**. For function keys and other special keys on the keyboard, you need the X Window **keysym**, the symbolic key name for that key. For example, **Delete**, **Return**, **Next** (instead of *Page Down*), and so on. (Table 4.4 lists the most important keysyms.)

To bind an event to **Alt-a**, use <Alt-Key-a>.

Binding Mouse Events

Binding mouse events is just like binding keyboard keys. For example,

```
bind all <Button-3> {
  puts "You pressed Button-3"
}
```

```
# bind1.tcl
```

Use source to load in the **bind1.tcl** script into the **wish** interpreter. If you click the rightmost mouse button over the Tk window, you should see the simple message printed out.

On UNIX, most users have a three-button mouse. Most mice have two buttons on Windows, and the Macintosh is famous for its one-button mouse.

WINDOWS Because of this, you'll need to be careful when depending on mouse button bindings, because the particular mouse button you're binding may not exist on the user's system.

The tricky part is that Button-3 is actually the rightmost mouse button with a two-button mouse on Windows. Button-2 is apparently gone.

Class Bindings

In addition to binding an event to a widget, you can bind it to a class of widgets, such as all button widgets. (The class name for such widgets is Button. You can find the class name for any type of widget in the on-line manual pages for that widget.)

Getting at Event Data in the Tcl Script

In your Tcl script for a particular event, you normally don't need access to data such as which button was pressed. If the script is bound to Button-1, you know that Button-1 was pressed. You may need to access other data associated with the event, such as the X, Y coordinate location of the mouse click, the widget in which the event occurred, and so on.

Through a strange syntax, you can access this event data. If you script has any percent signs, %, in it, then the Tcl interpreter will replace the percent sign (and the character following it), with data from the event. Tcl actually makes a new script for your binding each time the binding gets invoked. (This can be a performance issue.) Table 4.3 lists the most important % options. Other, more obscure options are described in the on-line manual information for the bind command.

Table 4.3 Percent sign options for event data in bindings.

Sequence	Use
%%	Used to place a real percent sign in the script.
%b	The button number for ButtonPress or ButtonRelease events.
%c	Counts down to zero with Expose (redraw) events. A count of zero means all Expose events in the same sequence have arrived.
%h	Height field for resizing (Configure) and redrawing (Expose) events.
%k	Keycode for key events, value depends on keyboard and operating system.
%w	Width field for resizing (Configure) and redrawing (Expose) events.
%x	X position (of mouse for button events, etc.)
%y	Y position (of mouse for button events, etc.).
%A	The ASCII value of the key pressed.
%K	Keysym name for event, such as "Delete" for Delete key.
%N	The keysym for the event, but stored as a decimal number, e.g., 65 for "A".
%T	The event type.
%W	The window (widget) on which the event was reported.

There are many more percent sign options, which you can see in the on-line manual pages for the bind command. Most pertain only to UNIX and the X Window System. The most useful set is the %x and %y to get the mouse position for button events. Try the following script:

```
# Use of %x %y in bind
```

```
bind all <Button-3> {
  puts "You pressed at %x %y"
}
```

bind2.tcl

Source the **bind2.tcl** into the **wish** interpreter. Now, if you click the right-most mouse button in the Tk window, the script prints the X, Y location of the mouse. Note that for Tcl/Tk, X values start on the left and increase going right, whereas Y values start at the top of the window and increase going down.

The %K option is handy to figure out what name Tk uses for a particular key. The following binding can be used to see what Tcl thinks is on your keyboard:

```
bind all <Key> { puts "Key %K pressed" }
```

bind3.tcl

After entering this command, try typing keys on the keyboard, when the **wish** window is active. You'll find some interesting key names, like **Prior** for *Page Down*, **L1** for *F11*, and so on. With key names, Tcl betrays its UNIX roots. Even so, bindings work well on Windows, as long as you use the names Tcl expects.

The most useful keys on the keyboard and their associated keysyms are listed in Table 4.4.

Table 4.4 The most useful keys and keysyms.

Key	Keysym as Used in Tcl
F1	F1 (and so on for F2..F12)
Up Arrow	Up
Down Arrow	Down

continued

Table 4.4 continued

Left Arrow	Left
Right Arrow	Right
Insert	Insert
Delete	Delete
Backspace	BackSpace
Home	Home
End	End
Page Up	Prior
Page Down	Next
Enter	Return
Esc, Escape	Escape
`	grave
~	asciitilde
?	question
/	slash
\	backslash
|	bar
+	plus
=	equal
_	underscore
-	minus
!	exclam
@	at
#	numbersign
$	dollar
%	percent
^	asciicircum
&	ampersand
*	asterisk
(	parenleft

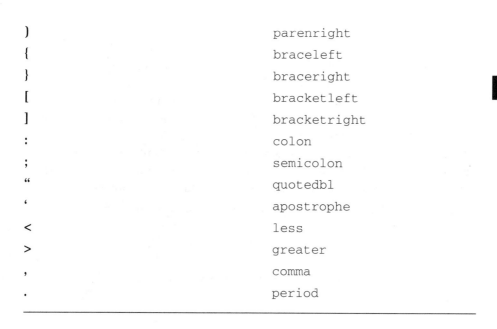

)	parenright
{	braceleft
}	braceright
[	bracketleft
]	bracketright
:	colon
;	semicolon
"	quotedbl
'	apostrophe
<	less
>	greater
,	comma
.	period

Table 4.5 lists the keypad keys, which have special keysyms.

Table 4.5 The keypad keys and keysyms.

Key	Keysym as Used in Tcl
0	`KP_0`
1	`KP_1` (and so on through `KP_9`)
/	`KP_Divide`
*	`KP_Multiply`
-	`KP_Subtract`
+	`KP_Add`
Enter	`KP_Enter`

On Windows, you may see the keypad keys as normal keys. For example, the + key on the keypad may return the same keysym as the normal + key, `plus`.

WINDOWS

Special Events

To better support operating system differences, Tk, starting with version 4.2, provides the ability to create virtual events with the event command. A **virtual event** is a name—any arbitrary name—you choose that is connected to one or more event sequences. For example, the three most common virtual events are <<Cut>>, <<Copy>>, and <<Paste>>. Each of these virtual events is usually tied to a set of keyboard events, for example, the operating system keyboard events for a cut, copy, and paste operation, respectively. A virtual event uses the special double angle bracket syntax.

You can add a virtual event with the event add command:

```
event add <<virtual_event>> key_sequence1 key_sequence2 ...
```

The <<virtual_event>> can be any name you come up with. For example, a common UNIX binding for the <<Paste>> virtual event follows:

```
event add <<Paste>> <Control-Key-v> \
    <Key-F18> <Control-Key-y>
```

The Control-y comes from the popular **emacs** text editor.

On Windows, the <<Paste>> virtual event gets set to the following: <Control-Key-v> <Shift-Key-Insert>.

After executing this command, Tk will generate the <<Paste>> event on any of these key sequences. Now, the event add command just sets up an event, not a binding on the event. Thus, after executing this command, we now have a new event, <<Paste>>, but nothing is bound to the <<Paste>> event. To do that, you have to use the bind command as described previously. For example,

```
bind all <<Paste>> {paste_proc %W}
```

Virtual events provide you with two interesting capabilities. First, you can set up events for common tasks, especially the cut, copy, and paste used so far, making your scripts more portable across operating systems. Second, you can define some new type of event to make it easier to have multiple key sequences call a particular procedure. For example, you can use the event add mechanism to provide users with the ability to redefine the key sequences used by your scripts. (The scripts work off the virtual events, and the users just redefine the virtual events. Of course, you can do this with other Tk constructs—particularly just using bind—but virtual events make this easier.)

Virtual events have lower precedence than the real thing, i.e., <Control-Key-v> has higher precedence than <<Paste>>.

The event delete command removes a particular key binding for a virtual event. For example,

```
event delete <<Paste>> <Control-Key-v>
```

The event info command returns the virtual events that have been defined:

```
% event info
<<Copy>> <<Paste>> <<Cut>>
```

When you pass a virtual event to the event info command, you get the actual binding on that event.

```
% event info <<Cut>>

<Control-Key-x> <Shift-Key-Delete>
```

WINDOWS

```
% event info <<Cut>>

<Control-Key-x> <Key-F20> <Control-Key-w>
```

U N I X

N O T E

You can combine these special events with the widget class bindings discussed previously under Class Bindings to create a general binding for all widgets of the same class. The two most useful classes for this are Entry and Text, for the entry and text widgets, respectively, which are covered in depth in Chapter 5.

224

For example, you can bind the <<Paste>> for all entry and text widgets with the following commands:

```
bind Entry <<Paste>> {puts "Paste in %W"}
bind Text <<Paste>> {puts "Paste in %W"}
```

Note how the %W allows us to get at the widget name. Of course, in your bindings you'd like to actually paste data. See Chapter 5 for more on pasting data and the clipboard.

Testing with the event Command

You can also use the event command to help your testing. The event generate command generates an event, either a real event or a virtual event. The syntax uses the following form:

```
event generate widget_name event options...
```

The *widget_name* refers to the Tk widget you want the event generated on. The *event* is the name of the event. The *options* fill in the data for the event and are listed in Table 4.6. You need to fill in at least some data for most events.

Table 4.6 Most useful options for the event generate command.

Option	Usage
-button *number*	Sets mouse button *number* (counting from leftmost) for button events; %b.
-count *number*	Sets count field for Expose events; %c.
-height *size*	Sets height for Configure events; %h.
-keycode *number*	Sets O.S.-dependent keyboard code for keyboard events, %k.
-keysym *name*	Sets *name* of key hit for keyboard events, %K.

-width *size*	Sets width for Configure events; %w.
-when *when*	Controls when event is processed: now, head, tail, or mark.

See Table 4.3 for a description of the % values associated with the bind command.

The -when option allows you to control when the event is generated and has one of the following values: now (immediately), head (place new event at the front of the event queue), tail (place new event at the end of the event queue), and mark (place new event at the front of the event queue, but after all other events with -when mark set).

There are even more, but obscure, options listed in the on-line documentation for the event command.

Bindings for Accelerators and Keyboard Shortcuts

Now that you know how to bind events, it's time to create a set of bindings for menu shortcuts and accelerators.

The *Edit* menu uses some common options, including the ones listed in Table 4.7, which the following code example will show how to set up.

Table 4.7 Some *Edit* menu choices.

Choice	Shortcut	Accelerator	Old Accelerator	Virtual Event
Cut	t	**Ctrl-X**	**Shift-Del**	<<Cut>>
Copy	C	**Ctrl -C**	**Ctrl-Ins**	<<Copy>>
Paste	P	**Ctrl -V**	**Shift-Ins**	<<Paste>>

There are two main reasons for a standard set of accelerators: to allow users to control software without a lot of mouse interaction, especially important for those who aren't able to easily control a mouse, and to allow power users a quicker way to engage menu choices.

The old accelerators come from earlier versions of Windows. Many Windows applications support both the old and the new (which come originally from the Macintosh).

Even though both the Windows and Motif (UNIX) interface standards agree on the Cut, Copy, and Paste accelerators, you should use the newer virtual event mechanism, if available, for the greatest portability between operating systems. Unfortunately, virtual events don't exist in older versions of Tk, so you again need to check for versions. The following code uses the `tk_version` variable to control this.

To set up the choices from Table 4.7 in Tcl, you need to display both the shortcut and the accelerator. Tk will automatically set up the key binding for the shortcut, if you use the `-underline` option. That's rather nice of Tk.

It is up to you to set up the accelerator. The `-accelerator` option just sets up the text, not the binding, to display.

Implementing Cut, Copy, and Paste Menu Items

I use a procedure for each of the *Cut*, *Copy*, *Paste*, and all other menu actions. Why? Because the `-command` option on the menu choice needs to call a Tcl script, and so does the binding on the keyboard accelerator. Furthermore, your toolbar may provide cut, copy, and paste buttons. To avoid these multiple sets of code from getting out of sync, I ensure that all means to invoke the action call the same Tcl script. The easiest way to do this is to create a procedure for each menu choice and have both the binding and the `-command` option call the same procedure.

Tk also automatically sets up a binding on **Alt-Key-e** to pull down the *Edit* menu when you use the `-underline` option. Sometimes, Tk is just really friendly.

To put all this together and create a partial *Edit* menu, you can use the following code:

```
#
# Binding keyboard accelerators.
#

  # Handle Cut
proc cut_proc { widget } {
  puts "Cut on $widget"
}
```

```
  # Handle Copy
proc copy_proc { widget } {
  puts "Copy on $widget"
}

  # Handle Paste
proc paste_proc { widget } {
  puts "Paste on $widget"
}

  #
  # Bind Cut, Copy, Paste, based on Tk version.
  #
if { $tk_version >= 4.2 } {
    if { [event info <<Paste>>] != "" } {
        event add <<Paste>> <Control-Key-v> <Control-Key-y>
    }
    bind all <<Paste>> {paste_proc %W}

    if { [event info <<Copy>>] != "" } {
        event add <<Copy>> <Control-Key-c> <Meta-Key-w>
    }
    bind all <<Copy>> {copy_proc %W}

    if { [event info <<Cut>>] != "" } {
        event add <<Cut>> <Control-Key-x> <Control-Key-w>
    }
    bind all <<Cut>> {cut_proc %W}

} else {
    bind all <Control-v> {paste_proc %W}
    bind all <Control-c> {copy_proc %W}
    bind all <Control-x> {cut_proc %W}
}
bind all <Shift-Key-Insert> {paste_proc %W}
bind all <Control-Key-Insert> {copy_proc %W}
bind all <Shift-Key-Delete> {cut_proc %W}

  # Old way to create a menubar.
```

```
frame .menubar -relief raised -borderwidth 1

 # Edit menu.
menubutton .menubar.edit -text "Edit" \
   -menu .menubar.edit.menu -underline 0
pack .menubar.edit -side left

menu .menubar.edit.menu

.menubar.edit.menu add command -label "Cut" \
   -underline 2 -accelerator "Ctrl+X" \
   -command { cut_proc . }

.menubar.edit.menu add command -label "Copy" \
   -underline 0 -accelerator "Ctrl+C" \
   -command { copy_proc . }

.menubar.edit.menu add command -label "Paste" \
   -underline 0 -accelerator "Ctrl+V" \
   -command { paste_proc . }

 # Create a faked main area.
label .main -text "Main Area"

pack .menubar -side top -fill x -expand true

pack .main -pady 100 -padx 200

# bind4.tcl
```

Notice the use of the event info command to see if the <<Cut>>, <<Copy>>, and <<Paste>> virtual events exist. If these don't exist, we set an arbitrary key bindings that should appease **emacs** users as well as normal UNIX or Windows users.

With the **bind4.tcl** example, you should be able to create Windows-compliant accelerators.

There's a lot to the bind command. You'll probably want to look up the on-line manual information on bind if you're trying anything tricky.

Standard Menus

Both the Windows and Motif (on UNIX) style guides place a lot of emphasis on the menu bar. Every application should sport a menu bar, and the menus should follow a common theme. Motif is the de facto interface standard on UNIX and the X Window System. And, of course, the Windows interface guidelines rule on the Windows 95 and NT platforms.

The Macintosh also requires a menu bar but follows a slightly different style. The next section describes the Windows and Motif styles. Macintosh users will need to modify the discussion for their platform. (For example, the last choice in the MacOS *File* menu is *Quit*, not *Exit*.)

To start with, both Windows and Motif follow the basic rules in the IBM Common User Access document (which describes how user interfaces should act), so both interfaces look virtually the same, with only a few minor differences. Most of these minor differences are taken care of by the native widgets provided by Tk starting with version 8.0. Both Windows and Motif style guides require a menu bar and mandate the following menu names, as listed in Table 4.8.

Table 4.8 Standard menus.

Menu Name	Keyboard Shortcut
File	F
Edit	E
View	V
Options	O
Window	W
Help	H

Only the *File* menu is required. If the application allows editing, you should also include an *Edit* menu. Every application should provide help and a *Help* menu.

The File Menu

The *File* menu should always be the first menu on the menu bar. This menu has choices that, obviously, pertain to files, including loading, saving, and printing files. This assumes that your application deals with files (which most do, including spreadsheets, word processors, and database managers).

The standard choices in the *File* menu are listed in Table 4.9.

Table 4.9 File-menu choices.

Menu Choice	Keyboard Shortcut	Purpose
New	N	Creates an empty new file for the user to act on.
Open...	O	Opens a file that already exists.
Save	S	Saves the current file to its current name.
Save As...	A	Saves the current file to a different name.
Print...	P	Prints the current file.
Close	C	Closes the window.
Exit	x	Quits the application.

Use common sense when building your menus. If your program has nothing to do with printing, for example, then skip the *Print...* menu choice.

A few of the choices include ellipses, such as the "..." after *Open*. The ellipses tell the user that this menu choice will call up a dialog box, requiring further action from the user to complete the menu choice. (See Chapter 7 on dialog boxes.) In the case of *Open*, a file-selection dialog box should appear so that the user can choose a file.

For the *File* menu, if you use the *Open...* choice to open a file named **hello.tcl**, the *Save* choice would save your work back to the file **hello.tcl**.

230

This implies that file-based programs always maintain a current file name, the name of the file the user has currently loaded.

For the *Save As...* menu choice, the ellipses implies that a dialog box will appear—again a file-selection dialog box. This choice allows you to save the file under a different name. After a *Save As...,* you should change the current file name to the new name the user selected.

The *Print...* menu choice can be *Print* or *Print...,* depending whether a print dialog box appears or not (to perhaps choose the printer, the print quality, and paper size).

Use the *Close* menu choice when your application has multiple independent top-level windows (again, see Chapter 7). The *Close* choice then closes one of these windows—the window from which the user makes the menu choice. If you don't use multiple top-level windows, skip the *Close* choice.

The *Exit* choice is required for all applications. You can use the Tcl `exit` command for this purpose. In addition, if the user asks to exit, but has modified a file without saving, your program should prompt the user to save the data before exiting. The main goal of all these interface guidelines is to help the user. You should place a menu separator before the *Exit* to clearly separate it from the rest of the *File* menu.

Many Tcl scripts use the term *Quit* instead of *Exit.* To make your scripts better fit into the existing user interface style guidelines on UNIX and Windows, stick to *Exit.* User interface guidelines exist not to restrict your personal creativity but to make it easier for users to learn your programs. Skills gained while learning other programs will aid users learning your programs, but only if your program follows the expected user interface style. No interface style is perfect (in fact, I consider most terrible), but the user gains from consistency among programs.

The Edit Menu

The *Edit* menu essentially provides a menu-driven cut, copy, and paste mechanism. The *Edit* menu should come second on the menu bar. Depending on the application, implementing *Undo* may be the toughest task for the whole program.

The standard *Edit* menu choices are listed in Table 4.10.

Table 4.10 Edit menu choices.

Menu Choice	Shortcut	Accelerator	Purpose
Undo	U	**Ctrl-Z**	Undoes the last thing the user did.
Redo	R	**Ctrl-Y**	Reverses last *Undo* operation.
Cut	t	**Ctrl-X**	Removes the selected material and puts it in the clipboard.
Copy	C	**Ctrl-X**	Copies selected material to clipboard.
Paste	P	**Ctrl-V**	Pastes contents of clipboard to current location.
Clear	l	**Del**	Clears selected material.
Select All	none	**Ctrl-A**	Selects everything.
Deselect All	none	none	Deselects all selected items.
Find…	F	**Ctrl-F**	Finds items in current file.
Replace…	e	**Ctrl-H**	Substitutes items after being found.

There's a lot of menu choices here. The key idea is to use only the ones that make sense for your application. *Undo*, *Cut*, *Copy*, and *Paste* are the most commonly used choices.

With *Undo*, you may also want to modify the text displayed (the -`label` option for the menu choice). For example, the *Undo* choice in many applications may read *Undo Typing* or *Undo Paste*. If you can tell the user more information about what will be undone, this can help the user see what is allowed for *Undo* and what isn't. To change this text dynamically, you need to get at the menu choice.

To modify the first (zeroeth) entry in a menu, use the `entryconfigure` option. If the menu is named *.menubar.edit.menu*, you can use the following Tcl command to modify the text of the first menu choice:

```
.menubar.edit.menu \
    entryconfigure 0 \
    -text "Undo Paste"
```

If you use a tear-off menu, then entry 0 is the tear-off dashed line. The *Undo* choice would then be entry number 1.

WARNING

Cut removes the selected (highlighted) material and places that material (text, spreadsheet cells, whatever) into the clipboard. See Chapter 5 for more on Tcl clipboard commands.

Copy copies the selected material to the clipboard but doesn't remove the material from where it was originally.

Paste pastes the contents of the clipboard at the current location (usually where an insertion cursor is).

Everything after *Paste* is an optional choice.

Clear, an optional choice, removes the selected material but doesn't copy the material to the clipboard—potentially a dangerous operation. The *Clear* choice is supposed to leave a gap where the old material was. The *Delete* choice is also optional.

The Windows 95 interface pushes for a unified *Find and Replace...* menu choice, even though it defines separate Find and Replace dialog boxes (discussed in Chapter 7), while older software (such as MS Word 7.0) and UNIX keeps two separate choices. Use your best judgment.

The View Menu

The *View* menu controls "views" of the data. That is, the *View* menu allows the user to adjust what is viewed in the main window of your application. Some examples of this include choosing how to sort the data (by name, by size, by date, and so on), if the data should be sorted at all, and how much detail to show (file name only or file name, size and owner, etc.). An outlining application or example, could use the *View* menu to control how many levels of the outline are visible at one time. A *Zoom* menu choice, if appropriate, should go on the *View* menu.

View menus are highly dependent on what your application actually does. A spreadsheet *View* menu will look a lot different than the *View* menu on an SQL query-by-forms application.

The Options Menu

The *Options* menu is essentially a miscellaneous menu. Into this menu go various choices that allow the user to customize the application, such as choosing the fonts and colors that the application uses. As with the *View* menu, the *Options* menu is highly dependent on what your application actually does.

The Window Menu

If your application supports multiple top-level windows, it should have a *Window* menu to allow the user to select any of the active windows.

The Help Menu

These days, few users actually read manuals anymore. Because of this, it is essential to provide on-line help in some format or other. Users expect to see a *Help* menu. When users see windows and pull-down menus, their expectations on user-friendliness go way up. Adding a good on-line help system is an effective way to improve productivity with software you create.

The choices on the *Help* menu are really up to you. What makes the most sense for your application? Some common choices do exist, though, that you probably want to take advantage of, as shown in Table 4.11.

Table 4.11 Help menu choices.

Menu Choice	Keyboard Shortcut
Contents...	C
Index...	I
Tutorial...	T
About Application...	A

If your application doesn't provide a certain type of help, such as an on-line tutorial, then you should skip that menu choice, obviously. The *Contents* choice should provide a high-level table of contents for all the on-line help.

The most fun choice is the *About* choice. It lists information about your application. If your application is named WunderWord, this menu choice should read *About WunderWord*. Typically, this choice will call up a dialog box that shows a great bitmap logo for your software, the version number, and copyright information. Often you'll see customer support numbers in this type of dialog window as well.

Placing the Help Menu

On UNIX, the *Help* menu should appear at the far right of the menu bar. On Windows, the *Help* menu merely needs to be the rightmost menu, but it does not have to appear on the right edge of the menu bar.

With the new method for creating menus, you should name your menu *help* (as in *.menubar.help*, etc.). The new menu creation methods will ensure your menu appears on the far right of the menu bar on UNIX. You can try the script below to test this:

```
#
# Using menus and menu bars.
#
source menubar.tcl
source menu.tcl

CreateMenubar . .menubar
```

```
#
# You must use the name returned from
# CreateMenu as the menu name.
#
set menu_name [CreateMenu .menubar \
    filemenu "File" 0]

$menu_name add command -label "Open" \
    -command { puts "Open" } -underline 0
$menu_name add command -label "Exit" \
    -command { exit   } -underline 1

set menu_name [CreateMenu .menubar \
    editmenu "Edit" 0]

$menu_name add command -label "Undo" \
    -underline 0

set menu_name [CreateMenu .menubar \
    help "Help" 0]

$menu_name add command -label "Undo" \
    -underline 0

# menu2.tcl
```

The **menu2.tcl** script is just a slightly modified version of the **menu1.tcl** script.

On Windows, the *Help* menu will just appear as the rightmost menu.

WINDOWS

If you use the older method for creating a menu bar (creating a `frame` widget), you can manually place the *Help* menu to the far right of the menu bar.

To get the *Help* `menubutton` to appear on the far right edge of the menu bar, use the `-side right` option for the `pack` command:

```
pack .menubar.help -side right
```

For all the other menubuttons, use `-side left` when packing. You'll also want to pack the *Help* `menubutton` last.

Naming and Arranging Menu Choices

Menu choices should have descriptive, easy-to-understand names. You may want to repeat parts of the text to help group related menu choices, for example, *Zoom In* and *Zoom Out*, as well as *Print Setup...* and *Print....*

You should group like menu choices together and use separators to add further cohesion to the groups. Use separators to highlight destructive or nonreversible actions like *Exit* and *Delete.*

As a general rule of thumb, a group of menu choices should include no more than five to seven menu choices. The menu itself should not get too long. Remember that the menu must appear on the screen, and too many choices will simply fall off the screen for suitably large menus or low screen resolutions.

Avoid too many cascaded submenus, even though this may contradict the advice above. Each level of cascading makes it harder for the user to pick the right menu choice and requires longer and longer times to select.

Sometimes, you don't have much choice. As always, use your best judgment for user interface issues. The goal is to make your software as easy to learn and as easy to use as possible while providing an interface that is consistent with other applications.

The Main Window

In addition to a standard menu bar, just about every windowed application sports some sort of main area. In a word processor application, for example, this main area contains the document and a scrollbar. You can also add a toolbar of bitmap buttons just beneath the menu bar. See Chapter 8 for more on bitmaps and toolbars.

The basic layout of most applications includes a menu bar at the top, a main area for the application, and a status area at the bottom. Usually this status area is a `label` widget, sometimes in a `frame`, although you may want to include a `text` widget as well (see Chapter 5 for more on `text` widgets).

The Status Area

Use the **status area** to place general status messages, such as that a document was printed. Critical errors, though, should appear in an error dialog box, as discussed in Chapter 7. You can place short help messages in the status area, using `Enter` and `Leave` event bindings to display and erase, respectively, short one-line help messages as the mouse moves over buttons and other widgets.

You can create a status area as a `label` widget, packed at the bottom of the main window. I often use a sunken relief to indent the status area. For example,

```
#
# A simple status area.
#

  # Create a faked main area.
label .main -text "Main Area"

pack .main -pady 100 -padx 200

#
# Status area.
#
label .status -relief sunken \
  -anchor w -borderwidth 1
pack .status -fill x -side bottom

#
# Store a status message.
#
.status config -text "This is a status message."

# status1.tcl
```

This status area is shown in Figure 4.8.

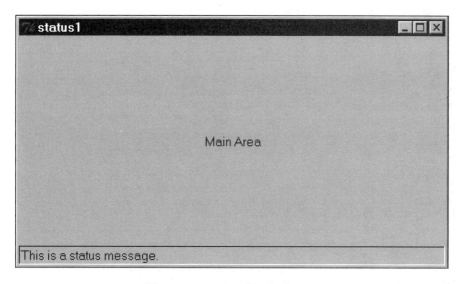

Figure 4.8 A simple status area.

To set a status message, you can use the `configure` option on the `label` widget to set in a new `-text` value:

```
.status config -text "This is a status message."
```

Pack the status area with the `-fill  x` option to ensure that it stretches to fit across the entire window.

Because most status messages don't require the entire width of the main window, you may want to pack in more data to avoid wasting space. To do so, you can create a `frame` widget for the status area and then child widgets for each individual element you want to display. For example,

```
#
# A more complicated status area.
#

  # Create a faked main area.
label .main -text "Main Area"
```

```
pack .main -pady 100 -padx 200

#
# Status area.
#
frame .status -borderwidth 0

label .status.l1 -relief sunken \
  -anchor w -borderwidth 1 \
  -text "Page 1 of 15"

label .status.l2  -relief sunken \
  -anchor w -borderwidth 1 \
  -text "Column 5    Line 32"

label .status.l3  -relief sunken \
  -anchor w -borderwidth 1 \
  -text "OVR"

label .status.l4  -relief sunken \
  -anchor w -borderwidth 1 \
  -text "           "

label .status.l5  -relief sunken \
  -anchor w -borderwidth 1 \
  -text "100%"

label .status.l6  -relief sunken \
  -anchor w -borderwidth 1 \
  -text "           "

pack .status.l1 .status.l2 .status.l3 \
    .status.l4 .status.l5 .status.l6 \
    -side left -padx 2 -pady 1 -fill x

# Last label fills in remaining area.
pack .status.l6 -side left -padx 2 -pady 1 -expand 1
```

```
pack .status -fill x -side bottom

# status2.tcl
```

This status area is shown in Figure 4.9.

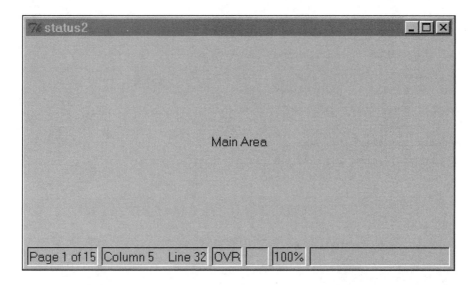

Figure 4.9 A more complicated status area.

Pulling this all together, you can create a sample main window using the following code as a guide:

```
#
# Example main window.
#


  # Old way to create a menubar.
frame .menubar -relief raised -borderwidth 1


#
# File menu.
```

```
#
menubutton .menubar.file -text "File" \
    -underline 0 -menu .menubar.file.menu
pack .menubar.file -side left


menu .menubar.file.menu

.menubar.file.menu add command -label "New" \
  -underline 0 -command { puts "New" }
.menubar.file.menu add command -label "Open..." \
  -underline 0 -command { puts "Open" }

.menubar.file.menu add separator
.menubar.file.menu add command -label "Exit" \
  -underline 1 -command { exit }


 # Edit menu.
menubutton .menubar.edit -text "Edit" \
  -menu .menubar.edit.menu -underline 0
pack .menubar.edit -side left

menu .menubar.edit.menu

.menubar.edit.menu add command -label "Cut" \
  -underline 2 -accelerator "Ctrl+X"

.menubar.edit.menu add command -label "Copy" \
  -underline 0 -accelerator "Ctrl+C"

.menubar.edit.menu add command -label "Paste" \
  -underline 0 -accelerator "Ctrl+V"

 # Create a faked main area.
label .main -text "Main Area" -background white \
    -relief sunken -bd 1

pack .menubar -side top -fill x -expand true
pack .main -ipady 100 -ipadx 200 -expand true
```

```
#
# Status area.
#
frame .status -borderwidth 0

label .status.l1 -relief sunken \
  -anchor w -borderwidth 1 \
  -text "Page 1 of 15"

label .status.l2  -relief sunken \
  -anchor w -borderwidth 1 \
  -text "Column 5      Line 32"

label .status.l3  -relief sunken \
  -anchor w -borderwidth 1 \
  -text "OVR"

label .status.l4  -relief sunken \
  -anchor w -borderwidth 1 \
  -text "          "

label .status.l5  -relief sunken \
  -anchor w -borderwidth 1 \
  -text "100%"

label .status.l6  -relief sunken \
  -anchor w -borderwidth 1 \
  -text "          "

pack .status.l1 .status.l2 .status.l3 \
    .status.l4 .status.l5 .status.l6 \
    -side left -padx 2 -pady 1 -fill x

# Last label fills in remaining area.
pack .status.l6 -side left -padx 2 -pady 1 -expand 1

pack .status -fill x -side bottom

# mainw1.tcl
```

Figure 4.10 shows this sample main window.

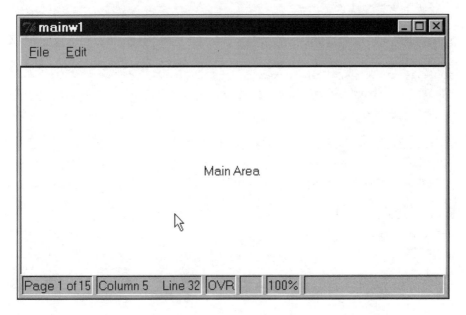

Figure 4.10 A typical main application window.

Option Menus

An **option menu** is a lot like a set of radiobuttons, but in a more compact placement. This menu displays a current value, the value of the last choice picked. The user can display the option menu and then select a choice. The choice then appears in the menubutton associated with the option menu. An option menu is not like normal menus. It is more like a special widget that sets a variable value.

Option menus come from Motif on UNIX. The closest analog to an option menu in the Windows environment is called a Drop-Down Combo Box.

The command to create an option menu is tk_optionMenu:

```
tk_optionMenu w varname value1 value2 value3 ...
```

When the user selects a new choice, the option menu changes the variable
to hold the proper value for that choice. For example,

```
tk_optionMenu .option units \
inches millimeters centimeters furlongs
set units inches

pack .option
```

The option menu, *.option*, uses the global variable *units* and allows the user
to set it to the following values: inches, millimeters, centimeters, and fur-
longs (for supporters of old English measurements or horse racing fans).

Placing an option menu tends to be a problem, because it changes size
to match the current value. You also normally place a `label` next to the
option menu to tell the user what the choice is for, as shown here:

```
#
# Option menu.
#
label .label -text "Set units to: "
tk_optionMenu .option units \
    inches millimeters centimeters furlongs

# Default value
set units millimeters

pack .label .option -side left

# option1.tcl
```

This example is show in Figure 4.11.

Figure 4.11 An option menu.

Different versions of Tk display option menus slightly differently.

When to Use Option Menus

Because option menus are so like radiobuttons, at least in the end result, their use tends to overlap. Choose an option menu when you think it looks better or when screen space is tight, because an option menu takes up much less space than a set of radiobuttons for the same choices.

Option menus are implemented entirely with Tcl commands. You can look at the tk_optionMenu procedure to get some very interesting ideas. For example, the current option menu just changes a variable. What if you want to have it execute a procedure on changes? It's not that hard to copy the tk_optionMenu procedure and add your extensions. Look in the file **tk/optMenu.tcl**. This file is part of the run-time Tk library. On Windows, this should be located in the **\TCL\TK** directory, assuming you installed Tcl/Tk under the **\TCL** directory. On UNIX, this is likely to be in **/usr/local/lib/tk8.0** directory.

Pop-up Menus

A *pop-up menu* is a menu without a menubutton to call it up. Normally, you'll use the rightmost mouse button (depending on the platform—button 1, 2, or 3) to call up a pop-up menu. Pop-up menus often contain shortcut options or allow you to change the properties of an item.

You create a pop-up menu the same way you'd create any other menu, with the menu command. Then, when the proper moment comes (more on this later), you post the pop-up menu with the tk_popup command. The syntax for tk_popup is

```
tk_popup menu x y entry
```

The optional *entry* parameter specifies the index of which menu choice to activate.

The reason you need to post the menu yourself is because there is no menubutton widget to do the job for you.

A common way to post a pop-up menu is to create a binding on the rightmost mouse button.

WINDOWS

On a two-button mouse in Windows, Tcl treats the rightmost mouse button as Button 3, not Button 2. So, you can bind Button 3 to call up pop-up menus and expect this to work on Windows and UNIX.

The main trick with pop-up menus is to get the pop-up to appear at the precise mouse location. Because the pop-up will appear in from a binding on <Button-3>, you can use the %x and %y syntax to get the current mouse position. Unfortunately, this position is in local coordinates, local to the application window.

So, the next step is to get the global coordinates for the application window and then add this to the values in the %x and %y, as given by the Tk binding.

We can use the winfo command, described in more detail in Chapter 7, to retrieve the global (or root) coordinates of a widget, as show later. The following command returns the global X coordinate for a given widget:

```
winfo rootx .widget
```

The rooty option works similarly:

```
winfo rooty .widget
```

The next step is to determine what widget to use. If the event occurs over a widget, then we need to use that widget and get its global coordinates (of position 0, 0 in that widget). To do so, we use the %W syntax (see Table 4.3) to get the widget in which the event occurred.

To pull this together, we have the following binding for <Button-3>:

```
#
# Pop-up menu.
#
```

```
# Pop up our menu on rightmost button.
bind all <Button-3> {

    # Get global X position of app.
    set gx [winfo rootx %W]

    # Get global Y position of app.
    set gy [winfo rooty %W]

    # Add to local mouse positon.
    set mx [expr $gx + %x]
    set my [expr $gy + %y]

    # Display pop-up menu.
    tk_popup .popup $mx $my
}

# Create pop-up menu.
menu .popup

.popup add command -label "Popup Choice 1" \
    -command { puts "Popup 1" }
.popup add command -label "Popup Choice 2" \
    -command { puts "Popup 2" }

.popup add separator
.popup add command -label "Exit" \
    -command { exit }

# popup.tcl
```

Note how this Tcl code adds the global X value of origin of the widget to the %x value of the mouse position within the widget.

The pop-up menu, named *.popup*, will then appear at the current mouse position. This pop-up menu is created like any other menu.

You don't pack menus. In this case, the tk_popup command will handle this task.

NOTE

When you create pop-up menus, you should be very careful because there's no indication to new users that a pop-up menu exists. You'll want to ensure that all the choices on the pop-up menu are also available elsewhere in the interface. The pop-up menu should be a shortcut feature for expert users, not an essential part of the application's interface.

Summary

This chapter covers a major component of all graphical applications: menus and the menu bar.

A menu bar is a sideways menu. Prior to Tk 8.0, a menu bar is merely a `frame` widget, configured horizontally. On this `frame` widget, you place `menubutton` widgets to pull down menus, packed from the left.

A `menu` widget must be a child of the `menubutton` that pulls it down, or the menu it cascades from.

You can add menu choices to a menu via the `add` option. Use the `bind` command to set up keyboard accelerators. Both Windows and UNIX have similar conventions for what menus and menu choices should appear on an application's menu bar.

To create an option menu, a different kind of menu, use the `tk_optionMenu` command with variable name and a set of values. An option menu is not like normal menus.

For a pop-up menu, use the `tk_popup` command to make it appear.

Chapter 5 continues on working with graphical applications and covers text editing, Tcl string functions, and scrollbars.

Tcl/Tk Commands Introduced in This Chapter

```
bind
event
menu
menubutton
tk_optionMenu
tk_popup
winfo
```

Text Editing with Tcl and Tk

This chapter covers:

- The `entry` widget for single-line text entry
- The multiline `text` widget
- Scrolled `text` widgets
- The `scrollbar` widget
- Controlling scrollbars
- String-handling commands in Tcl
- Creating a Tcl text editor that executes commands

Entering Text

Just about every graphical program requires some form of text-entry widget that allows users to enter file names, values, and other data. Tk provides two main widgets for this purpose: `entry` and `text`.

The `entry` widget provides a one-line entry area and is more like a single-value entry field. The `text` widget can be scrolled with many lines of text entry and is more like a text editor.

Creating Entry Widgets

For the `entry` widget, the `-width` option determines how wide you want the `entry` widget—in characters. Thus, a width of 30 specifies an `entry` widget that can show 30 characters at once. This is very useful for cases where you need to control the input, or if you simply want a larger entry area.

When to Use an `entry` Widget

The `entry` widget allows you to type in a value, such as a last name, file name, address, or phone number. Use an `entry` widget when you require only limited amounts of data and the data are somewhat freeform. If you have only a limited number of choices or a fixed syntax, try to use a `list-box` or option menu instead of the `entry`.

To create an `entry` widget, all you need is the following:

```
entry .ent_1 -width 30
pack .ent_1

# entry1.tcl
```

In most cases, though, you'll want to specify more options.

The `-textvariable` option sets a variable to hold the data the user enters. You can use this both to set an initial value and to get at the contents of the user input later on.

The `entry` widget has no `-command` option, so the normal way you associate Tcl code with an `entry` widget is to set up a binding, often on the **Return** key. You also want to use the `-textvariable` option.

N O T E

On its own, an `entry` widget provides no prompts to the user, so `entry` widgets are usually associated with `label` widgets. The `label` then provides the prompt.

To set up an `entry` widget with a binding on the **Return** key and an associated `label` prompt, you can use the following to base your code on:

```
label .label -text "Enter user name: "
entry .ent -width 30 -textvariable entry1

pack .label .ent -side left

# Capture Return/Enter key.
```

```
bind .ent <Key-Return> {
    global entry1

# Your code goes here...
    puts $entry1
}

# entry2.tcl
```

You can see this widget combination in Figure 5.1.

Figure 5.1 An entry widget with a label for a prompt.

Even if you don't set up the -textvariable option, you can still retrieve the text in the widget by using the get option:

widgetname get

For example, using the entry widget named *.ent*,

set var   [.ent get]

Password Entry

The -show option allows you to specify a character to show instead of the default—the characters entered. For example, the following label and entry can be used for a password entry, as shown in Figure 5.2.

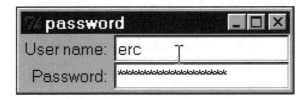

Figure 5.2. An example password entry.

The code for this example follows:

```
#
# Password entry aligned with
# grid command.
#
label .user -text "User name: "
entry .username -width 20 \
    -textvariable username
label .pass -text "Password: "
entry .password -width 20 \
    -textvariable password -show "*"

grid config .user -column 0 -row 0 -sticky e
grid config .pass -column 0 -row 1 -sticky e

grid config .username -column 1 \
    -row 0 -sticky snew
grid config .password -column 1 \
    -row 1 -sticky snew

# password.tcl
```

The widgets in the **password.tcl** example script use the `grid` command to align everything. Even though you could play around with the `pack` command to line things up, `grid` is more appropriate for this example because `grid` helps you align the labels, which have a variable width and less height than an `entry` with the entries, both of which are the same size. The `grid` command is especially useful any time you have a set of labels with `entry` widgets, creating a data-entry form.

Data-Entry Forms

The `entry` widget forms the backbone of all data-entry forms. In most cases, you'll use the `grid` command to lay out the `entry` and `label` widgets in the form. The following example creates a data-entry form:

```
#
# Data-entry form using grid command.
```

```
#
frame .fr -borderwidth 1 -relief raised


# Name
label .fr.l_name_first -text "First"
label .fr.l_name_last  -text "Last"

label .fr.l_name -text "Name: "
entry .fr.name_first -width 15
entry .fr.name_last  -width 30

set row 0
grid config .fr.l_name_first -column 1 \
    -row $row -sticky w
grid config .fr.l_name_last  -column 2 \
    -row $row -sticky w


set row [expr $row + 1]
grid config .fr.l_name -column 0 \
    -row $row -sticky e
grid config .fr.name_first -column 1 \
    -row $row -sticky snew
grid config .fr.name_last  -column 2 \
    -row $row -sticky snew

# Street
label .fr.l_street -text "Street"
label .fr.l_address -text "Address: "
entry .fr.street -width 30

set row [expr $row + 1]
grid config .fr.l_street -column 1 \
    -row $row -sticky w
set row [expr $row + 1]
grid config .fr.l_address -column 0 \
    -row $row -sticky e
grid config .fr.street -column 1 \
   -row $row -sticky snew -columnspan 2
```

```
#
# City, State, Zip
#
# Note use of frm variable and
# child frame widget.
#
set frm .fr.city_frame
frame $frm -bd 0

label $frm.l_city  -text "City"
label $frm.l_state -text "State"
label $frm.l_zip   -text "Zip"

entry $frm.city  -width 20
entry $frm.state -width 2
entry $frm.zip   -width 5


grid config $frm.l_city  -column 0 \
    -row 0 -sticky w
grid config $frm.l_state -column 1 \
    -row 0 -sticky w
grid config $frm.l_zip   -column 2 \
    -row 0 -sticky w

grid config $frm.city   -column 0 \
    -row 1 -sticky snew
grid config $frm.state   -column 1 \
    -row 1 -sticky snew
grid config $frm.zip     -column 2 \
    -row 1 -sticky snew

# Necessary to make frame properly fit.
grid columnconfigure $frm 0 -weight 1

set row [expr $row + 1]
grid config $frm -column 1 -row $row \
    -sticky snew -columnspan 2
```

```
# E-Mail
label .fr.l_email -text "Email: "
entry .fr.email

set row [expr $row + 1]
grid config .fr.l_email -column 0 \
    -row $row -sticky w
grid config .fr.email   -column 1 \
    -row $row -sticky snew


# Bottom part of form.
frame .exit_frame -bd 0
button .exit_frame.exit -text "Exit" -command exit
pack .exit_frame.exit

pack .fr -side top -fill x -ipady 6 -ipadx 4
pack .exit_frame -side top -pady 6

# dataform.tcl
```

This extensive example provides a typical data-entry form, as shown in Figure 5.3.

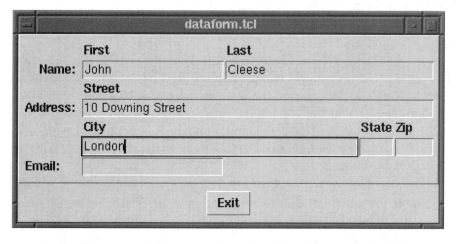

Figure 5.3 A data-entry form using the grid command.

In the **dataform.tcl** script, notice how the `label` widgets are made sticky to either the East (e) or West (w). This aligns the labels either to the left (e) or right (w). The `entry` widgets are normally made sticky to all four directions, `snew`.

WARNING

Don't mix `pack` and `grid` in the same `frame` widget. The two commands will both try to take over leading to a conflict that may prevent your Tcl scripts from operating properly.

Notice how the **dataform.tcl** script uses either the `grid` or the `pack` commands in each `frame`, but never both.

Working with the `entry` Widget

After you've created an entry `widget`, there are a number of ways to manipulate the text in the widget, as shown in the following sections.

Deleting All Text in an `entry` Widget

The following command deletes all the text in an `entry` widget:

```
widgetname delete 0 end
```

For example, using an `entry` widget named *.ent*, you could delete all the text in the widget with the following command:

```
.ent delete 0 end
```

The `delete` option requires two parameters, the character index of where to start deleting and the index of the last character to delete. Thus, 0 indicates the first character in the widget, because most areas of Tcl—but not all as you'll see with the `text` widget's line numbers—start counting with 0. The last index is the special keyword `end`. The keyword `end` indicates the end of the text in the widget, as you'd expect. Using the keyword `end` frees you from having to know how many characters are stored in the `entry` widget.

You'll probably call the `delete` option a lot. The user expects many `entry` fields to clear their input when the user enters a file name, user name; or other such entry. You can change the **Return** key binding from the **entry2.tcl** example to clear out the data using the following Tcl code:

```
bind .ent <Key-Return> {
    # Your code goes here...
    puts $entry1
```

```
# Clear contents of widget.
    .ent delete 0 end
}
```

The Insertion Cursor

Each entry widget has an insertion cursor. This cursor appears in the gap between two characters. When you enter new text, Tk inserts the new text after (to the right of) the insertion cursor.

You can position the insertion cursor with the icursor option:

widgetname icursor *position*

For example, with an entry widget named *.ent*, you can move the insertion cursor to the start of the widget text with the following command:

.ent icursor 0

The position is the character index where to place the insertion cursor. (Indices usually start with 0 in Tcl.) You can use a direct number or one of the entry widget's built-in positions such as end, listed in Table 5.1.

Table 5.1 Special insertion positions for the entry widget.

Position	Meaning
end	Just after the last character
insert	Just after the insertion cursor
sel.first	Start of selected text, if any is selected.
sel.last	End of selected text, if any is selected.

If you want to move the insertion cursor to the end of the text, use the following command:

```
.ent icursor end
```

The `icursor` option moves the insertion cursor, which controls where the user adds text. To move the insertion cursor, the user can also click the mouse at a different location as well as use the left and right arrow keys. Inside a Tcl script, though, you're not limited by the position of the insertion cursor. You can insert text anywhere with the `insert` option:

```
widgetname insert start_position text_string
```

The *start_position* identifies where to start the insertion of the new text string. This is an index to a character position, the same as that passed to the `icursor` option.

To insert the string "Inserted into the middle" into the text in an `entry` widget at, say, position 5, you can use the following command:

```
.ent insert 5 "Inserted into the middle"
```

If the text is too long for the widget's display, you'll only see part of the text, as shown in Figure 5.4.

Figure 5.4 An entry widget holding a lot of text.

Don't worry, the `entry` widget still holds the text, even if all of it is not visible at any time. You can use the left and right arrow keys to move the insertion cursor back and forth in the window.

Entry Widget Selections

The X Window System, so popular on UNIX, provides for the concept of a **selection**, a highlighted piece of data in some program on the screen. For a given selection (you can name alternate selections, although just about every program uses the selection named PRIMARY), only one program can own it at a time.

Tk works well within the X environment and allows you to copy text from a terminal window and paste it into a Tcl entry or text widget. The reverse operation is also possible.

To set this up, you need to set the -exportselection option to true. You almost always want to do this, so that the entry widget works well in the surrounding window environment.

On UNIX, you can select text with the mouse and paste it without going through an intermediary—the clipboard. Thus, the -exportselection option is very important so the user can select data in the window and paste it into another window.

On Windows, you need to copy the data to the clipboard, unless you only use **wish**. See the section on Cut, Copy and Paste for more on this.

In the entry widget, the position sel.first is set to the first character in the selection, and sel.last, to the end of the selection. You can use these positions with the delete option and so on.

In addition, the selection option allows you to control the contents of the selection. For example, the selection clear option clears the selection, obviously. For this, you need the widget name:

```
widgetname selection clear
```

For example,

```
.ent1 selection clear
```

Note that this clears the text *highlighting*, *not* the highlighted *text* itself.

The selection present option returns one if a selection is active in the widget. For example,

```
% .ent1 selection present
0
```

Scrolling in the `entry` Widget

You can control scrolling in the `entry` widget with the `xview` option. The `xview scroll` option moves the text back and forth in the window, presuming the text goes beyond the `entry` window.

The following command scrolls the visible text back to show previous text by 10 units, an amount based on the average character size:

```
.ent1 xview scroll -10 units
```

To scroll the text forward to the end, use positive numbers.

Describing this scrolling is tough, because moving forward causes the text to move to the left, so that text that was off to the right now becomes visible. The best way to figure this out is to try the commands.

There's a lot more to the `entry` widget. You'll want to look up the on-line manual information for `entry`.

With the `entry` widget, you can make a *File Open* dialog box, you can ask for user names and passwords. In fact, you can allow users to enter most of the data items required in your program. But sometimes, a single line of text is not enough. For those cases, you can use the `text` widget.

Multiline `text` Widgets

While the `entry` widget provides only one line of text, the `text` widget allows for many lines in a scrolled widget. This is useful for editing text, viewing files, sending electronic mail messages, and all sorts of fun things, including creating the simple Tcl editor at the end of this chapter.

The following example shows a `text` widget and a `scrollbar` (more on that in the section on scrollbars below) inside a `frame` widget:

```
#
# Very simple text editor in Tcl.
#
frame .tx
```

```
text .tx.text -yscrollcommand ".tx.scroll set"
scrollbar .tx.scroll -command ".tx.text yview"

# Pack scrollbar first.
pack .tx.scroll -side right -fill y
pack .tx.text -side left
pack .tx -side top
# text1.tcl
```

The above commands create a window like the one shown in Figure 5.5.

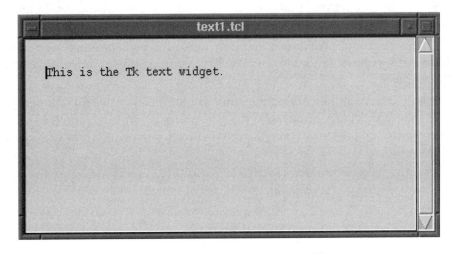

Figure 5.5 A text widget and a scrollbar.

The scrollbar needs to be connected to the text widget. When the user moves the scrollbar, the text widget needs to update as well. Similarly, the text widget needs to be connected to the scrollbar, so that when the text widget moves its text (via Tcl commands or on user input), the scrollbar gets updated as well.

The text widget and the scrollbar are linked by their widget names via the -ycommand and -command options, respectively. This is how you connect a scrollbar to a text widget. For more on this, see the section on Connecting the Text Widget to the Scrollbar.

When to Use a `text` Widget

The `text` widget provides a simple text editor inside a widget. You should use the `text` widget whenever you want large amounts of freeform text. For example, if you have a window page that allows the user to enter comments, you could use a `text` widget.

Controlling the Text Widget Display

The `-height` option controls the height of the `text` widget, in characters. The `-width` sets the width of the `text` widget, again in characters. In most cases, the defaults work fine.

The `-wrap` option takes a value of `none` for no wrapping, `char` for character-by-character wrapping, or `word` for wrapping only on word boundaries.

The `-state` option controls whether or not the `text` widget will accept input. With a `-state` of `normal`, the `text` widget works as you'd expect. You can disable user input, making the text read-only, with a `-state` value of `disabled`.

To disable user input for the `text` widget created in the **text1.tcl** you can use the following command:

```
.tx.text configure -state disabled
```

To restore the `text` widget back to normal, you can use the following command:

```
.tx.text configure -state normal
```

When a `text` widget is disabled, you cannot add any text to it, even from Tcl commands.

Controlling Spacing Between Lines

The `text` widget provides a number of confusing options for controlling the spacing between lines, as shown in Table 5.2.

Table 5.2 Text Widget Line Spacing Options

Option	Meaning
`-spacing1` *value*	Adds additional space above each line.
`-spacing2` *value*	Adds additional space between all lines but wrapped lines (assumed to be single lines for this spacing).
`-spacing3` *value*	Adds spacing after each line.

Deleting Text

Like with the `entry` widget, you can delete text with the `delete` option:

widgetname `delete` *start_index end_index*

The `delete` option deletes the text from the *start_index* to just before, but not including, the *end_index*. If you omit the *end_index*, `delete` deletes just one character.

The start and end positions are a bit more complicated than for the `entry` widget, though. For the `text` widget, you need to define a starting index, which allows a great deal of flexibility at a price in complexity.

Defining Positions in the Text

Tk calls a position within a text widget an **index**. The whole point of indices is to allow you to use symbolic names for the text to delete, much like the `sel.first` and sel.end positions for the `entry` widget, which indicate the starting and ending positions of the selection. The syntax for a `text` widget index is

`{ base modifiers }`

Or just

base

Table 5.3 lists the available values for the base part of the index.

Table 5.3 Base Values for Text Widget Indices

Value	Meaning
line.char	Character *char* (starting at 0) on line *line* (starting at 1).
@*x,y*	The character under the mouse at local position *x,y* (in pixels).
end	The character just after the last newline.
markname	The character just after the mark *markname*.
tagname.first	The first character in the given tag.
tagname.last	The character just after the last in the given tag.
windowname	The position of the embedded window of that name.
imagename	The position of an embedded image of that name.

The reason these indices are so complicated is that Tk allows you to define arbitrary positions within the text widget, called *tags*, *marks*, and *embedded windows*. Even though they are complicated, these neat features provide the basics for a full-blown hypertext system as well as a word processor with different text formats.

You can adjust the base part of an index with the following modifiers, as shown in Table 5.4.

Table 5.4 Text Index Modifiers

Modifier	Meaning
+ *value* chars	Adjust the base index forward by *value* characters.
- *value* chars	Adjust the base index backward by *value* characters.

+ *value* lines	Adjust the base index forward by *value* lines.
- *value* lines	Adjust the base index forward by *value* lines.
linestart	Adjust index to first character on the line.
lineend	Adjust index to last character on the line (the newline character).
wordstart	Adjust index to first character in word.
wordend	Adjust index to just after the last character in word.

So, based on these text indices, to delete all the characters in the text widget
.tx.text, you can use the following command:

```
.tx.text delete 1.0 end
```

The 1.0 specifies the first line (1) and the first character (0) in that line.

 Lines start counting with 1; characters in a line, with 0. The rationale for lines starting with 1 is to maintain compatibility with a number of UNIX commands that also count lines starting with 1. Most other counts in Tcl

N O T E start with 0.

You can use the index option to convert an index of one type into the
line.char form that is easiest to understand:

```
widgetname index index_to_convert
```

This converts the *index_to_convert* and returns the same position, but in
line.char format.

To show a more complicated example of using text indices, we can
modify the **text1.tcl** script as follows:

```
# Test of text widget indices.
# Create text widget.
```

```
frame .tx

text .tx.text -yscrollcommand ".tx.scroll set"
scrollbar .tx.scroll -command ".tx.text yview"

# Pack scrollbar first.
pack .tx.scroll -side right -fill y
pack .tx.text -side left
pack .tx -side top

# Bind mouse button to delete entire line of text.
bind .tx.text <Button-3> {

set pos [.tx.text index @%x,%y]
.tx.text delete "$pos linestart" "$pos lineend"
}

# text2.tcl
```

The **text2.tcl** script binds the rightmost mouse button, Button 3, to delete an entire line of text. To do this, you need to convert the position the mouse button was clicked into a text widget index. For this, the **text2.tcl** script uses the @x,y format for a text index. The `%x` and `%y` are special markers in a mouse button binding that expand to the current mouse position. Thus, the Tcl interpreter will expand `@%x,%y` into the coordinates where the button was clicked. This then becomes a `text` widget index indicating the character underneath the mouse.

When we have this index, we can use the `linestart` and `lineend` (note the *ee*) modifiers to extend the index to the start and end, respectively, of the line underneath the mouse. The `delete` option then deletes the text.

Try out the **text2.tcl** script. Enter some text and click the rightmost mouse button over a line of text. The line should disappear.

Text indices are kind of hard in theory but much easier in practice. You'll also need these indices for most other `text` widget commands, such as for inserting text.

Inserting Text

The basic form of the insert option is:

```
widgetname insert index characters
```

For example, to insert the string "In Xanadu did Kublai Khan a stately pleasure dome decree" into the beginning of a text widget, use the following command:

```
.tx.text insert 1.0 \
  "In Xanadu did Kublai Khan a
  stately pleasure dome decree."
```

(This command includes a newline before the word *stately*.)

You can also complicate the insert command with a list of tags, using the following syntax:

```
widgetname insert index characters taglist
```

This associates the tags in taglist with the new characters to be inserted. If you omit the taglist, the new characters will get any tags that are present on both ends of the insertion point.

You can add even more tags with repeated characters and taglist options:

```
widgetname insert index characters1 taglist1 characters2 taglist2
...
```

You can repeat the pattern as long as you desire.

These tags are discussed in the section on marks, tags and embedded windows.

The insert option won't work if the -state of the text widget is disabled.

Retrieving Text

You can retrieve the text with the get option, which uses the following syntax:

```
widgetname get start_index end_index
```

The *end_index* is optional.

The get option retrieves all the text from the *start_index* to the *end_index* (or a single character if you omit the *end_index*). To get all the text, use the following command, keeping with an example text widget named *.tx.text*:

```
% .tx.text get 1.0 end
In Xanadu did Kublai Khan a
  stately pleasure dome decree.
```

Connecting the text Widget to a Scrollbar

The scrollbar widget, used in some earlier examples, provides a number of options that you may want to exercise. You'll typically create a scrollbar with an associated widget, such as the text widget.

When the user moves the scrollbar thumb, the scrollbar executes its -command Tcl script. When the scrollbar executes its -command script, it appends the current position within the scrollbar to the Tcl script, along with the particular xview (if horizontal) or yview (vertical) command. That is, if the scrollbar's -command Tcl script is ".tx.text yview", then the real Tcl code that gets executed is: ".tx.text yview command", where *command* is the amount to scroll, formatted using a special scrolling command.

Typically, the -command script is tied to a listbox (see Chapter 6) or text widget's yview command, which expects the hidden value parameters the scrollbar passes to it.

What this really means is that to make a scrollbar work properly, you need to follow some conventions, which are outlined next.

For a vertical scrollbar, the text widget must have a -yscrollcommand formatted as follows:

```
-yscrollcommand { scrollbar_name set }
```

For a horizontal scrollbar, the text widget must have a -xscrollcom-
mand formatted as follows:

```
-xscrollcommand { scrollbar_name set }
```

For the scrollbar, a vertical scrollbar must have a -command formatted
as follows:

```
-command { textwidget_name yview }
```

A horizontal scrollbar must have a -command formatted as follows:

```
-command { textwidget_name xview }
```

To make a horizontal scrollbar, use the -orient option.

To get text to scroll horizontally, you must also set the -wrap option for
the text widget to none; otherwise, the text widget will wrap to the available size. You can try the following code:

```
#
# Horizontal and vertical scrollbars.
#

# Create text widget.
frame .tx

# Turn off text wrapping.
text .tx.text \
    -wrap none \
    -yscrollcommand ".tx.v_scroll set" \
    -xscrollcommand ".tx.h_scroll set"

# Vertical scrollbar.
scrollbar .tx.v_scroll -command ".tx.text yview"

# Horizontal scrollbar.
scrollbar .tx.h_scroll -orient horizontal \
    -command ".tx.text xview"
```

```
# Pack scrollbars first.
pack .tx.v_scroll -side right -fill y
pack .tx.h_scroll -side bottom -fill x
pack .tx.text -side left
pack .tx -side top
# scroll.tcl
```

Note that you almost always need to place a `text` widget and its scrollbars alone inside a `frame` widget, so that the scrollbars get positioned properly. This means that most Tcl scripts tend to have a number of `frame` widgets, one for each `text` widget and a number of frames to connect things properly with the `pack` or `grid` commands.

When you `pack` a `text` widget and a `scrollbar`, you'll need to pack the scrollbar first. This is because the `text` widget normally wants all available space. So, to avoid crowding, pack the `scrollbar` first so it gets its fair share of the space.

Setting the Keyboard Focus

If your application has a main `text` widget, I usually like to set that widget to have the keyboard `focus` when the application starts up. To do this, use the focus command:

```
focus widgetname
```

For example,

```
focus .tx.text
```

The `focus` command won't work until the widget exists, so another handy command is `update`, which waits until all pending events are handled. Generally, `update` ensures that widgets get redrawn and that all windows appear. With the `update` command, the Tcl code to set the widget focus looks more like

```
update
focus .tx.text
```

Marks, Tags, and Embedded Windows

The `text` widget complicates Tk once you start getting into the concepts of marks, tags, and embedded windows. These items allow you to turn a plain old `text` widget into a hypertext browser or support compound documents. You have to, however, do a lot of work on your own.

The next sections introduce the theory behind marks, tags, embedded windows, and embedded images. After that, you'll see how to apply the theory and create hypertext links or embedded graphics.

Marks

A **mark** marks a position in the text with a symbolic name. This position appears in the gap between two characters. Thus, marks are invisible. You can use marks as an index position in the `text` widget, as shown in Table 5.3.

A special mark named `insert` identifies the position of the insertion cursor. Moving this mark moves the insertion point. You can move the insertion cursor by using the `mark set` option with a mark named `insert` and specifying a new position. For example,

```
.tx.text mark set insert 2.7
```

A special mark named *current* identifies the current mouse position, when translated to an index value in the `text` widget. This position is not updated while a mouse button is held down.

To create a mark, use the `mark set` option:

```
widgetname mark set markname index
```

The *index* indicates the position to set the mark. If the given *markname* already exists, this command moves the mark to a new position.

To get rid of a mark, use the `mark unset` option:

```
widgetname mark unset markname
```

You can unset a number of marks at once:

```
widgetname mark unset markname1 markname2...
```

You can query the names of all marks in a `text` widget with the `mark names` option:

```
widgetname mark names
```

Using Tags To Control Fonts

Unlike a mark, a tag has a beginning and an end. *Tags* associate special attributes or behavior with a section of text. For example, you can tag a section of text and then make the tagged text appear underlined or in a different font. (This is how you get multiple fonts in a `text` widget.)

Furthermore, you can bind events within a tagged area. For example, if you create a tagged area as a hypertext link, you can make the link appear underlined. You can also bind the Button-1 event to the tag and execute Tcl code to jump to the link when the user presses the Button-1 (usually the leftmost mouse button) over the tagged area. You can build a hypertext system with the `text` widget, but you must do it by hand. (See Chapter 11 for more on hypertext and HTML.)

A common use for tags is simply to display some text in a different font.

You can create a tag with the `tag add` option:

```
widgetname tag add tagname start_index end_index
```

You determine the *tagname*. For example, the following command adds a tag named *underline1* to the widget named *.tx.text*. This new tag starts on line 2 at the start of the word in column 1 (count beginning at 0) and goes to the end of the word. The Tcl command follows:

```
.tx.text tag add underline1 \

   {2.1 wordstart} {2.1 wordend}
```

If you omit the *end_index*, the tag spans a single character.

If you want the same tag, say for a font change, to apply to many areas in the text, you can pass multiple start and end indices:

```
widgetname tag add tagname \
  start_index1 end_index1 \
  start_index2 end_index2 \
  ...
```

Controlling Display Attributes with Tags

After you create a tag, you can control the display attributes with the tag configure option:

```
widgetname tag configure tagname option value
```

For example, to set our *underline1* tag above to underline the text, we can use the following command:

```
.tx.text tag configure \
  underline1 -underline 1
```

You can see the text underlined in Figure 5.6.

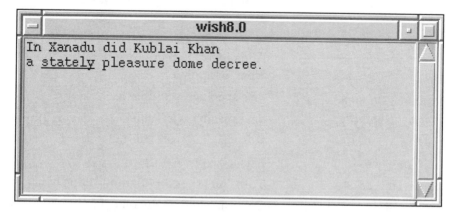

Figure 5.6. A text widget tag with underlined text.

Table 5.5 lists the options you can pass with tag configure. You can pass more than one option at a time.

Table 5.5. Tag configuration options.

Option	Meaning
`-background` *color*	Sets background color for tag.
`-bgstipple` *bitmap*	Uses *bitmap* as a background stipple (brush pattern).
`-borderwidth` *pixels*	Sets border width of tagged area.
`-fgstipple` *bitmap*	Uses *bitmap* as a foreground stipple (brush pattern).
`-font` *fontname*	Sets font for tag.
`-foreground` *color*	Sets foreground color for tag.
`-justify` *justify*	Justifies the line `left`, `right` or `center`.
`-lmargin1` *pixels*	Adds *pixels* to left margin for first line of tag only.
`-lmargin2` *pixels*	Adds *pixels* to left margin for all remaining lines of tag.
`-offset` *pixels*	Offsets the text baseline vertically by *pixels*.
`-overstrike` *boolean*	Turns on (1) or off (0) overstrike mode.
`-relief` *relief* ridge	Sets relief to `flat`, `groove`, `raised`, or `sunken`.
`-rmargin` *pixels*	Adds *pixels* to right margin, only applies when wrapping.
`-spacing1` *pixels*	Sets spacing, see Table 5.2.
`-spacing2` *pixels*	Sets spacing, see Table 5.2.
`-spacing3` *pixels*	Sets spacing, see Table 5.2.
`-tabs` *tablist*	Sets tab stops within tag.
`-underline` *boolean*	Turns on (1) or off (0) underlining of tag.
`-wrap` *mode*	Controls wrap mode, one of `none`, `char`, or `word`.

Binding Events to Tags

You can bind events that occur within a tag to execute a Tcl script, but you are limited to mouse and keyboard events. They include Enter, Leave, ButtonPress, ButtonRelease, (mouse) Motion, KeyPress and KeyRelease events.

You can bind events inside tags to actions using the tag bind option and the following syntax:

```
widgetname tag bind tagname event tcl_script
```

For example, when the user presses the leftmost mouse button, you can make a tag jump to a hypertext link. To set up such a binding, use the following template as an example:

```
.tx.text tag bind underline1 <Button-1> {
# Pretend to jump.
  puts "Jumping."

}
```

Of course, it's up to you to add the actual hypertext behavior. (Again, see Chapter 11 for HTML and Chapter 13 for URLs.) Press the leftmost mouse button over the underlined tag and you should see the following text printed out: *Jumping*.

In addition to jumping to a hypertext link, many Web browsers, such as Microsoft Internet Explorer or Netscape Navigator, display the jump location in a widget at the bottom of the window. This allows you to see where a hypertext link (think *tag*) will go. Normally, this appears when you move the mouse over the particular tag (hypertext link). To do something like this in Tcl, you can start with a label widget to display the jump-to location:

```
label .status \
   -text "Status Area"
pack .status -side bottom -anchor w
```

Next, you'll need to bind both the Enter and Leave events. On Enter, we need to extract the jump address (the Web's Universal Resource Locator) and set the text in the label widget to that value. The following code shows only how to set up the binding, not how to work with URLs (Chapter 13 covers Tcl and the Web):

```
.tx.text tag bind underline1 <Enter> {

# Display link.
  .status configure \
      -text "Over link."

}
```

We normally would bind the Leave event to clear the text in the label widget. In this case, though, we'll set this event to display a message. The purpose of this message is to allow you to experiment with the tag bindings and better see how the Enter and Leave events operate.

```
.tx.text tag bind underline1 <Leave> {

# Clear display of link.
  .status configure \
      -text "No longer over link."

}
```

Now, move the mouse over the underlined tag. The text in the *status* label should change. Move the mouse away. The text should change again.

You could also change the background color of the tagged area to provide even more indication to the user which tag is the "active" one. For example,

```
# text widget tags.

# Create text widget.
frame .tx

text .tx.text -yscrollcommand ".tx.scroll set"
scrollbar .tx.scroll -command ".tx.text yview"
```

```
# Pack scrollbar first.
pack .tx.scroll -side right -fill y
pack .tx.text -side left
pack .tx -side top

# Status area.
label .status -text "Status area" -justify left
pack .status -side bottom -fill x -anchor w

# Set up text, tags and colors.
.tx.text insert 1.0 "In Xanadu did Kublai Khan\n"
.tx.text insert 2.0 "a stately pleasure dome decree."

# Create tags.
.tx.text tag add underline1 \
    {2.2 wordstart} {2.2 wordend}

.tx.text tag add underline2 \
    {1.4 wordstart} {1.4 wordend}

# Configure tags to underline text.
.tx.text tag configure underline1 -underline 1
.tx.text tag configure underline2 -underline 1

# Set up actions for mouse events.
proc mouse_over_tag { widgetname tag color message } {
    # Change color of tag.
    $widgetname tag configure $tag \
        -background $color

    # Display link.
    .status configure -text $message

}


# Bind mouse events over the underlined tags.
.tx.text tag bind underline1 <Enter> {
    mouse_over_tag .tx.text underline1 \
        lightsteelblue "Over link."
```

```
}


.tx.text tag bind underline1 <Leave> {
    # Restore color of tag.
    mouse_over_tag .tx.text underline1 \
        lightgray "No longer over link."

}


.tx.text tag bind underline2 <Enter> {
    mouse_over_tag .tx.text underline2 \
        limegreen "Over link."

}


.tx.text tag bind underline2 <Leave> {
    # Restore color of tag.
    mouse_over_tag .tx.text underline2 \
        lightgray "No longer over link."
}

# tag.tcl
```

Notice how each link has its own named tag. This allows the Tcl code to keep each tag separate. For example, you could bind the leftmost mouse button, Button-1, to jump to the given hypertext link. Without separate tags, it would be harder to implement (but you could use an array for storing the separate data perhaps).

As you run the **tag.tcl** script and move the mouse over the window, the colors of the tagged areas should change as the mouse moves.

Deleting Tags

To delete a tag, use tag delete:

widgetname tag delete *tagname*

If you don't want to delete a tag, but just want to stop it from applying to a particular index, you can use the tag remove option:

```
widgetname tag remove tagname index
```

You can include multiple indices with this option.

You can query what tags exist with tag names:

```
widgetname tag names index
```

The *index* is optional. If omitted, you'll get the list of all tag names. if you use an *index*, you'll get back only the tags active at that position in the text.

Emebedded Windows

While tags allow you to place special formatting on a section of text, *embedded windows* allow you to place a whole widget at a position (index) in the text.

If you think about creating a World Wide Web browser in Tcl, you can use embedded windows to create the widgets used in Web-based forms. Chapter 13 covers more about Tcl and the Web. For now, though, we'll concentrate on the basic building blocks that make up embedded windows and images.

Creating Embedded Windows

You can create an embedded window at a particular location, an index, within a text widget, using the window create option:

```
widgetname window create index option value...
```

The *index* identifies where the new window is to be placed.

Table 5.6 lists the options you can use to configure the new embedded window at either creation time or later with the window configure command.

Table 5.6 Text Widget Embedded Window Options

Option	Usage
-align *where*	Set *where* to one of top, center, bottom or baseline, if the embedded window is shorter than a line of text.
-create *tcl_script*	Execute *tcl_script* to create the embedded window; won't work with -window.
-padx *pixels*	Extra space on each side of embedded window.
-pady *pixels*	Extra space on each side of embedded window.
-stretch *boolean*	If true (1), stretch embedded window vertically to fit line of text.
-window *widgetname*	Gives the widget name to display.

For example, we can embed a window inside the text widget. In this case, we'll use a button widget, but you can use any widget you want.

```
# Embedded window inside text widget.

# Create text widget.
frame .tx

text .tx.text -yscrollcommand ".tx.scroll set"
scrollbar .tx.scroll -command ".tx.text yview"

# Pack scrollbar first.
pack .tx.scroll -side right -fill y
pack .tx.text -side left
pack .tx -side top

# Status area.
label .status -text "Status area" -justify left
pack .status -side bottom -anchor w
```

```
# Fill in some text.
.tx.text insert 1.0 "In Xanadu did Kublai Khan\n"
.tx.text insert 2.0 "a stately pleasure dome decree."


# Create embedded widget as child of text widget.
button .tx.text.embed1 -text "Embedded button"

# Embed button widget inside text widget.
.tx.text window create {1.0 lineend} \
    -window .tx.text.embed1

# Don't pack embedded widgets.
# embed1.tcl
```

WARNING

Don't pack the widget you intend to embed. The text widget takes care of this for you.

Figure 5.7 shows this embedded button widget in the text widget.

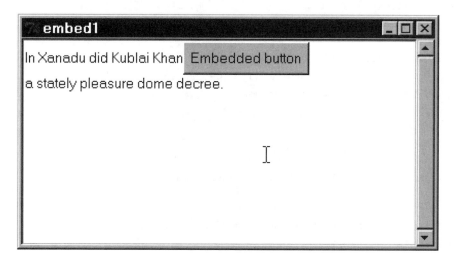

Figure 5.7. An embedded button widget.

One of the best things about embedded windows (and embedded images, discussed following this section) is that the text widget maintains the proper place in the text as the widget scrolls and new text gets added. Thus, your embedded windows are properly managed inside the text widget at the textual position you provide.

You could also use embedded widgets to create a data entry form often used in *Hyper Text Markup Language*, or HTML, documents, the *lingua franca* of the Web. To do this, you can create a frame and then create a label and entry widget within the frame. Then, embed the parent frame widget within the text widget:

```
# Embedded window inside text widget.

# Create text widget.
frame .tx

text .tx.text -yscrollcommand ".tx.scroll set"
scrollbar .tx.scroll -command ".tx.text yview"

# Pack scrollbar first.
pack .tx.scroll -side right -fill y
pack .tx.text -side left
pack .tx -side top

# Status area.
label .status -text "Status area" -justify left
pack .status -side bottom -anchor w


# Fill in some text.
.tx.text insert 1.0 "In Xanadu did Kublai Khan\n"
.tx.text insert 2.0 "a stately pleasure dome decree."


# Create embedded widgets as child of text widget.
frame .tx.text.embed2

label .tx.text.embed2.lbl -text "Enter name: "
```

```
entry .tx.text.embed2.ent -width 30 \
    -textvariable name

pack .tx.text.embed2.lbl .tx.text.embed2.ent -side left

button .tx.text.embed1 -text "Embedded button"

# Embed button widget inside text widget.
.tx.text window create {2.0 linestart} \
    -window .tx.text.embed2

# Don't pack embedded widgets.
# embed2.tcl
```

You need to pack subwidgets within the widget you embed, e.g., *.tx.text.embed2.lbl* and *.tx.text.embed2.ent*. But, again, don't pack the widget you intend to embed, that is, *.tx.text.embed2*, the parent frame widget.

The embedded frame widget, with its label and entry child widgets, appears in Figure 5.8.

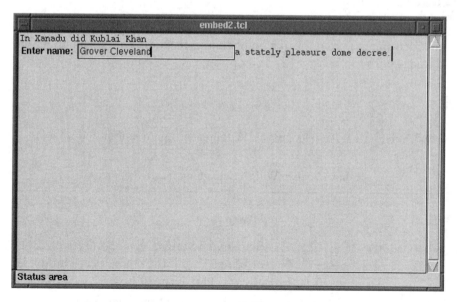

Figure 5.8 An embedded frame widget with child widgets.

286

You can modify an embedded window with the `window configure` command, which uses the following syntax:

```
widgetname window configure index option value
```

You can use `window configure` with multiple options at the same time.

If you want to know the names of all embedded windows, the `window names` command returns the name of each embedded window in the widget.

```
widgetname window names
```

Embedded Images

In addition to embedding windows—widgets—inside a `text` widget, you can also embed images directly.

NOTE You must have Tk 8.0 or higher to use embedded images. Prior to this version, you can embed a `label` widget and then place the image inside the `label` widget.

Embedded images are a lot like embedded windows. You create an embedded image with the `image create` option:

```
widgetname image create index option value...
```

Table 5.7 lists the options available when creating an embedded image.

Table 5.7 `text` Widget Embedded Image Options

Option	Usage
`-align` *where*	Set *where* to one of `top`, `center`, `bottom` or `baseline`, if the embedded window is shorter than a line of text.
`-image` *image*	Uses the image of the given name.

-name *image_name*	Provides a name to refer to the image within the text widget.
-padx *pixels*	Extra space on each side of embedded window.
-pady *pixels*	Extra space on each side of embedded window.

The most important thing you need to embed an image is the image file itself. Tk supports a number of image formats, including the common GIF format. To embed a GIF image in a text widget, you can use the following code as an example:

```
# Embedded image inside text widget.

# Create text widget.
frame .tx

text .tx.text -yscrollcommand ".tx.scroll set"
scrollbar .tx.scroll -command ".tx.text yview"

# Pack scrollbar first.
pack .tx.scroll -side right -fill y
pack .tx.text -side left
pack .tx -side top

# Status area.
label .status -text "Status area" -justify left
pack .status -side bottom -anchor w


# Fill in some text.
.tx.text insert 1.0 "In Xanadu did Kublai Khan\n"
.tx.text insert 2.0 "a stately pleasure dome decree."


# Create the image.
image create photo ring_brodgar -file rngbrod5.gif
```

```
# Embed image inside text widget.
.tx.text image create {2.0 linestart} \
    -image ring_brodgar -name ring
```

```
# embed3.tcl
```

This example image appears in Figure 5.9.

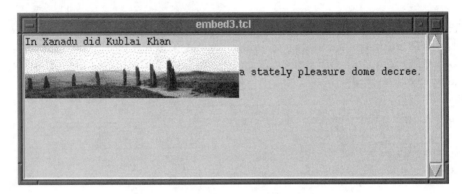

Figure 5.9 An embedded image inside a `text` widget.

You can find out more about the `image create` command in the section on Photo Images in Chapter 8.

You may embed the same image at multiple places inside the `text` widget. You can refer to embedded images via the name you can provide using the `-name` option.

Making Hypertext Links in the Text

Note that you can use marks, tags, and embedded windows to create a hypertext system quickly.

For example, a program called **plume**, shown in Figure 5.10, uses the `text` widget (and a lot of customized code) to create a World-Wide Web browser. The `text` widget provides the basics for a hypertext system. Tags can outline links, and embedded windows can provide graphics.

Figure 5.10 The Plume Web browser.

NOTE

Plume is available on the Internet from **http://tcltk.anu.edu.au/**, and on the CD-ROM in the **contrib/www** directory.

To do this, you'll want to set up a tag for each hypertext link. You'll then need to bind the tags to `Enter`, `Leave` and `Button-1` events. You can also use tags for the more mundane text formatting commands found in most hypertext systems, such as the World Wide Web.

Cut, Copy, and Paste with the `text` Widget

Taking a step away from the hypertext examples, any real work with a `text` widget requires use of the clipboard. That is, if you want to make a usable interface. You can make the Tk `text` widget support cut, copy, and paste operations using a few simple Tk commands, including `clipboard` and `selection`.

290

The Clipboard

The **clipboard** provides a landing spot for data exchange. You can copy the selected text (or data in whatever form) to the clipboard from one application and then paste it from the clipboard into another application.

The Clipboard and the Selection

The clipboard exists in limbo. You can't see its contents (without a clipboard-viewing program at least). The selection, however, is usually visible, unless the user scrolls out of the way or covers up a window.

The **selection** is just a fancy name for the text that is selected on the screen. You can often select other things than just text, but for the text widget, we'll concentrate on selecting text, copying the selected text, and so on.

All the standard operations of cut, copy, and paste involve the clipboard for data storage and the selection. For a copy operation, the selected text is copied into the clipboard. A paste reverses this and copies the clipboard text to the text widget (and overwrites any selected text).

Getting the Selected Text

There are two main ways to get at the selected text. First, in a text widget, you can access the special tag Tk sets up for the selection. You can also use the more general selection command.

Accessing the Selection Tag

In a text widget, if the selection is in the widget, a special tag named sel (much like that for the entry widget) will indicate the span of the selection.

The Selection Command

While the special sel tag can prove useful, I normally stick to the more general selection command. This allows you to create a more general cut, copy, and paste mechanism, where you don't have to worry about which widget the selection resides in at any time.

To get the current selection, use the following command:

```
set var [selection get]
```

N O T E

If no data are selected, then the `selection get` command generates an error. To avoid this, you can wrap the `selection get` command inside the `catch` command, which catches errors, as shown here:

```
catch {
    set var [selection get]
}
```

Chapter 9 covers the `catch` command in greater detail.

The `selection get` command returns the current selection. By default, the data are in text format. You can use the `-type` option to request the data in a different format. The default value is STRING for text string format.

U N I X

These types come from the X Window System's concept of selections. In X, you can play a game of 20 questions with the current selection. The idea is that you may want more than the actual selected data. You may want to know what window the data reside in. You may want the length of the data, as well as the actual contents of the data. The X Window System handles this with the concept of the **target type** of data you ask for.

For example, you can ask the application that owns the selection for the window ID of the window in which the selection appears (`-type CLIENT_WINDOW`). You can ask for the data as an integer (`-type INTEGER`), although this often causes an error.

You can ask for the length of the selected data (normally the number of characters in the selected text, but for other data formats this is undefined) with the `-type LENGTH` option. You can ask for the character position within the data where the selected text resides with the `-type CHARACTER_POSITION` option.

To find out what available types the application which owns the selection supports, use the `-type TARGETS` option. This returns the name of all the target types supported. Note that different applications support different target types.

For example, try the following commands:

```
% selection get
```

```
These types come from the X Window System's concept
% selection get -type CLIENT_WINDOW
0x80000e
% selection get -type INTEGER
PRIMARY selection doesn't exist or form "INTEGER" not defined
% selection get -type LENGTH
0x13
% selection get -type CHARACTER_POSITION
PRIMARY selection doesn't exist or form "CHARACTER_POSITION"
not defined
% selection get -type TARGETS
STRING TEXT COMPOUND_TEXT LENGTH
LIST_LENGTH TIMESTAMP HOSTNAME
IP_ADDRESS USER CLASS NAME CLIENT_WINDOW
```

In virtually all cases, you use the -type STRING option, the default, or skip the -type option altogether. See Appendix A for a list of books on the X Window System that will explain selections in the UNIX environment.

WINDOWS

If you try the above commands on Windows, you're likely to get errors. Even so, Tk applications will work with selections and work very well with the clipboard, which is where UNIX is weakest.

In addition to different data target types, there's also different selections. The default selection is called the PRIMARY selection. This is the one that just about every application uses. On UNIX, you'll also see SECONDARY and CLIPBOARD selections. You can also define your own selections, using any name you want. The rules that apply to the PRIMARY selection apply to all: Only one application at a time may own any *particular* selection. Your application may own the PRIMARY selection, but another application may own SECONDARY.

You can use the -selection option to indicate the selection you want:

```
selection get -selection PRIMARY
```

The main problem with multiple selections is finding programs to exchange data with. Virtually all UNIX programs support the default PRIMARY selection. Very few support an arbitrarily named selection called FRAMROD.

Only in rare circumstances will you need a different selection, unless you're retrieving data from the clipboard, in which case you'll use the CLIPBOARD selection.

The on-line documentation for the selection command lists a host of other options, most useful only in the UNIX environment.

Clearing the Selection

To clear the current selection, use the selection clear command:

```
selection clear
```

Again, you can use the -selection option if you want to specify a different selection than PRIMARY.

This only clears the fact that something was selected. It does *not* delete the selected data.

Checking Who Owns the Selection

To check if your application owns the selection, use the selection own command:

```
selection own
```

If your application owns the selection, the selection own command will return the name of the widget that owns the selection. Otherwise, selection own returns a NULL string.

To see if your application owns the selection, you can use the following code:

```
if { [selection own] != "" } {
# Have selection.

} else {
```

```
    # Don't have selection.
}
```

The selection, though, is just the first part of cut, copy, and paste operations. The remaining part is working with the clipboard.

Putting Text in the Clipboard

The `clipboard append` command places data in the clipboard.

```
clipboard append data
```

This *data* is appended to whatever data were already in the clipboard. Because of this, you may want to clear the data out first (as shown later).

 If the *data* starts with a dash, -, then you'll want to use the -- option prior to the *data*, for example:

N O T E

```
clipboard append -- ---
```

The above command appends three dashes, ---, to the clipboard. Without the -- option, Tk would treat the data as an option, a bad option at that.

Clearing Text in the Clipboard

The `clipboard clear` command clears the data in the clipboard and asserts ownership:

```
clipboard clear
```

Retrieving Data from the Clipboard

To retrieve data from the clipboard, you need to use the `selection get` command with a `-selection CLIPBOARD` option. The following commands clear the clipboard, append text, and then retrieve it:

```
% clipboard clear
% clipboard append "Hello Clipboard"
% selection get -selection CLIPBOARD
Hello Clipboard
```

With these commands, you can now put together the cut, copy, and paste operations discussed at the beginning of this section.

Copy

The copy operation is the easiest. What you need to do is outlined here.

1. Check if any text is selected.
2. If so, get the selected text.
3. Clear the clipboard.
4. Place the selected text in the clipboard.

All these tasks can be accomplished with just the selection and clipboard commands, as shown in the following edit_copy procedure:

```
# Handle the copy action for a text widget.
proc edit_copy { textwidget } {

# Check if any text is selected in textwidget.
    set owner [selection own]

    if { $owner == $textwidget } {
        # Clear clipboard.
        clipboard clear

        catch {
            clipboard append [selection get]

        }

    }

}
```

It's a good idea to always wrap the `selection get` command inside the `catch` command as shown in the `edit_copy` procedure.

Cut

The cut operation is essentially the same as a copy, with an extra deletion.

1. Check if any text is selected.
2. If so, get the selected text.
3. Clear the clipboard.
4. Place the selected text in the clipboard.
5. Delete the selected text.

To implement this, we use code similar to the `edit_copy` procedure. The cut operation is nearly the same as the following copy operation:

```
# Handle the cut action for a text widget.
proc edit_cut { textwidget } {

# Check if any text is selected in textwidget.
    set owner [selection own]

    if { $owner == $textwidget } {
        # Clear clipboard.
        clipboard clear

        catch {
            clipboard append [selection get]

            # Delete selected text.
            $owner delete sel.first sel.last
        }

    }

}
```

In this `edit_cut` procedure, the `sel` tag is used to create the indices for the starting and ending positions of the selection.

Paste

The paste operation reverses (sort of) the copy operation.

1. Get the text from the clipboard.
2. Check if any text is selected.
3. If so, delete the selected text.
4. Insert the clipboard text at the current insertion position.

To implement this, you can use the following code example.

In the code, there are two main cases to deal with. If the user selected data in the window, the paste operation will replace the selected data with the contents of the clipboard. Otherwise, paste will merely insert the data at the current insertion point. Both alternatives require the name of the widget you want to paste in.

The following code implements a paste operation on a given widget:

```
# Handle the paste action for a text widget.
proc edit_paste { textwidget } {

# Get text from clipboard.
    catch {
        set clip [selection get -selection CLIPBOARD]
    }


# Default location to insert data.
    set idx [$textwidget index insert]

# Check if any text is selected in textwidget.
    set owner [selection own]

    if { $owner == $textwidget } {
```

```
catch {
    # Save index where selection starts.
    set idx [$owner index sel.first]

    # Delete selected text.
    $textwidget delete sel.first sel.last
}

}


catch {
    # Paste in selected text.
    $textwidget insert $idx $clip
}

}
```

Binding Events for Cut, Copy, and Paste

After you've set up procedures to handle cut, copy, and paste operations, the next logical step is to set up menu choices and **Control**-key accelerators to call the edit_cut, edit_copy, and edit_paste procedures, respectively.

Chapter 4 covered how to set up menu choices and accelerators, so this should be old hat. Watch out, though. There's a tricky problem. The text widget already comes with a set of bindings for cut, copy, and paste (although the default paste binding never seems to work for me). So, there's the danger that two sets of routines will get called for the same event. The way to stop this is with the break command at the end of the binding for the various control keys.

Within a key binding, the break command stops Tcl from executing any other bindings on the same event. Normally, Tcl executes each binding in turn, one after another. You can stop this with break:

```
bind .tx.text <Control-Key-x> "edit_cut    .tx.text; break"
bind .tx.text <Control-Key-c> "edit_copy   .tx.text; break"
bind .tx.text <Control-Key-v> "edit_paste .tx.text; break"
```

Note how the break command goes at the end of the actual binding. You can't put break inside the edit_cut, edit_copy, or edit_paste procedures because within a procedure, break must go inside a loop.

I spent a lot of time trying to figure this one out. So, to avoid wasting your time, always set up the break command at the end of common key bindings.

We'll use these techniques in the section on A Tcl-Based Text Editor, later in this chapter.

text Widget Efficiency

Each character in a text widget requires about 2 or 3 bytes of memory. With modern computers (and modern memory-eating operating system requirements), you should be able to display a large amount of text before running into memory problems.

Dumping the Contents of a text Widget

You can use the dump option to extract the full contents of the text widget. The marks, tags, and images make this more interesting than just the text alone. For example, to dump the contents of the text widget set up in the **emebed3.tcl** script, you can use the following command:

```
% .tx.text dump -all 1.0 end
text {In Xanadu did Kubl} 1.0 mark anchor 1.18 mark insert 1.18 text
{ai Khan
} 1.18 mark current 2.0 image ring 2.0 text {a stately pleasure dome
decree.
} 2.1
```

The syntax is

```
widgetname dump options start_index end_index
```

The options include -all to get all information, -image to just dump information on images, -mark for information on marks, -tag for information on tags, -text for just the text, and -window for information on embedded windows. There's also a special option, -command, with which you provide a Tcl script to execute for each item found. The -command script will get three items appended for each—item, the key, the value, and the index. These data come from the data returned by the dump option.

The data returned use the following format:

```
key1 value1 index1 key2 value2 index2...
```

The key tells you what type of data are described. The value provides the text or other information and the index the position. From this example, one entry follows:

```
text {In Xanadu did Kubl} 1.0
```

Here, the key is text, the value is {In Xanadu did Kubl}, and the index is 1.0, the start of the text widget. The valid keys include image, mark, tagon, tagoff, text, and window.

The dump option is useful if you want to save the state of a text widget and later restore it to the original state.

Searching Within the text Widget

The search option allows you to search for a text string within the contents of the text widget. The syntax is

```
widgetname search options search_for start_index stop_index
```

The search option searches for the *search_for* text string beginning at the *start_index* and going up to the end or the optional *stop_index*, if one is provided.

If found, you get back the index where the searched-for text starts.

There are a number of options you can provide to control the nature of the search, as listed in Table 5.8.

Table 5.8 text Widget Search Options

Option	Meaning
-forward	Searches in the forward direction, the default.
-backward	Searches backward.
-exact	Characters must match pattern exactly, the default.
-regexp	Use pattern as a regular expression (see Chapter 2).
-nocase	Ignore case when searching.
-count *variable*	If a match is found, place the number of characters into *variable*.
--	Stops options.

The -- option seems kind of strange at first glance. Tcl interprets all items starting with a dash, -, as an option. The problem is then searching for an item that starts with a dash (sort of like deleting a file named "-i" on UNIX). The double-dash, --, stops all parsing for options and allows the pattern to start with a -.

With the -regexp option, you can use all the power of regular expression searches to find text in the widget.

One of the most common uses for the search option is implementing search and replace in a text widget.

Search and Replace

The search option provides the basic capability to search for text in the text widget. Once found, though, you need to perform some operations to make that text visible to the user.

To make the text visible, you need to tag it with a tag that provides for some form of highlighting. You could use any tag you want and configure that tag to highlight the text in a manner you prefer. What I usually do, though, is tag the searched-for text with the sel tag. This special tag marks the selected text in the widget. So, if you mark the text with the sel tag, you're selecting the text. The user sees the text highlighted in the same way any selected text is highlighted. The user can then cut or copy the text to the clipboard or simply delete the text. If you don't use the special sel tag, then you need to write custom code to handle all these activities. Because you already need to write cut, copy, and paste code, why don't you reuse that by sticking to the sel tag?

The following example shows a text widget with a search window at the bottom. Type in a text string in the search window, press the **Return** (**Enter**) key, and the script should search for the text.

```
# Example of searching in a text widget.

# Create text widget.
frame .tx

text .tx.text -yscrollcommand ".tx.scroll set"
scrollbar .tx.scroll -command ".tx.text yview"

# Pack scrollbar first.
pack .tx.scroll -side right -fill y
pack .tx.text -side left
pack .tx -side top -expand 1

# Create search area.
frame .sr

label .sr.label -text "Search: "
entry .sr.search
button .sr.again -text "Find Again" \
    -command { find_text .sr.search .tx.text }

pack .sr.label -side left -fill y
pack .sr.search -side left -fill x -expand 1
pack .sr.again  -side left -fill y

pack .sr -side top -fill x
```

```
# Bind Return in the entry widget to search.
bind .sr.search <Key-Return> {
    find_text .sr.search .tx.text

}


# Global position where last search left off.
global find_last_indx
set find_last_indx 1.0

# Procedure to search text widget.
proc find_text { entrywidget textwidget } {
    global find_last_indx


    # Get text to search for.
    set search_for [$entrywidget get]

    set length [string length $search_for]

    # Search for text.
    set indx [$textwidget search - \
            $search_for $find_last_indx end]

            if { $indx == "" } {
        set find_last_indx 1.0

        set indx [$textwidget search - \
            $search_for $find_last_indx end]

    }


            if { $indx != ""} {
        #
        # Clear tag for any text that was selected.
        # Inside catch because it may generate an error.
        catch {
```

```
        $textwidget tag remove sel sel.first sel.last
    }


    #
    # Select the found text.
    #
    $textwidget tag add sel $indx "$indx + $length chars"
    #
    # Place insertion cursor at start of selected data.
    #
    $textwidget mark set insert $indx

    #
    # Make sure text is visible.
    #
    $textwidget see $indx

    # Keep index for next search.
    set find_last_indx "$indx + 1 char"

} else {
    # Reset to search from beginning.
    set find_last_indx 1.0
    puts "$search_for not found"


    }


}

# textfind.tcl
```

In this example, the searching is performed by the find_text procedure. Going through this procedure in depth should explain how to perform search operations with Tk.

The find_text procedure first extracts the text to search for from the entry widget that you typed the text into. Then, find_text gets the length of this text. We need the length to control the amount of the text to select—if found, of course.

The next step is to search for the text in the `text` widget. The starting index is stored in the global variable *find_last_indx*. This allows the *Find Again* button to search for the next occurrence of a text string. Each time the text is found, the global variable *find_last_indx* gets updated with the index, plus one character, so that the next search takes place after the initial text that was found.

If not found, the `find_text` procedure searches again from the beginning of the `text` widget. This allows the search to wrap around the end of the text.

If found, the `find_text` procedure removes the previous selection. It is very possible that no text is selected, so this command is wrapped inside the handy `catch` command, which catches any errors. You'll use `catch` a lot in making robust Tcl scripts.

After the old selection, if any, is removed, the `tag add` option sets the `sel` tag to the new location, the location of the search text.

The next step is to move the insertion cursor to this location, by moving the special mark called `insert`. (The `text` widget supports a number of special marks and tags, which you can see with the `dump` option described previously.)

Finally, we must deal with the case where the text is found but isn't visible in the window. For example, the user may have scrolled away from the area around the selected text. To deal with this, the `see` option makes a given index visible in the window. The syntax is

```
widgetname see index
```

Note that this command just makes sure that the text is in the visible area of the window. You can still cover this up by placing another window on top.

Replacing Text Once Found

A common option in most text editors is to extend the search to include the ability to replace the searched-for text with another text string.

You can replace text in the `text` widget by deleting the old text and inserting the new. To delete the search `text`, you need the index in the text widget where the text was found as well as the length of the search text. With that, you can delete the `text` widget using a command like:

```
$widgetname delete $indx "$indx + $length chars"
```

You then insert the new text at the same starting index. For example,

```
$widgetname insert $indx $replace_text
```

You can see another example, which includes text searching in the simple text editor created, at the end of this chapter. In addition, Chapter 7 covers a find and replace dialog box.

Tcl String-Handling Commands

In addition to the text and entry widgets that display strings on the screen, Tcl provides a large number of text string-handling commands, which come in handy when you start retrieving strings from widgets and need to parse the string in some way.

This next section covers the most important string-handling commands. You can use these commands when you need to extract a substring from a string, closely examine the data held in a string, (and much more.)

Extracting Substrings

To get the length of a string, use the string length command:

```
% set str1 "1234567890"
1234567890
% string length $str1
10
```

Remember to use the $ with variable names, so the string commands don't interpret the variable name as a text string itself.

NOTE

To get the character at a particular position, use the string index command, which uses the following format:

```
string index $string char_position
```

The *char_position* starts counting at 0. For example,

```
% string index $str1 4
5
```

To extract a range of characters, use the `string range` command, which uses the following format:

```
string range $string first last
```

For example,

```
% string range $str1 2 5
3456
```

To get the index of the start or end of a word, use the `string wordstart` and `string wordend` commands:

```
string wordend $string index
string wordstart $string index
```

To get a hang of this, you should try an example:

```
% set str1 "In Xanadu did Kublai Khan"
In Xanadu did Kublai Khan
% string wordend $str1 4
9
% string wordstart $str1 4
3
```

Starting with version 8.0, Tcl provides a number of extra word-handling routines, mostly to deal with different assumptions on different operating systems. For example, in Windows, a space, tab, and newline separates words. But, on UNIX, anything except for a number, letter, or underscore can be considered to separate a word. These rules come from the Windows and Motif (UNIX) interfaces and the following routines are used in the `text` widget to determine how much text is selected when you double-click on a word.

`tcl_endOfWord` returns the index where the current word ends. You pass in a starting index, and `tcl_endOfWord` searches for an end-of-word character (which may differ by platform) following the first word character following the starting index. That is, if you pass in the index of a space character, `tcl_endOfWord` will go forward to the next word and find that word's end.

`tcl_startOfNextWord` returns the index of the start of the next word after the given starting index.

`tcl_startOfPreviousWord` reverses this and returns the index of the start of the previous word.

`tcl_wordBreakAfter` returns the index of the next word break after the starting index.

`tcl_wordBreakBefore` reverses this and returns the index of the word break before the starting index.

All these commands return minus one if the searched-for item was not found. These commands also follow similar syntax:

```
tcl_endOfWord string starting_index
tcl_startOfNextWord string starting_index
tcl_startOfPreviousWord string starting_index
tcl_wordBreakAfter string starting_index
tcl_wordBreakBefore string starting_index
```

You can test these commands with the following example script:

```
# Tcl 8.0 word-searching commands.

# Test data.
set string "What a word_finding tool this is."
puts "Test string is <$string>."

# Should return end of "What"
set indx [tcl_endOfWord $string 1]

puts "Should return end of word <What>."
```

```
puts "\t <[string range $string $indx end]>"

# Should return end of "word_finding".
# Note start index is a space.
set indx [tcl_endOfWord $string 6]

puts "Should return end of <word_finding>."
puts "\t <[string range $string $indx end]>"

# Should return start of word after <What>.
set indx [tcl_startOfNextWord $string 1]

puts "Should return start of word after <What>."
puts "\t <[string range $string $indx end]>"

# Should return start of word before <word_finding>.
set indx [tcl_startOfPreviousWord $string 6]

puts "Should return start of word before <word_finding>."
puts "\t <[string range $string $indx end]>"

# Should return the word break before <word_finding>.
set indx [tcl_wordBreakBefore $string 7]

puts "Should return the word break before <word_finding>."
puts "\t <[string range $string $indx end]>"

# Should return the word break after <word_finding>.
set indx [tcl_wordBreakAfter $string 7]

puts "Should return the word break after <word_finding>."
puts "\t <[string range $string $indx end]>"
# word.tcl
```

When you run the **word.tcl** script, you should see the following output:

```
Test string is <What a word_finding tool this is.>.
Should return end of word <What>.
```

```
            < a word_finding tool this is.>
```

Should return end of <word_finding>.
```
            < tool this is.>
```

Should return start of word after <What>.
```
            <a word_finding tool this is.>
```

Should return start of word before <word_finding>.
```
            <a word_finding tool this is.>
```

Should return the word break before <word_finding>.
```
            <word_finding tool this is.>
```

Should return the word break after <word_finding>.
```
            < tool this is.>
```

N O T E You must have at least version 8.0 of Tcl to use these commands.

Comparing Strings

The string compare command compares two strings.

```
string compare string1 string2
```

It returns minus one, 0, or 1. If both strings are the same, then string compare returns 0. if *string1* is less than *string2*, using the comparison of the ASCII characters in the string, then string compare returns minus one. Otherwise, string compare returns 1, indicating that *string2* is greater than *string1*, in terms of ASCII sort order.

```
% set string1 "ABCDEF"
ABCDEF
```

```
% set string2 "abcdef"
abcdef
% string compare $string1 $string2
-1
% string compare $string2 $string1
1
```

Searching in Strings

The `string match` command returns 1 if the given pattern matches the string:

```
string match pattern $string
```

The pattern can contain a `*` as a wildcard to match anything (or nothing), a `?` to match any one character, patterns in square brackets such as `[a-z]` or an escaped character with a backslash. Tcl introduces yet another pattern-matching scheme (in addition to the `glob` and `regexp` methods described in Chapter 2) to mimic the UNIX C-shell, **csh**.

The `string first` command searches a string for the first occurrence of the characters in another string and returns the index position within the string of the first match:

```
string first characters_to_match string_to_check
```

For example,

```
% string first "not" "I am not a crook."
5
```

If there is no match, `string first` returns minus one.

The `string last` command works the same but returns the last match:

```
string last characters_to_match string_to_check
```

Changing Case

The `string tolower` command returns a string with all characters lower-case. It does not modify the original string.

```
% string tolower "aaaBBBaaa"
aaabbbaaa
```

Similarly, the `string toupper` command returns a string with all characters uppercase.

```
% string toupper "aaaBBBaaa"
AAABBBAAA
```

Trimming Strings

The `string trimleft` command trims a set of characters from the start of the string. By default, `string trimleft` trims all leading whitespace from the string, returning the new string. Again, the original string is not modified.

```
string trimleft $string characters
```

With the optional characters, you can specify which characters to trim. For example, to trim all leading e's:

```
% string trimleft "eeeeStart of string" "e"
Start of string
```

If you skip the *characters* argument, `string trimleft` trims all leading whitespace characters: spaces, tabs, returns, newlines, etc.

The `string trimright` command works the same, but from the end of the string working in.

Finally, the `string trim` command works from both ends: front and back. If you need to perform even more complicated string manipulation, there's even more in the on-line manuals for the `string` command.

A Tcl-Based Text Editor

One of the most troublesome aspects to writing Tcl applications on the Windows platform is the lack of a good environment. On UNIX, you create Tcl scripts inside an **xterm** shell window and can use the selection to copy and paste into the **wish** command prompt.

On Windows, though, the Console window created by **wish** supports only limited editing capabilities. The fact of the matter is that Tcl on Windows does not yet work as well as it does on UNIX. (Things are getting better with each release, though.)

NOTE

If you're running an older version of **wish**, the default text widget bindings are **Ctrl-Y** for pasting, **Ctrl-W** for cutting and **Alt-W** for copying. Newer versions of the Tcl console support the standard Windows **Ctrl-X**, **Ctrl-C** and **Ctrl-V** for cut, copy, and paste, respectively.

To help alleviate this problem, you can use the Tcl text widget to create a Tcl-oriented editor. Furthermore, you can add in Tcl commands to evaluate either the selected text or the whole contents of the text widget. With this, development on Windows becomes a much more positive experience. (This example also pulls together all the lessons in this chapter into one Tcl script.)

The key to making this work lies in being able to execute the text typed in.

Executing Tcl Scripts within Tcl

Remember the mantra that everything in Tcl is text, even Tcl commands. Because of this, you can create new Tcl scripts from within a Tcl script and execute them. The key is the eval command.

The eval command concatenates all its arguments together and then passes these to the Tcl interpreter. For example,

```
eval { puts "In eval." }
```

In a Tcl editor, you could create a `button` widget that, when invoked, will call `eval` on the selected text in a given `text` widget. Another `button` widget may call `eval` on all text in the given `text` widget.

WARNING

With `eval`, you can make Tcl scripts that modify themselves. This is not always a good idea and can easily lead to problems. Because of that, you'll want to perform extra testing on any script in which you use `eval`.

Creating the Script

We've already covered a lot of Tcl commands that help build a text editor. First of all, there's the `text` widget, which forms the basis for the whole thing. In this chapter, we've covered using cut, copy, and paste and searching for text. Chapter 4 covered how to set up menus, including the necessary *Edit* menu. Thus far, the two main missing areas include working with files to read and write text and creating dialog boxes to allow the user to select a file to open. Chapter 6 covers files and Chapter 7, dialog boxes. For now, we'll cheat and include some commands that give you a preview of what's to come in the following chapters.

The **textedit.tcl** script creates a menu bar that includes *File*, *Edit*, and *Help* menus.

The *File* menu includes choices for *New*, *Open*, *Insert* (at insertion cursor), *Save*, *Save As*, and *Exit*. Most of these choices use examples from Chapters 6 and 7.

The *Edit* menu includes the ubiquitous *Cut*, *Copy*, and *Paste* choices.

The *Help* menu displays only an *About* dialog box.

Beneath the menu bar, a toolbar provides buttons for executing the selected text using the `eval` command, as well as executing all the text in the widget. At the end of the toolbar, the search widgets from the **textfind.tcl** script are included to allow you to search for text in the widget.

Beneath the toolbar comes the main application area, the `text` widget itself.

The whole script creates an interface as shown in Figure 5.11. Note how many extra widgets are required to support the one basic `text` widget where all the action lies. You'll find you need to create a lot of supporting widgets in most graphical applications.

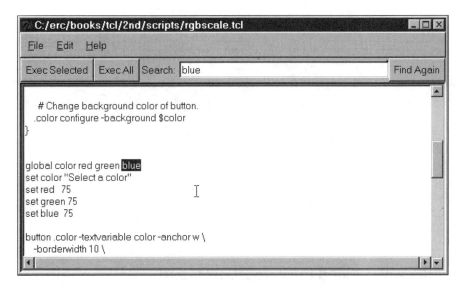

Figure 5.11 A Tcl editor/executer program.

For this program, we need the `edit_cut`, `edit_copy`, and `edit_paste` procedures created in the section on Cut, Copy, and Paste. We also need to create some new procedures.

To execute the selected text within a given widget, you can use the following procedure:

```
# Executes selected text as Tcl commands.
proc exec_sel { textwidget } {

if { [selection own] == $textwidget } {
        catch {
            set sel [selection get]

            if { $sel != "" } {
                eval $sel

            }

        }

    }
```

```
}
```

To execute all the text in a given widget, you can use the following:

```
# Executes all text in a text widget.
proc exec_all { textwidget } {

    # Get all text from widget.
    set all [$textwidget get 1.0 end]

    # Execute text as Tcl commands.
    eval $all
}
```

Issues with Calling the `eval` Command

There are a few issues you must deal with if you call the `eval` command in your scripts, especially from a Tcl text editor. The first and most important issue is that you are modifying the text editor itself, as all your commands apply to the same Tcl interpreter.

Thus, if you create a `button`, it could appear in the text editor interface. To help avoid this, the `textedit_create` procedure creates a `toplevel` widget that serves as the top widget for the text editor. Because the text editor doesn't use the widget named . any widgets you create as children of the widget named . should not interfere with the text editor.

This leads to a good rule: In general, you don't want to create your widgets as children of the top-level widget named . to avoid these conflicts.

Another problem is name conflicts for global variables and procedures. Most of the global variables in the **textedit.tcl** script are elements inside the global array named *textedit*. This helps to eliminate conflicts in variable names. It would also be a good idea to use some form of naming prefix for all procedure names. (The **textedit.tcl** script does not do this, but for any larger Tcl script, you should provide some way to make your procedure names unique. Furthermore, starting in Tcl 8.0 you can use name spaces to help separate your names from those of others. See Chapter 14.)

One way to help with all these potential conflicts is to create a new Tcl interpreter. The `interp` command creates a new Tcl interpreter that is distinct from the main interpreter we've been using so far.

One of the main uses for `interp` is to create a special environment to execute commands. The `-safe` option for the `interp create` command creates a safe interpreter that restricts which commands can get executed inside the new interpreter.

To create a new restricted—safe—interpreter, use the following syntax:

```
interp create -safe name
```

To create a regular interpreter, use the following syntax:

```
interp create name
```

In both cases, the *name* refers to the new interpreter. You can use any name you like, such as

```
interp create eval_env
```

After you create the interpreter, you can execute the *name* as its own command. The following `eval` option allows you to execute commands inside the new interpreter:

```
#
# Use of interp to create a new Tcl interpreter.
#
  # Test variable.
set a 2
interp create eval_env
eval_env eval { set a 1 }

puts "Outside value is a=$a"
eval_env eval { puts "Inside value is a=$a" }
# interp.tcl
```

When you run this script, the variable *a* has two values: one inside the child, or slave interpreter, *eval_env*, and a separate value outside in the main interpreter. The output follows:

```
Outside value is a=2
Inside value is a=1
```

By default, the `interp` command does not provide access to Tk commands, just the base Tcl language. To use Tk, you need to run commands like the following:

```
# Loading Tk inside another interpreter.

interp create eval_env
load {} Tk eval_env

eval_env eval {
    button .b -text "Inside interp"
    pack .b
}

# interptk.tcl
```

The `interp` command has many of options discussed in the on-line documentation. Most of these options exist to enforce security. One of the main uses for slave interpreters is with the Tcl plug-in for Web browsers discussed in Chapter 12. Because you don't always know the origin of a Web page, Tcl imposes strict security on slave interpreters, so you want to use the `-safe` option when creating the interpreter.

A number of Tcl freeware applications use the `interp` command to create a software development environment. The **TkCon** script, for example, creates a console window, much like that for **wish** on Windows, that allows you to edit and execute scripts. **TkCon** appears in Figure 5.12 and on the CD-ROM in the **contrib/scripting** directory.

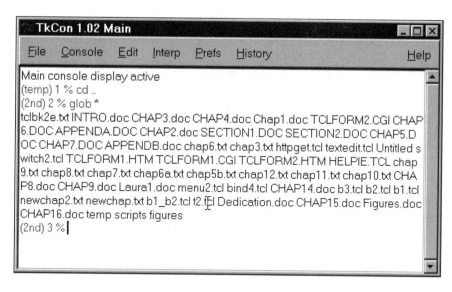

Figure 5.12 The TkCon console window.

If you like the **textedit.tcl** script, you may want to look into **TkCon**.

The Sample Text Editor

The **textedit.tcl** script is the most complicated script so far in this book. It shows a number of concepts you may want to use in your own scripts. The code for **textedit.tcl** follows:

```
# Tcl-based text editor.
#


###############################
## Global option defaults.
###############################
```

```
set textedit(text_fore) black
set textedit(text_back) white
set textedit(intf_fore) black
set textedit(intf_back) lightsteelblue


    # Start in current directory.
set textedit(last_directory) [pwd]

    # Default name to save to.
set textedit(save_name) "Untitled"
global textedit


#
# Creates an old-style menubar.
# toplevel = name of toplevel widget, e.g., "."
# menubar = name of menubar to create, e.g., ".menubar"
#
# See menu.tcl.
proc menubar_create { toplevel menubar } {

    frame $menubar -borderwidth 2 -relief raised
    pack $menubar -side top -fill x
}


# Creates a menubutton and its associated menu.
#
# menubar = name of menubar
# text = text to display for menubutton.
# menu = name of menu to create and associate with button.
#   This should be a child of menubar.
# mnemonic = character to underline, or < 0 to ignore this option.
#
proc menu_create { menubar menu button text mnemonic } {
    global  tk_version

    if { $mnemonic >= 0 } {
        menubutton $button -text $text \
```

```
            -menu $menu -underline $mnemonic

    } else {
        menubutton $button -text $text -menu $menu
    }


    pack $button -side left
    menu $menu
}


# Reads a text file.
# filename = name of text file to read in.
#
proc file_read { filename } {

# Default value.
    set data ""

    if { [file readable $filename] } {

        set fd [open $filename "r"]

        set data [read $fd]

        close $fd
    }


    return $data
}


#
# Saves data to disk.
#
proc file_write { filename data } {

return [catch {
```

```
        set fileid [open $filename "w"]

        puts -nonewline $fileid $data
        close $fileid

    }]

}


# Loads up a file into text widget.
# filename = name of file.
# toplevel = name of toplevel widget, gets filename in title.
# textwidget = name of text widget to place text.
#
proc file_load { toplevel textwidget filename } {

set data [file_read $filename]

if { $data != "" } {

        # Delete all existing text.
        file_new $toplevel $textwidget $filename

        # Store text in textwidget.
        $textwidget insert end $data
    }

}


#
# Deletes all text in text widget, sets toplevel to
# have given title.
#
proc file_new { toplevel textwidget title } {


# Delete all tags.
```

```
    set names [$textwidget tag names]
    foreach tagname $names {
        $textwidget tag delete $tagname
    }


    # Delete all text.
    $textwidget delete 1.0 end

    # Set title.
    wm title $toplevel $title

    focus $textwidget
}


proc file_open_get {  } {
    global textedit

    set file_types {
        { "Tcl Files"    { .tcl .TCL .tk .TK } }
        { "Text Files"   { .txt .TXT } }
        { "All Files"    * }

    }


    set filename [tk_getOpenFile -initialdir \
        $textedit(last_directory) \
        -filetypes $file_types \
        -title "Select a file to load" \
        -parent .]

    # Store last directory for loading next time.
    set $textedit(last_directory) [file dirname $filename]

    return $filename
}
```

```
# Asks user for filename, loads it.
proc file_open { toplevel textwidget } {
    set filename [file_open_get]

    if { $filename != "" } {
        file_load $toplevel $textwidget $filename
        focus $textwidget

    }

}


#
# Loads in a file and inserts data at cursor. Does
# not delete old data.
#
proc file_insert { toplevel textwidget } {

    set filename [file_open_get]
    if { $filename != "" } {
        set data [file_read $filename]

        if { $data != "" } {
            # Store text in textwidget at insertion cursor.
            $textwidget insert insert $data
            focus $textwidget

        }

    }

}


proc file_save { textwidget } {
    global textedit

    set data [$textwidget get 1.0 {end -1c}]
```

```
        # Remove any ending newlines.
        set text [string trimright $data]

        return [file_write $textedit(save_name) $data]
}


proc file_save_get {   } {
        global textedit

        set file_types {
            { "Tcl Files"    { .tcl .TCL .tk .TK } }
            { "Text Files"   { .txt .TXT } }
            { "All Files"    * }

        }


        set filename [tk_getSaveFile -initialdir \
            $textedit(last_directory) \
            -filetypes $file_types \
            -title "Select file name to save" \
            -parent .]

        # Store last directory for loading next time.
        set textedit(last_directory) [file dirname $filename]

        return $filename
}


proc file_save_as { toplevel textwidget } {
        global textedit

        set filename [file_save_get]

        if { $filename != "" } {
            # Store file name.
            set textedit(save_name) $filename
```

```
        # Save file.
        file_save $textwidget

        # Change window title.
        wm title $toplevel $filename
    }

}



#
# Called to exit editor. You can expand this procedure
# to prompt the user to save to a file and then exit.
#
proc file_exit { } {
    exit
}



# Handle the cut action for a text widget.
proc edit_cut { textwidget } {

# Check if any text is selected in textwidget.
    set owner [selection own]

    if { $owner == $textwidget } {
        # Clear clipboard.
        clipboard clear


    catch {
            set text [selection get]
            clipboard append $text

    # Delete selected text.
            $owner delete sel.first sel.last

        }

    }
```

```
}


# Handle the copy action for a text widget.
proc edit_copy { textwidget } {

    # Check if any text is selected in textwidget.
    set owner [selection own]

    if { $owner == $textwidget } {
        # Clear clipboard.
        clipboard clear

        catch {
            clipboard append [selection get]
        }

    }

}


# Handle the paste action for a text widget.
proc edit_paste { textwidget } {

    # Get text from clipboard.
    catch {
        set clip [selection get -selection CLIPBOARD]
    }


    # Default location to insert data.
    set idx [$textwidget index insert]

    # Check if any text is selected in textwidget.
    set owner [selection own]

    if { $owner == $textwidget } {
        catch {
```

```
            # Save index where selection starts.
            set idx [$owner index sel.first]

            # Delete selected text.
            $textwidget delete sel.first sel.last
        }

    }


catch {
        # Paste in selected text.
        $textwidget insert $idx $clip
    }

    }


#################################################
######## Code for executing text
#################################################


# Executes selected text as Tcl commands.
proc exec_sel { textwidget } {

if { [selection own] == $textwidget } {
        catch {
            set sel [selection get]

            if { $sel != "" } {
                eval $sel
            }

        }

    }

    }
```

```
# Executes all text in a text widget.
proc exec_all { textwidget } {

    # Get all text from widget.
    set all [$textwidget get 1.0 end]

    # Execute text as Tcl commands.
    eval $all
}



#################################################
######## Search
#################################################


# Global position where last search left off.
global find_last_indx
set find_last_indx 1.0

# Procedure to search text widget.
proc find_text { entrywidget textwidget } {
    global find_last_indx

    # Get text to search for.
    set search_for [$entrywidget get]

    set length [string length $search_for]

    # Search for text.
    set indx [$textwidget search - \
        $search_for $find_last_indx end]

    if { $indx == "" } {
        set find_last_indx 1.0

        set indx [$textwidget search - \
            $search_for $find_last_indx end]
    }
```

```
if { $indx != ""} {
        #
        # Clear tag for any text that was selected.
        # Inside catch because it may generate an error.
        catch {
            $textwidget tag remove sel sel.first sel.last
        }


        #
        # Select the found text.
        #
        $textwidget tag add sel $indx "$indx + $length chars"

        #
        # Place insertion cursor at start of selected data.
        #
        $textwidget mark set insert $indx

        #
        # Make sure text is visible.
        #
        $textwidget see $indx

        # Keep index for next search.
        set find_last_indx "$indx + 1 char"

} else {
        # Reset to search from beginning.
        set find_last_indx 1.0
        puts "$search_for not found"
    }

}

#
# Displays a box about this program.
proc help_about { toplevel } {
```

```
tk_messageBox -default ok -icon info -message \
{TextEdit,
a simple Tcl text editor
by Eric Foster-Johnson} \
        -parent $toplevel -title "About TextEdit" -type ok
}


# Creates a text editor.
# height = number of lines in text widget.
proc textedit_create { height } {
    global argc argv
    global textedit

    # Create a toplevel widget.
    toplevel .edit

    # The text widget name is used throughout.
    set textname .edit.main.text


    ##############################
    # Create menubar.
    ##############################


    menubar_create .edit .edit.menubar
    menu_create .edit.menubar .edit.menubar.file.filemenu \
        .edit.menubar.file "File" 0
    menu_create .edit.menubar .edit.menubar.edit.editmenu \
        .edit.menubar.edit "Edit" 0
    menu_create .edit.menubar .edit.menubar.help.helpmenu \
        .edit.menubar.help "Help" 0


    ##############################
    # File menu.
    ##############################
```

```
set men .edit.menubar.file.filemenu
$men add command -label "New" -underline 0 \
    -command "file_new .edit $textname Untitled"
$men add command -label "Open..." -underline 0 \
    -command "file_open .edit $textname"
$men add command -label "Insert..." -underline 0 \
    -command "file_insert .edit $textname"
$men add separator

$men add command -label "Save" -underline 0 \
    -command "file_save $textname"
$men add command -label "Save As..." -underline 5 \
    -command "file_save_as .edit $textname"

$men add separator
$men add command -label "Exit" -underline 1 \
        -command {file_exit}


#############################
# Edit menu.
#############################


set men .edit.menubar.edit.editmenu

$men add command -label "Cut" -underline 2 \
        -command "edit_cut $textname" \
        -accelerator "Ctrl+X"

$men add command -label "Copy" -underline 0 \
    -command "edit_copy $textname" \
    -accelerator "Ctrl+C"

$men add command -label "Paste" -underline 0 \
    -command "edit_paste $textname" \
    -accelerator "Ctrl+V"
```

```
##############################
# Help menu.
##############################


set men .edit.menubar.help.helpmenu
$men add command -label "About…" -underline 0 \
    -command "help_about .edit"


##############################
# Toolbar.
##############################


set frm .edit.toolbar
frame $frm -bd 1 -relief flat

button $frm.exec_sel -text "Exec Selected" \
    -command "exec_sel $textname"
button $frm.exec_all -text "Exec All" \
    -command "exec_all $textname"
pack $frm.exec_sel $frm.exec_all -side left

# Create search area.
label $frm.label -text "Search: "
entry $frm.search
button $frm.again -text "Find Again" \
        -command "find_text $frm.search $textname"

pack $frm.label -side left -fill y
pack $frm.search -side left -fill x -expand 1
pack $frm.again  -side left -fill y

# Bind Return in the entry widget to search.
bind $frm.search <Key-Return> \
   "find_text $frm.search $textname"
pack $frm -side top -fill x
```

```
###############################
# Text widget in main area.
###############################


set frm .edit.main
frame $frm -bd 4 -relief sunken

text $frm.text -width 80 -height $height -wrap none -bg white \
    -yscrollcommand "$frm.vscroll set" \
    -xscrollcommand "$frm.hscroll set"

scrollbar $frm.vscroll -command "$frm.text yview"
scrollbar $frm.hscroll -command "$frm.text xview" \
    -orient horizontal
pack $frm.vscroll -side right  -fill y
pack $frm.hscroll -side bottom -fill x
pack $frm.text -side left -fill both -expand 1
pack $frm -side right -fill both -expand 1

bind $frm.text <Control-Key-x> "edit_cut $frm.text; break"
bind $frm.text <Control-Key-c> "edit_copy $frm.text; break"
bind $frm.text <Control-Key-v> "edit_paste $frm.text; break"

#
# Any command-line parameter is assumed to
# be the name of a file to load.
#
if { $argc > 0 } {
    set filename [lindex $argv 0]
    file_load .edit $textname $filename

}


# Pack main area.
pack  $frm -side top -fill both -expand 1

# Wait for a while for all widgets to exist.
```

```
    update

    # Set keyboard focus to text widget.
    focus $textname
}


#
#
tk appname "TextEdit"
textedit_create 32
# textedit.tcl
```

Try out this script, especially if you work on the Windows platform. You should have a better editor to work in, and you should be able to paste data from other text-editing programs, such as **Notepad**, or your favorite Windows text editor. Even Microsoft Word works with Tcl.

If you get ambitious, you may want to extend this editor and such add things as undo, and font control.

Summary

The chapter covered `text` widgets and commands related to working with text.

The `entry` widget provides a single-line text entry area. When you need a larger text area, you can use the multiline `text` widget.

In addition to text editing, the handy `text` widget allows you to tag areas of text and modify display attributes, such as switch to an italic font. With tags, you can also bind events within the tag to execute Tcl code. This allows you to easily create a Hypertext system out of the `text` widget.

Continuing on this vein, you can embed widgets within the `text` widget, to display graphic images, for example.

The `scrollbar` widget allows the user to scroll about the text displayed in a `text` widget.

The `string` command, with zillions of options, allows you to manipulate and extract from strings.

The `eval` command evaluates its arguments as a Tcl script, executing the script.

Finally, if you're getting tired of the poor text-input capabilities that Tcl provides on Windows with its Console window, you now have enough Tcl and Tk commands to create a viable Tcl editor and execute the code you type in. You can also copy and paste from other applications, such as your favorite editor.

Continuing on the scrolling theme, Chapter 6 covers scrolled `listbox` widgets and Tcl list-handling commands. It also discusses Tcl file and directory commands, including how to read a file into a `text` widget.

Tcl/Tk Commands Covered in This Chapter

```
catch
clipboard
entry
eval
focus
interp
scrollbar
selection
string
tcl_endOfWord
tcl_startOfNextWord
tcl_startOfPreviousWord
tcl_wordBreakAfter
tcl_wordBreakBefore
text
update
```

Lists, Files, and Directories

This chapter covers:

- Tcl list variables and commands
- Special lists that hold command-line arguments
- The `listbox` widget
- Creating multicolumn listboxes
- Accessing files
- Scanning directories
- Building a file and directory browser

Lists

After the complications of the `text` widget, you'll find the `listbox` widget and list variables an easy undertaking, in general. This chapter covers Tcl lists; then it delves into a `listbox` widget for displaying lists. After that, this chapter shows how to access files and directories on both Windows and UNIX.

A **list** in Tcl is just a collection of elements, such as 1 2 3 4 5 six. All the elements are text, as is everything in Tcl.

So, a list variable is just a plain Tcl variable. The only fact that makes it a list is the fact that you store a number of elements in it. You can use the list commands described in this chapter on any regular Tcl variable. Unlike arrays, which use a special syntax, lists are normal Tcl variables and use normal Tcl syntax.

Building Lists

The `list` command builds a list out of all its arguments, returning this new list. It may modify the arguments if you have items like backslashes in the list.

```
% set l1 [list arg1 arg2 arg3]
arg1 arg2 arg3
% puts $l1
arg1 arg2 arg3
set l2 [list {arg1} {{arg2} {arg3}} ]
arg1 {{arg2} {arg3}}
% puts $l2
arg1 {{arg2} {arg3}}
```

Note how some of these examples have lists within lists. `{{arg2} {arg3}}` is one list element, even though the list element is made up of a list itself (of two items).

You can also use the `concat` command to build a list:

```
set l1 [concat arg1 arg2 arg3]
```

The `concat` command simply concatenates its arguments together, placing a space character between each item. The `list` command, on the other hand, will build up a proper list. That is, if one of the arguments to `list` is a multi-item element, the `list` command will ensure that it becomes a single element in the new list (a list may hold lists).

For example, compare the following:

```
% list {1 2 3} 4 "five six"
{1 2 3} 4 {five six}
% concat {1 2 3} 4 "five six"
1 2 3 4 five six
```

Notice the differing output.

The `list` command makes each of its arguments an item in the new list, even if the argument was itself a list (leading to lists of lists). The `concat` command, on the other hand, simply places all arguments together into a list, separated by spaces; it removes the sublists and promotes all elements into the same list. Because of this, you need to choose carefully which command to call.

Inserting Elements into a List

Use the `linsert` command to insert items into a list:

```
linsert listvar index element
```

You can pass more than one *element* to insert. These elements are inserted at a given *index* position. You can use the special position named `end` for appending to a list. Note that `linsert` does not modify the original list.

Try the following examples:

```
% set l1 { dog cat }
 dog cat
% set l2 [linsert $l1 end platypus]
 dog cat platypus
% puts $l2
 dog cat platypus
```

You can also add data to the list itself:

```
% set l2 [linsert $l2 1 wolverine]
 dog wolverine cat platypus
% puts $l2
 dog wolverine cat platypus
```

To get the number of items in a list, use the `llength` command:

```
llength listvar
```

For example,

```
set l1 { dog cat snake }
set len [llength $l1]
```

The list length in this case is 3. This is different from the `string length` command, which returns a value of 15 (characters rather than list elements) in this case. Also, note the *ll* in `llength`.

Appending Elements to a List

The `lappend` command appends a number of items (as many as you want) onto the end of a list, using the following syntax:

```
lappend listvar item1 item2 item3 ...
```

This command is much like the `append` command (with no *l*), but items are assumed to be added to the list identified by *listvar*.

You can replace elements in a list with the `lreplace` command:

```
lreplace listvar first_index last_index newdata1 newdata2 ...
```

The `lreplace` command replaces all the items in the list from the *first_index* to the *last_index*, using all remaining parameters as the data items to fill in the list. Pass 0 for the first element and `end` for the last.

If no new data are provided, then the list elements in the range are merely deleted.

Pulling Out Elements from a List

To pull out a given element from a list, use the `lindex` command:

```
lindex listvar index
```

As with `lreplace`, pass 0 for the first element of a list and `end` for the last. Try the following commands:

```
% set ll { 1 2 3 4 5 6 7 8 nine }
 1 2 3 4 5 6 7 8 nine
% lindex $ll end
nine
% lindex $ll 0
1
% lindex $ll 5
6
```

To pull out a sublist, use the `lrange` command:

```
lrange listvar first_index last_index
```

You must provide both the *first_index* and the *last_index*. For example,

```
% set ll { 1 2 3 4 5 6 7 8 nine }
 1 2 3 4 5 6 7 8 nine
% lrange $ll 2 5
3 4 5 6
% lrange $ll 6 end
7 8 nine
```

Breaking Up Lists

You can break up lists with the `split` command and build them back together with the `join` command.

The `split` command looks for a set of special split characters given in its arguments and splits the value into multiple list elements. The syntax is,

```
split string split_chars
```

For example, if you have an XBase database and a set of comma-delimited data, you can use `split` to separate the elements, as shown here:

```
% set data "Eric Foster-Johnson, St. Paul, cat owner"
Eric Foster-Johnson, St. Paul, cat owner
% split $data ,
```

```
{Eric Foster-Johnson} { St. Paul} { cat owner}
%
```

In this example, the split character is a comma. Note that the list elements get the leading space that appeared after the comma. (To strip this out, you can use the `string trimleft` command introduced in Chapter 5.)

You can undo the effect of `split` with `join`, which takes the following syntax:

```
join listvar separator
```

The `join` command connects all the list elements in the list and places the separator character between each item. Note that because `join` takes the *listvar* as one argument, if you have separate data items, you must enclose them in curly braces or double quotation marks.

To undo the `split` example, you can use the following commands:

```
% set data "Eric Foster-Johnson, St. Paul, cat owner"
Eric Foster-Johnson, St. Paul, cat owner
% set split_data [split $data ,]
{Eric Foster-Johnson} { St. Paul} { cat owner}
% join $split_data ,
Eric Foster-Johnson, St. Paul, cat owner
```

You can also work on the data directly. Remember that you must provide the data to `join` as one argument (hence the enclosing curly braces), as shown here:

```
% join {{Eric Foster-Johnson} { St. Paul} { cat owner}} ,
Eric Foster-Johnson, St. Paul, cat owner
```

Searching Through Lists

The `lsearch` command searches through a list and takes the following syntax:

```
lsearch mode listvar pattern
```

The *mode* controls the type of search, familiar from the string searches described in Chapter 2. It can be one of -exact, -glob, or -regexp. See the section on regular expressions in Chapter 2 for more on the modes. You can omit the *mode*, which defaults to -glob.

Sorting Lists

The lsort command returns a sorted list, generated from its input list. The syntax is

lsort *options listvar*

You can modify the method used to sort, as listed in Table 6.1.

Table 6.1 Sort methods.

Method	Meaning
-ascii	Use ASCII string comparisons to sort.
-integer	Convert values to integers and sort in numerical order.
-real	Convert values to floating-point numbers and sort in numerical order.
-command *tcl_script*	Use the *tcl_script* to compare items.
-increasing	Sort in increasing order, with the smallest items first.
-decreasing	Sort in decreasing order, with the largest items first.
-dictionary	Sort like ASCII, but ignore case except to break a tie between two items and treat numbers as integers.
-index *index*	Treats list as a list of sublists. Instead of sorting all thedata, lsort extracts the index element from each sublist with lindex and then sorts based on that element alone. Useful if you want to sort on a key value that is part of each sublist.

344

The default options are -ascii and -increasing.

With the -command option, your *tcl_script* should accept the two values to compare and should return a value based on the comparison. A return value of 0 means that the items are considered equal. Whatever Tcl code you provide will get the two values appended at the end. The -command option allows you to write your own comparison routine, which is useful if you have specially formatted data you want to sort. You Tcl code must return a value as expected by lsort.

A return value less than 0 means that the first element is less than the second. A return value of greater than 0 means that the first element is greater than the second.

Special Lists for Accessing the Command Line

Tcl provides some special variables that contain the arguments passed on the DOS or UNIX command line. Familiar to most C programmers, these arguments mimic the argc, argv, and environment parameters passed to the C main function, but with a twist.

Table 6.2 lists these special variables for accessing command-line and environment data.

Table 6.2 Command-line variables.

Variable	Type	Holds
argc	integer	Number of command-line arguments in argv.
argv	list	Command-line arguments, but not command itself.
argv0	string	Name of file passed to **wish** or **tclsh**.
env	array	Holds UNIX or Windows environment variables.

See Chapter 2 in the section on Special Arrays for Environment Variables for more on the env variable.

If you invoke a Tcl script with the following arguments, 1 2 3 4 5 6 seven, the special *arg* variables will hold the values shown in Table 6.3. The following command shows an example of the syntax:

```
wish pr_argv.tcl 1 2 3 4 5 6 seven
```

Table 6.3 Contents of arg variables for args 1 2 3 4 5 6 seven.

Variable	Holds
argc	7
argv	1 2 3 4 5 6 seven
argv0	pr_argv.tcl

The argc value holds the number of command-line arguments, in this case, *seven*. argv holds the arguments passed to the Tcl script, *1 2 3 4 5 6 seven*.

Unlike the UNIX and DOS tradition, argv does *not* hold the full command line (which would include **wish** and **pr_argv.tcl**). Instead, it just holds all the *arguments* to the Tcl script you're executing.

The **pr_argv.tcl** script mentioned in the preceding example merely prints out all the command-line arguments. The script follows:

```
#
# Tcl script prints out number of
# command-line arguments.
#
puts "Number of arguments is: $argc"
puts "Full command line is: $argv"
for {set i 0} {$i < $argc} {incr i} {
    set curr_arg [lindex $argv $i]
    puts "Arg $i is: $curr_arg"
}
```

```
exit
# pr_argv.tcl
```

WINDOWS

On Windows, you should remove the `exit` command at the end of the **pr_argv.tcl** script. With the Windows version of **wish**, the console where you see the output is part of **wish**. On UNIX, the console is the terminal window you launched **wish** from.

When you run this script with some command-line arguments, you'll see the following output:

```
% wish pr_argv.tcl 1 2 3 4 5 6 seven
Number of arguments is: 7
Full command line is: 1 2 3 4 5 6 seven
Arg 0 is: 1
Arg 1 is: 2
Arg 2 is: 3
Arg 3 is: 4
Arg 4 is: 5
Arg 5 is: 6
Arg 6 is: seven
```

WINDOWS

On Windows, you typically don't run commands from a command-line (DOS) shell, especially for Windows programs like **wish**. You can associate the file extension, such as *.tcl* or *.tk* with the Windows Explorer so that Windows will launch your Tcl scripts when you double-click on them. See Chapter 1 for instructions for how to set up this association (which is normally set up when you install Tcl).

If you're still using Windows NT 3.5 or Windows 3.1, you can set up a Program Manager items for each Tcl script. You just need to use the proper **wish** executable name, set up the working directory to the location you installed Tcl, and set the script to run as the command name.

After all this work on lists, it's time to use them in a widget.

Listbox Widgets

The `listbox` widget provides a list of items from which the user can select. You can configure the list for multiple or single selection.

Create a `listbox` with the `listbox` command, such as:

```
listbox .list -height 10
pack .list
```

The `-height` option controls how many rows high to make the `listbox`. A corresponding `-width` option controls how many characters wide to make the `listbox`. With a proportional width font, the `-width` option controls the width based on the size of the character *0*.

The `-selectmode` option controls how items may be selected in the list. Table 6.4 shows the possibilities.

Table 6.4 `listbox` selection modes.

Mode	Meaning
single	Only one item may be selected at a time.
browse	Only one item may be selected, but you can select by dragging.
multiple	Multiple items may be selected, one at a time.
extended	Multiple items may be selected.

With a `-selectmode` of `multiple`, clicking mouse Button 1 over an item toggles whether it is selected. Many items may be selected.

With a `-selectmode` of `extended`, clicking mouse Button 1 with the **Shift** key down extends the existing selected items by including all items between the mouse position and the previously selected item. Clicking mouse Button 1 with the **Control** key down toggles whether the item under the mouse is selected or not. **Shift-Up Arrow** and **Shift-Down Arrow** also extend the current selection. The default -selectmode is browse, which allows only a single item to be selected at a time.

Like the text widget, you want to set the -exportselection option to true, which allows the selected list item to be copied and pasted elsewhere.

There is no -command option for a listbox widget. You therefore need to connect a list to either a binding, like a double-click or a button widget and then use the selection get option to extract the selected items.

N O T E

When to Use a listbox Widget

The listbox widget, naturally, displays lists of data. Because you can add a scrollbar to the listbox, you can display very large lists of data in a small area. The listbox provides an alternative to a large set of label or button widgets. Use a listbox when you have a large or variable amount of data. The text widget can also display scrolled data. Use a listbox instead of a text widget when each line of data is a distinct item and you want to select an item. Use a text widget when you want to treat the data merely as text.

Working With the listbox-Widget

To add new items to a listbox, use the insert option:

widgetname insert *index element*

You need to do this to fill in the original values in the listbox. In most cases, you want to append items or insert them at the end. You can use a special index value of end for this purpose:

widgetname insert end *element*

For example,

```
# listbox example.
listbox .list -height 10
.list insert end "Minnesota"
.list insert end "Alabama"
.list insert end "Oregon"
.list insert end "New York"
.list insert end "Maryland"
.list insert end "Georgia"
pack .list
# minnlist.tcl
```

It is more efficient to insert items into the listbox before packing the widget. This is because the listbox is not yet visible so it is faster to insert items.

N O T E

See the section on List Indices for more options when creating the index.

Connecting a Listbox to a Scrollbar

Virtually all listbox widgets have an associated scrollbar widget. You connect a listbox to a scrollbar in much the same way as for the text widget, shown in Chapter 5. An example follows:

```
# Scrolled listbox example.
listbox .list -height 10 -yscrollcommand ".scrl set"
.list insert end "Minnesota"
.list insert end "Alabama"
.list insert end "Oregon"
.list insert end "New York"
.list insert end "Maryland"
.list insert end "Georgia"
.list insert end "Ohio"
.list insert end "Alaska"
.list insert end "Washington"
.list insert end "Virginia"
.list insert end "North Dakota"
```

```
.list insert end "Iowa"
.list insert end "Texas"
scrollbar .scrl -command ".list yview"
pack .scrl -side right -fill y
pack .list -side left
# scrlist.tcl
```

You can see this scrolled `listbox` in Figure 6.1.

Figure 6.1 A scrolled listbox.

Listbox Indices

Like the `text` widget, the `listbox` widget allows you to specify an item by its index within the `listbox`. You can use the item number, with 0 for the first item. Or, you can use a more symbolic place, much like that of the text widget.

Table 6.5 lists the available index values.

Table 6.5 List item indices.

Index	Meaning
number	Item number, starting with 0.
end	Last item in list.
@*x,y*	Item under local *x, y* position.
active	Item with location cursor.
anchor	Item at selection anchor.

The anchor is the fixed part at the end or beginning of the selection.

List Indices

You can convert other forms of indices into the standard numeric format with the index option:

widgetname index *index_to_convert*

This command returns a new index generated from the *index_to_convert*. The new index is in numeric format.

Armed with these indices, you can identify an individual item in a list or a range of items.

Accessing Listbox Items

To get the number of items in a listbox, use size:

widgetname size

This returns the number of items in the listbox.

352

To delete items in a list, use `delete`:

widgetname delete *first last*

This command deletes all items from the *first* index to the *last*. You may omit the *last* index, in which case, only one item gets deleted.

To retrieve a `listbox` item, use `get`:

widgetname get *first last*

If you ask for only one item (and skip the *last* index), you will get the item (the text string displayed). If you ask for a range of items, you'll get a Tcl list of the items in the range.

The `activate` option activates an item in the `listbox`, identified by its index:

widgetname activate *index*

The active item gets drawn in a special way. It also controls the index named `active` shown in Table 6.5.

Finding Out Which Items Are Selected

You can find out which `listbox` items are selected by using the `curselection` option, which has the following syntax:

widgetname curselection

N O T E This command returns a list of all the indices of the selected items, not the selected items themselves. For example, if the item at `listbox` index 5 is selected, the `curselection` option will return 5, not the text of the item.

If you have a `-selectmode` of `single`, then `curselection` can return only one item, the index of the selected item. To then retrieve the selected item, you can use the following procedure:

```
# Returns selected item for a single-select list.
proc list_selected { listname } {
    set indx [$listname curselection]
    if { $indx != "" } {
        set item [$listname get $indx]
        return $item
    } else {
        return "";
    }
}
```

Note that if no item is selected, the curselection option will return nothing.

WARNING

You may see problems getting the item currently selected in the listbox. The problem is the order of the bindings and the fact that sometimes the current selection hasn't been updated by the time your binding runs.

One way around this is to use the lixtbox index of the form @x,y. This format refers to the listbox item that covers the point *x, y*. You can get the *x, y* values from the %x and %y in the binding. Thus, you can get the list item underneath the mouse pointer using the following command in your Button-1 binding for a listbox:

```
set item [.list get @%x,%y]
```

The binding fills in the %x and %y with the *x, y* coordinates of the mouse. The **histlist.tcl** script, which follows, uses this method.

Use selection clear to clear the selection in the listbox:

widgetname selection clear *first last*

This clears all selections between the first and the last indices. The *last* index is optional.

To see if an item is selected, use selection includes:

widgetname selection includes *index*

This command returns 1 if the selection includes the given *index*.

To select items in the listbox, use selection set:

widgetname selection set *first last*

Again, the *last* index is optional.

Making an Item Visible

To make a listbox item visible, you can use the see option:

widgetname see *index*

This option takes the index of the item you want to make visible.

Listbox Examples

The following Tcl script creates a listbox and allows you to select items from it. The listbox holds a form of command history, from which you can select a previous command. Double-clicking on a list element re-executes that command. If you single-click on a list element, then the element appears selected. The selected item also gets placed into the entry widget. This allows you to edit a previous command. Pressing the **Return** key in the entry widget also executes the command and appends it to the listbox. The Tcl code follows:

```
#
# Command history listbox example.
#
  # History list.
frame .hist
listbox .hist.list -height 10 -width 40 \
    -selectmode single \
    -yscrollcommand ".hist.scrl set"
scrollbar .hist.scrl -command ".hist.list yview"
```

```
pack .hist.scrl -side right -fill y
pack .hist.list -side left -fill x -fill y
   # Command entry.
frame .cmd
entry .cmd.entry -width 30 -textvariable entry_var
label .cmd.label -text "Command: "
pack .cmd.label -side top -anchor w
pack .cmd.entry -side bottom -fill x -expand 1
   # Command results.
frame .res
text .res.text -width 40 -height 6 -wrap none \
    -yscrollcommand ".res.v_scroll set" \
    -xscrollcommand ".res.h_scroll set"
scrollbar .res.v_scroll -command ".res.text yview"
scrollbar .res.h_scroll -command ".res.text xview" \
   -orient horizontal
pack .res.v_scroll -side right -fill y
pack .res.h_scroll -side bottom -fill x
pack .res.text -side left -fill x -fill y -expand 1
pack .res -side top -fill x
pack .hist -side top -fill y -expand 1
pack .cmd -side bottom -fill x
   # Procedures.
# Returns selected item for a single-select list.
proc list_selected { listname } {
    set indx [$listname curselection]
    if { $indx != "" } {
        set item [$listname get $indx]
        return $item
    } else {
        return "";
    }
}
#
# Executes a Tcl command with eval.
# Requires the name of an entry, listbox and
# text widget.
#
```

```
proc exec_cmd { entryname listname textname cmd } {
    set results [eval "$cmd"]
    # Put results into text widget.
    $textname insert end "$results\n"
    # Add command to history list.
    $listname insert end "$cmd"
    # Clear text of entry widget.
    $entryname delete 0 end
}

# Key bindings for listbox and entry widgets.
bind .hist.list <Double-Button-1> {
    set cmd [list_selected .hist.list]
    if { $cmd != "" } {
        exec_cmd .cmd.entry .hist.list \
            .res.text $cmd
    }
}
bind .hist.list <Button-1> {
    global entry_var
    set cmd [.hist.list get @%x,%y]
    if { $cmd != "" } {
        set entry_var $cmd
    }
}

bind .cmd.entry <Key-Return> {
    exec_cmd .cmd.entry .hist.list \
        .res.text $entry_var
}
# histlist.tcl
```

You can see this command-history script in Figure 6.2.

Figure 6.2 Using a listbox for a command history.

The **histlist.tcl** script uses a `text` widget to display the results of the commands you enter into the command `entry` widget.

The `exec_cmd` procedure executes commands from within the context of a procedure. Consequently, most variables won't be accessible, because the `global` statement was not executed first.

A Multicolumn List

A common problem with listboxes is creating two or more separate lists and having them all work off a single `scrollbar`. For example, lists of files, sizes, and modification dates often use three columns in a list. In Tk, the way to do this is to use separate listboxes and then tie them together to the same scrollbar.

To set up multiple listboxes like this, you create the listboxes the same way as always, but set each listbox's -yscrollcommand option to the same command on the same scrollbar, as shown here:

```
listbox .frame.list1 \
   -borderwidth 1 \
   -relief raised \
   -selectmode single \
   -yscrollcommand ".frame.scroll set"
listbox .frame.list2 \
   -borderwidth 1 \
   -relief raised \
   -selectmode single \
   -yscrollcommand ".frame.scroll set"
```

The key to making this work is in the scrollbar's -command. Normally, each scrollbar is tied to a single listbox (or text) widget. What you need to do is tie this scrollbar to a number of listboxes. The tricky part is that the scrollbar appends data onto the Tcl command it executes. And, we don't know exactly what data this is until the scrollbar moves. (The amount of this data has also changed between versions of Tk.)

To take care of this problem, create a procedure called multi_scroll, as shown next:

```
#
# This proc scrolls a number of listboxes all together
# from one scrollbar.
#
# The scroll_list holds a list of the widgets
# to scroll. This must be a list. The args
# hold all the remaining arguments, which
# come from the scrollbar. All these are
# passed to each widget in the scroll_list.
#
proc multi_scroll { scroll_list args } {
  # Get info on list of listboxes.
```

```
set len [llength $scroll_list]
for {set i 0} {$i < $len} {incr i} {
    set temp_list [lindex $scroll_list $i]
    eval $temp_list yview $args
}
}
```

The key to this procedure is that the *scroll_list* argument *must* be a list, the list of all the widget names we want to scroll at once. The list requirement comes from the special args argument. This special argument holds a variable-length list of all the remaining arguments. The problem is that it holds *all* the remaining arguments. Our problem is that we don't know how many lists will be tied together. That's one variable-length list of values (the names of the listbox widgets to scroll together). Also, the scrollbar appends an unknown amount of data to the arguments, which makes another variable-length list. This procedure uses the special args argument for this second list.

For the first variable-length list of listbox widgets to scroll, the multi_scroll procedure requires that it be called with a list. So, you need to follow the method below when creating the scrollbar:

```
scrollbar .frame.scroll \
    -command \
    { multi_scroll {.frame.list1 .frame.list2} }
```

Note that the two listbox widget names appear within curly braces, to make the two items into one list (and one argument to multi_scroll).

The full source for this example follows:

```
#
# Tcl script that creates multiple listboxes
# with one scrollbar.
#
#
# This proc scrolls a number of listboxes all together
# from one scrollbar.
#
# The scroll_list holds a list of the widgets
```

```
# to scroll. This must be a list. The args
# hold all the remaining arguments, which
# come from the scrollbar. All these are
# passed to each widget in the scroll_list.
#
proc multi_scroll { scroll_list args } {
 # Get info on list of listboxes.
 set len [llength $scroll_list]
 for {set i 0} {$i < $len} {incr i} {
     set temp_list [lindex $scroll_list $i]
     eval $temp_list yview $args
 }
}


#
# Fill in list with various data.
#
proc FillList { listvar } {
  for {set i 0} {$i < 40} {incr i} {
    set str [format "Item %d" $i]
    # Curly braces make str into one item.
    eval $listvar insert end {$str}
  }
}


# Use a frame around all lists.
frame .frame -relief groove -borderwidth 3
listbox .frame.list1 \
  -borderwidth 1 \
  -relief raised \
  -selectmode single \
  -yscrollcommand ".frame.scroll set"
listbox .frame.list2 \
  -borderwidth 1 \
  -relief raised \
  -selectmode single \
  -yscrollcommand ".frame.scroll set"
listbox .frame.list3 \
```

```
  -borderwidth 1 \
  -relief raised \
  -selectmode single \
  -yscrollcommand ".frame.scroll set"
 # Fill lists with data.
FillList .frame.list1
FillList .frame.list2
FillList .frame.list3
pack .frame.list1 .frame.list2 \
   .frame.list3 -side left
scrollbar .frame.scroll \
   -command \
   { multi_scroll {.frame.list1 .frame.list2 .frame.list3} }
pack .frame.scroll -side right -fill y
pack .frame
# multlist.tcl
```

This program creates three `listbox` widgets, as shown in Figure 6.3. All the lists should scroll together.

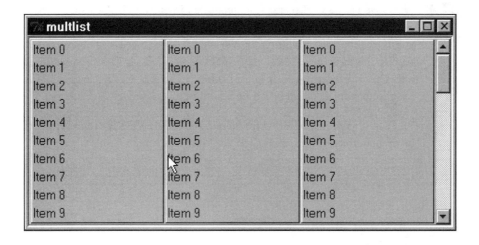

Figure 6.3 Multiple listboxes with one scrollbar.

Accessing Files

Most applications read, modify, and write files. Tcl provides a number of commands to help perform these mundane tasks.

To read a file, you need to open it and then read data from the file. When done, you need to close the file. Writing to a file works the same way, but you write data instead of reading, obviously. If the file doesn't exist, the open command, with the right parameters, will create it.

For both operations, you first need to open the file with the open command:

```
open filename access permissions
```

File Names

The *filename* must be a valid file name on your system; otherwise, an error will result. See Chapter 9 for more on errors and handling them.

CROSS-PLATFORM

In addition, Tcl has a few problems with the Windows idea of file names. Windows uses a backslash, \, to separate directories. UNIX uses a forward slash, /. In fact, Tcl treats the backslash as a line continuation marker, so you normally need to *escape* the backslash by using two. For example, to specify the directory \USERS\ERC, use \\USERS\\ERC. The \\ construction tells the Tcl interpreter to ignore other meanings for the backslash and insert one real backslash (not a line continuation marker) into the text.

You can also use UNIX-style file names on Windows. For example, the following commands both change to the same directory:

```
cd /tcl/bin
cd \\tcl\\bin
```

File names entered on a Windows system, though, are likely to contain backslashes.

WINDOWS

The DOS file system, called FAT for File Allocation Table, allows only file names in the form of a maximum of eight characters, a single period, and a maximum three-character file extension. Any files stored under Windows 3.1 must follow these conventions. The same goes for Windows NT using a FAT file system (the NT file system, NTFS, allows for longer file names). Windows 95 also allows for longer file names.

Windows uses a backslash to separate directories. UNIX uses a forward slash, and the MacOS uses a colon. The colon causes extra grief because a Windows file name may include a disk drive, indicated by the drive letter and then a colon, such as **C:\TCL\BIN**. (Remember to use double back-slashes when entering this into Tcl.)

The situation is further complicated. On UNIX, multiple forward slashes are taken to mean a single slash. UNIX and Windows support two special directory names, . for the current directory and . . for the parent of the current directory. Windows also supports special UNC file names for network-mounted directories in the following format:

```
\\hostname\share_partition\filename
```

Note the double-backslash for the *hostname* needs to be expanded for Tcl to four backslashes: \\\\hostname

To help with file-naming problems, Tcl offers the file join and file split commands.

The file join command joins parts of a file name and places in the proper directory separator, / for UNIX and Windows, : for MacOS. The file join command returns the new path. For example,

```
% file join dir filename
dir/filename
```

This example shows a relative path, from the current directory. If you want an absolute path, you need to start with a forward slash, as shown here:

```
% file join /dir filename
/dir/filename
```

```
% file join / dir filename
/dir/filename
```

The `file join` command uses the forward slash for both Windows and UNIX.

N O T E

With `file join`, you can include as many elements as necessary. For example,

```
% file join / usr local lib tk demos
/usr/local/lib/tk/demos
```

There's a strange quirk to `file join`. If you include a slash in any argument, `file join` ignores any previous arguments. For example,

N O T E

```
% file join ignored / usr local lib tk demos
/usr/local/lib/tk/demos
```

You can include slashes in elements, as long as you start with a slash. For example,

```
% file join / usr/local lib tk demos
/usr/local/lib/tk/demos
```

The `file split` command acts the reverse of the `file join` command, returning the elements that make up a full path name. For example,

```
% file split /dir/filename
/ dir filename
% file split /usr/local/lib/tk/demos
/ usr local lib tk demos
```

With relative names, though, `file split` removes slashes, as shown here:

```
% file split dir/filename
dir filename
% file split ../usr/local/lib/tk/demos
.. usr local lib tk demos
```

For the most portable Tcl scripts, you should use file join and file split. If you just need to work with Windows and UNIX, or you're using an older version of Tcl, you can use the forward slash. Users on Windows systems, though, will expect to be able to enter file names with backslashes, so your Tcl scripts will need to handle this special character.

After you set up the file name, the next step is the access mode.

File Access Modes

The *access* argument to open must have an *r* (for read), *w* (for write), or *a* (append). Table 6.6 shows further modifications of this.

Table 6.6 File access codes for the open command.

Code	Meaning
r	Open file for reading only. File must exist.
r+	Open file for reading and writing. File must exist.
w	Open file for writing, destroying any existing data.
w+	Open file for reading and writing; destroying any existing data.
a	Open file for writing. File must exist. New data are appended to the end.
a+	Open file for reading and writing. New data are appended to the end. The file does not have to exist.

If you're used to programming in the C language, the access codes in Table 6.6 are slightly different.

If you don't like the values in Table 6.6, you can use an alternate set of access codes. In this format, you must include one of the following flags: RDONLY (read only), WRONLY (write only), or RDWR (reading and writing). You can also add in other flags, providing a list of options. The other available flags are listed in Table 6.7.

Table 6.7 Flags for access codes.

Flag	Meaning
APPEND	Start at end of file.
CREAT	Create file if it doesn't exist.
EXCL	With CREAT, returns an error if the file exists.
NOCTTY	Prevents file from becoming controlling terminal (for terminal devices).
NONBLOCK	Prevents process from blocking while opening file.
TRUNC	If file exists, truncate all data in it.

If you use the modes in Table 6.7, you need to provide all the modes as a list. For example, { WRONLY CREAT }.

If you open a file for both reading and writing, you must use the seek command for positioning in the file. See the section on Seeking Data in Files for more information.

The *permissions* argument applies only to new files you create. The default permissions are 0666 (you knew Tcl was possessed, didn't you?), which means read and write permissions for all users. The leading zero indicates this is an octal (base 8) number.

The permissions follows the UNIX model for file permissions. See Appendix A for books on UNIX if this concerns you.

U N I X

The `open` command returns a file ID, for use with `read` or `puts` commands. The main way to work with a file ID is to set it into a variable and then use this variable for all subsequent file operations. For example,

```
set fileid [open report.txt r]
```

The actual contents of a file ID shouldn't matter (and may well differ on Windows, UNIX, or Macintosh systems).

CROSS-PLATFORM

Built-In File IDs

Three file IDs always exist for all Tcl programs: `stdin` for input from the terminal or Console window, `stdout` for output to the Console window, and `stderr` also for output to the Console window, but intended for error messages. These file IDs come from the UNIX and C language conventions.

You should avoid using Console input and output on Windows. Windows users expect to see graphical programs. UNIX users tend to be more lenient, but the whole point of writing graphical applications is to get beyond the limitations of the text-only programs of the past.

WINDOWS

The Console window has proven essential for debugging Tcl applications, but you shouldn't burden the end user with the Console window. In addition, if you run a Tcl script from the Explorer or Program Manager, the script will not have the Console window that **wish** creates when run without a script to execute. In this case, output to `stdout` (or just a `puts` command without a file ID) will generate an error.

To read in data from a file, first `open` the file and then use the `read` command, which takes many forms:

```
read $fileid
```

```
read -nonewline $fileid
read $fileid number_bytes
```

If you don't specify the number of bytes, read will pull in the entire file. The -nonewline option tells read to skip any final newline character at the end of the file, commonly put there by the text widget.

To write data to a file, use the familiar puts command with an expanded syntax:

```
puts -nonewline $fileid string
```

The -nonewline argument is optional. Up to now, we've skipped the *fileid* argument with puts. When you do this, puts writes its data to the terminal or Console window, to the stdout file ID.

With puts, you need to know that Tcl uses buffered file output routines. For speed, any operating systems delay writing data to a file until enough has been buffered up in main memory. This is because writing to disk is typically a very slow operation when compared to writing to memory. When enough data are collected, the buffering routines automatically write the data to disk.

In most cases, this works well. But, it has the unfortunate side effect that after you call puts, your data may not yet be stored in the file. If this matters (in most cases it does not), you can use the flush command:

```
flush $fileid
```

The flush command will force all the buffers to write out to disk. This may take some time, and the flush command will not return until it finishes, which may introduce delays in your Tcl scripts.

When you're done with a file, close it with the close command:

```
close $fileid
```

The close command also flushes all buffers, so you normally don't need to call flush.

To read in all the data in a presumably small file and store it in the variable named *data*, use the following procedure:

```
# Reads a text file.
# filename = name of text file to read in.
#
proc file_read { filename } {
    # Default value.
    set data ""
    if { [file readable $filename] } {
        set fd [open $filename "r"]
        set data [read $fd]
        close $fd
    }
    return $data
}
```

The problem with this procedure is that it reads the whole file at once. This may cause problems with a multimegabyte file.

To get around this, you may read files in increments. For example, a common block size is 2 kilobytes, or 2048 bytes. You can then create a while loop to read in the file in blocks of this size. Of course, few files are arranged to have an exact multiple of 2048 (or any other amount of) bytes. So, with each call to read, you need to test whether you're at the end of the file. The eof command, short for end of file, does this:

```
eof $fileid
```

The eof command returns one at the end of the file and 0 otherwise. So, to read all the bytes in a large file, a block at a time, you can use the following code snippet as a guide:

```
if { [file readable $filename] } {

  set fileid [open $filename "r"]

  # Are we at the end of the file?

  while { [eof $fileid] != 1 } {

    # Read one block.
```

```
    set data [read $fileid 2048]

    # Process data.

    # ...insert your code here...

  }

  close $fileid
}
```

NOTE If there are fewer bytes left in the file than you ask for, the read command will return only those bytes that are in the file. Thus, in this example, at least one call to read will return less than 2048 bytes, unless the file is an exact multiple of 2048 bytes in size.

Reading a File Line by Line

A more common approach toward reading data from files is to read text files a line at a time. This is very common if you want to process each line, such as send it to the Tcl interpreter with the eval command. To read files this way, you can use the gets command:

```
gets $fileid varname
gets $fileid
```

There are two forms of gets, seemingly just to confuse you. The first form, and the one I recommend, stores the line read into the given variable. In this form, gets returns the number of bytes read in, or a minus one if the end of the file was reached.

In the second form, gets returns the characters read in, and an empty string if the end of the file was reached.

In both forms, gets removes the newline character that terminates the line.

So, to read in an entire file line-by-line, you can use the following code:

```
if { [file readable $filename] } {
  set fileid [open $filename "r"]
  # Are we at the end of the file?
  while { [gets $fileid data] >= 0 } {
    # Process data.
    # ...insert your code here...
    puts $data
  }
  close $fileid
}
```

Seeking Data in Files

In most cases, read and puts work sequentially through a file. But sometimes you need to access a particular location in a file. For this, you can use the seek command:

```
seek $fileid offset starting_location
```

What seek does is move the file pointer, the indicator that stores where you are in a file. The read and puts commands both work from the current position of the file pointer. When completed, read and puts both update the file pointer (to the end of the data read in or written, respectively). The seek command moves the file pointer to an arbitrary location, so that the next read or puts command uses this new position.

With seek, the offset argument is the number of bytes to move the file pointer. The optional *starting_location* can be one of start (for the beginning of the file), current (for the current position of the file pointer), or end (for the end of the file). The *starting_location* defaults to start.

If you want to seek to a position 4096 bytes into a file, use the following command:

```
seek $fileid 4096 start
```

This moves the file pointer 4096 bytes from the beginning of the file.

If you want to position the file pointer 4096 bytes from the end of the file (assuming the file is longer than 4096 bytes), use the following command:

```
seek $fileid -4096 end
```

Note the use of a negative number, because we want to move backwards relative to the end of the file. (Trying to go forward beyond the end of the file is not recommended and usually results in an error. Trying to go backward beyond the beginning of a file also results in an error.)

To seek into the file 10 bytes forward from the current position of the file pointer, use the following code:

```
seek $fileid 10 current
```

You'll usually use the seek command with the file size command (see Table 6.9), so that you know the size of the file.

If you aren't sure where the file pointer is located, use the tell command, which tells the current position:

```
set varname [tell $fileid]
```

Table 6.8 summarizes the commands to work with files.

Table 6.8 Commands that work on files.

Command	Usage
close $fileid	Closes open file.
eof $fileid	Returns 1 at end of file; 0 otherwise.
gets $fileid varname	Reads line of text into *varname*, returns minus one on end of file.
flush $fileid	Forces all buffered data for file to disk.
gets $fileid	Reads line of text, returns the text or an empty string on end of file.

`open` *filename mode*	Opens a file, returns file ID.
`puts` -nonewline *$fileid string*	Writes data to file.
`read` *$fileid*	Reads entire file into memory.
`read` -nonewline *$fileid*	Reads entire file into memory, skips ending newline.
`read` *$fileid number_bytes*	Reads given amount of file into memory.
`seek` *$fileid offset starting_at*	Moves file pointer to given position.
`tell` *$fileid*	Returns current byte position in file.

Channels

In Tcl terminology, a file is a channel. Networking sockets, discussed in Chapter 12, are also channels. The commands listed in Table 6.8 work on sockets as well as files.

Reading a File into a `Text` Widget

To read a text file and store its data into a `text` widget, you can use the following code, based on the `read_file` procedure:

```
proc read_file { filename } {
  # Default value.
  set data ""
  if { [file readable $filename] } {
    set fileid [open $filename "r"]
    set data [read $fileid]
    close $fileid
  }
  return $data
}
proc read_into_text { textwidget filename } {
    # Read in file.
    set data [read_file $filename]
    # Check if we have any.
```

```
    if {$data != "" } {
        # Delete all existing text in widget.
        $textwidget delete 1.0 end
        # Insert new text.
        $textwidget insert end $data
    }
}
```

The `read_into_text` procedure deletes all the text in the `text` widget but does not remove any of the tags. If your `text` widget has a lot of tags, the results with the new text could look bizarre with old tags but new text. So, you may want to delete all the tags, too. The following procedures, combined with the `read_file` procedure, do that:

```
#
# Deletes all text in text widget, sets toplevel to
# have given title.
#
proc file_new { toplevel textwidget title } {
    # Delete all tags.
    set names [$textwidget tag names]
    foreach tagname $names {
        $textwidget tag delete $tagname
    }
    # Delete all text.
    $textwidget delete 1.0 end
    # Set title.
    wm title $toplevel $title
    focus $textwidget
}
# Loads up a file into text widget.
# filename = name of file.
# toplevel = name of toplevel widget, gets filename in title.
# textwidget = name of text widget to place text.
#
proc file_load { toplevel textwidget filename } {
    set data [file_read $filename]
    if { $data != "" } {
```

```
        # Delete all existing text.
        file_new $toplevel $textwidget $filename
        # Store text in textwidget.
        $textwidget insert end $data
    }
}
```

This code comes from the **textedit.tcl** script in Chapter 5.

If you think the file will be large, you may want to read in the file in blocks, as shown previously (2048 bytes makes a good block size). In that case, use the text widget's insert end command with each block read.

Saving the Contents of a Text Widget to Disk

To store out all the text from a text widget to a disk file, you can use the following example code:

```
#
# Saves data to disk.
#
proc file_write { filename data } {
    return [catch {
        set fileid [open $filename "w"]
        puts -nonewline $fileid $data
        close $fileid
    }]
}

proc save_text { textwidget filename } {
    set data [$textwidget get 1.0 {end -1c} ]
    file_write $filename $data
}
```

The {end -1c} retrieves all data from the text widget skipping the last character, since we know this character is a newline character.

Of course, you may want to check for errors. See Chapter 9 for more on this topic.

NOTE If the first letter of the file name passed to open is a | character (often called a pipe character), then open assumes the file name is a command to execute and to connect via a pipe. See Chapter 10 for more on pipes and launching programs from within Tcl scripts. For now, don't use the | character in file names.

File Commands

Tcl offers a whole family of commands related to files with the file command, listed in Table 6.9.

Table 6.9 file commands.

Command	Usage
file atime *filename*	Returns time file was accessed, as integer.
file attributes *filename options*	Returns file attributes.
file attributes *filename option value*	Sets file attributes.
file copy *source target*	Copies *source* file to *target*.
file delete *filename*	Deletes *filename*.
file dirname *filename*	Returns all characters in file name, up to the last slash, or a period, if there are no slashes.
file executable *filename*	Returns 1 if the file is marked as an executable.
file exists *filename*	Returns 1 if the file name exists; 0 otherwise.
file extension *filename*	Returns the file extension (e.g., ".txt").
file isdirectory *filename*	Returns 1 if the file name is a directory.
file isfile *filename*	Returns 1 if the file name is not a directory.

`file join` *name name name*	Joins file name parts into a platform-specific path.
`file lstat` *filename*	Same as file `stat`, but if file name is a link, returns information on the link, not the linked-to file.
`file mkdir` *directory*	Creates directory.
`file mtime` *filename*	Returns time file was last modified, as integer.
`file nativename` *filename*	Returns native file name, sometimes needed on Windows and MacOS
`file owned` *filename*	Returns 1 if the file name is owned by the current user.
`file pathtype` *filename*	Returns information on the *filename*, one of `absolute`, `relative`, or `volumerelative`.
`file readable` *filename*	Returns 1 if the file name is readable; 0 otherwise.
`file readlink` *filename*	Returns the file a given symbolic link points to.
`file rename` *source target*	Renames file *source* to *target*.
`file rootname` *filename*	Returns the base part of the file name, up to the first period (.).
`file size` *filename*	Returns the size of the file, in bytes.
`file split` *filename*	Splits *filename* into component parts. Opposite of `file join`.

continued

Table 6.9 continued

`file stat` *`filename varname`*	Invokes the stat() system call.
`file tail` *`filename`*	Returns all the characters in file name after the last forward slash.
`file type` *`filename`*	Returns `blockSpecial`, `characterSpecial`, `directory`, `file`, `fifo`, `link`, or `socket`.
`file volume`	Returns list of mounted values on Windows such as a:/ c:/ d:/; / on UNIX.
`file writable` *`filename`*	Returns 1 if the file name is writable; 0 otherwise.

Many of these file commands have to do with file permissions. Windows 3.1 doesn't support much of this, but Windows NT and UNIX do.

Working with File Names

One of the most common tasks with file names is extracting the base part of the name from the directory and extension. The `file` command provides a number of ways to extract parts of a file name, as shown here:

```
% file join / usr local lib tk demos colors.tcl
/usr/local/lib/tk/demos/colors.tcl
% file extension /usr/local/lib/tk/demos/colors.tcl
.tcl
% file dirname /usr/local/lib/tk/demos/colors.tcl
/usr/local/lib/tk/demos
% file rootname /usr/local/lib/tk/demos/colors.tcl
/usr/local/lib/tk/demos/colors
% file tail /usr/local/lib/tk/demos/colors.tcl
colors.tcl
```

Detecting the Type of File

You can use the `file` command to provide information about the type of the file, whether it is a directory and so on, even whether or not a given file name represents a file. For example,

```
% file pathtype /usr/local/lib/tk/demos/colors.tcl
absolute
% file pathtype usr/local/lib/tk/demos/colors.tcl
relative
% file type /usr/local/lib/tk8.0/demos/colors.tcl
file
% file type /usr/local/lib/tk8.0/demos
directory
% file isdirectory /usr/local/lib/tk8.0/demos
1
% file isdirectory /usr/local/lib/tk8.0/demos/colors.tcl
0
% file exists /usr/local/lib/tk/demos/colors.tcl
0
% file exists /usr/local/lib/tk8.0/demos/colors.tcl
1
% file readable /usr/local/lib/tk8.0/demos/colors.tcl
1
% file writable /usr/local/lib/tk8.0/demos/colors.tcl
0
```

The most useful `file` commands include `file isdirectory`, `file exists`, and `file readable`. You can use the `file exists` command to verify that a file name is valid before trying to open it. The `file writable` command tells you whether or not you can write to a file, and so on.

Getting Information on the File

The `file size` command returns the size of the file, in bytes:

```
% file size /usr/local/lib/tk8.0/demos/colors.tcl
5071
```

380

With the `file stat` command, the variable *varname* filled with data is an array. The following array elements are filled in: `atime`, `ctime`, `dev`, `gid`, `ino`, `mode`, `mtime`, `nlink`, `size`, `type`, and `uid`.

Copying, Renaming, and Deleting Files

The `file copy` command copies a file. Similarly, the `file delete` command removes a file from a directory. The `file rename` command renames or moves a file. All three commands accept a `-force` option. For `file copy` and `file rename`, the `-force` option allows the commands to overwrite an existing file. Without the `-force` option, neither `file copy` nor `file rename` will overwrite an existing file. For `file delete`, the `-force` option allows you to delete a directory that still has files, a condition that otherwise generates an error.

Working with Serial Ports

With Tcl, you can open up serial ports as files, reading and writing data.

The ability to open Windows serial ports requires Tcl 8.0 or higher.

Because the serial port is not a regular file, you can use the `fconfigure` command to set up communication options like baud rates. The syntax is

```
fconfigure $fileid -mode baud,parity,data_bits,stop_bits
```

The value for the `-mode` option is a comma-separated list of four values: the baud rate, such as 14400; the parity, one of the following letters, `e` (even), `n` (none), `o` (odd), `m` (mark), or `s` (space); data bits, the number of data bits, usually 7 or 8; and the number of stop bits, usually 1 or 2.

WINDOWS

For Windows, the serial ports have a name in the format of **com1:** for the first serial port, **com2:**, and so on, usually through **com4:**. For Tcl, the communications port name requires the colon. In addition, you should be careful about which ports you try to open as the mouse takes up a serial port on many Windows systems.

UNIX already treats all devices as files. Usually, the file name for serial ports is something like **/dev/ttya** for the first port and **/dev/ttyb** for the second, and so on. Some systems provide special names like **/dev/modem** that refer to particular ports. The device files should be located in the **/dev** directory so you can figure out which ports your system supports.

In addition to file operations, Tcl provides a number of disk directory-scanning commands.

Scanning Directories

To list the files in a directory, Tcl uses the `glob` command, not the familiar **ls** or **DIR** commands, as shown in Table 6.10.

Table 6.10 File-listing commands.

System	Command
UNIX	ls
DOS	DIR
Tcl	glob

With Tcl, you can always use the `exec` command to run the UNIX **ls** program (provided your script is running on UNIX). But, in most cases, `glob` will work fine. The `glob` command takes the following syntax:

```
glob -nocomplain pattern
```

The *pattern* is any valid glob-style search pattern, as discussed in Chapter 2 in the section on the `switch` command. The most common pattern is *, to list all the files. The `-nocomplain` option tells `glob` not to generate an error if the return list is empty, that is, if no files were found. You'll almost always want to use this option.

To list all the files in a directory, you can use the following code:

```
# Use of glob to list files in a directory.
```

```
set files [glob -nocomplain *]
if { $files != "" } {
    foreach filename $files {
        puts $filename
    }
}
# glob1.tcl
```

You can sort the list returned by glob using the lsort command:

```
# Use of glob to list files in a directory.
set files [glob -nocomplain *]
if { $files != "" } {
    set sorted [lsort $files]
    foreach filename $sorted {
        puts $filename
    }
}
# glob2.tcl
```

This results in easier to read output.

You can also use glob to return only some files, based on the search pattern. For example, you can use a pattern of *.txt* to return all file names ending in *.txt*, such as **chap03.txt** and **report.txt**.

Changing Directories

In addition to listing directories, you may need to change to a different working directory and then scan the files located there.

The pwd command returns the current working directory:

```
% pwd
/home/erc/tcl
```

On Windows, this looks more like

```
tcl> pwd
C:/ERC/TCL
```

The `cd` command allows you to change the current working directory:

```
% cd /home/erc
% pwd
/home/erc
```

You can go up one level in the directory hierarchy by using the shorthand name `..` for the parent directory:

```
cd ..
```

This works on Windows and UNIX.

The `cd` command accepts the standard UNIX usage for directory names. A tilde character, `~`, specifies the user's home directory, as in

```
% cd ~
% pwd
/home/erc
```

On this system, home directories are located in /home. This location may vary on different UNIX systems.

If you use a tilde with a user's name, such as ~kevin, `cd` takes you to that user's home directory:

```
% cd ~kevin
% pwd
/home/kevin
```

WINDOWS

Windows 3.1 doesn't support user names, while Windows NT does. So, don't depend on tilde substitution working on Windows. On Windows 95, you may end up in a directory such as **C:/.**

Creating Directories

You can create a directory with the `file mkdir` command:

```
% file mkdir temp
% cd temp
% pwd
/home/erc/tcl/book/temp
```

You can remove a directory with the `file delete` command. Without the `-force` option, the `file delete` command will not delete a directory that still has files inside. You can normally (without `-force`) delete an empty directory.

A Tcl Directory Browser

We can build on the commands introduced in this chapter to build a Tcl directory browser. If you've ever tried this in another programming language, such as C, you'll appreciate how easy Tcl makes this.

For this browser, we'll have a list of subdirectories in the current directory, and a list of files. The file list will really show two `listbox` widgets connected to the same `scrollbar`. The first `listbox` will show the file name, the second its size.

The listboxes will appear in frames, with a `label` on top to show what the is held in the list. Note the use of nested `frame` widgets to get things to line up.

When you run this script on UNIX, you'll see a window like that shown in Figure 6.4.

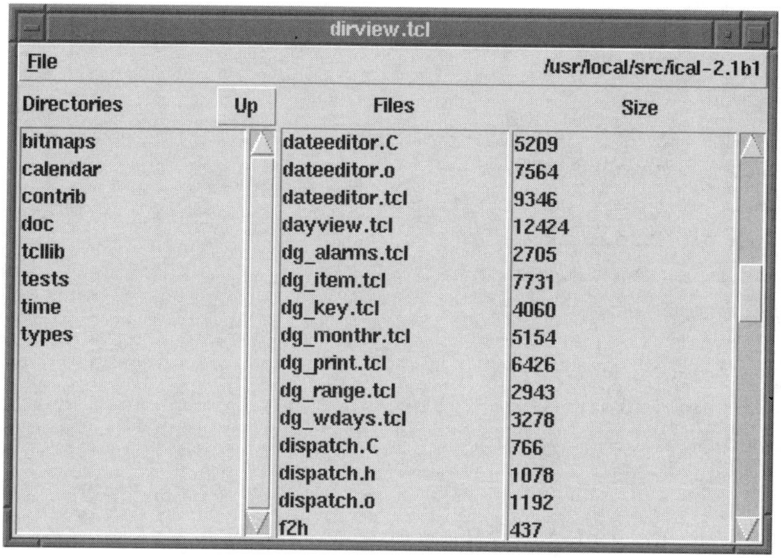

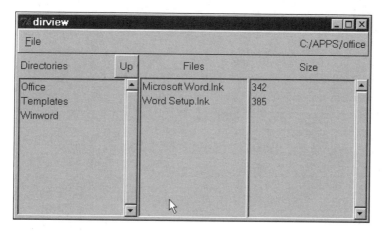

Figure 6.4 The **dirview.tcl** script on UNIX.

If you run it on Windows, you'll see something more like that in Figure 6.5.

Figure 6.5 The **dirview.tcl** script on Windows.

The **dirview.tcl** script follows:

```
#
# Tcl/Tk Directory Viewer
#
# File menu
frame .menubar -bd 1 -relief raised
menubutton .menubar.file -text "File" \
   -underline 0 -menu .menubar.file.menu
menu .menubar.file.menu
.menubar.file.menu add command -label "Exit" \
   -underline 1 -command exit

 # Place a label here, too.
label .menubar.curdir -text "Dir"
pack .menubar.file -side left
pack .menubar.curdir -side right

 # Frame for everything under menubar.
frame .main -bd 0
frame .main.dir -bd 1
frame .main.dir.text -bd 0
label .main.dir.text.label -text "Directories"
button .main.dir.text.up -text "Up" \
   -command go_up

pack .main.dir.text.label -side left
pack .main.dir.text.up -side right
frame .main.dir.f -bd 0
listbox .main.dir.f.list -height 20 \
   -selectmode single \
   -yscrollcommand ".main.dir.f.scrb set"
scrollbar .main.dir.f.scrb \
   -command ".main.dir.f.list yview"
pack .main.dir.f.list .main.dir.f.scrb \
   -side left -fill y
pack .main.dir.text -anchor w \
    -side top -fill x
pack .main.dir.f -side bottom
```

```
# Frame for file names.
frame .main.files -bd 0
label .main.files.files -text "Files"
listbox .main.files.file_list -height 20 \
  -selectmode single \
    -yscrollcommand ".main.sizes.f.scrb set"
pack .main.files.files \
  -side top -fill x -pady 4
pack .main.files.file_list -side bottom

 # File size area.
frame .main.sizes -bd 0
label .main.sizes.size -text "Size"
frame .main.sizes.f
listbox .main.sizes.f.size_list -height 20 \
  -selectmode single \
    -yscrollcommand ".main.sizes.f.scrb set"
scrollbar .main.sizes.f.scrb \
 -command { multi_scroll \
    {.main.files.file_list .main.sizes.f.size_list} }

pack .main.sizes.f.size_list -side left
pack .main.sizes.f.scrb -side right -fill y
pack .main.sizes.size -pady 4 \
  -side top -fill x
pack .main.sizes.f -side bottom
pack .main.dir .main.files .main.sizes -side left

# Pack top-level widgets.
pack .menubar -side top -fill x -expand true
pack .main -side left

 # Procedures
proc multi_scroll { scroll_list args } {
 # Get info on list of args.
 set len [llength $scroll_list]
 for {set i 0} {$i < $len} {incr i} {
    set temp_list [lindex $scroll_list $i]
    # Uncomment next line for debugging.
    # puts "Command: $temp_list yview $args"
```

```
        eval $temp_list yview $args
  }
}

# Fill lists with filenames.
proc read_dir { dirlist filelist sizelist } {
    # Clear listboxes.
    $dirlist delete 0 end
    $filelist delete 0 end
    $sizelist delete 0 end

    set unsorted [glob -nocomplain *]
    if {$unsorted != "" } {
        set files [lsort $unsorted]
        # Separate out directories.
        foreach filename $files {
            if { [file isdirectory $filename] != 0 } {
                # Is a directory.
                $dirlist insert end "$filename"
            } else {
                # Is a file.
                $filelist insert end "$filename"

                # Fill in size.
                set sz [file size $filename]
                $sizelist insert end $sz
            }
        }
    }

# Now, store current dir in label.
  .menubar.curdir configure -text [pwd]
}
 # Go up one directory.
proc go_up { } {
  # Go up one.
  cd ..

  # Read directory.
  read_dir .main.dir.f.list \
```

```
        .main.files.file_list .main.sizes.f.size_list
}

# Change dir on double-click.
bind .main.dir.f.list <Double-Button-1> {
    # Get selected list item.
    set diritem [.main.dir.f.list curselection]
    set dir [.main.dir.f.list get $diritem]

    # Change directories.
    cd $dir
    # Fill lists.
    read_dir .main.dir.f.list \
        .main.files.file_list .main.sizes.f.size_list
}
read_dir .main.dir.f.list \
        .main.files.file_list .main.sizes.f.size_list
# dirview.tcl
```

The read_dir procedure reads a directory and separates its elements into files and subdirectories, each going to a separate list. The file isdirectory command determines whether a file name read is a directory. Directory names go in one list and normal files in another.

For normal files, the file size command returns the size, and that value goes into another list. Both the file name and file size lists are tied to the same scrollbar, so that the proper size value will be synchronized with its corresponding file name.

The **dirview.tcl** script cheats in a few regards. First, it places a label widget on the menu bar (to display the current directory). That's a no-no. You should place only menubutton widgets or menu cascades on a menu bar. In a test program, it's OK to cheat a little.

Summary

This chapter introduced Tcl's lists, which are normal Tcl variables (unlike arrays shown in Chapter 2). Tcl provides a number of list-handling commands, such as lsort to sort a list, lindex to extract an element from a list, and list to build lists.

To display a list on the screen, you can use the `listbox` widget. Normally tied together with a `scrollbar`, the `listbox` can be configured with a `-selectmode` of `single`, `multiple`, `browse`, or `extended`.

Tcl provides a number of file commands, such as `open`, `read`, and `close`. To write data to a file, use the `puts` command, which defaults to writing to the terminal or Console window if you don't specify a file ID.

The `glob` command lists the files in a directory that matches a pattern, including the all-inclusive `*` pattern. The `cd` command changes to a different working directory, and the `pwd` command returns the current working directory.

The next chapter shows how to make dialog boxes, such as a file open dialog boxes, as well as how to create other top-level application windows.

Tcl/Tk Commands Introduced in This Chapter

cd

close

concat

eof

file

flush

glob

join

lappend

lindex

linsert

list

listbox

lrange

lreplace

lsearch

lsort

open

puts

pwd

read

seek

split

tell

CHAPTER 7

Dialog Windows

This chapter covers:

- Dialog windows
- Modal and nonmodal dialog windows
- Convenience dialog windows
- Creating top-level application windows
- Positioning dialog windows
- Handling the close window manager option
- Building your own convenience dialog windows
- Error dialog windows
- Drop-down lists

Dialog Windows

In user interface terminology, a **dialog window** is a window that gathers information from the user for a particular purpose. For example, most applications include print dialog windows to control printing options, file open dialog windows to select a file to load, and error dialog windows to alert the user to serious problems.

Tk provides the means to create all these types of dialog windows and more. This chapter covers dialog windows as well as all sorts of other types of top-level windows including application windows and pop-up windows.

We'll start with the handy convenience dialog windows, because they save you a lot of time; then we'll go into the commands necessary to create your own dialog windows.

Convenience Dialog Windows

There are number of special dialog windows, called **convenience dialog windows**, that Tk provides. These handy dialogs save you a lot of work and make your Tk applications better fit into the interface style guides on various platforms.

Table 7.1 lists the convenience dialog windows and the commands necessary to create them.

Table 7.1 Convenience dialog windows.

Dialog Type	Command	Usage
File Open	tk_getOpenFile	Asks user to select a file to open.
File Save As	tk_getSaveFile	Asks user to select a file name to save to.
Error	tk_messageBox	Displays an error message.
Information	tk_messageBox	Presents important information.
Question	tk_messageBox	Asks a question. No longer recommended.
Warning	tk_messageBox	Warns about a serious condition.
Color	tk_chooseColor	Allows user to select a color.

WINDOWS

The Windows style guide recommends against using question dialog windows.

All the dialog windows listed in Table 7.1 follow user interface guidelines on each platform. That is, on Windows you'll see a native Windows file dialog window, for example. On UNIX, the dialog windows follow—roughly—the Motif style guide.

There are two important dialog windows missing from this list: font and search/replace. Near the end of this chapter, you'll see the Tcl commands necessary to make these two useful dialog windows.

The convenience dialog windows form three groups: message dialog windows created with tk_messageBox, file dialog windows, and the color dialog window.

N O T E

All these convenience dialog windows require Tk 4.2 or higher. If you're using an older version of Tk, you can use the tk_dialog command, which is described later.

Message Dialog Windows

The simplest set of convenience dialog windows use the tk_messageBox command. The tk_messageBox command creates a simple dialog window with a message, a bitmap icon, and a set of buttons at the bottom. The dialog window appears, and then tk_messageBox waits for the user to respond. Such dialog windows are called *modal*, because they force the program into a mode awaiting user response. (See the section on Modal Dialog Windows for a longer discussion of these types of dialog windows.)

The basic format of the tk_messageBox command is

```
tk_messageBox -icon icontype -message your_message \
  -parent main_window -title title -type type
```

The tk_messageBox command uses symbolic names for each button, such as ok, cancel and so on. These buttons may not have the exact text, depending on the user interface style. The tk_messageBox command returns the symbolic name of the button the user clicked on, such as ok. This lets you know the user's choice.

To create a dialog window with tk_messageBox, you need to make a number of choices, starting with the icon image to display. The -icon option needs a value, one of `error`, `info`, `question`, or `warning`. The `question` icon, a question mark, is no longer recommended in the Windows style guide.

The `-parent` option lists the name of the main window for which this dialog window applies, usually the widget named `.`, or some other top-level window.

The `-message` option sets up the message to display, and the `-title` option controls the dialog window's title.

The `-type` option is a bit more tricky. It determines the buttons that appear at the bottom of the dialog window. Table 7.2 lists the available types.

Table 7.2 Types for the `tk_messageBox` command.

Type	Usage
abortretryignore	Displays three buttons: `abort`, `retry`, and `ignore`.
ok	Displays a single `ok` button.
okcancel	Displays an `ok` and a `cancel` button.
retrycancel	Displays a `retry` and a `cancel` button.
yesno	Displays `yes` and `no` buttons.
yesnocancel	Displays `yes`, `no`, and `cancel` buttons.

One of the advantages of the `tk_messageBox` command is that the dialog windows appear to follow the style guidelines of each platform. The examples that follow alternate between Windows and UNIX dialog windows, to give you some of the platform-specific flavor of these dialog windows. Note that the same Tcl code works on all supported platforms. You don't have to change a thing.

Error Dialog Windows

Error dialog windows describe some problem to the user. Good error dialog windows describe what you can do to try to get around the problem or where you can go for help.

For example, if the user requested a program from a CD-ROM and the CD-ROM has not been inserted, you could display a dialog window like that shown in Figure 7.1.

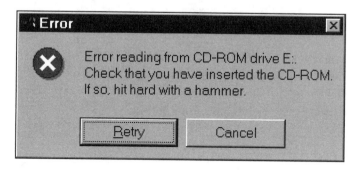

Figure 7.1 An error dialog window.

The code for this dialog window follows:

```
# Error dialog window.

set result [tk_messageBox -parent . \
     -title Error -type retrycancel \
     -icon error \
     -message \
"Error reading from CD-ROM drive E:.
Check that you have inserted the CD-ROM.
If so, hit hard with a hammer."]

# dlgerr.tcl
```

Information Dialog Windows

Information dialog windows should provide information to the user, such as the result of a database query. You should offer the user no choices, so set the -type option to ok. Figure 7.2 shows an information dialog window.

Figure 7.2 An information dialog window.

The source code for this dialog window follows:

```
# Info dialog window.


set result [tk_messageBox -parent . \
    -title {Query Result} -type ok \
    -icon info \
    -message "Found 1001 matches."]

# dlginfo.tcl
```

Warning Dialog Windows

Warning dialog windows alert the user to a condition that requires a user choice before going on or could result in some action that cannot be undone, such as overwriting a file. Oftentimes, the message is a question, such as "Overwrite YearlyReport?". Figure 7.3 shows a warning dialog window.

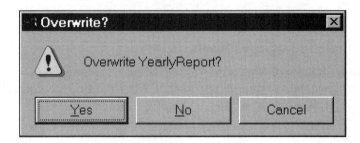

Figure 7.3 A warning dialog window.

The source code for this example follows:

```
# Warning dialog window.

set result [tk_messageBox -parent . \
    -title {Overwrite?} -type yesnocancel \
    -icon warning \
    -message "Overwrite YearlyReport?"]

# dlgwarn.tcl
```

Other Options for the `tk_messageBox` Command

The `-default` option to the `tk_messageBox` command specifies the symbolic name of the button to mark as the default button. The default button is engaged if you press **Return** when a `tk_messageBox` dialog window is visible.

NOTE

There's an older form of tk_messageBox called tk_dialog, discussed in the section on the tk_dialog command.

File Dialog Windows

Most operating systems, especially MacOS and Windows, support standard file open and file save as dialog windows. The commands that support these dialog windows are tk_getOpenFile and tk_getSaveFile.

The file open dialog window supports the *Open* choice on the *File* menu, as discussed in Chapter 4.

The basic method for calling tk_getOpenFile is as follows:

```
# Tk file dialog window.

set initialdir [pwd]
global initialdir

# Selects a Tcl file.
```

```
proc file_open_get { title } {
    global initialdir


    set file_types {
        { "Tcl Files"    { .tcl .TCL .tk .TK } }
        { "Text Files"   { .txt .TXT } }
        { "All Files"    * }
    }


    set filename [tk_getOpenFile \
        -initialdir $initialdir \
        -filetypes $file_types \
        -title "$title" \
        -parent .]


    if {$filename != ""} {
        set initialdir [file dirname $filename]
    }


    return $filename
}


set filename [file_open_get "Open"]

puts "Selected <$filename>"

# filedlg.tcl
```

When you run the **filedlg.tcl**, you'll see a file dialog window based on the style guide for your system. On Windows 95, you'll see a dialog window as shown in Figure 7.4.

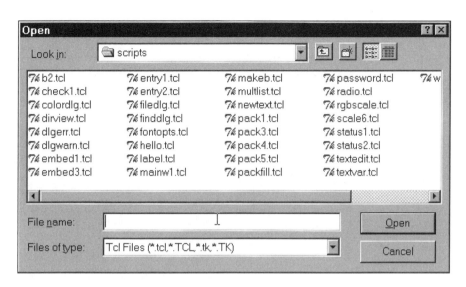

Figure 7.4 The file dialog window on Windows 95.

A UNIX example for the `tk_getSaveFile` appears in Figure 7.5.

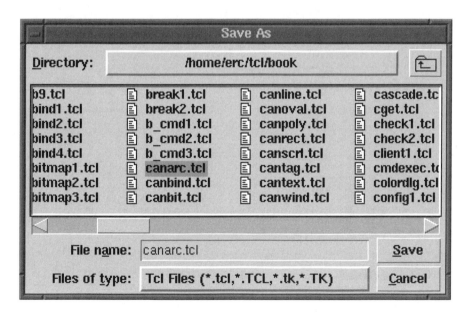

Figure 7.5 The save as dialog window on UNIX.

The save as dialog window supports the *Save As* choice on the *File* menu, also discussed in Chapter 4. For this dialog window, use the tk_getSaveFile command. The options are identical to the tk_getOpenFile command:

```
# Tk save as dialog window.

set initialdir [pwd]
global initialdir

# Selects a Tcl file.

proc file_save_get { title } {
    global initialdir

    set file_types {
        { "Tcl Files"   { .tcl .TCL .tk .TK } }
        { "Text Files"  { .txt .TXT } }
        { "All Files"   * }
    }

    set filename [tk_getSaveFile \
        -initialdir $initialdir \
        -filetypes $file_types \
        -title "$title" \
        -parent .]

    if {$filename != ""} {
        set initialdir [file dirname $filename]
    }

    return $filename
}
```

```
set filename [file_save_get "Save As"]

puts "Selected <$filename>"

# savedlg.tcl
```

With the `tk_getSaveFile` dialog window, if the user selects a file that already exists, the user gets to choose whether or not to overwrite the file.

Both `tk_getSaveFile` and `tk_getOpenFile` return the file name chosen. If the user selected Cancel, then both `tk_getSaveFile` and `tk_getOpenFile` return a NULL string.

Both `tk_getSaveFile` and `tk_getOpenFile` also take the same options. The main ones include `-initialdir`, which sets the initial directory to start in; `-title` which sets the title of the dialog window; `-parent` for the parent top-level window, usually `.`; and `-filetypes`, which contains a list of lists of file types.

I use the `-initialdir` option to start the file dialog window in a known location and then save the last directory the user visited, keeping this value for the next time. This means that if the user browsed through the directory tree, the next time the dialog window appears, it will appear in the same directory the user last used. With large hard disks the norm these days, this could save the user a lot of frustration repeatedly going back to the same directory.

The `-title` option should be "Open" for `tk_getOpenFile` and "Save As" for `tk_getSaveFile`, according to the Windows interface style guide (which is close enough to the Motif style guide on UNIX that you can safely follow these instructions on both operating systems). These are is for English interfaces, of course.

The `-filetypes` is a special case and contains a formatted list, such as the one that follows:

```
set file_types {
    { "Tcl Files"   { .tcl .TCL .tk .TK } }
    { "Text Files"  { .txt .TXT } }
    { "All Files"   * }
}
```

Each element in the list is a list itself. Each of these sublists starts with a type name, such a "Text Files", a list of extensions and an optional (skipped here) MacOS file type, such as GIFF for GIF image files and TEXT for text files.

The Color Dialog

The color dialog window allows the user to select a color. Many programs allow users to select foreground and background colors, to customize the interface. Whenever you need the user to select a color, you should use the tk_chooseColor command. tk_chooseColor creates the dialog window style appropriate for your operating system.

You can use the following code as a guide for calling tk_chooseColor:

```
# Tk color dialog window.

proc color_get { parent initialcolor } {

    set color [tk_chooseColor \
        -parent $parent \
        -initialcolor $initialcolor \
        -title "Color"]


    return $color
}

set color [color_get . maroon]

puts "Color=<$color>"

# colordlg.tcl
```

The title for the color dialog window should always be "Color".

On Windows 95, the color dialog window appears as shown in Figure 7.6.

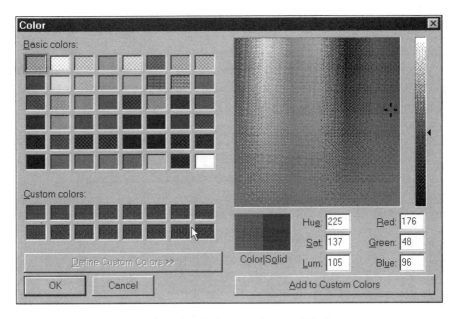

Figure 7.6 The color dialog window on Windows 95.

On UNIX, you'll see a dialog window that looks vaguely like the Silicon Graphics color-selection widget, as shown in Figure 7.7.

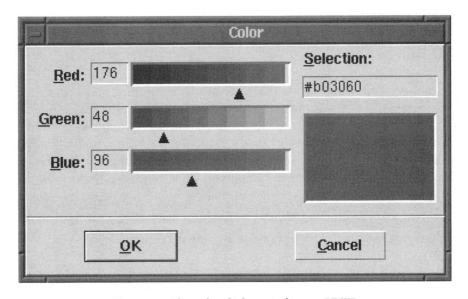

Figure 7.7 The color dialog window on UNIX.

The `tk_dialog` Command

Prior to Tk 4.2, the only convenience dialog windows were created by the `tk_dialog` command. You can still call `tk_dialog`, but you won't get the operating system-specific dialog windows created by `tk_messageBox`.

Dialog windows created with `tk_dialog` show a bitmap, a text message, and a number of buttons, as shown in Figure 7.8.

Figure 7.8 A dialog window created by `tk_dialog`.

Like `tk_messageBox`, the dialog window created by `tk_dialog` is modal. The execution of your script will stop until the user responds to the dialog window.

`tk_dialog` uses the following syntax:

```
tk_dialog name title text bitmap default_button label1 label2 ...
```

The *name* is the name of the dialog window to create, usually something like *.warning*. The *title* is the window title and the text is the message to display. The *bitmap* is one of the built-in monochrome bitmaps supported by Tk, usually `error`, `info`, or `warning`. The *default_button* holds the number of which button is marked as the default, starting with 0 for the first button. Button names, one for each button you want, following the *default_button* in order. `tk_dialog` will create as many buttons as you provide labels.

`tk_dialog` returns the number of the button selected, starting with 0.

You can use the following code as a guide for calling `tk_dialog`:

```
# Old-style tk_dialog dialog windows.
```

```
set result [tk_dialog .warning "Warning" \
    "This is a warning dialog." \
    warning \
    0 \
    OK Cancel]
puts "Result is <$result>"

# olddlg.tcl
```

The **olddlg.tcl** script creates the dialog window shown in Figure 7.8. This dialog window diverges a bit from the Windows interface style guide, but it is good enough for most uses. The `tk_dialog` routine is written in Tcl, so you can build your own if you'd like (see Building Your Own Dialog Windows, for more on this).

Many dialog windows require a lot more interaction with the user and many more widgets that are allowed in dialog windows created by `tk_dialog`. For these more advanced dialog windows, you'll need to build them yourself.

Building Your Own Dialog Windows

To create your own dialog windows, you need to create a `toplevel` window and then set up the proper window manager options to make this widget into a dialog window. Then, you need to fill in the `toplevel` widget with whatever widgets you want inside the dialog window, usually including listboxes and `entry` widgets.

Creating Top-Level Application Windows

To create a top-level window, you need to make a `toplevel` widget. You can use this widget as both a top-level application window or as a dialog window. Some applications require multiple top-level windows, beyond the top-level widget (`.`). Each top-level window has a window title bar and can be moved about the screen by the user.

Most applications require only one such window, but some require more. For example, a multiple-document interface, or MDI, application on

Windows supports multiple top-level windows. With Tk, these are multiple `toplevel` widgets.

To create such a window, use the `toplevel` command:

```
toplevel .top
```

The `toplevel` widget must be created as a child of the root widget, named with a . so that your `toplevel` widgets will have a name of the form *.name*.

Once created, you can fill in the `toplevel` widget with any of the standard Tk widgets we've been using so far. For example,

```
# toplevel widget.

toplevel .top

label .top.label -text "Top-level window"
button .top.button -text "Push Me" -command exit

pack .top.label .top.button -side left

# top1.tcl
```

You don't `pack` a `toplevel` widget. Much like the main widget named ., when the child widgets get packed, you'll see the new `toplevel` widget. You can also use the `-width` and `-height` options if you want to specify a particular size for the new `toplevel` widget.

NOTE

You can see this `toplevel` widget in Figure 7.9.

Figure 7.9 A simple toplevel widget.

You can fill in your `toplevel` widget with any Tk widgets you desire. The `toplevel` acts a lot like the `frame` widget, only the `toplevel` widget has a title bar and can be moved about the screen.

To specify that a `toplevel` widget is a dialog window, you can use the `-class` option:

```
toplevel .dlg -class Dialog
```

Don't use `class Dialog` if your `toplevel` widget is not a dialog window.

There's a number of other options you may want to set to turn a `toplevel` widget into a dialog window.

Setting Window Manager Options

The main options you need to set lie with the window manager. Under the X Window System on UNIX, the **window manager** program owns the window title bars. The window manager creates these windows (for title bars are windows themselves) and places the text therein. So, to control the title bar, you need to send specially formatted messages to the window manager.

On Windows, however, the title bar is considered part of the application's window. Luckily, Tcl hides most of these platform differences.

To set a title into the title bar, you need to use the `wm title` command:

```
wm title widgetname titlestring
```

The `wm` command contains a zillion options for communicating with the window manager or configuring your own windows. For a dialog window, you are supposed to register the fact that the dialog window is a **transient** window for the main application window. On doing this in Tk, however, you'll sometimes lose the title bar completely.

This should depend on the window manager program in use on UNIX. The **fvwm** window manager, common on Linux, for example, removes the title bars for these transient `toplevel` widgets (by default; this is configurable, with the *DecorateTransients* option in the **.fvwmrc** file). The **mwm** and **dtwm** window managers, however, do not.

To mark a `toplevel` widget as a transient window (really a dialog window), use the following syntax:

```
wm transient dialogname main_window
```

The *main_window* is almost always the top-level . widget. The *dialogname* is the name of your dialog window to mark as transient.

Positioning Dialog Windows

You can position a dialog window with the `wm geometry` command:

```
wm geometry widgetname geometry_spec
```

This command takes a widget name and a *geometry_spec*. The *geometry_spec* uses a rather strange X Window format of *widthXheight+x+y*. You can omit the size (*widthXheight*) or position (+*x*+*y*) if you want. An easier way to set the size is to use the `-width` and `-height` options on the `toplevel` widget.

To create a dialog window and position it, you can use the following commands as an example:

```
# Tk dialog window with window manager hints.


toplevel .dlg -class Dialog
wm title .dlg "Dialog"

wm transient .dlg .

wm geometry .dlg +200+300
```

```
button .dlg.b -text "Button"
pack .dlg.b -side left
```

```
# dialog1.tcl
```

These commands create a dialog window and position it at 200 pixels from the left and 300 pixels down from the top.

In X, the geometry specifications also allow you to figure positions from any edge of the screen, with odd origin values for each of the four corners, as shown in Table 7.3.

Table 7.3 Specifying the corner of the display.

Geometry	Location
+0+0	Upper left corner.
-0+0	Upper right corner.
+0-0	Lower left corner.
-0-0	Lower right corner.

Try the following commands:

```
wm geometry .dlg -0-0
wm geometry .dlg -0+0
wm geometry .dlg +0+0
wm geometry .dlg +0-0
```

You may want to center your dialog window within the main application window or on the screen. To get the screen size, you can use the following commands:

```
set width  [winfo screenwidth  .]
set height [winfo screenheight .]
```

For example,

```
% set width  [winfo screenwidth  .]
1024
% set height [winfo screenheight .]
768
```

The following procedure positions a dialog window in approximately the center of the screen:

```
proc dialog_position { dlg } {


    set width  [winfo screenwidth  .]
    set height [winfo screenheight .]


    set x [expr ($width/2)  - 200]
    set y [expr ($height/2) - 200]


    wm geometry $dlg +$x+$y
}
```

Getting Window Positions

In Tk, widgets are positioned in terms of relative coordinates. Each window has its own origin, located at the upper-left corner. Coordinate values increase from 0, 0 going to the right and down.

To place a dialog window, though, you need to use global, or screen, coordinates. To do this, you can use the winfo rootx and winfo rooty commands, as discussed in Chapter 4:

```
set x [winfo rootx $associated_widget]
set y [winfo rooty $associated_widget]
set y [expr $y + [winfo height $associated_widget]]
```

To help keep the similar winfo, info, and wm commands apart, you can think of them in the following way: winfo is short for widget info and provides information on widgets. info returns information about the Tcl interpreter. wm is short for window manager. wm helps your program work better in a windowed environment.

The winfo width and winfo height commands return a widget's width and height. At creation time, the width and height are likely to be incorrect, because the grid or pack geometry manager has yet to lay out the widgets. Because of this, you may want to call other winfo options:

```
winfo reqwidth widgetname
winfo reqheight widgetname
```

The winfo reqwidth returns the requested width of the widget. winfo reqheight similarly returns the requested height. This is useful for checking the size of newly created widgets that have yet to be displayed.

The winfo x and winfo y commands return the location of the given widget, in terms of local coordinates of the widget's parent:

```
winfo x widgetname
winfo y widgetname
```

Finding Out More About Widgets

The winfo command goes even farther. The winfo exists command returns 1 if the given widget exists; 0 otherwise:

```
if { [winfo exists $widgetname] == 1 } {
  # The widget exists...
}
```

The winfo toplevel command returns the name of the toplevel widget associated with the given widget:

```
winfo toplevel widgetname
```

The `winfo manager` command returns the name of the geometry manager, such as `pack`, associated with the given widget:

```
winfo manager widgetname
```

And, the `winfo children` command returns the list of child widgets for a given widget:

```
winfo children widgetname
```

Table 7.4 lists the main options for the `winfo` command.

Table 7.4 The `winfo` command.

Command	Usage
`winfo children widgetname`	Returns list of child widgets.
`winfo containing rootx rooty`	Returns name of widget containing given global coordinates.
`winfo exists widgetname`	Returns 1 if widget exists; 0 otherwise.
`winfo geometry widgetname`	Returns size and location in geometry format.
`winfo height widgetname`	Returns height of widget. Widget must be displayed.
`winfo id widgetname`	Returns UNIX X window ID for widget, HWND on Windows.
`winfo interps`	Returns list of all Tk applications running. Does not run on Windows as of Tk 8.0.
`winfo ismapped widgetname`	Returns 1 if widget is mapped; 0 otherwise.
`winfo manager widgetname`	Returns geometry manager, e.g., `pack`.

`winfo name widgetname`	Returns name within parent widget.
`winfo parent widgetname`	Returns name of parent widget.
`winfo pixels widgetname distance`	Returns number of pixels corresponding to *distance*, which can be in centimeters, etc., as described in Chapter 3.
`winfo pointerx widgetname`	If mouse is in window, returns X global coordinate.
`winfo pointery widgetname`	If mouse is in window, returns Y global coordinate.
`winfo reqheight widgetname`	Returns requested height of widget.
`winfo reqwidth widgetname`	Returns requested width of widget.
`winfo rootx widgetname`	Returns global coordinate for origin.
`winfo rooty widgetname`	Returns global coordinate for origin.
`winfo screenheight widgetname`	Returns height of screen that widget is on.
`winfo screenwidth widgetname`	Returns width of screen that widget is on.
`winfo toplevel widgetname`	Returns `toplevel` for widget.
`winfo viewable widgetname`	Returns 1 if widget is mapped; 0 otherwise.
`winfo width widgetname`	Returns width of widget. Widget must be displayed.
`winfo x widgetname`	Returns X coordinate for widget, in terms of parent.
`winfo y widgetname`	Returns Y coordinate for widget, in terms of parent.

414

Showing and Hiding Dialog Windows

Top-level widgets appear on the screen when you add child widgets to the `toplevel`. Sometimes, though, you don't want the `toplevel` to appear. For one reason, you may want the `toplevel` to appear later and only build up the widgets early. For performance, even if you want a `toplevel` widget to appear right away, you may want to hide the `toplevel` and then add all the child widgets, finally showing the `toplevel` widget when you're all done.

The reason for the performance issue is that as you `pack` widgets, Tk must make a number of calculations as well as move and resize existing windows (all the widgets you've packed so far).

 The same performance considerations apply to the `grid` geometry manager.

N O T E

If the widget isn't visible yet, Tk doesn't have to move the physical windows, an expensive operation. So, for best performance, hide a `toplevel` widget right after creation, fill in all the child widgets, and then show the `toplevel` widget.

To hide a `toplevel` widget, call `wm withdraw`:

`wm withdraw` *widgetname*

To show the `toplevel` widget again, call `wm deiconify`:

`wm deiconify` *widgetname*

The `wm deiconify` command deiconifies the `toplevel` widget, which is the same as showing the widget. (This command comes from low-level X Window functions.)

The `winfo ismapped` command returns 1 if the given widget is mapped; 0 otherwise:

`winfo ismapped` *widgetname*

A mapped widget should be visible on the screen. The term mapped also comes from the X Window System as well. The `winfo ismapped` command helps to tell whether or not you need to call `wm withdraw` or `wm deiconify`.

The `wm iconify` command turns a top-level window into an icon:

```
wm iconify widgetname
```

See Chapter 14 for more on icons.

Positioning the Main Widget

You can also position the main application widget with the `wm geometry` command, but you also may need to lie to the window manager and claim the user picked the position for the window. If you try the `wm geometry` command and nothing happens, try the following command first, and then execute the `wm geometry` command:

```
wm positionfrom . user
```

The reason for this is that many window manager programs don't honor positions specified by the program (the default). Instead, your program has to claim the user actively chose the location.

Handling the Close Window Manager Option

Most window managers provide for a window menu, and usually this menu has a choice labeled "Close" or "Quit". Typically, when the user chooses this, Tk will terminate your program, sometimes not very gracefully.

There is a way to get around this. Of course, when the user asks for a window to close, you should close it, even if this means stopping the application. The user should be in charge after all.

But, you may want to confirm with the user. You may need to prompt the user to save a file before quitting. Or, you may merely want to execute some clean-up code before abrupt termination.

To do all this, you need to set up a protocol handler to handle the WM_DELETE_WINDOW protocol (this is an X Window term). For this, call the wm protocol command, which uses the following syntax:

```
wm protocol widgetname protocol tcl_script
```

The *widgetname* should be a toplevel widget, as well as the . widget. (So, you'll need to call this for all top-level widgets.) The *protocol* is WM_DELETE_WINDOW, and you provide the *tcl_script*.

To query the user to confirm quitting the program, you can use the following code, which sets up the procedure handle_close to handle all dialog window and main window close messages:

```
# Handles window manager Close choice.


proc prompt_close { widgetname } {


    # If main window, prompt.
    if { $widgetname == "." } {
        set result [tk_messageBox -parent . \
                -title {Exit?} -type yesno\
                -icon warning \
                -message "Do you really want to quit?"]


        if { $result == "yes" } {
            exit
        }
    } else {
        # Not the main window, destroy it.
        destroy $widgetname
    }


}
```

```
wm protocol . WM_DELETE_WINDOW "prompt_close ."
```

```
# wmclose.tcl
```

Note that the WM_DELETE_WINDOW protocol does not trap every means to stop an application. On UNIX, many window managers provide a means to kill an application's windows, something you cannot trap with wm protocol.

The prompt_close procedure destroys any dialog windows it gets sent. This is based on the idea that what the user says, goes. But, if the user asks to close the widget named ., then the prompt_close procedure prompts the user with a dialog window like the one show in Figure 7.10.

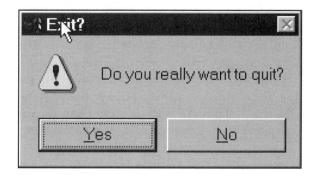

Figure 7.10 Querying the user whether to quit.

You'll want to set something like the prompt_close procedure for all toplevel widgets you create.

Modal and Nonmodal Dialog Windows

Once you've created your dialog window, the next question you must answer when creating a dialog window is whether to make it modal or non-modal. A **modal** dialog window requires that the user interact with it right now. A **nonmodal** dialog window just sits there; if the user wants to interact with it, the user will.

Although many application developers make frequent use of modal dialog windows, I tend to shy away from them. A major point of graphical user interfaces is to put the user in control, but modal dialog windows take away a measure of that control. The user should be able to choose when to respond and what to respond to. So, if you can avoid making a dialog window modal, do so.

There is a place for modal dialog windows, though. When used with care—and not overused—you can put modal dialog windows to good use. If there's something the user absolutely has to respond to, or something in which it makes no sense to continue until the user responds, then consider using a modal dialog window if you run out of alternatives.

NOTE Coming from a background in factory automation, I'm always extremely careful about having a program decide the user must respond. If your plant is burning down, you shouldn't be stopped by a modal dialog window demanding that you complete a file name properly, for example.

If you do need to create a modal dialog window, you can use the `tkwait` command to make the dialog window modal. The `tkwait` command waits until one of three conditions happens: a variable's value changes, a widget becomes visible on the screen, or a widget gets destroyed. The three forms follow:

```
tkwait variable varname
tkwait visibility widgetname
tkwait window widgetname
```

Normally, you'll use only the `variable` and `window` (destroyed) forms of `tkwait`. The `visibility` form is intended for use with the `grab` command, something that is required for very few applications and is inherently not portable in all its subtleties. (If you're interested, you can look up the on-line manual information on `grab`. Generally, you won't need this command.)

In most cases, you'll create a dialog window using the `toplevel` widget command. You'll place `button`, `label` and `message` widgets inside the `toplevel` widget.

To make `tkwait` work, you need either to have the all `button` widgets' `-command` option `destroy` the `toplevel` widget, or to have each `button` set a chosen variable to a different value. Which method you choose determines which form of `tkwait` to use.

Then, call `tkwait` with the name of the `toplevel` widget.

The `tkwait` command allows you to build a modal dialog window by hand. You often don't even have to go to this much work, if you need only a simple convenience dialog window. In this case, use `tk_messageBox`.

Now, we have enough tools to start building dialog windows.

Creating Your Own Convenience Dialog Windows

In most complex applications, you'll need to make one or two dialog windows. This section shows how to create useful dialog windows by focusing on two common examples: search/replace and font dialog windows. These are real examples you can use in your code.

The first example, the search/replace dialog window, creates a non-modal `toplevel` window. The second, a font dialog window, creates a modal window and uses `tkwait`, which was described previously.

Search and Replace Dialog Windows

The search and replace dialog window handles the *Replace* choice on the *Edit* menu of most text editors. (You can add this to the **textedit.tcl** editor in Chapter 5 if you'd like.)

The code looks long, mostly because it allows a great deal of control over the search options. You can, for example, use the regular expression style of searching from this dialog window.

A typical search and replace dialog window appears in Figure 7.11.

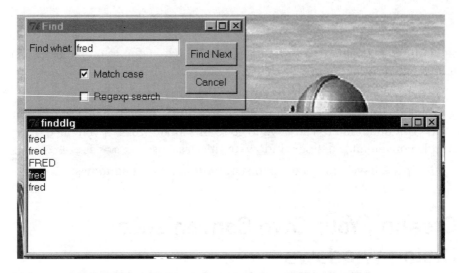

Figure 7.11 The search and replace dialog window.

The format of the dialog window follows the Windows style guide. The code follows:

```
# Find dialog window for searching a text widget.
#


#
# Creates a Find dialog for searching a text widget.
# Pass in the name of the text widget to search.
#
proc FindDialog { textwidget } {
    global find_case find_regexp find_last_indx


    # Don't require exact case match.
    set find_case 0


    # Don't use regexp-style searches.
    set find_regexp 0
```

```
    # Last place searched, line 1 column 0 (start).
set find_last_indx 1.0


    #
    # Create font dialog window.
    #
set dlg .finddialog
toplevel $dlg
wm protocol $dlg WM_DELETE_WINDOW "destroy $dlg"


wm title $dlg Find


label $dlg.l_findwhat -text "Find what:" -anchor w
entry $dlg.findwhat


bind $dlg.findwhat <Key-Return> \
    "FindText $dlg.findwhat $textwidget"


grid config $dlg.l_findwhat -column 0 -row 0 \
  -sticky "w" -pady 8
grid config $dlg.findwhat    -column 1 -row 0 \
  -sticky "snew" -pady 8


checkbutton $dlg.matchcase -text "Match case" \
  -variable find_case
grid config $dlg.matchcase -column 1 -row 1 \
  -sticky "w"


checkbutton $dlg.regexp    -text "Regexp search" \
  -variable find_regexp
grid config $dlg.regexp    -column 1 -row 2 \
  -sticky "w"
```

```
    set fr $dlg.buttons
    frame $fr -bd 0
    button $fr.findnext -text "Find Next" \
        -command "FindText $dlg.findwhat $textwidget"


    button $fr.cancel -text "Cancel" \
          -command "destroy $dlg"
    pack $fr.findnext -side top -fill x
    pack $fr.cancel    -side top -fill x -pady 6


    grid config $fr -column 2 -row 0 -rowspan 4 \
       -padx 8 -pady 8
}



#
# Called by Find dialog window to search textwidget.
# entrywidget has the text to search for.
#
proc FindText { entrywidget textwidget } {


    global find_case find_regexp find_last_indx


    # Get pattern to search for.
    set pattern [$entrywidget get]


    # Get length of pattern.
    set length [string length $pattern]


    set options "-forwards"
    if { $find_case == 0 } {
        append options " -nocase"
    }
```

```
if { $find_regexp == 1 } {
    append options " -regexp"
}


set cmd [format \
  "$textwidget search %s — $pattern \"$find_last_indx\"" \
  $options]


set indx ""
catch {
    set indx [eval $cmd]
}


if { $indx != ""} {
    catch {
        #
        # Remove old tag placement for any currently
        # selected text.
        #
        $textwidget tag remove sel sel.first sel.last
    }


    #
    # Select text found.
    #
    $textwidget tag add sel $indx "$indx + $length chars"


    #
    # Place insertion cursor at start of selected data.
    #
    $textwidget mark set insert $indx


    #
    # Make sure text is visible.
```

```
    #
    $textwidget see $indx


    #
    # Set focus back to text widget
    # to show selected text.
    #
    focus $textwidget


    # Keep index for next search.
    set find_last_indx "$indx + 1 char"
} else {


    #
    # Display not found dialog window.
    #
    tk_messageBox -type ok -icon info -parent $textwidget \
        -title "Not Found" -message \
        "Sorry, but <$pattern> was not found."
    }
}


proc test_code { } {
    text .text -width 80 -height 24
    .text insert end "fred\nfred\nFRED\nfred\nfred"
    pack .text


    FindDialog .text
}


# Comment out test code for real usage.
test_code

# finddlg.tcl
```

In the **finddlg.tcl** script, the `FindDialog` procedure creates the dialog window and sets up the interface. The `FindText` procedure does the actual searching. Notice how complicated this procedure is due to the many available options. Each time you allow the user an extra option, you'll find your code gets more complicated. The `test_code` procedure creates a find dialog window for testing. You can comment out the last line that calls `test_code` to avoid the testing code.

WINDOWS

The `FindText` procedure uses the `focus` command to set the keyboard focus back to the `text` widget. This is because on Windows, the selected text won't appear highlighted unless the window is active.

Creating a Font Dialog Window

The Windows interface supports a standard font dialog window, which allows you to select a font, a font size, and other attributes of the font. Tk doesn't offer such a dialog window, which provides an opportunity to create one ourselves, as shown in Figure 7.12.

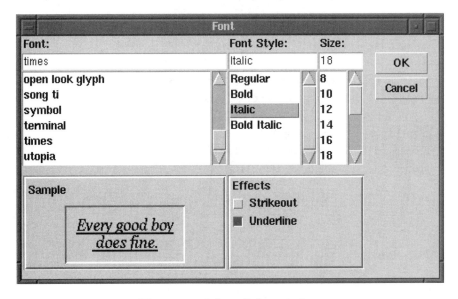

Figure 7.12 A font dialog window.

The font dialog window requires the `font` commands described in Chapter 3. These commands allow you to create a virtual font and set its attributes in a way that eliminates platform differences.

You'll need Tk version 8.0 or higher to use the font command.

The `FontDialog` procedure, shown in the **fontdlg.tcl** script, creates a `toplevel` widget and then fills in that `toplevel` widget with a number of `listbox` and `entry` widgets, to allow you to select the font, style, and size. Notice all the effort spent with the `grid` command to get everything to line up. Even simple dialog windows can take a long time to put together.

The code for the **fontdlg.tcl** script follows:

```
#
# Creates a font dialog window to select a font.
#
# Comment out test code at end of file for real usage.
#


#
# Creates a font dialog window like that in Windows 95.
# returns 1 if user chose a font; 0 otherwise.
#
proc FontDialog { font_name } {
    global fd_family fd_style fd_size fd_close
    global fd_strikeout fd_underline


    set fd_family {}
    set fd_style  {}
    set fd_size   {}
    set fd_strikeout 0
    set fd_underline 0
    set fd_close  -1
```

```
set unsorted_fam [font families]


set families [lsort $unsorted_fam]


#
# Get current font's family and so on.
#
    # Calculate font style.
set slant    [font actual $font_name -slant]
set weight   [font actual $font_name -weight]


    # Default style.
set fd_style "Regular"


if { $slant == "italic" } {
    if { $weight == "bold" } {
        set fd_style "Bold Italic"
    } else {
        set fd_style "Italic"
    }
} else {
    if { $weight == "bold" } {
        set fd_style "Bold"
    }
}


set family [font actual $font_name -family]
set fd_family $family
set size   [font actual $font_name -size]
set fd_size  $size
set strikeout [font actual $font_name -underline]
set fd_strikeout $strikeout
set underline [font actual $font_name -overstrike]
set fd_underline $underline
```

```
#
# Create font dialog window.
#
set dlg .fontdialog
toplevel $dlg
wm protocol $dlg WM_DELETE_WINDOW "set fd_close 0"


wm title $dlg Font


label $dlg.family_lbl -text "Font:" -anchor w
entry $dlg.family_ent -textvariable fd_family \
    -background white
bind  $dlg.family_ent <Key-Return> \
    "FontDialogRegen $font_name"
grid config $dlg.family_lbl -column 0 -row 0 \
    -sticky w
grid config $dlg.family_ent -column 0 -row 1 \
    -sticky snew


label $dlg.style_lbl  -text "Font Style:" -anchor w
entry $dlg.style_ent  -textvariable fd_style \
    -width 11 -background white
bind  $dlg.style_ent  <Key-Return> \
    "FontDialogRegen $font_name"
grid config $dlg.style_lbl  -column 1 -row 0 \
    -sticky w
grid config $dlg.style_ent  -column 1 -row 1 \
    -sticky snew


label $dlg.size_lbl    -text "Size:" -anchor w
entry $dlg.size_ent    -textvariable fd_size \
    -width 4 -background white
bind  $dlg.size_ent    <Key-Return> \
    "FontDialogRegen $font_name"
grid config $dlg.size_lbl    -column 2 -row 0 \
```

```
        -sticky w
grid config $dlg.size_ent    -column 2 -row 1 \
        -sticky snew


# Font family listbox.
set fr $dlg.family_list
frame $fr -bd 0
listbox $fr.list -height 6 -selectmode single \
    -yscrollcommand "$fr.scroll set" \
     -width 30 -background white


scrollbar $fr.scroll -command "$fr.list yview"


foreach f $families {
    $fr.list insert end $f
}


bind $fr.list <Double-Button-1> \
 "FontDialogFamily $fr.list $font_name $dlg.family_ent"


pack $fr.scroll -side right -fill y
pack $fr.list -side left
grid config $fr -column 0 -row 2 -rowspan 16


# Font style listbox.
set fr $dlg.style_list
frame $fr -bd 0
listbox $fr.list -height 6 -selectmode single \
    -yscrollcommand "$fr.scroll set" \
    -width 11 -background white


scrollbar $fr.scroll -command "$fr.list yview"
```

```
$fr.list insert end "Regular"
$fr.list insert end "Bold"
$fr.list insert end "Italic"
$fr.list insert end "Bold Italic"


bind $fr.list <Double-Button-1> \
  "FontDialogStyle $fr.list $font_name $dlg.style_ent"


pack $fr.scroll -side right -fill y
pack $fr.list -side left
grid config $fr -column 1 -row 2 -rowspan 16


# Font size listbox.
set fr $dlg.size_list
frame $fr -bd 0
listbox $fr.list -height 6 -selectmode single \
    -yscrollcommand "$fr.scroll set" \
    -width 4 -background white


scrollbar $fr.scroll -command "$fr.list yview"


set i 8
while { $i <= 32 } {
    $fr.list insert end $i
    set i [expr $i + 2]
}


bind $fr.list <Double-Button-1> \
  "FontDialogSize $fr.list $font_name $dlg.size_ent"


pack $fr.scroll -side right -fill y
pack $fr.list -side left
grid config $fr -column 2 -row 2 -rowspan 16
```

```
    # OK/Cancel.
    set fr $dlg.ok_cancel
    frame $fr -bd 0


    button $fr.ok -text "OK" -command "set fd_close 1"
    button $fr.cancel -text "Cancel" \
    -command "set fd_close 0"
pack $fr.ok -side top -fill x
pack $fr.cancel -side top -fill x -pady 2
grid config $fr -column 4 -row 1 -rowspan 2 \
        -sticky snew -padx 12


    # Effects.
    set fr $dlg.effects
    frame $fr -bd 3 -relief groove


    label $fr.effects -text "Effects" -anchor w
    checkbutton $fr.strikeout -variable fd_strikeout \
        -text "Strikeout" -anchor w \
        -command "FontDialogRegen $font_name"
    checkbutton $fr.underline -variable fd_underline \
        -text "Underline" -anchor w \
        -command "FontDialogRegen $font_name"


    pack $fr.effects $fr.strikeout $fr.underline \
        -side top -fill x


    grid config $fr -column 1 -columnspan 2 -row 20 \
        -rowspan 2 -sticky snew -pady 10


    # Sample text.
    set fr $dlg.sample
    frame $fr -bd 3 -relief groove
    label $fr.l_sample -text "Sample" -anchor w
```

```
label $fr.sample -text "Every good boy\n does fine." \
    -font $font_name -bd 2 -relief sunken


pack  $fr.l_sample -side top -fill x -pady 4
pack  $fr.sample -side top -pady 4 -ipadx 10 -ipady 10


grid config $fr -column 0 -columnspan 1 -row 20 \
    -rowspan 2 -sticky snew -pady 10 -padx 2


# Make this a modal dialog window.
tkwait variable fd_close


# Get rid of dialog window and return value.
destroy $dlg


#
# Restore old font characteristics on a cancel.
#
if { $fd_close == 0 } {
        font configure $font_name -family $family \
                -size $size -underline $underline \
                -overstrike $strikeout -slant $slant \
                -weight $weight
}


    return $fd_close
}


proc FontDialogFamily { listname font_name entrywidget } {


    # Get selected text from list.
    catch {
```

```
        set item_num [$listname curselection]
        set item [$listname get $item_num]

        # Set selected list item into entry for font family.
        $entrywidget delete 0 end
        $entrywidget insert end $item


        # Use this family in the font and regenerate font.
        FontDialogRegen $font_name
    }
}


proc FontDialogStyle { listname font_name entrywidget } {


    # Get selected text from list.
    catch {
        set item_num [$listname curselection]
        set item [$listname get $item_num]

        # Set selected list item into entry for font family.
        $entrywidget delete 0 end
        $entrywidget insert end $item


        # Use this family in the font and regenerate font.
        FontDialogRegen $font_name
    }
}


proc FontDialogSize { listname font_name entrywidget } {


    # Get selected text from list.
    catch {
        set item_num [$listname curselection]
```

```
        set item [$listname get $item_num]


        # Set selected list item into entry for font family.
        $entrywidget delete 0 end
        $entrywidget insert end $item


        # Use this family in the font and regenerate font.
        FontDialogRegen $font_name
    }
}


    # Regenerates font from attributes.
proc FontDialogRegen { font_name } {
    global fd_family fd_style fd_size
    global fd_strikeout fd_underline


    set weight "normal"
    if { $fd_style == "Bold Italic" || $fd_style == "Bold" } {
        set weight "bold"
    }


    set slant "roman"
    if { $fd_style == "Bold Italic" || $fd_style == "Italic" } {
        set slant "italic"
    }


    #
    # Change font to have new characteristics.
    #
    font configure $font_name -family $fd_family \
        -size $fd_size -underline $fd_underline \
        -overstrike $fd_strikeout -slant $slant \
        -weight $weight
}
```

```
# Test code. Comment out for real usage.
proc FontTest { } {

    wm withdraw .
        # Create a dummy font for use.
    font create testfont -family helvetica


    # Ask user to select font.
    set status [FontDialog testfont]


    if { $status == 1} {
        puts "User selected font."
    } else {
        puts "User did not select a font."
    }


    # Verify font family.
    puts "Font family [font actual testfont -family]"


    font delete testfont
}


    # Test code. Comment out for real usage.
FontTest


# fontdlg.tcl
```

The FontDialog procedure creates a modal dialog window and uses the tkwait variable command with a global variable named *fd_close*. If *fd_close* is set to 0, then the user has canceled the dialog window. If *fd_close* is set to 1, then the user selected a font. On the cancel, the end of the FontDialog procedure restores the original font settings. This is necessary because the FontDialog procedure is actually changing the attributes for the passed-in font.

The code that makes this a modal dialog window is very simple:

```
# Make this a modal dialog window.
tkwait variable fd_close
```

The font dialog window expects that you have already created a font. The test procedure, FontTest, does this for you. After you have the font set up, you can pass the name of this new font to the FontDialog procedure to have a font dialog window setting options for that font. This way, you can reuse the font dialog window to set different fonts in the application.

You can call the font dialog window with code like the following:

```
set status [FontDialog your_font]
```

```
if { $status == 1} {
    # User selected font...
} else {
    # User did not select a font...
}
```

The FontDialog procedure returns 1 if the user selected a font.

In order to use this dialog window in your code, you need to create a font and use that font for any text. You may have multiple fonts, for headings, text, fixed-width text, menus, and so on. You can reuse the FontDialog procedure to allow the user to change any of these fonts.

Drop-Down Lists

More common in the Windows environment, drop-down lists are also part of Motif 2.0 and the Common Desktop Environment on UNIX. Tk doesn't support drop-downs lists—not directly, but you can build one on your own, using a toplevel widget.

First of all, an option menu using the `tk_optionMenu` command may do the trick for you. See Chapter 4 for more on this. You could save yourself some work.

The main problem with an option menu is the lack of space. An option menu doesn't scroll, so you're limited by the screen size. If you use a `list-box` widget, though, you can scroll the choices and conceivably present thousands of choices.

You can put the `listbox` in a `toplevel` widget to make the `listbox` appear like it is floating on the screen. In this case, we want the `toplevel` widget to have no window manager title bar at all, much like a menu. While you could try playing with the menu widget itself, you can also use another option to the wm command:

```
wm overrideredirect widgetname 1
```

The `overrideredirect` (that's override redirect) option specifies that the given window not be given any decorations, like the title bar, from the window manager. Under the X Window System, this is what menus use. To turn this option off, use

```
wm overrideredirect widgetname 0
```

For the entry part of the widget, we can use a `label` prompt, an `entry` widget, and then a `button` to call up the `listbox`. To follow the Windows style, you should place a down-pointing arrow bitmap in the `button`. Such bitmaps in buttons are covered in Chapter 8.

When we put all this together, we have an entry area that looks like what is shown in Figure 7.13.

Figure 7.13 The drop-down list entry area.

The code to create the drop-down list is a bit complex. First, we must determine the position of the `listbox`, which should be beneath the `button` and `entry` widgets. We can use the `entry` widget's position.

To convert the `entry` widget's position to global coordinates, you can use the `winfo rootx` and `winfo rooty` commands, as shown here:

```
set x [winfo rootx .entry]
set y [winfo rooty .entry]
```

We can then create the whole drop list widget using the following code. Look over the code to see what it is trying to do. There are a few new commands, especially for the bitmap button, as a preview of Chapter 8. The code for **droplist.tcl** follows:

```
# Drop-down list code.
#
# The main procedure to use is DropListCreate.
# The test_drop_list procedure shows how to use
# the drop list. The rest of the procedures are
# private to the drop list.
#


# Creates a drop-down list and a few interface widgets
# (label, entry, and drop-button) from your supplied basename.
#
# basename = base name for frame that holds entry widget.
# text = text for label widget.
# height = number of visible lines in list.
# width = number of columns in list and entry widget.
# variable = name of variable that gets the selected value.
# initial_value = first value.
#
# Returns name of actual listbox widget,
# so you can fill in the listbox.
#
proc DropListCreate {
```

```
basename text width height variable initial_value } {


upvar #0  $variable var
set var "$initial_value"


# Name of top-level widget to create.
set top $basename.top


#
# Widgets to enter data.
#
frame $basename -bd 0
label $basename.lbl -text $text -anchor e
entry $basename.ent -width $width
$basename.ent insert 0 "$initial_value"
DropButton $basename.drop $basename.top $basename.ent


bind $basename.ent <Return> \
    "DropListSetVal $basename.ent $variable"


bind $basename.ent <Key-Escape> "wm withdraw $top"


pack $basename.lbl -side left -fill y
pack $basename.ent -side left -expand 1 -fill y
pack $basename.drop -side left -fill y


#
# Drop-list is a top-level temporary window.
#
toplevel $top -cursor top_left_arrow
wm overrideredirect $top 1
wm withdraw $top
```

```
# Create list.
set frm $top.frame
frame $frm -bd 4 -relief sunken


listbox $frm.list -height $height -width $width \
    -selectmode single \
    -yscrollcommand "$frm.scrollbar set"


bind $frm.list <Key-Escape> "wm withdraw $top"


# Create scrollbar.
scrollbar $frm.scrollbar \
    -command "$frm.list yview"


pack $frm.scrollbar -side right -fill y
pack $frm.list       -side left
pack $frm -side top


bind $frm.list <ButtonRelease-1> \
    "DropListClick $top $basename.ent $variable"


pack $basename


#
# Return list widget so you can fill it.
#
return $frm.list
}


# Returns selected item for a single-select list.
proc list_selected { listname } {
    set indx [$listname curselection]
```

```
        if { $indx != "" } {
            set item [$listname get $indx]


            return $item
        } else {
            return "";
        }


    }



    # Places value in global variable.
    proc DropListSetVal { entry variable } {
        upvar #0 $variable var


        set value [$entry get]


        if { $value != "" } {
            set var $value
        }



    }



    # Handles click on drop-list widget.
    proc DropListClick { basename entry variable } {


        catch {
            set selected [list_selected $basename.frame.list]


            if { $selected != "" } {
                #
                # Put item into entry widget.
                #
```

```
            $entry delete 0 end
            $entry insert 0 "$selected"

            DropListSetVal $entry $variable
        }
    }


    wm withdraw $basename
}


# Makes drop list visible. Create with DropListCreate.
proc ShowDropList { basename associated_widget } {
    set x [winfo rootx $associated_widget]
    set y [winfo rooty $associated_widget]
    set y [expr $y + [winfo height $associated_widget]]


    wm geometry $basename "+$x+$y"


    wm deiconify $basename
    raise $basename


    focus $basename.frame.list
}


# Creates a button with a drop-down bitmap.
proc DropButton { name toplevel entry } {


    button $name -image dnarrow \
        -command "ShowDropList $toplevel $entry"


    return $name
}
```

```
#
# Bitmap data for down arrow bitmap.
#
set dnarrow_data "
#define dnarrow2_width 18
#define dnarrow2_height 18
static unsigned char dnarrow2_bits[] = {
    0x00, 0x00, 0x00, 0x00, 0x00, 0x00,
    0xfc, 0xff, 0x00, 0xf8, 0x7f, 0x00,
    0xf8, 0x7f, 0x00, 0xf0, 0x3f, 0x00,
    0xf0, 0x3f, 0x00, 0xe0, 0x1f, 0x00,
    0xc0, 0x0f, 0x00, 0xc0, 0x0f, 0x00,
    0x80, 0x07, 0x00, 0x80, 0x07, 0x00,
    0x00, 0x03, 0x00, 0x00, 0x00, 0x00,
    0x00, 0x00, 0x00, 0xfc, 0xff, 0x00,
    0xfc, 0xff, 0x00, 0x00, 0x00, 0x00};
"
image create bitmap dnarrow -data $dnarrow_data


set drop_test_var "Unset"
global drop_test_var


proc test_value { } {
    global drop_test_var


    puts "Value of variable=$drop_test_var"
    exit
}


# Test procedure creating a drop-down list.
proc test_drop_list { } {
    global drop_test_var


    #
```

```tcl
    # This drop list holds font families.
    #
set families [font families]
set sorted [lsort $families]


    #
    # Determine initial value.
    # Enclose in quotes because it may
    # have spaces in the value.
    #
set initial_value [lindex $sorted 0]


    # Create drop list.
set list [DropListCreate .font "Font: " \
    40 8 drop_test_var "$initial_value"]


    # Fill in drop list with font families.
foreach family $sorted {
    $list insert end $family
}


    button .quit -text "Exit" -command test_value
    pack .quit -side bottom
}


    # Comment out next line to remove test code.
test_drop_list


# droplist.tcl
```

To create a drop-down list, you call the DropListCreate procedure with the name of the frame widget to create in the interface, the width and height of the drop-down list to create, the name of a global variable that gets the results, and an initial value.

The DropListCreate procedure returns the name of the list widget it creates so you can fill in the list with values. The test_drop_list procedure calls DropListCreate and then fills in the list with font family names, a handy source of test data.

The DropListCreate procedure creates a frame widget, and then a label, entry, and button for the main part of the interface. DropListCreate then creates a toplevel widget for the drop-down list. The wm withdraw command hides the window, so it does not appear on the display. You can reverse this process by calling wm deiconify.

Note the use of upvar when accessing a variable that you have only the name of.

The DropListClick procedure, private to the internals of the drop list routines, handles a button click in the listbox. The selected list value is placed into the entry widget. The DropListSetVal procedure takes the value in the entry widget and fills in the global variable.

When the user clicks on the down-arrow button, the ShowDropList makes the drop list visible. It uses the winfo rootx and winfo rooty commands to get the global coordinates of the associated entry widget. This makes the drop list appear wherever the entry widget is located. The main reason for this code is to take care of the case where the entry widget gets moved to another screen location. This happens if the user moves the main toplevel window the entry widget is part of.

When the user makes a selection, the global variable passed to DropListCreate gets set with the new value.

All together, this makes a workable drop-down list. When pulled down, this list looks like what is shown in Figure 7.14.

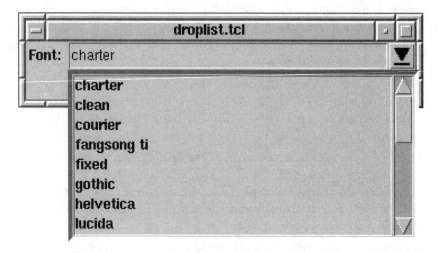

Figure 7.14 A drop-down list with the list pulled down.

There are a number of other means to create drop-down lists. If you don't like the behavior of the widgets shown, you can experiment to see if you get the behavior and look you want.

Summary

This chapter introduced the `toplevel` widget, used to make dialog windows and other top-level application windows.

The `tk_messageBox` command creates modal convenience dialog windows, such as error, warning, and information dialog windows. The `tk_getOpenFile` command creates a open file dialog window and `tk_getSaveFile` creates a save as file dialog window.

To make a dialog window into a modal dialog window, you can use the `tkwait` command. The `tkwait` command waits until one of three conditions happens: a variable's value changes, a widget becomes visible on the screen, or a widget gets destroyed.

The `wm geometry` command allows you to position any `toplevel` widget.

The `wm protocol` command allows you to trap the `WM_DELETE_WIN-DOW` message, which is really the *Close* choice on the window menu.

You can build drop-down lists using `wm overrideredirect` to make the `toplevel` widget not have any window manager decorations.

The next chapter covers bitmap images (briefly introduced in this chapter), color images, and the canvas widget.

Tcl/Tk Commands Introduced in This Chapter

```
tk_chooseColor
tk_dialog
tk_getOpenFile
tk_getSaveFile
tk_messageBox
tkwait
toplevel
winfo
wm
```

Bitmaps, Images and the canvas Widget

This chapter covers:

- Bitmaps
- Creating bitmaps From X bitmap files
- Images
- Creating images from GIF files
- Creating images from PPM files
- Toolbars
- The `canvas` widget
- Creating drawing items in the `canvas` widget
- Generating PostScript output from the `canvas` widget
- Displaying thumbnail images

Images and Bitmaps

Modern graphical interfaces display a plethora of small images in toolbars, product logos, and just about everything else. Tk supports two types of images, called `bitmap` and `photo`. The `bitmap` type supports only images with a foreground and background color, called **monochrome images**. The `photo` type supports GIF and PPM color images with up to 24 bits of color, more than you need for most programs.

Tcl extensions such as the Img extension on the CD-ROM, provide additional images formats, especially JPEG. See the **contrib/extend** directory.

You create both kinds of images with the `image create` command. The next sections show how to create monochrome bitmaps and then images. After that, you'll find a number of commands for manipulating images.

Image Names

Every requires a unique name (if you don't provide one, Tk will). To use an already created image, you need to know this name. To create one, you provide the new name. To delete one, you also need this name.

Built-In Bitmaps

You can create a `bitmap` with the `image create bitmap` command. Or, you can use one of the built-in bitmaps supplied by Tk. Table 8.1 lists these bitmaps.

Table 8.1 Tk's built-in bitmaps.

Name
error
gray12
gray25
gray50
gray75
hourglass
info
questhead
question
warning

N O T E   The `gray75` bitmap is only available starting with Tk 8.0.

To show all Tk's built-in bitmaps and their names, you can use the following code:

```
# Displays Tcl's built-in bitmaps.

#
# Displays a bitmap inside a frame with
# a label describing the name.
#
proc display_bitmap { widgetname bitmap } {

    frame $widgetname -bd 0

    label $widgetname.bitmap -bitmap $bitmap
    label $widgetname.text -text $bitmap

    pack $widgetname.bitmap -side top -fill x
    pack $widgetname.text -side bottom

    pack $widgetname -side left -padx 10
}

set bitmap_list \
  { error hourglass info question questhead warning }

lappend bitmap_list gray12 gray25 gray50

if { $tk_version >= 8.0 } {
    lappend bitmap_list gray75
}

foreach bit $bitmap_list {
```

```
        display_bitmap .$bit $bit
}
```

```
# bitmap1.tcl
```

This leads to a window like that shown in Figure 8.1.

Figure 8.1 Tk's built-in bitmaps.

As shown in the **bitmap1.tcl** example, you can display a bitmap inside a widget such as a `label` widget. Tk allows you to display bitmaps inside `button`, `checkbutton`, `radiobutton`, `label` and `menubutton` widgets; however, you should not place a bitmap on the menu bar, because this violates both the Windows and Motif style guides. Inside menus, you can use bitmaps with the menu's `add` command. You can also place bitmaps in the `text` and `canvas` widgets.

To place a bitmap into most widgets (`menu`, `canvas`, and `text` widgets are exceptions), you use the `-bitmap` option in place of the more common `-text` option. For example, to place a bitmap inside a `label` widget, you can use the following code as an example:

```
label .label -bitmap error
```

If the built-in bitmaps shown in Figure 8.1 don't appeal, you can create your own. Either you can use the `-bitmap` option with a file name or you can create a bitmap with the `image` command and use the `-image` option. If you use the `-bitmap` option, you need to follow a special syntax:

```
-bitmap built_in_name
-bitmap @filename
```

If you don't use a built-in bitmap, you must precede the *filename* with an @ character. The *filename* must be the name of a validly formatted X bitmap file.

If you use the *@filename* syntax, remember that the bitmap file must be available when your script gets executed. This usually means you have to install the bitmap files to a known location and then provide a full file name path with the *@filename* syntax. For example,

```
@/usr/local/lib/wunderword/logo.xbm
```

Windows users are at a loss with X bitmap files, because there are few Windows tools that can create or convert X bitmaps. Your best bet is to create such images on UNIX.

WINDOWS

Creating Bitmaps from X Bitmap Files

For bitmap images, Tk supports the X Window System's bitmap file format. This format is quite simple in nature, and a bitmap file looks like a snippet of C code, as follows:

```
#define warning_width 6
#define warning_height 19
static unsigned char warning_bits[] = {
 0x0c, 0x16, 0x2b, 0x15,
 0x2b, 0x15, 0x2b, 0x16,
 0x0a, 0x16, 0x0a, 0x16,
 0x0a, 0x00, 0x00, 0x1e,
 0x0a, 0x16, 0x0a};
```

This format is quite convenient because it is entirely made up of ASCII text and you can include the data directly in C and C++ programs.

To create a bitmap from a file of this type, you can use the `image create bitmap` command, which takes the following form:

```
image create bitmap name options
```

The *name* is a unique name you give to refer to the bitmap.

There are a number of options to control the new bitmap, as shown in Table 8.2.

Table 8.2 Bitmap creation options.

Option	Usage
-background *color*	Sets image background color.
-data *datastring*	Uses data in *datastring*, must be in X Bitmap format.
-file *filename*	Loads data from file.
-foreground *color*	Sets image foreground color.
-maskdata *datastring*	Specifies bitmap data to use as a mask; must be in X Bitmap format.
-maskfile *filename*	Specifies a bitmap file to use as a mask; must be a file in X Bitmap format.

To create a bitmap image from raw bitmap data, you can use the following code:

```
set bitmap_data "
#define peace16_width 16
#define peace16_height 16
static unsigned char peace16_bits[] = {
    0xf0, 0x07, 0xb8, 0x0e,
    0x8c, 0x18, 0x86, 0x30,
    0x83, 0x60, 0x83, 0x60,
    0x81, 0x40, 0x81, 0x40,
    0xc1, 0x41, 0xa3, 0x62,
    0x93, 0x64, 0x8e, 0x38,
    0x8c, 0x18, 0xb8, 0x0e,
    0xf0, 0x07, 0x00, 0x00};"

# Create bitmap.
image create bitmap peace16 -data $bitmap_data

# Use bitmap within label widget.
label .bitmap -image peace16
```

```
label .label -text "16-by-16 pixel Peace sign"

pack .bitmap .label

# bitmap2.tcl
```

In the **bitmap2.tcl** script, you should pay attention to a few points:

- The bitmap data gets enclosed with double quotes to allow the data to span multiple lines. You could also use curly braces for the same effect.

- The label widget has its -image option set to the newly created image's name. Note that this is not the -bitmap option. Images created with the image command require the -image option, an important distinction. It's sometimes hard to keep track of whether a bitmap image was created with the image command, which requires the -image option or using the -bitmap option.

When you execute these commands, you'll see a bitmap like the one shown in Figure 8.2.

Figure 8.2 Creating a bitmap label.

Note that we use a -image option (not a -bitmap option), because we created the bitmap with the image command and didn't use a built-in bitmap, like error. This can be confusing, because both commands are used to specify bitmaps in this case.

To create a bitmap image from an X Bitmap file, you can use the following code, which is almost exactly the same, except from the source of the data:

```
# Create bitmap.
```

```
image create bitmap peace16 -file peace16.xbm

# Use bitmap within label widget.
label .bitmap -image peace16

label .label -text "16-by-16 pixel Peace sign"

pack .bitmap .label

# bitmap3.tcl
```

To make this work, you must have a file with the bitmap data, such as the following one (and in the earlier example, the file must be named **peace16.xbm**):

```
#define peace16_width 16
#define peace16_height 16
static unsigned char peace16_bits[] = {
    0xf0, 0x07, 0xb8, 0x0e,
    0x8c, 0x18, 0x86, 0x30,
    0x83, 0x60, 0x83, 0x60,
    0x81, 0x40, 0x81, 0x40,
    0xc1, 0x41, 0xa3, 0x62,
    0x93, 0x64, 0x8e, 0x38,
    0x8c, 0x18, 0xb8, 0x0e,
    0xf0, 0x07, 0x00, 0x00};
```

The data string specified from the -data option and the contents of the file specified from the -file option must be in the same format.

NOTE

Many of the example bitmaps that come with Tk use a *.bmp* file extension, short for bitmap. The problem is that these Tk bitmap files are really stored in X Bitmap format, not the more recognizable Windows BMP format. If you try to use a BMP image in Tk (without custom programming) or treat a Tk *.bmp* file as a BMP image, you'll experience problems due to the differing image file formats.

WARNING

Following Internet convention, I name all my X Bitmap files with a *.xbm* extension to avoid confusion.

Creating X Bitmap Files

You can create the files used for Tk bitmaps from the X Window program called **bitmap**. You can also use a number of image file conversion programs, including **PBM** (mentioned in more detail in the section on PPM images), **ImageMagick** or **xv**. These are UNIX utilities. There are very few Windows or Macintosh programs that create images in X bitmap format. Virtually every Web browser will read them, however.

Photo Images

Tk calls color images **photo** images. For this type, you can use images in CompuServe GIF format or the PPM from the Portable Bitmap (PBM) suite of image conversion programs. To create such an image, the basic syntax follows:

```
image create photo name options
```

Photo images are stored internally using 24 bits of color per pixel, which can use up a lot of memory. On low-color systems, Tk automatically dithers the images.

Table 8.3 lists the options when creating a photo image.

Table 8.3 Photo image options.

Option	Usage
`-channel` *channel_id*	Provides the ID of an open channel for reading the data.
`-data` *datastring*	Specifies image data is held in *datastring*; must be in base64 format.
`-format` *type*	Specifies the image format: `gif`, `ppm`, or `pgm`.
`-file` *filename*	Uses the given *filename* for the image data.

continued

Table 8.3 continued

-gamma *gammavalue*	Tells the image command to perform gamma correction with the given value, which defaults to 1 (no correction).
-height *size*	Controls the size of the image, in pixels.
-palette *colorpalette*	Controls the color palette.
-width *size*	Controls the size of the image, in pixels.

Creating Images from GIF Files

GIF images are extremely common—much more so that PPM images, especially due to the World Wide Web. To load a GIF image from a file named **rngbrod6.gif**, you can use the following command:

```
image create photo ring_brodgar -file rngbrod6.gif
```

You can then display this image in a label widget (or any other widget that accepts a -image option), as shown here:

```
# Creating a photo image from a GIF file.
image create photo ring_brodgar -file rngbrod6.gif

label .image -image ring_brodgar
pack .image

# image1.tcl
```

With large images, you'll experience a noticeable delay when executing these commands. Figure 8.3 shows the completed widget.

Figure 8.3 The Ring of Brodgar in Orkney in a Tk label widget.

Using Base64 Encoding

The advantage of X bitmap files is that you can include the bitmap data in your Tcl script. By placing the image data in your Tcl script, you do not require an external file. Every external file requires the ability to find the file based on the current installation and complicates your scripts. If you can avoid having extra files beyond the one script file, your code can be a lot simpler. (Most of my Tcl scripts require some external files. The key is to keep the list as small as possible.)

To go along with the main advantage of X bitmap files, you have two disadvantages. First, X bitmap files are monochrome. You lose the ability to display a colored image. Second, X bitmap files are hard to create on Windows. (UNIX systems should have the program **bitmap**. Other good programs include **xv** and **ImageMagick**.)

Starting with Tk versions higher than 4.2, you can include color image data in your Tcl scripts, if that data are encoded in **base64** format, a format commonly used with e-mail attachments.

So, you can convert GIF images to base64 encoding. In this format, the image data is all ASCII text, so you can include the data in your Tcl script file, as shown here:

```
# Example of base64 encoding for a GIF image.

set data "
```

```
R0lGODdhUgBsANUAAP///wgICBAQEBgYGCkpKUJCQlJSUmtra3Nzc3t7e4SEhJSUlKWlpa2trcbG
xufn5/f39721ta2lpWJZWUk4MCAPB2I4F4tZMGtCIcakhMWTYkoxGINRIMV6MEIpEK1qKeesa7WT
a9WkasaLQoxyUotiKNabQq16MeasUd61Ss2TODAgB96kQpNyMGtRIda8hOa8Sda1SjAoD/bVUbWb
Of/uY4ODciEpIUl6cmOlpVKMjDljYyhJSTkxOQAAAAAACwAAAAAUgBsAEUG/0CfcEgsGo/IpHLJ
ZAaa0KhOOiwsesPB40YkOIqMQXdBjBQPCAWxcCAeDMOeg1F8PIqTCbVJ2PtVGz4dFz4DJH5DEQAP
NgJVABCRDxBfVRIAAHBMBpAQDwARJSgqJjEwMzU1MzQzLS0oLBx9iEUFkJOSRTe4nlm3EABPnJIQ
ZkMvIj0tLBcvJgQBFgm0R7bEvV2/kw9PQwE9fcO4DmLUTAKdwIsOke2SEYrpED4IC7zAsz49ODpD
Ajw8upmbwiDdJzVK2EnKROQShAmOBiIq6CkSgGkJ2x30wesTHYkgQ4ocKaSCkQACjwQwWYQlyZcD
K3DAkBKmTSQolQTw4MHCBv8LK1b4qPChBIajgYh4wODSBwcVFnwG4vCBpQUVHoR0sCAEKFcfGIQO
8cChyNYmu4jcgNCAyACGQ8KMUQshopC2RLAJedOwkhABCz4KMeBXpY+aNxNL2SGGhxgCXBCDJMHi
BQhSKFz5iDEjhQkVI7DsKVdrEbE7iIZVxOtABQsWG1pg4JwihmcVIOyas8ar8AJt85Rw6i3ZpgCU
x1EqX65byPKcRJA/hw5zgAPEFBciBDNLoScAonns4EHgH0DIxW8W5AVgOxLvn/LcwqsYyY0C8TDp
1//gAGKGkhBBS0HyZX+PAbJPvRl5gMMqzk3BMMbMBVINLEFsIEHTdVHxYUXJOX/wQYVHCWDcxj4AGJJ
HHAFYgUbcHCBDBaM6ANPM3JQw1A+1CBDBBR9GEcANAQzAABdECNBcITpJEcCRUAwQgQwfXBCADGJp
```

aCUSVRHRQVY+fABUB2UNUYFYG3wwxAYdpETWWGZqFQhRGQpRohAlfJUjl1fmqdMD+ViHgB4AJiCY
D3INQQAZiRjRxhqA7qWJPnMUqQCiQijQ6BENLNAnN3MRwYBoAFLqgxVuMCBqAQgQgcCjAyhgzBB2
FOkAqHqG9CNIxw3BhWj5vCQDCB2IMEIKJ5hggmcfEEDBf1IIykADDcAjLTwOVFvtA9c6MEkBS1Tw
yYBkGGAsCzC04IILNNTQ/8IGMnDAggkdxMmEA4MKYU1FsRoBwKVJDPedAgmkoEIKNLRQQgsyUEAD
Kyik0AEIGEg5kC24bHMEAfFcp88ikIjm7ydtNYOBBqQYq8IyLKgQApO0UNxbHe4U5sN9oKoGTASI
ESCavBL18IsnqMG6jUfCmRaJAyzDpDMFCtnxnabgDEHBNu0g+ABeAyCwyDb7MlvrQAHs4AN59QUQ
yaNCrFdRe0UMM0TTwGARQA6O6NDr191Z5N4R8ME1AQOTKjDpAhjpmd0kbGe0EKAGRHI33p0gvrcR
3mlUUSS0Qs7e5EVUDgGiAjgt+dekl2766c6VVEQ31MHEIJQyLBXhSjKAyP9uBbWntBOPPKooowcB
0HSYjKgX7w8F4KRn/GEFJDDAAAVUECc4oKTEQz9C8JCFrkWMh8QAOAgRvnM6OHJe9kLcAJAQYnsD
oADQLC///E5U0DpK0kNh/0qsu6Rc6tF5UABXp7whcKBKQ+nGB7hUpugEgCoC8UCbZuKDFYRpRm0S
RCBWcKMjrCArHLigUxCYBKII5EVC4EBSLMCBblhAICXwECGUMicMKpBLZGFdVjBEhAOmEE94+toT
hogcAUjviEhMovQYNKbXrSA934hOAYjknAKk5G4BuBuQiJC5AlBALbq5wX9+dLfMFQEdVNTCARpF
ABsMigG6ORQRFIA2H0j/oBZoW1UcIuWPBYiqQEpoQJ+K4RYIuAeOnUpbEXrQA25J7VJ6FIIcRBUA
BRTGSUqARz68dcW9IdJQf+zVARwgqh4sylF7rJde7MW5SlXgUQKQQEoGwK8DLEAgA0DbAG4Zh0aq
5Ytx6BWqomMAtDWPfsi0UgAO4YMJMJMkuQqA9mzywBsQYFgkM8ECRnACaghgBzfoAUrUF7YBTBOa
h1mGazDQApPBSwMgmOFLWDedJizJSPh8AgZUMDAWnMAFMOBmu+AlggkUEAmKAIYdrnYPi0RgAdr6
BDDqeIQbHGBrC/3AsFKQglNswAXqikEpTsCCNO2hARDo4tY0YgQFwGUJ/8NBHBkWAAsUrCIAMVBF
DGRAg3epoKBU+CQXf0aJIxhAVP36BQAy8IEPmIAFKcBAuhbWghk0LGXPnBhRZdaFCBQDopNQABX9
BYw7DsA1JaNBCWBAgxS85gRUqeFuInc0IxBAoRBY1FsuJ4yf4SxXL+gAR586MA10AAU8Q8S9hlYE
rYluDcB4yGBWWgyBuEAIJBiBDyigWQCCxGeWC5o+KrZKo95iEhrT02JzMQQEuONsRQMaJZJ2E4oR
Q2a/cccWkko1pNXKZ6R9ALMmYBBKKKAABHBVBPTwMU/QdiQEGJA6EKSfS/6Gau3JRwOoS93CJbNJ
jvAaTKZjpOmgZADJWf9OIdD7nCIQAAflLVs7HGAAAphku+4AABm+YQDGCoEdVJvFDggAPm8kzzgA
cKSn5JE4IjTubZdLqRB0wAUB4GB8PsBndWxwBIrgosFEWIAmANwOBWd4gLXysN6WADcIaMIe39ra
q/KkYmC0EsK8OGUCIPE4wzH4xv8lBgDacFEFma7GIObbNRLaDoqm+McsNhoEEKC1y4HnyAZJMuWu
QYbQ5ZfDQvTqNYSrOFzQh7ga2deVCqAABBzgzXCG8wQOoIDMTcDNcX6zHteYhz4b4AAH/a6gBz2S
QJtuf6wTQuzyNyX+Ee+7GLjQUXzSgaG8iBAMeqKMLsCBnnwoKcGLhv2znMIVF4EleI8myUpwh5IG
uWRFJaJdmHZkEvvxaCgssR1LWDS/pOBIJUM83QY6dJgNbMBCxxYCu2rCoCkNbwBNwd9hkDjtwxia
0NgOCQUmYAMK9Nhe3Hqu8UwSPK44KDoyeMsDFCCQHuzAjO07AkBYRpqIDGAHTxiAGNNnKH/YZQPc
WtKqEFOAHlA0OSARwxUNkz27nJMIGhBhtudpTwIeJnWJvrhy0puTjps3J474nxAQEAQAOw==
"

```
image create photo tcltkcov -data $data
label .l -image tcltkcov
pack .l

# base64.tcl
```

When you run the **base64.tcl** script, you should see a small image.

To get your GIF image to base64 encoding, you can often take advantage of MIME-compliant e-mail programs. Convert your image to an attachment and save the attachment data. In addition, I find the freeware programs **uudeview** and **uenview** very helpful.

The UNIX version of **uudeview/uenview** is located on the CD-ROM in the **contrib/uudeview** directory. You can also look on the Internet at: **http://zeus.informatik.uni-frankfurt.de/%7Efp/uudeview/**. The Windows version is available on the Internet at **http://www.miken.com/uud/**.

CD-ROM

Using base64 image data requires a Tk version higher than 4.2.

N O T E

Creating Images from PPM Files

In addition to GIF images, which are very popular for the Windows and Macintosh platforms (and are used heavily in World Wide Web pages), you can create images from PPM and PGM data files. Both formats are internal formats used by the PBM, or portable bitmap, suite of freeware image conversion programs. To convert an image file from one format to another, PBM works by having you convert the image, say in GIF format, to a PBM internal format, such as PPM, and then converting the data to the desired output format, such as Windows BMP format. The PPM and PGM formats hold the intermediary data.

The reason for this was to avoid having to write a GIF to BMP converter, then a GIF to Macintosh PICT converter, and then a BMP to Macintosh PICT converter, and so on. Instead, each program in the PBM suite converts to and from the PBM internal formats. This allows a very small number of programs to convert data from almost any image file format to any other.

To create an image in one of these formats, you use the same command as before—only you use a file in a different format, as shown here:

```
# Creating a photo image from a PPM file.
image create photo eric_face -file ericface.ppm

label .face -image eric_face
```

```
pack .face

# image2.tcl
```

You can see the representation of a face in Figure 8.4.

Figure 8.4 A PPM image in a label widget.

There are two main formats for PPM and PGM images: **raw** and **ASCII**. For the image command, your images must be in PPM and PGM raw data format.

N O T E

Commands on Images

When a photo image is created, you can use the name of the image as a command, just like for widgets. Photo images support a number of options, including blank, copy, and write.

To blank an image, which makes it transparent, use blank:

```
imagename blank
```

To copy parts of an image, use the following:

```
imagename copy sourceimagename
```

With the copy option, you can control what part is copied and where it will appear in the image. Table 8.4. lists some of these options.

Table 8.4 Image copy options.

Option	Usage
`-from` *x1 y1 x2 y2*	Copy the given area from the source image.
`-to` *x1 y1 x2 y2*	Place the source data in the given area in the target image.
`-shrink`	Shrink the target image data.
`-zoom` *mag_x mag_y*	Magnify the width by a factor of *mag_x*, height by a factor of *mag_y*.
`-subsample` *x y*	Shrinks image by skipping pixels; only uses every *x*th pixel in X direction and *y*th pixel in Y direction.

You can also use the common `configure` option to change values in an image. The `configure` option supports the same options as the `create` option, listed in Table 8.3.

The main commands on images are listed in Table 8.5.

Table 8.5 Commands on created images.

Command	Usage
imagename `blank`	Blanks the image
imagename `cget` *option*	Returns value for given option.
imagename `configure` *option value*	Changes the image in some way.
imagename `copy` *source_image*	Copies *source_image*. See Table 8.4 for options.
imagename `get` *x y*	Returns value of color at x,y; returns list of red, green, blue values, from 0 to 255 each.

continued

Table 8.5 continued

imagename put *data* \ -to *x1 y1 x2 y2* to	Changes colors in a part of image to that of *data*; optional -to specifies exact area (defaults whole image).
imagename read *filename options*	Reads in data from file name and applies it to image. See Table 8.6 for options.
imagename redither	Redithers image. (Images are stored internally with 24 bits of color per pixel.)
imagename write *filename options*	Writes data to disk. See Table 8.6 for options.

You can write out an image with the write option:

imagename write *filename options*

Table 8.6 lists the options for reading and writing.

Table 8.6 Image options for reading and writing.

Option	**Usage**
-format *format*	Defines format of image data, e.g., gif.
-from *x1 y1 x2 y2*	Specifies area of image read in to use.
-shrink	Shrink image, if necessary.
-to *x y*	Specifies area to place read in data.

The write option only supports -format and -from.

Deleting Images

You can delete a named image with the `image delete` command:

```
image delete name
```

Images, especially photo images, use a lot of computer memory. When you're done with an image, you should delete it.

N O T E

Querying Images

You can query the size or type of a given image. You can also check the available types of images and the images already defined.

To get the size of an image, use the `image width` and `image height` commands:

```
set w [image width name]
set h [image height name]
```

To get the type of an image, use the `image type` command:

```
set t [image type name]
```

To get a list of all available image types, use the `image types` command:

```
% image types
photo bitmap
```

Most Tk systems only support `bitmap` and `photo` image types.

Don't confuse the `image type` with the `image types` command.

WARNING

To get a list of all created images, use the `image names` command:

```
image names
```

The Main Window Revisited

Chapter 4 on menus covers style guide issues and common layouts for most application windows. Virtually all graphical applications start with a menu bar at the top, a main area underneath, and a status area at the bottom. With bitmaps under out belt, we can now extend this to include a toolbar under the menu bar. Many applications, such as Microsoft Word, sport a bitmap toolbar that gets placed, by default, immediately under the menu bar.

Creating Toolbars

In Tk, a toolbar is merely a set of `button` widgets inside a `frame` and packed horizontally (with the `-side left` option). Each `button` widget provides a shortcut to perform a task from the menus. Thus, creating a toolbar is relatively easy.

To group toolbar items, you can create `label` widgets that display a number of spaces as separators. Or, you can create sub-`frame` widgets and place all `button` widgets that form a group into the `frame`. I usually configure the `frame` to have zero border width and then `pack` the `frames` with the `padx` option to provide some space between the `frames`.

For example, you can use the following script as a guide for creating toolbars:

```
# Example toolbar.

#
# Create images for toolbar bitmaps.
# These files are on the CD-ROM.
#
image create bitmap tool_new -file toolbar/new.xbm
image create bitmap tool_open -file toolbar/open.xbm
image create bitmap tool_save -file toolbar/save.xbm
```

```
image create bitmap tool_cut -file toolbar/cut.xbm
image create bitmap tool_copy -file toolbar/copy.xbm
image create bitmap tool_paste -file toolbar/paste.xbm

  # Old way to create a menu bar.
frame .menubar -relief raised -borderwidth 1

#
# File menu.
#
menubutton .menubar.file -text "File" \
   -underline 0 -menu .menubar.file.menu
pack .menubar.file -side left

menu .menubar.file.menu

.menubar.file.menu add command -label "New" \
  -underline 0 -command { puts "New" }
.menubar.file.menu add command -label "Open..." \
  -underline 0 -command { puts "Open" }

.menubar.file.menu add separator
.menubar.file.menu add command -label "Exit" \
  -underline 1 -command { exit }

 # Edit menu.
menubutton .menubar.edit -text "Edit" \
  -menu .menubar.edit.menu -underline 0
pack .menubar.edit -side left

menu .menubar.edit.menu

.menubar.edit.menu add command -label "Cut" \
  -underline 2 -accelerator "Ctrl+X"

.menubar.edit.menu add command -label "Copy" \
  -underline 0 -accelerator "Ctrl+C"

.menubar.edit.menu add command -label "Paste" \
```

```tcl
  -underline 0 -accelerator "Ctrl+V"

  # Create a faked main area.
label .main -text "Main Area" -background white \
   -relief sunken -bd 1

pack .menubar -side top -fill x -expand true


  ##################################
  # Toolbar
  ##################################


frame .toolbar -bd 2 -relief raised

  # Group for new, open, save.
set frm .toolbar.file_group
frame $frm -bd 0

button $frm.new -image tool_new -command {puts new}
button $frm.open -image tool_open -command {puts open}
button $frm.save -image tool_save -command {puts save}
pack $frm.new $frm.open $frm.save -side left
pack $frm -side left

  # Set up short help.
bind $frm.new <Enter> \
  ".status configure -text {Clear and start new}"
bind $frm.new <Leave> \
  ".status configure -text { }"

bind $frm.open <Enter> \
  ".status configure -text {Open file}"
bind $frm.open <Leave> \
  ".status configure -text { }"

bind $frm.save <Enter> \
  ".status configure -text {Save file}"
bind $frm.save <Leave> \
```

```
  ".status configure -text { }"

  # Group for cut, copy, paste.
set frm .toolbar.clip_group
frame $frm -bd 0

button $frm.cut -image tool_cut -command {puts cut}
button $frm.copy -image tool_copy -command {puts copy}
button $frm.paste -image tool_paste -command {puts paste}
pack $frm.cut $frm.copy $frm.paste -side left

bind $frm.cut <Enter> \
  ".status configure -text {Cut}"
bind $frm.cut <Leave> \
  ".status configure -text { }"

bind $frm.copy <Enter> \
  ".status configure -text {Copy}"
bind $frm.copy <Leave> \
  ".status configure -text { }"

bind $frm.paste <Enter> \
  ".status configure -text {Paste}"
bind $frm.paste <Leave> \
  ".status configure -text { }"

  # Pack second group with X padding to space out.
pack $frm -side left -padx 10

pack .toolbar -side top -fill x

pack .main -ipady 100 -ipadx 200 -expand true -side top

#
# Status area.
#
label .status -relief sunken \
  -anchor w -borderwidth 1 \
```

```
    -text "Status"

pack .status -fill x -side bottom
```

```
# toolbar.tcl
```

When you run this script, you'll see a toolbar like that shown in Figure 8.5.

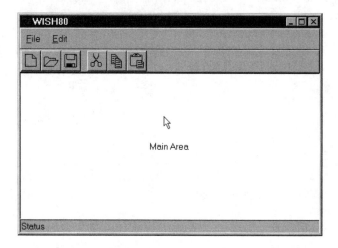

Figure 8.5 A toolbar.

The **toolbar.tcl** script creates a number of images from X Bitmap data, based on the Windows interface style guidelines (see Appendix A for books on interface guidelines). Note the two groups of bitmaps: one set for new, open, and save and the other for cut, copy, and paste. These images are in the **book/toolbar** directory on the CD-ROM.

Help On Toolbars

In addition to displaying a toolbar, it's also very common for graphical applications to provide short help on items inside the toolbar. Normally, this is done when the mouse enters the `button` in the toolbar. A short message appears in the status area (usually a `label` widget) that describes the toolbar `button`.

Another common form of help is where a small window pops up with a short help message. Called *tooltips* help, you can find out more on this in Chapter 11. For now, we'll stick to placing short help messages in the status area.

To implement short help on the toolbar, we can use the `bind` command to trap `Enter` events in each of the `buttons`. On the `Enter` event, the `bind` script should set the `-text` option for a `label` widget at the bottom of the window, used for the status area (see Chapter 4 for more of a discussion on the status area).

You also want to bind `Leave` events to clear the status area, so that the user doesn't think other widgets perform a given operation due to a tardy help message.

The following code, from the **toolbar.tcl** script, sets up help on a file open button:

```
bind $frm.open <Enter> \
  ".status configure -text {Open file}"
bind $frm.open <Leave> \
  ".status configure -text { }"
```

You need to bind `Enter` and `Leave` events for all buttons on the toolbar to create this kind of short help message.

One of the main places you'll use images in Tcl scripts is in the `canvas` widget.

The `canvas` Widget

Tcl, even with Tk, does not make a full-fledged drawing package. You're not going to create AutoCAD or a 3D solid modeling package in Tcl, although you may well want to embed Tcl as an application customization language in such an application.

Even though Tcl is a not a graphics drawing system, you can a do a lot with the `canvas` widget, with a remarkably small number of commands.

The `canvas` widget gives you a canvas on which to place drawing items, including lines, rectangles, bitmaps, and even widgets. Once placed, the `canvas` widget takes care of drawing the items, sort of like a display list of structured graphics in 3D graphics systems. The structured graphics model means that you don't—directly—draw into the `canvas`. Instead, you place graphics items such as lines and ovals. When necessary, the `canvas` widget displays all items in the display list, going from the beginning to the end. That means that the first item created is the first to be drawn. If a later item obscures the first item, you may never even see it. Thus, it's important to watch the order in which you create drawing items. Once created, you may move graphics drawing items, change their colors, and so on.

To create a `canvas` widget, use the `canvas` command:

```
canvas .can
pack .can
```

You can control the size of the `canvas` widget with the `-width` and `-height` options, as shown here:

```
canvas .can -width 300 -height 250
pack .can
```

Creating Drawing Items in the `canvas` Widget

You can fill the `canvas` widget with a number of drawing items, such as lines and rectangles. To draw into a `canvas` widget, then, you create structured graphic items such as lines, arcs, rectangles, and so on; the `canvas` widget takes care of the rest.

The `canvas` widget uses the model of a display list for drawing. It maintains a list of items to display.

To create drawing items, use the `create` option:

```
widgetname create type x y options
```

When you create a drawing item, the command will return a number which you can use as an ID for the drawing item in subsequent commands.

Table 8.7 lists the available item types that you can create and the necessary arguments for that type of item.

Table 8.7 canvas item types.

Type	Required Data
arc	*widgetname* create arc *x1 y1 x2 y2*

bitmap	*widgetname* create bitmap *x y*
image	*widgetname* create image *x y*
line	*widgetname* create line *x1 y1 x2 y2* ...
oval	*widgetname* create oval *x1 y1 x2 y2*
polygon	*widgetname* create polygon *x1 y1 x2 y2* ...
rectangle	*widgetname* create rectangle *x1 y1 x2 y2*
text	*widgetname* create text *x y*
window	*widgetname* create window *x y*

In addition to the required data, you may add a number of options to each of the item types.

Arc Drawing Items

An arc item can draw an arc, a pie slice, or a piece of a circle (chord), bounded by a rectangle, using the following basic command:

widgetname create arc *x1 y1 x2 y2*

The *x1*, *y1*, *x2*, and *y2* arguments are for the rectangle that bounds the arc and helps define its shape.

You can specify a number of options, as shown in Table 8.8.

Table 8.8 Arc options.

Option	Usage
-extent *degrees*	The span of the arc, in degrees.
-fill *color*	If set, fills arc with given *color*; otherwise, arc is not filled.
-outline *color*	If set, outlines arc with given *color*; otherwise, arc is not outlined.

continued

Table 8.8 continued

`-start` *degrees*	Controls angle where arc starts, in degrees.
`-stipple` *bitmapname*	Fills arc by using *bitmapname* as a brush pattern.
`-style` *type*	One of `arc`, `chord`, or `pieslice` (the default).
`-tags` *taglist*	Applies all the tags in *taglist* to the item.
`-width` *outlinewidth*	Controls size of pen used to outline arc.

The following example shows how to create arc drawing items:

```
# Arc items in a canvas.
canvas .can -width 400 -height 300

.can create arc 10 20 100 200 \
    -start 45 -extent 180 \
    -fill maroon -style pieslice

.can create arc 100 20 200 200 \
    -start 0 -extent 180 \
    -outline blue -style arc \
    -width 10

.can create arc 200 20 300 200 \
    -start 180 -extent 90 \
    -outline orange -style chord

pack .can

# canarc.tcl
```

When you run the **canarc.tcl** script, you'll see arc variants as shown in Figure 8.6.

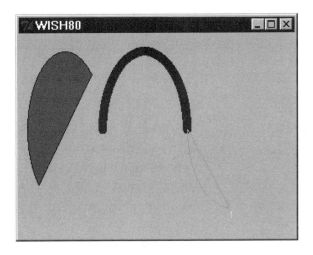

Figure 8.6 Arc drawing items.

 The way Windows and X draw items like `arcs` is slightly different, which means you won't see exactly the same arc on both systems. Windows and UNIX (really the X Window System) have different rules for how to choose which pixels lie in the outline of an arc and which lie inside.

Line Drawing Items

Lines are not the simple creatures you're used to, as reflected in the many options in Table 8.9.

Table 8.9 Line options.

Option	Usage
`-arrow none`	No arrow heads.
`-arrow first`	Arrow head on first point of line.
`-arrow last`	Arrow head on last point of line.

continued

Table 8.9 continued

-arrow both	Arrow head on both first and last point of line.
-arrowshape *shapelist*	List of three coordinates specifies how to draw arrow heads.
-capstyle *style*	How to draw ends of line. One of butt, projecting, or round.
-fill *color*	Controls line color. Defaults to black. No option creates a transparent line.
-joinstyle *style*	How to connect line segments, one of bevel, miter, or round.
-smooth 1	Draw line as a curve, with a series of Bezier splines.
-smooth 0	Draw line as a series of segments.
-splinesteps *number*	Uses *number* segments to approximate each spline.
-stipple *bitmapname*	Fills line by stippling given bitmap.
-tags *taglist*	Applies all the tags in *taglist* to the item.
-width *outlinewidth*	Controls size of pen used for drawing.

The basic command takes the following format:

```
widgetname create line x1 y1 x2 y2 ...
```

One really nice thing that Tk provides is arrow heads on either (or both) ends of the line. For example,

```
.can create line 100 10 100 100 -arrow both
```

You can use a line to go from point A to point B. Or, you can make a polyline, going from point A through point B through point C and so on. Just keep adding in coordinates, as shown in the following staircase example:

```
.can create line \
   110 10 \
   110 20 \
   120 20 \
   120 30 \
   130 30 \
   130 40
```

You can convert the lines into splines with the -smooth option:

```
.can create line \
   150 10 \
   200 45 \
   150 195 \
   -smooth 1
```

The following script shows a number of canvas line options.

```
# Line items in a canvas.
canvas .can -width 400 -height 300

.can create line 10 10 10 30 30 30 30 60 60 60 60 90 \
    -joinstyle miter -fill maroon -width 10

.can create line 110 10 110 30 130 30 130 60 160 60 160 90 \
    -joinstyle round -fill black -width 10

.can create line 210 10 210 30 230 30 230 60 260 60 260 90 \
    -joinstyle bevel -fill black -width 10

.can create line 10 210 10 230 30 230 30 260 60 260 60 290 \
    -arrow last -joinstyle round -fill maroon -width 10

.can create line 110 210 110 230 130 230 130 260 160 260 160 290 \
    -arrow first -fill black

.can create line 210 210 210 230 230 230 230 260 260 260 260 290 \
```

```
    -arrow both -fill black -smooth 1

pack .can

# canline.tcl
```

Figure 8.7 displays the lines from the **canline.tcl** script.

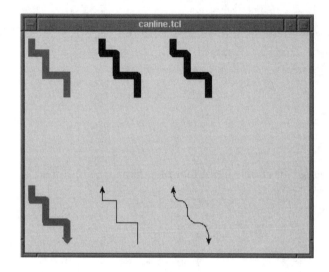

Figure 8.7 Canvas lines.

Oval Drawing Items

The oval drawing item creates an oval or a circle item from a bounding rectangle. You can fill an oval with the -fill option. This and other oval options appear in Table 8.10.

Table 8.10 Oval options

Option	Usage
-fill *color*	If set, fills oval with given *color*; otherwise, oval is not filled.
-outline *color*	If set, outlines oval with given *color*; otherwise, oval is not outlined.

-stipple *bitmapname*	Fills oval by stippling given bitmap.
-tags *taglist*	Applies all the tags in *taglist* to the item.
-width *outlinewidth*	Controls size of pen used to draw outline.

To create an oval, you can use the following command:

```
widgetname create oval  x1 y1 x2 y2
```

To try some of the options, you can use the following:

```
.can create oval 160 150 220 250 \
   -fill limegreen \
   -outline limegreen \
   -stipple gray50
```

Note the use of both the fill color and the outline color to get both to appear the same color. Otherwise, you could draw the outline in a different color.

A number of oval options are used in **canoval.tcl**:

```
# Oval items drawn in a canvas.
canvas .can -width 400 -height 300

.can create oval 160 150 220 250 \
    -outline red -fill maroon -width 10

.can create oval 10 10 200 100 \
    -outline blue

pack .can

# canoval.tcl
```

When you run this script, you'll see two ovals as shown in Figure 8.8.

480

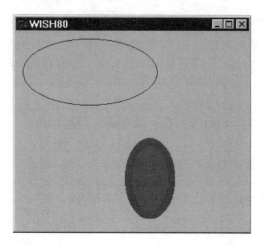

Figure 8.8 Canvas oval items.

Polygon Drawing Items

The `polygon` drawing item allows you to create many-sided figures or a smooth curved figure (using the `polygon` vertices as spline control points). Table 8.11 lists the allowed options.

Table 8.11 Polygon options

Option	Usage
-fill *color*	If set, fills polygon with given *color*; otherwise, polygon is not filled.
-outline *color*	If set, outlines polygon with given *color*; otherwise, polygon is not outlined.
-smooth 1	Draws each line in the polygon as a curve, with a series of Bezier splines.
-smooth 0	Draws each line as a series of segments.
-splinesteps *number*	Uses *number* segments to approximate each spline.

-stipple *bitmapname*	Fills polygon by stippling given bitmap.
-tags *taglist*	Applies all the tags in *taglist* to the item.
-width *outlinewidth*	Controls size of pen used to draw outline.

To create a polygon drawing item, use the following format:

widgetname create polygon *x1 y1 x2 y2 ...*

You can add as many vertices as you'd like, as shown here:

```
.can create polygon \
  220 10 \
  250 10 \
  250 30 \
  210 50 \
  220 80 \
  -fill orange
```

The following example shows the canvas polygon at work:

```
# Polygon items drawn in a canvas.

canvas .can -width 400 -height 200

.can create polygon 220 10 250 10 250 30 210 50 220 80 \
    -outline red -fill orange -width 10

.can create polygon 10 10 100 10 120 30 100 50 60 100 80 120 40 150 \
    -outline black -fill white -smooth 1
pack .can

# canpoly.tcl
```

Of the two polygons, one is smoothed and the other normal, as shown in Figure 8.9.

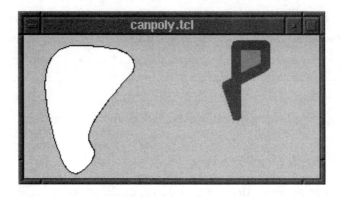

Figure 8.9 Canvas polygon items.

NOTE When working with event bindings, all points inside the `polygon`, whether it is filled or not, are considered to be inside the polygon. For `arcs`, `ovals`, and `rectangles`, the item must be filled for all points inside to be considered part of the item.

Rectangle Drawing Items

The `rectangle` drawing item allows you to create, as you'd expect, a rectangle. Table 8.12 lists the relevant options.

Table 8.12 Rectangle options

Option	Usage
`-fill` *color*	If set, fills rectangle with given *color*; otherwise, rectangle is not filled.
`-outline` *color*	If set, outlines rectangle with given *color*; otherwise, rectangle is not outlined.
`-stipple` *bitmapname*	Fills rectangle by stippling given bitmap.
`-tags` *taglist*	Applies all the tags in *taglist* to the item.
`-width` *outlinewidth*	Controls size of pen used to draw outline.

The `rectangle` command follows the usual form:

```
widgetname create rectangle x1 y1 x2 y2
```

For example,

```
.can create rectangle \
  265 200 300 230
```

Two rectangles appear in the **canrect.tcl** script:

```
# Rectangle items drawn in a canvas.

canvas .can -width 400 -height 200

.can create rectangle 20 10 150 110 \
    -outline red -fill orange -width 10

.can create rectangle 160 10 240 180 \
    -outline black

pack .can

# canrect.tcl
```

When you run the **canrect.tcl** script, you'll see rectangles as shown in Figure 8.10.

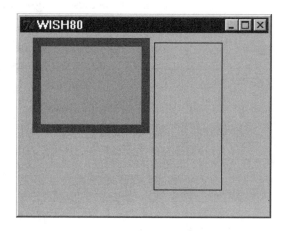

Figure 8.10 Canvas rectangles.

Text Drawing Items

The `text` item exists to place more than a display-only text string into the canvas. You can select text in a `text` drawing item. In your scripts, you can append, insert, and delete characters. As such, the `text` drawing item is a lot like the `entry` widget.

The basic `text` item command follows:

```
widgetname create text x y
```

The major options appear in Table 8.13.

Table 8.13 Text options

Option	Usage
`-anchor` *position*	One of `n`, `s`, `e`, `w`, `ne`, `nw`, `se`, `sw`, or `center`.
`-fill` *color*	If set, fills text with given *color*; otherwise, the default color is black.
`-font` *fontname*	Names font to use for the text. See Chapter 3 for more on fonts.
`-justify` *justification*	One of `left`, `right`, or `center`.
`-stipple` *bitmapname*	Fills text by stippling given bitmap.
`-tags` *taglist*	Applies all the tags in *taglist* to the item.
`-text` *textstring*	Sets text to *textstring*.
`-width` *linelength*	Controls maximum length of a line of text.

You can create a `text` item with the following command:

```
.can create text 150 130 \
  -text "Tk Canvas Widget"
```

For example,

```
# Text items drawn in a canvas.
```

```
if { $tk_version >= 8.0 } {
    font create textfont -family Helvetica -size 24

    set fontname textfont
} else {
    set fontname "-*-helvetica-bold-r-normal-24-*-*-*-*-*-*"
}

canvas .can -width 400 -height 200

.can create text 20 40 -anchor w \
    -text "Tk Canvas Widget" -fill orange

.can create text 100 160 -font $fontname \
    -text "Text item" -fill blue

pack .can

# cantext.tcl
```

The **cantext.tcl** script uses two fonts, the default and a larger size Helvetica font, as shown in Figure 8.11.

Figure 8.11 Canvas text items, showing different fonts.

The focus option sets the keyboard focus to a canvas item:

```
widgetname focus tag
widgetname focus id
```

The `focus` option takes either a tag name (described in the section on naming drawing items) or an ID number, such as returned by the `create text` option.

Bitmap Drawing Items

A `bitmap` item has a foreground and background color only. (For color images, use the `image` drawing item.) Table 8.14 lists the available options.

Table 8.14 Bitmap options

Option	Usage
`-anchor` *position*	One of n, s, e, w, nw, ne, sw, se, or `center`.
`-background` *color*	Controls background color.
`-bitmap` *bitmapname*	Specifies which bitmap to display.
`-foreground` *color*	Controls foreground color.
`-tags` *taglist*	Applies all the tags in *taglist* to the item.

You'll almost always need the `-bitmap` option to specify the actual bitmap to display. The command to create a `bitmap` item takes the following format:

```
widgetname create bitmap x y
```

The following example shows some of the built-in bitmap images, as well as how to use an X Bitmap file in a `canvas` bitmap item:

```
# Bitmap items in a canvas.
canvas .can -width 400 -height 100

set x 40
set y 30
set ty [expr $y + 30]

foreach bit {error warning question hourglass @tv.xbm} {
```

```
    .can create bitmap $x $y -bitmap $bit
    .can create text $x $ty -text $bit

    incr x 70
}

pack .can

# canbit.tcl
```

When you run this script, you'll see a number of bitmaps, like those shown in Figure 8.12. You'll need a bitmap file in the current directory named **tv.xbm**. This file resides on the CD-ROM.

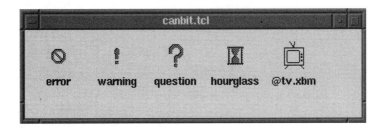

Figure 8.12 Canvas bitmap items.

Image Drawing Items

An `image` drawing item can hold a monochrome bitmap or a color image in a number of formats, including GIF and PPM (from the Portable Bitmap, or PBM, suite of image file utilities). Table 8.15 lists the relevant options.

Table 8.15 Image options

Option	Usage
-anchor *position*	One of n, s, e, w, nw, ne, sw, se, or center.
-image *imagename*	Names the image to display.
-tags *taglist*	Applies all the tags in *taglist* to the item.

The command to create an image is almost the same as for a bitmap:

```
widgetname create image x y
```

See the section on Images and Bitmaps previously in this chapter for more on how to set up an `image`.

Embedded Window Drawing Items

Much like the `text` widget, you can embed any Tk widget inside the `canvas` widget, using the `window` drawing type. Just about every `window` drawing item requires the `-window` option, which lists the name of the widget to embed. The options appear in Table 8.16.

Table 8.16 Window options

Option	Usage
-anchor *position*	One of n, s, e, w, ne, nw, se, sw, or center.
-height *size*	Controls size of window.
-tags *taglist*	Applies all the tags in *taglist* to the item.
-width *size*	Controls size of window.
-window *widgetname*	Embed *widgetname*.

The command to embed a `window` is rather simple:

```
widgetname create window x y
```

In real life though, this is a lot more complex, as the following short example shows:

```
# Embedded window items drawn in a canvas.
canvas .can -width 200 -height 100

button .can.b -text "Push Me" -command { puts ouch }
```

```
# Don't pack embedded widgets.

.can create window 100 50 \
    -window .can.b

pack .can

# canwind.tcl
```

Follow these rules when creating an embedded window:

- Don't pack the widgets you intend to embed.
- Create the widget as a child of the canvas widget.

See Chapter 5 in the section on Embedded Windows for more on the rules for embedding.

You can see an embedded widget in Figure 8.13.

Figure 8.13 An embedded widget inside a canvas.

Coordinate Positions for Drawing Items

All the drawing items require some coordinate arguments to specify where to place the item.

Unlike most windowing systems, all coordinates in the canvas widget are floating-point numbers. As usual, the origin is in the upper-left corner.

You can modify a coordinate position with one of the letters Tk accepts for units. Table 8.17 lists the available units.

Table 8.17 Units for coordinates in the canvas widget.

Letter	Meaning
m	Millimeters.
c	Centimeters.
I	Inches.
p	Points (used in publishing). Each point is 1/72 of an inch.

For example, `1.234p` means 1.234 points and `5.67i` means 5.67 inches. If you omit a units letter, the units default to pixels (e.g., `7.89`). The reason for the units is so that you can create a 2-inch square item on one screen and have it appear as 2 inches on all other systems.

WARNING

Graphical windowing systems like Windows and X are notoriously bad at generating true distances. The problem is in the monitor's screen size. You can, for example, swap a 15-inch monitor for a 17-inch monitor on a PC and not make any software changes. Because of this, Windows or X don't know how large your monitor's screen extends. Without this knowledge, Tk cannot generate a true distance. Thus, don't even pretend that `2.00i` will really generate a true 2-inch line. Assume the value will be off somewhat.

Scrolling the canvas Widget

To create a scrolled canvas widget, you must follow much the same rules as for the text and listbox widgets, as shown here.

```
# Scrolling canvas.
canvas .can -width 200 -height 200 \
    -scrollregion {0 0 1000 400} \
```

```
    -yscrollcommand ".v_scroll set" \
    -xscrollcommand ".h_scroll set"

scrollbar .v_scroll -command ".can yview"
scrollbar .h_scroll -command ".can xview" \
    -orient horizontal

# Fill in canvas.
for { set i 0 } { $i < 30 } { incr i } {
    set x1 [expr $i * 60 + 10]
    set y1 [expr $i * 36 + 40]
    set x2 [expr $x1 + 60]
    set y2 [expr $y1 + 30]

    .can create rectangle $x1 $y1 $x2 $y2
}

pack .v_scroll -side right -fill y
pack .h_scroll -side bottom -fill x

pack .can -side left -expand 1

# canscrl.tcl
```

The -scrollregion option contains a list of four coordinates, which identify the left, top, right, and bottom edges of the area on the canvas that can appear or be drawn into.

The scroll region is important to provide a fixed bounds for the scrolling area. What you'll usually need to do is place all the items on the canvas widget and then use the configure option to set the scroll region—you often won't know the extent of the scroll region in advance.

Naming Drawing Items

Each drawing item has a number that identifies it. You can use this number to refer to the drawing item for further manipulation. You can also provide a **tag name** for a canvas item. In fact, you can use the same tag name to identify a number of drawing items. The use of tags makes the canvas widget a lot like the text widget discussed in Chapter 5.

The special tag `all`, for example, is a special built-in tag name that refers to all the drawing items.

A special tag named `current` applies to the topmost item that is underneath the mouse cursor. Tk automatically updates this special tag when the mouse moves. Most drawing item commands accept either the numerical ID for an item or a tag name. The tag name may refer to one item or many.

For example, to delete a drawing item, or items if a tag name identifies many items, use the `delete` option. The syntax follows:

```
widgetname delete tag ...
widgetname delete id ...
```

All `canvas` items have an ID number, returned by the various `create` commands. A **tag** is merely a name that can refer to one or more drawing items. You can name the tag anything you want except for a number. Because IDs use numbers, this would confuse the `canvas` commands.

The easiest way to set up a tag is with the `-tag` option at creation time. The `-tag` option specifies a tag, or list of tags, that apply to the newly created `canvas` item. For example,

```
.can create line 10 10 10 30 \
    -joinstyle miter -fill maroon -width 10 \
    -tag line_tag
```

One of the advantages to tags is that you can group a number of items together.

If you didn't set up a tag with an item, you can also use the `addtag` option:

```
widgetname addtag tagname options
```

There's a number of ways to call the `addtag` option, depending on how you want to refer to the items to add to the tag. The simplest method is `all`:

```
widgetname addtag tagname all
```

The `all` option adds all drawing items to the given tag.

If you know an ID, or another tag, you can add items to a tag with the withtag option:

```
widgetname addtag tagname withtag tag
widgetname addtag tagname withtag id
```

You can either add all items within another tag or a particular item by its ID number.

You can select by stacking order with the above and below options:

```
widgetname addtag tagname above tag
widgetname addtag tagname above id
widgetname addtag tagname below tag
widgetname addtag tagname below id
```

The above and below options select canvas items that are just after (above) or before (below) in the canvas display list. Drawing items are added in the order of creation to the display list.

You can select all items that are enclosed within a rectangle with the enclosed option:

```
widgetname addtag tagname enclosed x1 y1 x2 y2
```

The enclosed option selects all items that are completely enclosed in the given rectangle, defined by the upper-left and lower-right corners.

The overlapping option selects all items enclosed within a rectangle or overlapping the area:

```
widgetname addtag tagname overlapping x1 y1 x2 y2
```

You can select the item closest to a given position with the closest option:

```
widgetname addtag tagname closest x y
widgetname addtag tagname closest x y halo
widgetname addtag tagname closest x y halo start
```

The canvas item closest to the x, y position gets added to the tag. The *halo* allows you to provide an numeric range. All items closer than the *halo* value from the x, y position are assumed to be within range. The item selected for the tag is the item closest to the end of the display list, usually the last-created item of the items within range. The *start* indicates a item number (or a tag) that is used to select the closest item that is below (before) the start item.

In addition to adding tags, you can delete tags with the dtag option:

```
widgetname dtag tag tag_to_delete
widgetname dtag id tag_to_delete
```

The dtag option deletes the *tag_to_delete* from the given item (a tag or ID number). That is, the *tag_to_delete* no longer applies to the item. If you just provide one tag name, then the dtag option removes that tag.

To determine what tags apply to a canvas item, you can use the get-tags option:

```
widgetname gettags tag
widgetname gettags id
```

These commands return the tags that apply to the given items.

The find option allows you to find items based on position, using the same options as addtag (above, all, below, closest, enclosed, over-lapping, and withtag), shown previously:

```
widgetname find options
```

Manipulating Canvas Items

To change a drawing item, you use the itemconfigure option, in one of two forms as shown here:

```
widgetname itemconfigure tag options
widgetname itemconfigure id options
```

The *options* are any of the allowed options for each drawing item, as shown in Tables 8.7 through 8.17.

The itemconfigure option is handy for changing canvas items once created, as shown in the **cantag.tcl** script:

```
# itemconfigure in a canvas.
canvas .can -width 200 -height 300

.can create line 10 10 10 30 30 30 30 90 \
    -joinstyle miter -fill maroon -width 10 \
    -tag red_tag

.can create line 110 10 110 30 180 30 \
    -joinstyle round -fill black -width 10 \
    -tag red_tag

.can create line 10 210 10 230 30 260 60 290 \
    -arrow last -joinstyle round -fill maroon \
    -width 10 -tag blue_tag

.can create line 110 210 110 230 130 230 160 290 \
    -arrow first -fill black -tag blue_tag

.can itemconfigure blue_tag -fill blue
.can itemconfigure red_tag -fill red

pack .can

# cantag.tcl
```

You can query the value of options for a canvas item using itemcget:

```
widgetname itemcget tag option
widgetname itemcget id option
```

The itemcget option works like the reverse of the itemconfigure option, using the same values from Tables 8.7 through 8.17.

The type option returns the type of a canvas item:

```
widgetname type tag
```

```
widgetname type id
```

If more than one item is identified by the tag, then the `type` option returns the type of the first item only.

To move an item, you can also use one of two forms of the command, as shown here:

```
widgetname move tag xoffset yoffset
widgetname move id xoffset yoffset
```

The *xoffset* and *yoffset* values must be valid coordinate amounts.

The `raise` and `lower` options allow you to adjust a `canvas` item in relation to other items. The `canvas` widget draws items from start to finish, so later items appear to be over earlier items. You can adjust this with the `raise` and `lower` options:

```
widgetname raise tag after_this
widgetname raise id after_this
```

The optional *after_this* ID or tag indicates an item to place the items after. The `lower` option works similarly:

```
widgetname lower tag below_this
widgetname lower id below_this
```

The optional *below_this* ID or tag indicates an item to place the items before.

Transforming Canvas Items

With the `canvas` widget, you can scale, but not rotate, drawing items. To scale, use one of the forms of the following command:

```
widgetname scale tag xorigin yorigin xscale yscale
widgetname scale id xorigin yorigin xscale yscale
```

The *xscale* and *yscale* values contain the scaling factors. A scaling factor of 2.0 generates an item twice the size. A scaling factor of 1.0 generates no scaling. The *xorigin* and *yorigin* values are used for the origin of the scaling operation.

Binding Events to Canvas Drawing Items

Like for the text widget, described in Chapter 5, you can bind events to items in the canvas widget, as shown here:

```
# Binding items in a canvas.

canvas .can -width 400 -height 300
pack .can

.can create text 200 20 -tag can_move \
   -text "Move Me"

.can create text 300 60 -tag can_move \
   -text "Move Me, Too"

.can create text 100 40 -text "Cannot Move"

  # Button 1 down stored initial position.
.can bind can_move <Button-1> {
   global x y

   set x %x
   set y %y
}

.can bind can_move <B1-Motion> {
   global x y

   set newx %x
   set newy %y

   set distx [expr $newx - $x]
   set disty [expr $newy - $y]
```

```
    .can move can_move $distx $disty

    # Store values for next time.
    set x $newx
    set y $newy
}

set x 0
set y 0
global x y

# canbind.tcl
```

These commands allow you to move a particular item about on the `canvas` by dragging with the leftmost mouse button.

The **canbind.tcl** script allows you to select one of two text items and move them about the `canvas` when dragging with the leftmost mouse button held down. The remaining text item will not move because it does not have the *can_move* tag. The event bindings are only on the items with the *can_move* tag.

The only events you can bind to canvas items are mouse and keyboard events, such as `Enter`, `Leave`, `Button`, `ButtonRelease`, `Motion`, `Key`, and `KeyRelease`.

Generating PostScript Output

You can generate PostScript output for all or part of a `canvas` widget. This is great for printing out your drawings. The basic format of the command is

widgetname postscript *options*

Table 8.18 lists the basic options for generating PostScript output.

Table 8.18 canvas widget PostScript options.

Option	Usage
-colormode *gray*	Generate a gray-scale image.
-colormode *color*	Generate a color image.

`-colormode` *mono*	Generate a monochrome image.
`-file` *filename*	Output to a file. Command then returns a NULL string.
`-height` *size*	Specify how high an area in the canvas to output.
`-rotate 1`	Specifies landscape mode.
`-rotate 0`	Specifies portrait mode, the default.
`-width` *size*	Specify how wide an area in the canvas to output.
`-x` *coord*	Specifies starting x coordinate to output.
`-y` *coord*	Specifies starting y coordinate to output.

Table 8.19 lists the options for controlling the output page.

Table 8.19 Canvas widget PostScript output page options.

Option	Usage
`-channel` *channel_id*	Write output to channel; leaves channel open for writing when done.
`-colormap` *color_array*	Use *color_array* to map colors. Each index is a color name, each element the PostScript code to generate values in that color.
`-fontmap` *font_array*	Map fonts according to array. Each index is a Tk font name, each element the PostScript commands for mapping that font.
`-pageanchor` *anchor*	Anchors the canvas output on the printed page.
`-pageheight` *size*	Scales the output to *size* height on the page.
`-pagewidth` *size*	Scales the output to *size* width on the page.
`-pagex` *position*	Controls the positioning point on the page.
`-pagey` *position*	Controls the positioning point on the page.

The `postscript` option creates Encapsulated PostScript (version 3.0) output. The `postscript` option returns the PostScript commands, unless you use the `-file` or `-channel` options to send the output to a file or open channel. (See Chapter 12 for more on channels.)

Displaying Thumbnail Images

To provide a flavor of the `image` command and a number of its options, you can use Tk for creating a neat GIF thumbnail image-viewer with very little code, from the **picdir.tcl** file:

```
#
# Sample image thumbnail-viewing program.
#

  #
  # Shrinks image for display
  # in a small button, maintaining
  # aspect ratio.
  #
  # im = image to shrink
  # max_width = max size of shrunken image.
  # max_height = max size of shrunken image.
  #
proc shrink_image { im max_width max_height } {

  # Determine proper aspect ratio to get size.
  set w [image width $im]
  set h [image height $im]

  # Determine size of small proportional image.
  set iw [expr ($w * $max_height)/$h]
  set ih [expr ($h * $max_width)/$w]

  # If iw is too big, use ih.
  if { $iw >= $max_width } {
     set iw $max_width
```

```
    } else {
        set ih $max_height
    }

    # Create new, blank, small image.
    image create photo $im.small \
        -format gif \
        -width $iw -height $ih

    if { $w > $h } {
        set samp_x [expr $w/$iw]
        set samp_y $samp_x
    } else {
        set samp_y [expr $h/$ih]
        set samp_x $samp_y
    }

    # We always shrink.
    if { $samp_x == 1 } {
        set samp_x 2
        set samp_y 2
    }

    $im.small copy $im \
        -subsample $samp_x $samp_y \
        -shrink \
        -to 0 0 $iw $ih

    return $im.small
}

#
# Returns 1 if GIF or PPM; 0 otherwise.
# filename = name of file to check.
#
proc identify_file { filename } {

    set ext [file extension $filename]
```

```
  switch $ext {
     .GIF { return 1 }
     .gif { return 1 }
     .PGM { return 1 }
     .pgm { return 1 }
     .PPM { return 1 }
     .ppm { return 1 }
   }

 return 0
}


 #
 # Creates toplevel window to show image in.
 # name = toplevel name
 # filename = image to display
 #
proc show_image { name filename } {

    image create photo $name.im \
       -file $filename

    toplevel .$name
    button .$name.im \
      -image $name.im \
      -command "destroy .$name"

    pack .$name.im

    wm title .$name $filename
}

 # Initialize
global fcount x y
set fcount 0
set x 50
set y 50
```

```
set doc_image "
#define document_width 32
#define document_height 32
static unsigned char document_bits[] = {
   0x00, 0x00, 0x00, 0x00,
   0x00, 0x00, 0x00, 0x00,
   0xf0, 0xff, 0x1f, 0x00,
   0x10, 0x00, 0x20, 0x00,
   0x10, 0x00, 0x60, 0x00,
   0x10, 0x00, 0xa0, 0x00,
   0x10, 0x00, 0x20, 0x01,
   0x10, 0x00, 0x20, 0x02,
   0x10, 0x00, 0x20, 0x04,
   0x10, 0x00, 0xe0, 0x0f,
   0x10, 0x00, 0x00, 0x10,
   0x10, 0x00, 0x00, 0x10,
   0x10, 0x00, 0x00, 0x10,
   0x10, 0x00, 0x00, 0x10,
   0x10, 0x00, 0x00, 0x10,
   0x10, 0x00, 0x00, 0x10,
   0x10, 0x00, 0x00, 0x10,
   0x10, 0x00, 0x00, 0x10,
   0x10, 0x00, 0x00, 0x10,
   0x10, 0x00, 0x00, 0x10,
   0x10, 0x00, 0x00, 0x10,
   0x10, 0x00, 0x00, 0x10,
   0x10, 0x00, 0x00, 0x10,
   0x10, 0x00, 0x00, 0x10,
   0x10, 0x00, 0x00, 0x10,
   0x10, 0x00, 0x00, 0x10,
   0x10, 0x00, 0x00, 0x10,
   0x10, 0x00, 0x00, 0x10,
   0x10, 0x00, 0x00, 0x10,
   0xf0, 0xff, 0xff, 0x1f,
   0x00, 0x00, 0x00, 0x00,
   0x00, 0x00, 0x00, 0x00};"

image create bitmap doc -data $doc_image
```

```
#
# Displays small image in canvas.
# can = canvas widget
# filename = image to shrink
#
proc disp_file { can filename } {

  global fcount x y

  # Debugging info.
  #puts "$filename"

   # Create frame, button, and label for file.
  frame $can.$fcount
  label $can.$fcount.tx -text $filename

   # Create image for the file if image file.
  if { [identify_file $filename] == 1 } {
  puts "$filename"

    # Create image.
    image create photo $fcount -file $filename

    # Shrink image.
    set small [shrink_image $fcount 100 60]

    button $can.$fcount.im -image $small \
      -command "show_image $fcount $filename" \
      -relief flat

    # Free memory.
    image delete $fcount

  } else {

    # Use question mark bitmap.
    button $can.$fcount.im \
      -image doc -relief flat
  }
```

```
    pack $can.$fcount.im $can.$fcount.tx -side top

    # Don't pack frame; embed it.

    $can create window $x $y -window $can.$fcount

    set x [expr $x + 110]

    if { $x > 800 } {

      set x 50
      set y [expr $y + 100]
    }

  set fcount [incr fcount]
}

# Create canvas.
canvas .can -width 300 -height 400 \
  -xscrollcommand ".hscr set" \
  -yscrollcommand ".vscr set"

scrollbar .hscr \
  -command ".can xview" \
  -orient horizontal
          .
scrollbar .vscr -command ".can yview"

# Pack scrollbars first.
pack .vscr -side right -fill y
pack .hscr -side bottom -fill x

pack .can -side left \
  -expand yes -fill both

# Fill in files.
set files [glob -nocomplain *]

if { $files != "" } {
```

```
set sorted [lsort $files]

foreach filename $sorted {
    disp_file .can $filename
}

# Configure scrollbar.
set w 900
set h [expr $y+80]
.can configure \
    -scrollregion "0 0 $w $h"
}

# picdir.tcl
```

You can see the output of this script in Figure 8.14.

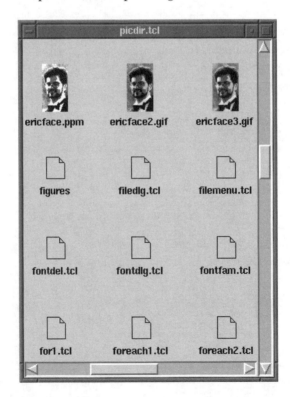

Figure 8.14 The **picdir.tcl** script displaying thumbnail images.

The **picdir.tcl** script, although small, is rather complex for a Tcl script. The shrink_image procedure creates a small image that is a shrunken version of a larger image passed to it. For best display, it tries to maintain the aspect ratio of the image.

The identify_file procedure is used for a simple test to see whether a file is a supported image file.

The show_image procedure creates a toplevel widget and a button inside that to display the image. When you click on the image's button, the toplevel widget gets destroyed.

The disp_file procedure is the workhorse command. It displays a file as three widgets embedded inside a canvas widget, a label to hold the file name, a button to display the image, and a frame to hold the other two. The disp_file procedure embeds this frame widget in the canvas, at a fixed distance so that each frame widget is separated.

There are a number of ways in which you may want to extend this script. First, it is terribly slow. Second, when the user clicks on text files, you could call up a scrolled text widget in a top-level window to edit the file. Clicking on a directory should scan that directory. You could add a button to go up to the parent directory, as well.

Furthermore, small images get tiled inside the display button. Images that aren't tiled do not appear as well as we'd like for thumbnail images. See if you can change this by working with the image options.

Summary

Tk provides a number of built-in bitmaps. You can also create your own bitmaps from data stored in X bitmap format, using the image create bitmap command. You can create color images out of GIF or PPM data using the image create photo command. You can use monochrome bitmaps or color images inside a toolbar in your programs.

Most graphical applications display a menu bar at the top, with a toolbar underneath. The image command is very useful for helping to set up your toolbars.

This chapter also introduced the multifaceted canvas widget. You can use the canvas as an area to draw on. In addition, you can place a lot of functionality within a canvas widget, turning it into something much more than a mere drawing canvas.

To draw in a `canvas` widget, you need to create drawing items, such as `arcs`, `rectangles`, and embedded `windows`. You can generate PostScript output from a `canvas` widget with the `postscript` option.

The next chapter shows how to find errors in your Tcl scripts and stamp them out.

Tcl/Tk Commands Introduced in This Chapter

canvas
image

SECTION II

Advanced Applications

Now that you've tackled the basics, this section delves into more advanced issues for creating cross-platform graphical applications with Tcl and the Tk toolkit.

Chapter 9 starts out by addressing the toughest issue of all: how to debug applications. It discusses a number of techniques to help find out what is wrong with your scripts and how to fix them, as well as how to avoid errors in the first place.

Because Tcl is a scripting language, you'll often want to launch UNIX or Windows applications from within your scripts. **Chapter 10** shows how to do this and covers some common pitfalls when trying to execute other applications from Tcl.

Every application should provide online help, both short messages and full-featured help. **Chapter 11** delves into tooltip help—also called balloon help—as well as using HTML to display your online help, with the handy html_library set of Tcl code.

Applications don't exist in limbo and **Chapter 12** shows how to communicate from Tcl to other applications, using the Tcl send command as well as TCP/IP socket communications.

Chapter 13 tackles the World Wide Web and how you can use Tcl to create Common Gateway Interface, or CGI, scripts, as well as Tcl applets with a Web browser plug-in.

Finally, **Chapter 14** wraps up the discussion by concentrating on miscellaneous commands to help round out robust applications. It covers ways to make more professional-looking interfaces, as well as how to package and install your Tcl code.

Tcl Tricks and Traps: Handling Errors and Debugging

This chapter covers:

- Handling errors
- Handling errors with `tkerror`
- Using `tkerror` to help debug your applications
- Reporting errors with the `error` command
- Catching errors with `catch`
- Defensive programming to avoid errors
- Tracing the execution of Tcl scripts for debugging
- Finding out more about the state of the Tcl interpreter
- Tcl debuggers

Handling Errors

Errors, unfortunately, are a fact of life. If you want your Tcl scripts to be robust, you must deal with errors. You need to announce some errors to the user; others can be dealt with silently inside your scripts.

Of course, we'd all prefer to eliminate all errors from the scripts during the development phase. This chapter discusses errors in Tcl, how to handle them, how to avoid them, how to defeat them, and how to help debug your code.

Foreground Errors and Background Errors

When the Tcl interpreter discovers an error in your script, especially when first reading in the file, you'll see an error message that includes as much of a stack trace as possible. A stack trace describes the set of procedures (procedure *A* calls procedure *B* calls procedure *C* and so on) where the error occurred. For example,

```
Error in startup script: missing close-brace
     invoked from within
"proc replace_angle_brackets { str } {


    if {$str != "" } {


    set start_idx [string first "<" $str]


    while { $start_idx > 0 } {
           #s ..."
(file "edoc2.tcl" line 97)
```

This error message is very helpful in that it gives you a line number within a file where the Tcl interpreter found the error. This is not always the true location of the error, but at least we're in the right area. In this case, a close brace, }, is missing somewhere in the script. (Most text editors can help you find which open brace has no close brace.)

The stack trace for this error is rather short, because the error lies within one procedure. Sometimes, though, the stack of called procedures appears longer, as in the following error message:

```
Error in startup script: domain error:
  argument not in valid range
     while executing
"

       set start_idx [string first "<" $str]
```

```
    set v [expr acos(-3) ]


    while { $start_idx > 0 } {
            #set start_idx [expr "$start_idx  ..."
    (procedure "replace_angle_brackets" line 1)
    invoked from within
"set textline [replace_angle_brackets $line_of_text]"
    (procedure "find_procs" line 1)
    invoked from within
"find_procs $filename $outfile"
    (procedure "process_files" line 1)
    invoked from within
"process_files"
    (file "edoc2.tcl" line 1)
```

The trick in reading the stack trace is that the top most messages are deepest in the code. The bottom most message describes where the error originated. Armed with this sometimes confusing information, you can try to step back through your script and find out where the error occurred.

This example leads us through procedure to procedure. Starting at the bottom, the procedure `process_files` calls the procedure `find_procs`. Note that the parameters passed to the procedures are printed. The `find_procs` procedure calls `replace_angle_brackets`, where the error occurs (a math error in this case).

Notice how the line numbers are all wrong. The Tcl interpreter is counting lines within a procedure and mostly displays line 1, no matter what real line of the Tcl file the error occurred in. (Can you think of a reason why? Hint: everything between { and } forms a single argument that Tcl treats as one line.) Whenever you see a similar stack trace, you cannot depend on the line numbers, but the printed parts of the code executed should help you to locate the error.

Most Tcl errors are reported immediately to the terminal or console window. But, a whole number of errors come from what is called **background code**. This code is executed for an event binding, or for a number of other situations where you set up a procedure in advance and the code is executed later, but not part of the standard flow of control in the Tcl script.

514

Even though the term background error may sound like a rarity, remember that the majority of the interaction in your Tcl scripts comes from users typing in data, selecting menu choices, clicking on buttons, and so on. All the Tcl code that gets executed from these situations is considered to run in the background.

Handling Background Errors with Tkerror

When any Tk procedure detects an error in a script called from `bind` or any other source of background processing, it executes a procedure called `tkerror`. Because you can redefine any procedure in Tcl with the `proc` command, you can override `tkerror` with your own routine.

The default `tkerror` displays a dialog box and provides a button to generate a stack trace of the error, as shown in Figure 9.1.

Figure 9.1 The result of the default `tkerror` procedure.

The Stack Trace

When you click on the *Stack Trace* button, you'll see a window like that shown in Figure 9.2.

The stack trace window in Figure 9.2 shows a number of commands:

```
invalid command name "llindex"
    while executing
"llindex"
    (procedure "proc9" line 1)
    invoked from within
```

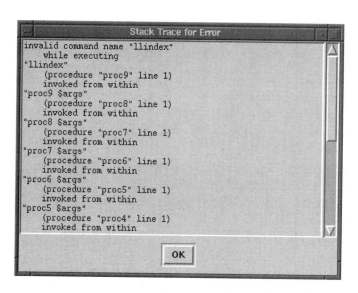

Figure 9.2 A stack trace.

```
"proc9 $args"
    (procedure "proc8" line 1)
    invoked from within
"proc8 $args"
    (procedure "proc7" line 1)
    invoked from within
"proc7 $args"
    (procedure "proc6" line 1)
    invoked from within
"proc6 $args"
    (procedure "proc5" line 1)
    invoked from within
"proc5 $args"
    (procedure "proc4" line 1)
    invoked from within
"proc4 $args"
    (procedure "proc3" line 1)
    invoked from within
"proc3 $args"
    (procedure "proc2" line 1)
```

```
    invoked from within
"proc2 $args"
    (procedure "proc1" line 1)
    invoked from within
"proc1 first second third fourth"
    invoked from within
".b invoke"
    ("uplevel" body line 1)
    invoked from within"uplevel #0 [list $w invoke]"
    (procedure "tkButtonUp" line 1)
    invoked from within
"tkButtonUp .b"
    (command bound to event)
```

In this stack trace, we can determine that the attempt to invoke a command named llindex failed. We can also tell that this command is called in a procedure named proc9. Furthermore, we can track this error to a widget named *.b* (based on the bottom lines of the stack trace).

The stack trace is especially helpful at tracking down problems in your scripts. It's not good, though, for end users, because chances are they won't know Tcl. So, robust applications should override tkerror and provide a more friendly error dialog window. The goal of an error dialog window is to provide the user with the knowledge to figure out what went wrong and how to work around the situation. Of course, this is never easy.

Some Tcl scripts override tkerror and present a dialog window allowing you to e-mail the stack trace to the program's author to let the author know about the problem.

The tkerror procedure takes one argument, the error message to display.

```
proc tkerror { errmsg } {


  # Your code goes here.


}
```

Now, you'll want to create a `tkerror` procedure that does more than this. For example, you may want to display an error dialog window to the user, to let the user know what happened. Before you can do this, though, you need to know more about the error information available through Tcl.

Reporting Errors in Your Code

If you detect an error in a procedure, you can use the expanded form of `return` to return an error code and assorted information about the error. From Chapter 2, the `return` command allows the following arguments:

```
return -code code -errorinfo info -errorcode code return_value
```

Going through the options one at a time, Table 9.1 shows the values allowed for the `-code` option.

Table 9.1 The `-code` value from the `return` command.

Code	Meaning
ok	Normal procedure return.
error	Error return; same as skipping `-code` entirely.
return	Causes calling procedure to return as well.
break	Acts like the `break` command, jumps out of innermost loop.
continue	Acts like `continue` command, jumps to top of innermost loop.
number	Returns this *number* as the completion code.

If a number of errors build up while processing inside your `tkerror` routine, `tkerror` will get called for each one. If this is a problem, you should return a `-code` of `break` from `tkerror`, which breaks this loop.

518

You can fill in stack trace information in the -errorinfo value. This value gets set into the global variable named *errorInfo*. This is used by the default tkerror procedure and should show the text of the actual lines of Tcl code where the error was detected.

The value set into the -errorcode option gets stored in the global variable *errorCode*. If you omit it, the value is set to NONE.

The *errorCode* variable contains a list of values, formatted a special way, as shown in Table 9.2. The first element in the list specifies how to interpret the data following.

Table 9.2 Data stored in the errorCode global list variable.

errorCode	Meaning
ARITH DIVZERO *message*	Arithmetic divide by zero error.
ARITH DOMAIN *message*	Arithmetic argument outside domain of a function error.
ARITH IOVERFLOW *message*	Integer overflow.
ARITH OVERFLOW *message*	Floating-point overflow.
ARITH UNKNOWN *message*	Unknown arithmetic error.
CHILDKILLED *pid* *signal message*	Child process killed by a signal.
CHILDSTATUS *pid code*	Child process exited with nonzero code.
CHILDSUSP *pid* *signal message*	Child process suspended by a signal.
NONE	No information available. Do not pass go.
POSIX *error message*	Error in POSIX kernel call.

Note that most of these errors come from the math routines that Tcl uses.

Setting Error Data

You can use the error command to store data in the global error variables. Don't set values in these variables directly, the Tcl interpreter assumes you'll follow the proper conventions, and it's always best to follow the established conventions. The `error` command uses the following syntax:

```
error message info code
```

The *message* is the text of the error message to return to the application. The *info* argument will get appended to the data in the global variable *errorInfo* (this is a list that gets appended to). The *code* argument will get placed in the *errorCode* global variable. See Table 9.2 for the format of the data. Both the *info* and *code* arguments are optional.

Many of these error values make a lot more sense if you're writing Tcl functions in C, as you'll see in Chapter 16. The math errors, for example, generally occur within the C function that implements a math procedure, rather than in Tcl code.

Building a New `tkerror` Procedure

With all this information on errors, you can now build a new version of `tkerror` that displays more data to the user, as shown below:

```
# Overriding tkerror procedure.
proc tkerror { errmsg } {

    global errorCode

    set msg [format "Error: %s\nResult: %s." \
        $errmsg $errorCode]

    tk_messageBox -parent . -title Error -type ok \
        -icon error -message $msg
}

    # Test bindings to generate errors.
bind all <Control-Key-e> {
    error "This is a simple error."
```

```
}


bind all <Control-Key-m> {
    # Math error in expression.
    set v [ expr acos(-3) ]
}



# tkerror.tcl
```

WARNING

It's very important that a routine called on errors doesn't generate errors itself. Can you find all the places the tkerror might fail? Just creating button widgets in the dialog window may fail with out-of-memory or out-of-color-cell errors.

To test this tkerror procedure, the **tkerror.tcl** script binds the following event:

```
bind all <Control-Key-e> {



    error "This is a sample error."
}
```

Then, press **Ctrl-E** in the **wish** window. Remember that tkerror is called for background errors. You'll see a dialog window like the one in Figure 9.3.

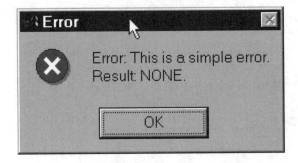

Figure 9.3 The new tkerror procedure.

To test other kinds of errors, you can bind **Ctrl-M** (for math) to generate another error, as shown here:

```
bind all <Control-Key-m> {
```

```
    set v [ expr acos(-3) ]
}
```

If you now press **Ctrl-M**, you'll see the error message shown in Figure 9.4.

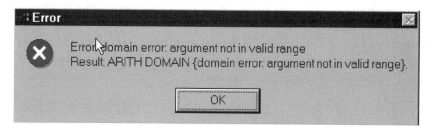

Figure 9.4 A math error trapped by our `tkerror` procedure.

The use of bound **Control** key combinations is just a convenience to generate the type of background error `tkerror` reports. There's nothing special about **Ctrl-E** or **Ctrl-M**.

N O T E

Trapping Errors

Reporting errors is never enough. The best way to deal with errors is to prevent them from happening in the first place. Of course, this, too, is never easy.

Catching Errors with `catch`

If a script causes errors, or you think it may, you can use `catch` to capture any errors from the script and continue processing normally. For example, many applications allow users to provide some form of customization file. With Tcl, it makes sense to keep this file in Tcl format, using the Tcl syntax

522

(because you already have a file parser—the Tcl interpreter). But, when you execute this file, you don't want a bad command in the user's customization file to stop the whole program. So, you can use `catch`. The syntax is

```
catch tcl_script varname
```

The `catch` command executes the given *tcl_script*, capturing any errors that occur. `catch` returns 0 on success, and a return code (from the `-code` option to the `return` command) if any errors occurred, as listed in Table 9.1.

The optional *varname*, if present, is used to store any values returned by the script (the normal return value) or an error message, if one is given.

catch quits the moment it detects an error, so multiline statements may show unanticipated problems. To get around this, you may need to use multiple calls to `catch`. For example,

```
catch {
  # First command...
}
catch {
  # Second command...
}
```

Defensive Programming

You can use a number of techniques in your scripts to try to avoid errors. Most of these techniques check for existence of variables, array elements, and widgets.

To check whether or not a variable exists, you can use the `info exists` command:

```
info exists varname
```

The `info exists` command returns 1 if the given variable exists in the current procedure; 0 otherwise.

For example,

```
% info exists emp
0
% set emp(name) Eric
Eric
% info exists emp
1
```

The variable *emp* didn't exist until set to a value.

NOTE Inside a procedure, a global variable does not exist unless you declared it `global`.

The `array names` command, described in Chapter 2, can be used similarly to `info exists` for elements in an array. Normally, you call `array names` with the name of an array to get a list of all elements in the array. You can pass another option, the name of an individual element, to see if that element exists in the array. For example, the following code checks that an array element exists before trying to access the element in the array:

```
if { [array names emp name] != "" } {
    puts "$emp(name)"
}
```

The `array names` command returns either the name of the element or a NULL string, hence the check for not equal to "". If you try to access an array element that does not exist, you'll get an error, so code like this can help stop errors from occurring.

The `winfo exists` command returns 1 if a given widget exists, and 0 if the widget does not exists, as shown next:

```
% winfo exists .
1
% winfo exists .not_created
0
```

I find all these commands useful in writing defensive Tcl code.

Debugging Tcl Applications

Tcl and Tk provide a number of hooks to help you debug your applications. First of all, because Tcl is a much simpler and a much higher-level language than C or C++, there's typically a lot less code to debug. A text editor in Tcl uses a lot less code than one written in C or C++. With less code, your debugging task becomes a lot easier.

Furthermore, due to the short cycle of edit/run, edit/run (rather than the edit/compile/link/run for C and C++ or edit/compile/run for Java), you can test out code and code snippets much more quickly. I've found the following techniques handy when debugging Tcl scripts, some old, some new:

- Use the simple `puts` command to print out a message, both that a procedure gets executed and also the value of variables you think you're having a problem with. This allows you to verify that the procedure is getting correct data.

- Split the problem in half using the divide and conquer method. Divide the area you think may be a problem in half, stopping the processing by placing an early `return` statement or commenting out the last half of the code. Then, verify that the first half of the code works correctly (I usually use `puts` to print out the values to verify them). If there is a problem in the first half, divide in half again. When you have the first half running properly, divide the remaining code in half and repeat the process.

- Create a scrolled `text` widget to act as a debugging log if you simply have too many messages to read as they scroll by. Placing the messages in a `text` widget allows you to scroll back and read the messages.

- Replace the procedure you find problematic, or suspect to be so. With Tcl, you can replace any procedure with the `proc` command. You can use this to gradually create a working procedure out of a nonworking one.

- Use the stack trace from the default `tkerror` procedure. While often not exact, this provides something close to the line that caused the error.

- Use the `trace` command to see how a variable is getting written to.

Tracing the Execution of Tcl Scripts for Debugging

You can use the `trace` command to execute a Tcl script whenever a variable changes. With global variables, the routine you suspect of causing a problem may be innocent; it may be that another procedure is causing the problem and writing bad data to the variable. This is especially an issue with global variables.

The `trace` command takes the following syntax:

```
trace variable varname operations tcl_script
```

The operations argument can be one or more of the values listed in Table 9.3.

Table 9.3 The available operations for the trace command.

Operation	Meaning
r	Execute *tcl_script* whenever *varname* is read.
w	Execute *tcl_script* whenever *varname* is written to.
u	Execute *tcl_script* whenever *varname* is unset.

A variable that is nonglobal, that is, local to a procedure, gets automatically unset when the procedure returns.

The *tcl_script* gets invoked with the following arguments:

```
tcl_script varname elementname operation
```

The *varname* is the variable that is changed. If *varname* is an array, then *elementname* holds the array element name that was changed (unless you're tracing the whole array).

The `upvar` command may access a variable under a different name. So, the name you see in your *tcl_script* may not always be the one you're looking for.

Furthermore, you may need to use upvar or uplevel to get at the value if your *tcl_script* is a procedure.

The following code sets up a tracing procedure and traces changes to the variable:

```
# Tracing changes to a variable.
proc trace_testvar { varname elementname operation } {


    # Upvar helps avoid recursive traces.
    upvar $varname var1


    puts "Tracing $operation: $varname holds <$var1>"
}


  # See if trace finds hidden changes via upvar.
proc hidden_change { varname value } {


    upvar $varname var1


    set var1 $value
}


trace variable testvar {rwu} trace_testvar


# Writing.
set testvar {Sample Value}


# Reading.
set x $testvar


# Can we track hidden changes?
```

```
hidden_change testvar 5
```

```
# trace.tcl
```

To turn off a `trace` on a variable, use the `trace vdelete` command:

```
trace vdelete varname operations tcl_script
```

The *varname*, *operations*, and *tcl_script* all must match the values originally passed to the `trace variable` command.

Finding Out More About the State of the Tcl Interpreter

You can use the `info` command to get information on the state of the Tcl interpreter. This can be useful if you think some procedure has been over-written with a new version or otherwise question what the Tcl interpreter thinks is going on.

Table 9.4 lists the many variants of the `info` command.

Table 9.4 The Tcl `info` command.

Command	Use
`info args procedure`	Returns the arguments, in order, for *procedure*.
`info body procedure`	Returns the body (code) of the given *procedure*.
`info cmdcount`	Returns number of commands executed by the interpreter.
`info commands`	Returns names of all Tcl commands.
`info commands pattern`	Returns names of all Tcl commands that match *pattern*.
`info complete command`	Returns 0 if *command* needs more input; 1 otherwise.

continued

Table 9.4 continued

`info default` *procedure* *argument varname*	If *argument* in *procedure* has a default value, returns 1 and places value in *varname*; returns 0 otherwise.
`info exists` *varname*	Returns 1 if *varname* exists in current procedure; 0 otherwise.
`info globals`	Returns list of all global variables.
`info globals` *pattern*	Returns list of all global variables matching *pattern*.
`info level`	Returns stack level number (0 is top level).
`info level` *number*	Returns parameters of current call at that stack level.
`info library`	Returns Tcl library directory (held in *tcl_library* global variable).
`info locals`	Returns all current local (inside procedure) variables.
`info locals` *pattern*	Returns all current local (inside procedure) variables that match *pattern*.
`info nameofexecutable`	Returns full pathname of executable.
`info patchlevel`	Returns current patch (revision) level of interpreter, same as *tcl_patchLevel* global variable.
`info procs`	Returns name of all Tcl procedures.
`info procs` *pattern*	Returns name of all Tcl procedures that match *pattern*.
`info script`	Returns name of innermost script file being executed, or NULL string if none.
`info sharedlibextension`	Returns shared library extension, such as `.dll` or `.so`.
`info tclversion`	Returns same data as global *tcl_version* variable.
`info vars`	Returns name of all currently active variables (local and global).
`info vars` *pattern*	Returns name of all currently active variables (local and global) that match *pattern*.

One of the most useful options to the `info` command is the `level` option. The `level` option returns the parameters passed with the current procedure call, to allow you to create a stack trace, very similar to the one displayed by the default `tkerror` dialog window.

The following code shows how to print out a stack trace:

```
#
# Utility to print calling stack for Tcl interpreter.
#


proc print_call_stack { } {
    set level [info level]


    set level [expr $level -1]


    puts "Tcl calling stack for [info script]"


    while { $level > 0 } {
        puts "\t [info level $level]"—


        incr level -1
    }
}



# stack.tcl
```

To generate a stack trace, call the `print_call_stack` procedure anywhere in your code. For example,

```
Tcl calling stack for edoc2.tcl
        output_html_header file6 edoc2.tcl edoc2.tcl
        find_procs edoc2.tcl edoc2.htm
        process_files
```

In this example, the procedure `process_files` calls the procedure `find_procs` with two arguments: *edoc2.tcl* and *edoc2.htm*. The `find_procs` procedure then calls `output_html_header` with the following arguments: *file6*, *edoc2.tcl*, and *edoc2.tcl*.

The `info script` command returns the name of the currently running script file.

Creating a Debugging Log

If you use the `puts` command to print out the value of variables, you may find that there is too much output, or that it's too hard to separate the debugging output from the regular output of your script. To help with this, you may want to create a debugging log.

Such a log is merely a `text` widget with scrollbars. You then create Tcl procedures to turn on and off the display of the debugging log as well to place a text message into the log. You can use the following code as an example of this:

```
# Text widget to display debugging output.
#
# To use:
# debug on
#   Creates debugging log window or shows it.
# debug off
#   Hides debugging window.
# debug_log message
#   Puts message at end of debugging window.
#


  # Global variable tells whether or not to debug.
set debuging off
global debuging


set debug_toplevel .debug
set debug_text .debug.frm.text
global debug_toplevel debug_text
```

```tcl
# Logs text message to debugging window.
proc debug_log { message } {
    global debuging debug_text


    if { $debuging == "on" } {
        $debug_text insert end "$message\n"
        $debug_text see end
    }
}



  #
  # Turns debugging "on" or "off".
  # Creates window if necessary.
  #
proc debug { on_or_off } {
    global debuging debug_toplevel


    # Only change if different.
    if { $debuging != $on_or_off } {


        if { $on_or_off == "on" } {


            #

            # Create debugging window.

            #

            if { [winfo exists $debug_toplevel] == 0 } {

                debug_create

            } else {

                wm deiconify $debug_toplevel
```

```
            }

        } else {

            wm withdraw $debug_toplevel
        }


        set debuging $on_or_off
    }
}


    # Private procedure. Creates debugging window.
proc debug_create { } {


    global debug_toplevel debug_text


    toplevel $debug_toplevel
    set frm $debug_toplevel.frm


    frame $frm -bd 0
    text $debug_text -yscrollcommand "$frm.v_scroll set" \
        -xscrollcommand "$frm.h_scroll set" \


    scrollbar $frm.h_scroll -orient horizontal \
        -command "$debug_text xview"
    scrollbar $frm.v_scroll -command "$debug_text yview"


    pack $frm.v_scroll -side right -fill y
    pack $frm.h_scroll -side bottom -fill x
    pack $debug_text -expand 1 -fill both


    pack $frm -side top
```

```
}
```

```
# debugtxt.tcl
```

After you `source` in these procedures, you can turn on the logging with the `debug on` command. This will create a logging window. You can append messages to the log with the `debug_log` command. The `debug off` command will hide the log.

Tcl Debuggers

A number of Tcl debuggers can help you track down errors in your code. A **debugger** is typically a program to provide information about another program, allowing you to stop the program and query the value of variables and so on. For most programming languages, debuggers are terribly complicated as they must understand the native machine code. Tcl is much easier in this regard, because you can use the `eval` command to execute code and the `info` command to get information on the state of the Tcl interpreter.

If you've never worked with a debugger before, you typically only use one as a last resort when there's some problem in your code (or in someone else's) that you just cannot figure out using the techniques described so far.

A debugger typically offers:

- The ability to stop the Tcl code at a given location, called a **break point**.
- The ability to query variable values and execute Tcl code after the code has stopped.
- Restart the Tcl script where it left off.
- Step through the code a line at a time, so that you can see what effects occur from each command.
- And much, much more....

The debuggers I like best are the ones written entirely in Tcl, because these tend to be more portable to Windows as well as UNIX.

In the next sections, you'll see a few of the available debuggers. Look in the **contrib/debug** directory on the CD-ROM for the actual debuggers.

None of these debuggers are part of the Tcl release. These freeware programs were written by very nice people in their spare time, so sometimes they'll work for you and sometimes they won't.

TDebug

The TDebug works in one of two modes. You can either start it with your Tcl script, or you can use the `send` command (see Chapter 12) to attach to a running Tcl script. For example, with a script named **textedit.tcl**, you can start TDebug with the following command:

```
TdChoose.tcl textedit.tcl
```

When the interface appears, select the *Popup* button. You'll always want this window.

Click the leftmost mouse button on a procedure name to prepare it for debugging (and move it to right list). (Left click on the procedure name in right list to remove from debugging list.)

When a debugged procedure gets entered, the second window will display the code and highlight the line executed. The *Next* button at the bottom of that window jumps to the next line of code. The variables window shows the value of variables at that time. Figure 9.5 shows the TDebug debugger.

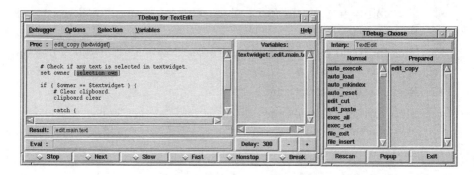

Figure 9.5 The TDebug debugger.

Juice

Juice is another Tcl-based debugger that allows you to place breakpoints at any location in a Tcl script. Juice also includes stack trace and variable watching windows. To run Juice, like TDebug, you run the **juice.tcl** script along with your script to debug. For example,

```
wish juice.tcl my_script_to_debug.tcl
```

When you run juice, you'll see a windows like that shown in Figure 9.6.

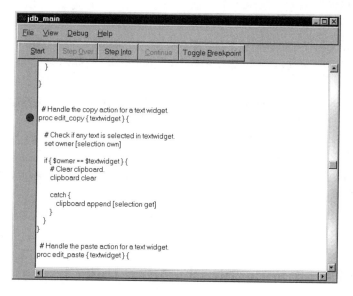

Figure 9.6 The Juice debugger.

Other Tcl-based debuggers include Tk-Inspect and TkDebug.

More Debugging Help

On the CD-ROM, you'll find a number of Tcl/Tk debugging programs in the **contrib/debug** directory.

Summary

This chapter covers techniques for trouble-shooting your Tcl applications. You can create a `tkerror` procedure to trap background errors generated by Tk, from things like event bindings. If you don't override `tkerror`, then Tk will display its own error window. This error window presents a stack trace if desired, a handy tool for debugging your Tcl scripts.

You can use the `catch` command to catch any errors coming from a Tcl script. This is very useful if you load in a file of Tcl commands and this file contains errors.

The `trace` command allows you to trace modifications and accesses to a variable.

The `info` command tells you what is stored inside the Tcl interpreter itself.

The best way to deal with errors is to prevent them from happening in the first place. To do this, you can code defensively to try to ensure that errors won't occur. If all else fails, you can use a Tcl debugger to help you find out what is going wrong.

All in all, handling errors is one of the hardest tasks for any graphical application.

After delving into things that stop your programs, the next chapter shows how to start programs from within your Tcl scripts.

Tcl/Tk Commands Introduced in This Chapter

```
error
info
return
trace
```

CHAPTER 10

Launching Applications from Tcl

This chapter covers:

- The `exec` command
- Tricks of combining `eval` with `exec`
- Redirecting input and output in commands
- Pipes
- Executing Tcl scripts from within Tcl
- Executing scripts after a time out

Executing Commands

Tcl is a scripting language, and launching applications from within scripts is a very common task. Luckily, Tcl provides a number of handy utilities to help.

The primary means of launching applications from within Tcl is the `exec` command, which uses the following basic syntax:

```
exec command arguments
```

The *command* executed must be a valid command for your system. Any *arguments* will be passed on to the *command*. If you end the arguments with an ampersand (&), the *command* will get executed in the background.

UNIX and Windows support a radically different set of commands, which means that cross-platform scripts are tough to create if you use exec.

CROSS-PLATFORM

The *command* argument must be by itself. The exec command takes the first argument and treats it as the name of the command. Thus commands such as {make all} will fail because exec expects the first argument to be a single command. To get around this problem, combine exec with eval.

Tricks of Combining Eval with Exec

One very common problem with the exec command is that it may not interpret its arguments the way you intend it to. On a UNIX system (the concepts are the same under Windows, but you'll use different commands), the following Tcl command probably won't do what you expect:

```
set command {date "+%d %B, %y"}
exec $command
```

From your knowledge of the Tcl interpreter, the above command will try to execute a UNIX command by the name of "date +%d %B, %y" (note the embedded spaces). The real intention is to execute a command called **date** (the UNIX **date** acts differently than the DOS one, by the way) with "+%d %B, %y" as its arguments. To separate the command name from the arguments in a Tcl variable, you can use something more like this:

```
set command {date "+%d %B, %y"}
eval exec $command
```

The use of eval allows for the variable *command* to be expanded to its component parts.

While the preceding example may seem contrived, many Tcl scripts need to execute programs and pass arguments to those programs. To deal with all the problems associated with separating the arguments from the command and yet passing the whole command—arguments and all—in a variable to the exec command, you can use the following procedure to execute commands from Tcl:

```
# Procedure to launch commands.

proc exec_cmd { command } {

    set result ""

    # Grab first argument as command.
    set check_cmd [lindex $command 0]

    set cmd [info commands $check_cmd]

    if { [string length $cmd] > 0 } {

# Command is a Tcl procedure.
        set result [eval $command]
    } else {

# Not a Tcl procedure, so exec it.
        set result [eval exec $command]

    }

    return $result
}

# cmdexec.tcl
```

The exec_cmd procedure first checks if the command is a Tcl procedure. If it is, a simple use of eval will execute that command. Otherwise, exec_cmd passes command to the operating system with the eval exec $command statement.

For example, the glob command is part of Tcl, so the info commands command will return that glob is a defined Tcl procedure. Passing glob to exec_cmd will call only eval, as shown here:

```
% exec_cmd {glob c*.tcl}
canarc.tcl canbit.tcl canline.tcl
canoval.tcl canpoly.tcl canrect.tcl
cantext.tcl canwind.tcl canscrl.tcl
```

`cmdexec.tcl`

On Windows 3.1, you'll likely see some special effects such as screen flashing when you run the `exec_cmd` procedure. Windows NT systems are better behaved when executing subprocesses. Windows 3.1 suffers from the fact that **wish** is a Win32 application and most Windows 3.1 applications are Win16 applications. You should only call `exec` to launch Win32 applications.

Because `exec` is platform-dependent, you'll need to run different code on UNIX or Windows.

Launching Commands on Windows

With the **cmdexec.tcl** script, you can launch a process, such as the **Notepad** text editor, in the foreground:

```
exec_cmd notepad.exe
```

This command launches **notepad.exe** in the foreground. That is, the command waits until you exit **Notepad** before going on. You can launch the program in the background by adding an ampersand, a UNIX convention that works with Tcl's `exec` command on Windows, too:

```
exec_cmd {notepad.exe &}
```

This command launches the **Notepad** editor in the background. In this case, you'll see the **wish** prompt and can enter more commands. If you launch commands in the foreground, you won't get the **wish** prompt until the command exits.

Note the use of curly braces to collect the arguments to `exec_cmd` together. The `exec_cmd` procedure was written to accept only one parameter. (You can, of course, change this.)

Many MS-DOS commands are not real programs that you can launch with `exec`. The **DIR** command, for example, is really handled internally by the MS-DOS shell, usually **cmd.exe** or **command.com**, depending on your version of Windows.

NOTE

For best results, try to exec only Win32 (32-bit) applications.

In trying to get Tcl applications to work on Windows, I started a list of frequently asked questions on Tcl/Tk usage on Windows (located at **http://www.pconline.com/~erc/tclwin.htm** and on the CD-ROM). A very large part of this list revolves around the exec command and problems with various flavors of Windows. Your best bet is to test everything to do with exec very carefully on as many versions of Windows as possible and be prepared for things not working as you'd like.

Launching Commands on UNIX

On UNIX, you probably want to exec all commands in the background, as shown here:

```
exec_cmd {xfd -fn cursor & }
```

This command launches the X font display program **xfd**, showing the cursor font.

Standard Input, Output and Error

Associated with your commands, UNIX includes the idea that all programs have at least three open files:

- stdin for input,
- stdout for output, and
- stderr for error output.

At a UNIX terminal (or terminal window), stdin usually comes from your keyboard. Data you enter at the keyboard gets sent to the application as if it came from the file ID of stdin. (UNIX treats almost everything as a file.) The stdout and stderr file IDs are similarly tied to the terminal's display. Data output via stdout or stderr is sent to the terminal. For example, the

Tcl `puts` command usually sends its output to `stdout`. In Tcl, `stdin`, `stdout`, and `stderr` are file IDs you can use.

Tcl on Windows supports these same concepts, but `stdin`, `stdout`, and `stderr` are part of the Tcl console window.

Error messages are sent to `stderr`, and normal output goes to `stdout`. This allows you to redirect the output of a command to a file while still seeing error messages on your screen.

N O T E

Redirecting Input and Output in Commands

Like the UNIX command line (and to a limited extent, the DOS command line), Tcl allows you to redirect the input and output for programs launched via the `exec` command.

Table 10.1 lists the various ways you can redirect input and output with `exec`.

Table 10.1 Redirecting input and output with exec.

Syntax	Meaning
|	Output (`stdout`) of one command is piped to next.
|&	Output (`stdout` and `stderr`) of one command is piped to next.
< *filename*	*Filename* is read in and passed as the standard input to command.
<@ *fileid*	Data from *fileid* is read in and passed as the standard input to command.
<< *data*	The *data* is passed to the first command as its standard input.
> *filename*	Output from last command gets sent to *filename*, not to screen.
>> *filename*	Standard error output from last command gets appended to *filename*.

>@ *fileid*	Output from last command gets sent to opened *fileid*, not to screen.
>& *filename*	Both standard error and output from last command gets sent to *filename*, not to screen.
>>& *filename*	Both standard error and output from last command gets appended to *filename*.
>&@ *fileid*	Both standard error and output from last command gets sent to opened *fileid*, not to screen.
2> *filename*	Standard error output from last command gets sent to *filename*, not to screen.
2>> *filename*	Standard error output from last command gets appended to *filename*.
2>@ *fileid*	Standard error from last command gets sent to opened *fileid*, not to screen.

CROSS-PLATFORM While it is nice to be able to redirect the output and input of commands, you'll generally only use this capability on UNIX, where such commands are commonplace. On Windows or the Macintosh, though, you'll find fewer commands that print data to a Console window. In fact, Tcl on Windows has to go so far as to create its own console window for stdin, stdout and stderr, because Windows doesn't really have a command line like UNIX does.

To make your applications portable, use I/O redirection sparingly.

Pipes

UNIX and DOS use the term **pipe** to describe sending the output of one command to the input of the next command in a sequence. For example, on UNIX, you can get a count of the number of files in a directory with the following compound command:

```
ls -1 | wc -1
```

544

This command line invokes two UNIX commands: **ls**, which lists the files in a directory, and **wc**, short for *word count*. The pipe symbol (|) causes the output of the **ls** command gets sent as the input to the **wc** command. The **ls** command gets a -1 (one) as its argument, which specifies to list all the file names one per line. The -l (ell) argument to the **wc** command, in turn, tells **wc** to report only a line count, not character and word counts. The **wc** command gets the output of the **ls** command, and counts the number of lines in that output.

Pipes allow you to combine a number of UNIX commands to create new commands. In addition, you can use pipes inside a Tcl script to allow your script to capture the output of a command, or control the data sent to it as input.

To set up a pipe in Tcl, use the open command and a filename that starts with | and ends with the command to execute. For example, on UNIX you can try the following command:

```
set fileid [open "|ls" r]
```

The "filename" passed to open is really a command name. This command sets up the *fileid* variable to reference a piped command. Any output from that command will get written to *fileid*.

To continue the example, you can read all the data associated with a piped command using the following procedure:

```
# Opening a pipe for reading.

#
# Opens command as a pipe for reading.
# Pass command without the leading | character.
#
proc read_pipe { command } {

    # Initialize
    set data ""

    # Start piped command.
    set fileid [open |$command r]
```

```
if { $fileid != "" } {

        # Read data.
        set data [read $fileid]

        close $fileid
    }

    return $data
}

# readpipe.tcl
```

On UNIX, you can test the `read_pipe` procedure with the following command:

```
read_pipe ls
```

You should see a listing of all the files in the current directory. Of course, a better—and more portable—way to generate a file listing in Tcl is to use the `glob` command.

If you want to use a command with arguments, you need to group the arguments, as shown here:

```
read_pipe {ls -CF}
```

On Windows NT, try the following command:

```
read_pipe {cmd /c dir}
```

This command executes the Windows NT MS-DOS command shell, **cmd.exe**, and asks it to run its internal **dir** command. On Windows 95, you can use the following command:

```
read_pipe {command.com /c dir}
```

In either case, the results will look like this:

```
% read_pipe {cmd /c dir}
 Volume in drive F is MS-DOS_6
 Volume Serial Number is 0000-0000

Directory of F:\erc\tcl\2nd_edition

06/05/97  11:08a  <DIR>          .
06/04/97  05:18p  <DIR>          ..
01/07/97  09:55a          515 novice_net.tcl
01/29/97  05:07p       15,193 tclbk2e.txt
01/31/97  05:44p        2,118 other.tcl.books
05/30/97  01:41p          362 canarc.tcl
05/30/97  02:00p          280 canbit.tcl
05/30/97  01:59p          878 tv.xbm
05/30/97  02:15p          703 canline.tcl
05/30/97  02:18p          218 canoval.tcl
05/30/97  02:23p          301 canpoly.tcl
05/30/97  02:33p          233 canrect.tcl
05/30/97  02:40p          416 cantext.tcl
05/30/97  02:48p          240 canwind.tcl
05/30/97  02:50p        8,346 tclbook.inf
05/30/97  02:58p          591 canscrl.tcl
06/04/97  05:14p        6,803 chap9.txt
06/03/97  04:14p          280 stack.tcl
06/04/97  03:26p        1,631 debugtxt.tcl
06/04/97  04:30p          518 trace.tcl
06/05/97  11:12a        2,581 launch.txt
06/05/97  10:35a          668 cmdexec.tcl
06/05/97  11:10a          356 readpipe.tcl
         23 File(s)    46,303 bytes
                   53,006,336 bytes free
```

Again, the best, most portable way to generate a file listing in Tcl is to use the glob command.

N O T E

In many situations, Windows 95 applications will experience strange behavior with pipes. Usually, you'll get synchronous output and the program won't return until the launched application exits. In other situations, applications may contend for the console, resulting in one or the other being delayed. See the on-line documentation for open for more on this and specific Windows versions.

You can also open pipes for writing, or both reading and writing. This is useful if you want to create an application that presents a graphical user interface on an older command-line program. See the on-line documentation on exec and open for more on pipes.

Getting the Process ID

Both UNIX and Windows use an ID number, called a **process ID**, to refer to each process. You can get the ID for the current process with the pid command:

```
% pid
4294012169
```

If you pass a file ID to the pid command that represents an open pipe, the pid command will return the process IDs for all processes in the pipeline.

Executing Tcl Scripts from within Tcl

In addition to exec and open, you can use the source command to execute files of Tcl scripts, as discussed in Chapter 1. The source command loads in a Tcl file and executes all the commands in it, using the following syntax:

```
source filename
```

With the open, gets, close, and exec commands, you could easily build your own version of the source command. See Chapter 6 for more on these file commands.

Using Tcl as a Customization Language

Many friendly applications provide users a means of customizing the applications and then store these customizations so that the user's customizations take effect every time the programs run. In Tcl, I've found the `source` command most useful for this purpose. Tcl executes Tcl commands quite well, so it makes sense to leave any customization file in Tcl format as well. That means you won't have to write a parser for a customization file. Instead, you just `source` it in.

What I usually do is write out the user's preferences as a series of variable settings. The trick is to write out valid Tcl commands, so that on reading in the user preferences, all you need to do is execute the preference file with the `source` command. I usually place all the variables as elements in one global array because you can list all the elements in an array without knowing in advance how many elements there are. Using a Tcl script for preferences provides a number of advantages:

- You don't need to write a special parser, the Tcl parser works fine.

- You can do more than set variables, as the preferences file could create dialog boxes, make buttons, extend menu choices, and so on. All of a sudden, your application becomes highly configurable.

It's very common to combine the `catch` command, described in Chapter 9, with `source` so that errors in the file "sourced in" don't stop your Tcl script.

Executing Scripts after a Timeout

You can use the `after` command to execute Tcl scripts, including the `exec` command, after a time out. You'll find this handy for commands that should execute on a given time cycle, such as a clock display (run the command once a minute), animation (draw each frame after very short but evenly spaced intervals), and so on.

The `after` command requires the following syntax:

```
after milliseconds tcl_script
```

The `after` command returns immediately. Later, at least after the given number of *milliseconds*, the *tcl_script* gets executed. Don't assume the time delays will be exact. Factors such as system load or simply poor-resolution system clocks can alter the actual amount of time delayed.

The *tcl_script* gets executed once, after the given time delay. This means that if you want to set up a periodic task, you need to call `after` again in your *tcl_script*.

For example, if you have a time-consuming task, you may want to display a message, such as *Working...*, to let the user know your program hasn't locked up. To continue showing that the program hasn't locked up, you may want to flash this message or alter its appearance in some way every so often. This will tell the user that the program is indeed continuing. Here's one way to do this using the `after` command:

```
# Use of after for a working... message

#
 # Status of whether (1) or not (0)
 # working message should be displayed.
 #
set working_active 0
global working_active


#
 # Displays a working message and
 # sets up a timer to display again.
 #
proc working_display { widget show_text fore back } {

global working_active

    # Check if we should proceed.
    if { $working_active == 0 } {
        return
    }

    if { $show_text > 0 } {
        $widget configure -fg $fore
```

```
            set show_text 0
      } else {
            $widget configure -fg $back

set show_text 1
      }


# Set up command to run again.
      after 500 "working_display $widget $show_text $fore $back"
}


  # Procedure to start working message.
proc working_start { widget fore back } {

global working_active

set working_active 1
      working_display .label 0 $fore $back


}


# Stops display of working message.
proc working_stop { widget fore } {

      global working_active

      set working_active 0

# Restore foreground color.
      $widget configure -fg $fore
}

set fore black
set back lightgray

label .label -bg $back -fg $fore -text "Working..."
button .start -text "Start Flashing" \
      -command "working_start .label $fore $back"
```

```
button .stop -text "Stop Flashing" \
    -command "working_stop .label $fore"

pack .label .start .stop -fill x

# after.tcl
```

When you run this script, you'll see a window like that in Figure 10.1.

Figure 10.1 Displaying a working message.

The **after.tcl** script makes the foreground and background colors the same on every other iteration. By doing this, the *Working...* message will appear to flash on and off.

You start the working message flashing by calling the `working_start` procedure with the name of a widget (assumed to be a `label`), with foreground and background colors. The `working_display` procedure changes the foreground color, every other time making the foreground and the background the same, for a flashing effect. At the end of the `working_display` procedure, the procedure calls the `after` command which will call the `working_display` procedure again after 500 milliseconds. This process repeats forever, until it is stopped (by calling the `working_stop` procedure).

Notice how the `working_start` procedure calls `after` to set up itself as a command to run again after a time out. This is how you set up multiple executions of the timer.

There are more variants to the `after` command. To wait for a while, without doing anything, you can omit the *tcl_script* argument to `after`. For example:

```
after 500
```

This command waits 500 milliseconds.

The `after cancel` command cancels an after script. The basic format is:

```
after cancel id
```

The *id* is a value returned by the original `after` command that set up the script to run. For example:

```
set id [after 500 {puts timed out}]
after cancel $id
```

If you want to wait until the Tk script is idle, that is, until after all incoming events have been handled, you can skip the time value and use `after idle`, as shown here:

```
after idle tcl_script
```

The `after info` command returns information on available `after` time outs:

```
after info
```

For example:

```
% set id [after 500000 {puts timed out}]
after#1
% after info
after#1
% after cancel   $id
% after info
%
```

The `after cancel` command removed the original time out.

Summary

The `exec` command allows you to execute programs on your system. These programs are likely to be very different between Windows and UNIX, which makes writing portable Tcl scripts with `exec` difficult.

You can combine the `eval` command with `exec` to break up a variable into its component parts and create a better command line for `exec`. This is often necessary if you have a command with parameters.

You can create a pipe to an application if you pass a pseudo file name of *| command* to the `open` command. The leading | indicates that the Tcl interpreter should open a pipe.

Tcl supports three standard file IDs for input and output to the console: `stdin` for input, `stdout` for output, and `stderr` for error output. On Windows, these three file IDs are part of the Tcl console window.

The `source` command allows you to execute Tcl script files from within Tcl.

The `after` command allows you to run a Tcl script after a given time out. This time out occurs only once. So, to set up a periodic command, you must call `after` in your Tcl script each time it gets invoked.

Tcl/Tk Commands Introduced in This Chapter

```
after
eval
exec
pid
source
```

CHAPTER 11

Hypertext and On-line Help

This chapter covers:

- On-line help
- Short help messages in the status area
- Tooltips help
- Using HTML for on-line help
- Launching Web browsers to display help
- Displaying HTML in the text widget
- Reading data from URLs with the Http package

On-line Help

On-line help is essential for any graphical application. No matter how easy you may think a program is, helpful information is always a plus for new users, as well as for experienced users who are using a feature for the first time or for casual users who do not use your program every day. On-line help cuts the amount of frustration time before a user becomes productive with your software. Furthermore, users expect on-line help with all modern applications. And, you'll find many options with Tcl that allow you to display on-line help.

This chapter covers how to display on-line help in a Tcl application. The focus is on short help messages, although longer help text in a window is also discussed. For the longer help information, HTML, the Hypertext Mark-Up Language, stands out as a natural format. So, this chapter covers launching Netscape Navigator or Internet Explorer to display HTML help files, as well as using Tcl to parse HTML help files and display HTML in the text widget. You'll also see how to use the Http package to acquire Web pages over a network.

Short Help Messages

Short help messages provide clues on how to use the interface. As the user moves the mouse over widgets, short messages appear. There are two main styles for this kind of help: tooltips help and messages in the status area. Both styles use similar techniques and both solve a similar problem: figuring out what the interface does, especially for modern interfaces sporting decks of toolbars containing cryptic icons that are somehow supposed to be faster than textual buttons.

Short Help Messages in the Status Area

Short help messages usually appear in a status area at the bottom of the main window. When you move the mouse about the window, messages appear and disappear as the mouse crosses Tk widget boundaries.

The main method to implement this comes from bindings on Enter and Leave events (as discussed in Chapter 8). The Enter event binding displays a message for the current widget under the mouse. The Leave binding clears the message. In Chapter 8, you saw the basics for button widgets on a toolbar:

```
button .open -text "Open"
label .status
pack .open .status -side top -fill x

# ...

bind .open <Enter> \
  ".status configure -text {Open file}"
```

```
bind .open <Leave> \
  ".status configure -text { }"
```

Tooltips Help

Tooltips help uses many of the same techniques as the short help messages displayed in a status area. Instead of a status area, though, **tooltips help** displays a small floating window by the widget in question. This small window holds the short help message. To avoid constant flashing and creating all sorts of small windows, you should impose a threshold time period. If the mouse enters a widget and remains there for the threshold time period, then the floating window should appear with the short help message.

The floating window goes away if you move the mouse outside the window.

To implement the threshold time period, you can use the `after` command discussed in Chapter 10 combined with a binding on the `<Enter>` event. The sequence goes like this:

1. When the mouse enters the widget; the `<Enter>` event binding calls the `after` command to display the tooltip window after the threshold time period.
2. Create a `toplevel` window to display the tooltips help if the mouse is still in the original widget after the threshold time period. The actual message can appear in a `label` widget. This window should not have a border (achieve this using `wm override`).
3. The window should go away if the mouse pointer leaves the tooltip window.

The following code implements a simple tooltips help system:

```
# Tooltips help.

 #
 # Call on <Enter> to set up a tooltips message.
 #
proc tooltip { widget message } {
```

```
    after 900 "tooltip_show $widget $message"


}

   # Private procedure to show tooltip.
proc tooltip_show { widget args } {

    # Check if mouse is still within widget.
    set mx [winfo pointerx $widget]
    set my [winfo pointery $widget]

    set has_mouse [winfo containing $mx $my]

    if { $has_mouse == $widget } {

        if { [winfo exists .tooltip] } {
            destroy .tooltip
        }

        toplevel .tooltip -cursor top_left_arrow

        # No border around window.
        wm override .tooltip 1

        # Hide until positioned.
        wm withdraw .tooltip

        #
        # Position window a little bit
        # down and to right of widget.
        #
        set x [expr \
            [winfo rootx $widget] + \
            ( [winfo width $widget] / 2) ]
        set y [expr \
            [winfo rooty $widget] + \
            ( [winfo height $widget] / 2) ]

    # Make window appear near mouse.
```

```
    if { $mx < $x } {
        set x [expr $mx - 3]
    }

    if { $my < $y } {
        set y [expr $my - 3]
    }

        wm geometry .tooltip "+$x+$y"

        label .tooltip.help -text "$args" -bg yellow
        pack .tooltip.help -ipadx 20

        # Close window when mouse leaves.
        bind .tooltip <Leave> {
            destroy .tooltip
        }

        # Show window.
        wm deiconify .tooltip
    }

}

# Create a few buttons for testing.
button .b1 -text B1
button .b2 -text B2
button .b3 -text B3
label .nothing -text "No tooltip help, sorry"

bind .b1 <Enter> {
    tooltip .b1 {Press for B1 functionality}
}

bind .b2 <Enter> {
    tooltip .b2 {Press for B2 functionality}
}

bind .b3 <Enter> {
```

```
    tooltip .b3 {Press for B3 functionality}
}
```

```
pack .b1 .b2 .b3 .nothing -fill y -side left
```

```
# tooltip.tcl
```

In this code, the `<Enter>` event bindings call the `tooltip` procedure to get everything set up. The `tooltip` procedure merely calls `tooltip_show` after a given threshold time period. The `tooltip_show` then checks the mouse position. If it's still in the widget, then `tooltip_show` creates a `toplevel` window and places the message inside a `label` widget. Note the use of the `wm override` command to prevent any window manager from placing a title bar or other decorations on the `toplevel` widget

To eventually get rid of the tooltip window, `tooltip_show` sets up an event binding on the `<Leave>` event. If the mouse leaves the window, then the tooltip window will get destroyed. (Just in case, `tooltip_show` will destroy any window named *.tooltip* if it exists already.)

When you run the **tooltip.tcl** script, you'll see a set of dummy button widgets as shown in Figure 11.1.

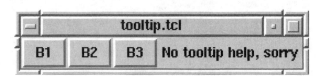

Figure 11.1 Before displaying tooltip help.

As the mouse moves into the widgets, tooltip windows will appear after the threshold time period, as shown in Figure 11.2.

Figure 11.2 Showing a tooltip help window.

The threshold time period is the real key to how this all works. If you have too small a threshold, the tooltip windows will appear too often, getting in the way. If you have too long a threshold, the user won't know that tooltip help is available.

Tooltip help is especially useful for toolbars of bitmap buttons.

Determining Which Kind of Short Help to Use: Tooltips or Short Messages to the Status Area

The status line form of short help is easier to implement than tooltip help. Most modern applications supports one of these two forms of short help messages. Very few applications support both. Both forms provide help on individual widgets.

There's another form of help for individual widgets, often called context-sensitive help. **Context-sensitive help** switches you into a mode where you to select a widget with the mouse and then get help on that widget. Usually the mouse cursor turns into a question mark to show that you're in a special mode. Chapter 14 covers cursors. For the actual context-sensitive help mode, you can use a binding on all widgets and then use the %W construct to retrieve the widget name. For example,

```
bind all <Button-1> {

    # Get widget mouse clicked in.
    set widget %W

    # Call up help related to widget...
}
```

In addition to short help messages, most applications require a longer form of help that is called up from the *Help* menu.

The Help Menu

On-line help exists to help the user make effective use of your program. No matter how intuitive the application appears—to its designer—you should still provide on-line help. In most applications, you call up help from the *Help* menu.

As discussed in Chapter 4, the *Help* menu may provide a number of help topics, such as a reference manual, help on the menus, a table of contents, an index, and even a tutorial. Use whatever topics are appropriate for your application.

Some help systems, notably Microsoft Windows help, provide special means to generate an index and table of contents. This means that the index is in one format, the contents are in another and individual help sections are in a third format. I've found it far easier to simply use HTML for all on-line help. The index is merely an HTML file, as is the table of contents and all help topics. This simplifies the format and allows you to make use of the many tools available for creating HTML. (Microsoft Windows help, as of this writing, is migrating to HTML as well.)

Using HTML for On-line Help

Unless you've been living in a cave, you're aware of the World Wide Web and the huge success of the Internet. Web pages are documents formatted in HTML.

Because of its great success, there's a plethora of software available for creating, modifying, and viewing HTML documents. Even though other document formats provide greater control over the exact formatting in the document, HTML is extremely portable and provides almost everything you need for on-line help.

In the sections that follow, I'll show how you can use HTML as the base format for your on-line help.

Launching Web Browsers to Display Help

Many large companies devote huge efforts to creating top-notch HTML viewers commonly known as Web browsers. So, instead of writing your own HTML viewer (even though I'll show how), it may make sense to call up a professional viewer to display your on-line help.

The advantages of this approach include:

- The latest Web browsers handle complicated HTML issues and the display of images, etc.
- Just about every computer has a Web browser.
- You can save a lot of time by reusing code.

The main disadvantages are the extra launch time to start up the Web browser (because Web browsers are large applications) and special configuration needed to identify which browser to call up and the command-line sequence for doing so.

The following simple script shows one way to display on-line help using one of the two most common browsers, Netscape Navigator:

```
# Example of on-line help
# launching a Web browser.
#

  # Calls up given help file in background.
proc help_exec { program helpfile } {

    set err ""

    catch {
        eval exec $program $helpfile &
    } err

    return $err
}

help_exec netscape helptest.htm

# helpexec.tcl
```

The **helpexec.tcl** script calls up Netscape Navigator to display an example help file named **helptest.htm** (the **helptest.htm** file is available on the CD-ROM).

The **helpexec.tcl** script makes a basic assumption that you'll have an executable named **netscape**, when in fact you may have an executable named slightly differently, such as **netscape3.01**, or use another Web browser, such as Microsoft Internet Explorer. Hence, there is a need for configuration that allows the user to select the browser.

What If the Browser Is Already Running?

Because of the long launch time required to start up a Web browser, you should take advantage of any browser already running. Some browsers allow you to communicate with a running browser and ask it to call up a new file—your help file.

With Netscape Navigator, you can use the -remote option to build up a command line like the following:

```
netscape -remote openFile(filename)
```

The *filename* should be the full root path to the file you want to call up. The reason for the full path is that **netscape** may have been launched from another directory.

We can modify the **helpexec.tcl** script to launch Netscape Navigator with the -remote option, as shown here:

```
#
# Example of on-line help
# launching Netscape Navigator.
#

   # Calls up given help file in background.
proc help_exec { program helpfile } {

    set err ""

    catch {
        eval exec $program $helpfile &
    } err

    return $err
}

 # Need full path to file.
set dir [pwd]
set filename $dir/helptest.htm

help_exec {netscape -remote} openFile($filename)

# helpnets.tcl
```

NOTE The `openFile($filename)` looks like a Tcl array value, but it isn't. The *openFile* is part of the syntax required for the `-remote` option to **netscape**.

Furthermore, for the `-remote` option to work, **netscape** must be running.

Using Microsoft Internet Explorer

With Internet Explorer, you need to launch the program **iexplore.exe**. Note that the default installation is in **\Program Files\Microsoft Internet\iexplore.exe**. The two spaces in the directory path can be a real pain because you need to group the full path as one Tcl argument.

The **helpie.tcl** script does that and launches Microsoft Internet Explorer to display on-line help:

```
# Example of on-line help
# launching Microsoft Internet Explorer.
#

  # Calls up given help file in background.
proc help_exec { program helpfile } {

    set err ""

    catch {
        eval exec $program $helpfile &
    } err

    return $err
}

  # Need full path to file.
set dir [pwd]
set filename $dir/helptest.htm

set err [help_exec \
   "{C:/program files/microsoft internet/iexplore.exe}" \
```

```
    $filename]

puts "$err"

# helpie.tcl
```

 NOTE These are not the only Web browsers available. You might want to look at Plume, a Web browser written in Tcl, as well as Amaya and Arena, two freeware programs that can display HTML files. In addition, in the fast-moving world of the Internet, commands that work for one release of a browser may no longer work on future releases.

Displaying HTML in `text` Widgets

Because of the long time it takes to launch a Web browser and the more complicated configurations required, you may want to display HTML inside a Tcl `text` widget within your own application and simplify matters. The `text` widget, as discussed in Chapter 5, provides tags that allow you to control the display of text. With tags, you can write Tcl code for the various formatting commands in HTML, such as bold, headings, and italic. Because you can bind events to tags, you can support HTML links.

All this is possible and fairly straightforward. You could write Tcl code to support HTML, but this has already been done for you (a number of times, in fact). One of the most common sets of HTML routines for Tcl is called the html_library, a set of freeware Tcl procedures to display HTML.

To use the html_library, you need to follow these steps:

1. Source in the file **html_library.tcl** (or include this file in your code, or convert it to a package, etc.).

2. Create a `text` widget. Normally this will be in a special help top-level window.

3. Initialize the `text` widget for HTML with the `HMinit_win` procedure.

4. Load an HTML file (or get HTML data from a Web server) and place all the HTML data into a global variable named *html*.

5. Call the `HMparse_html` procedure to convert the HTML to `text` widget tags. You can use the following command as a guide:

```
HMparse_html $html "HMrender $text"
```

That's all you need to do to call up an HTML file into a help `text` widget. Of course, there are a few more things you may want to set up.

Loading HTML Files

With the html_library, it's up to you to load an HTML file and place the data into a global variable named *html*. (Technically, you could get away with a different variable name, but this is easiest.)

To load a file, you can use the following procedure as a guide:

```
proc help_load_html { filename } {

    # Default data in case of errors.
    set data "<title>Bad file $filename</title>
        <h1>Error reading $filename</h1><p>"

    catch {
        set fileid [open $filename]

        set data [read $fileid]
        close $fileid
    }

        return $data
}
```

The `help_load_html` procedure returns the data from an HTML file, or an error message written in HTML for display to the user. (You could also extend this procedure to get HTML data from a Web server.)

Handling Links

One of the neat aspects to HTML is that you can have a link that will call up another HTML document (or run a script, load a sound bite, etc.). The html_library uses the idea of a callback procedure to handle links. When a link is selected, it calls a procedure named `HMlink_callback`.

```
 # Private procedure to handle a link.
proc HMlink_callback {win href} {
```

```
}
```

In the `HMlink_callback` procedure, the parameters are the name of the `text` widget that's displaying HTML, *win*, and the link data, *href*, usually a URL from the `<A HREF>` HTML anchor. (For more on HTML, see Appendix A.)

You need to write this procedure, to handle the links in your HTML files properly. For example, if all your help files are stored in a particular location—a location that the user specifies on installation—then your `HMlink_callback` procedure must look in the installation directory.

Your `HMlink_callback` procedure needs to load an HTML file and then reset the `text` widget display for the new data. You can use the `help_load_html` procedure to load the HTML file. The following commands then reset the `text` widget display:

```
HMreset_win $win
HMparse_html $html "HMrender $win"
```

All the procedure names in the html_library start with *HM*.

N O T E

Improving the Look of Links

The html_library by default highlights links with a 2-pixel-wide raised bevel. Such highlighting doesn't really look that good, so you may want to change it. To do so, you have two options. You can write your own `HMlink_setup` procedure, or you can change the *HMevents* array. The `HMlink_setup` procedure is rather complicated, so I found it easier to change the *HMevents* array.

The *HMevents* array holds the tag configuration options for a number of events, including Enter, Leave, Button-1 (down), and ButtonRelease-1. You can use the following code, from the **helpdlg.tcl** script, as an example for changing this highlighting to underline the link under the mouse cursor rather than showing a raised 3D bevel:

```
# Control look of links.
# The default is a raised 3D bevel.
```

```
global HMevents
array set HMevents {
    Enter   {-underline 1}
    Leave   {-underline 0}
    1               {-underline 0}
    ButtonRelease-1 {-underline 0}
}
```

Handling Images

Tk can display GIF images and so can the html_library. For JPEG images (the other common image format for Web pages), you need an extension to Tk, such as the Img extension on the CD-ROM in the **contrib/extend** directory.

Source Code for the HTML Viewer Help Window

Putting this all together, we can create an on-line help package that displays HTML files with very little Tcl code. In the **helpdlg.tcl** script, the help procedure creates a toplevel window to display the on-line help, loads the passed-in help HTML file, and then calls the html_library routines to display the HTML in a text widget.

To call the help procedure, all you need is the name of a file to call up. For example,

```
help helptest.htm
```

The rest of the procedures in the **helpdlg.tcl** script are considered private to the on-line help system. You can use the **helpdlg.tcl** script as an example for creating your own on-line help system.

The source code follows:

```
# Use of the html_library for on-line help.

 #
 # For this example, you must have
 # html_library.tcl in the current directory.
 #
puts "Loading html_library.tcl"
```

```
source html_library.tcl

#
# Control look of links.
# The default is raised bevel.
#
global HMevents
array set HMevents {
    Enter    {-underline 1}
    Leave    {-underline 0}
    1                {-underline 0}
    ButtonRelease-1 {-underline 0}
}

# Global variables.
set help_initialized 0
global help_initialized

# Creates a help window and calls up HTML help file.
proc help { helpfile } {
    global help_initialized
    global html

    set text [help_create $helpfile]

    # Load help file.
    set html [help_load_html $helpfile]

    # Initialize HTML.
    if { $help_initialized == 0 } {

        set help_initialized 1

        HMinit_win $text

        HMset_state $text -size 2
        HMset_indent $text 1.2
    } else {
```

```
        HMreset_win $text
    }

    HMparse_html $html "HMrender $text"
}


  # Handle the copy action for a text widget.
proc edit_copy { textwidget } {

    # Check if any text is selected in textwidget.
    set owner [selection own]

    if { $owner == $textwidget } {
        # Clear clipboard.
        clipboard clear

        catch {
            clipboard append [selection get]
        }
    }
}


  # Creates help window, called by help.
proc help_create { filename } {

    set top .helpwindow
    set frm $top.frm

    if { [winfo exists $top ] } {
        wm deiconify $top
        return $frm.text
    }

    toplevel $top
    # Set up wm options for .help  LATER....

    # Menubar.
    frame $top.menubar -bd 1 -relief raised
```

```
menubutton  $top.menubar.file -text "File" -underline 0 \
    -menu  $top.menubar.file.menu
menubutton  $top.menubar.edit -text "Edit" -underline 0 \
    -menu  $top.menubar.edit.menu

menu  $top.menubar.file.menu

    # Reset to original message.
$top.menubar.file.menu add command -label "Original Topic" \
    -command "help_disp_file $frm.text $filename"

$top.menubar.file.menu add command -label "Close" \
    -command "destroy  $top"

menu  $top.menubar.edit.menu
$top.menubar.edit.menu add command -label "Copy" \
    -command "edit_copy $frm.text"

pack  $top.menubar.file  $top.menubar.edit -side left
pack  $top.menubar -side top -fill x

# Main help area.
frame $frm -bd 0
text $frm.text -width 80 -height 20 \
    -yscrollcommand "$frm.v_scroll set"  \
    -xscrollcommand "$frm.h_scroll set"

scrollbar  $frm.v_scroll \
    -command "$frm.text yview"

scrollbar $frm.h_scroll -orient horizontal \
    -command "$frm.text xview"

pack $frm.v_scroll -side right -fill y
pack $frm.h_scroll -side bottom -fill x
pack $frm.text -expand 1 -fill both

pack $frm -side top -expand 1 -fill both
```

```
    # Return name of text widget.
    return $frm.text
}


 # Private procedure to handle a link.
proc HMlink_callback {win href} {
    global html

    #
    # If this is not a file link,
    # or if it has file://, you may
    # need to parse out the type
    # of URL.
    #
    # Load up HTML file.
    set html [help_load_html $href]

    # Display in text widget.
    help_disp_html $win $html


}


  # Private procedure to display HTML.
proc help_disp_html {win html} {

    # Display in text widget.
    HMreset_win $win
    HMparse_html $html "HMrender $win"


}


  # Private procedure to load HTML file and display.
proc help_disp_file {win filename} {

    set html [help_load_html $filename]

    help_disp_html $win $html
}
```

```
    # Private procedure to load HTML file.
proc help_load_html { filename } {

    # Default data in case of errors.
    set data "<title>Bad file $filename</title>
        <h1>Error reading $filename</h1><p>"

    catch {
        set fileid [open $filename]

        set data [read $fileid]
        close $fileid
    }

        return $data
}


# TEST CODE. COMMENT OUT FOR REAL USE.
help helptest.htm

# helpdlg.tcl
```

The test code displays a sample HTML file. Naturally, you should comment out the test call to the `help` procedure if you use this in your applications.

When you run the **helpdlg.tcl** script and call up on-line help, you'll see a window like that shown in Figure 11.3.

The menu bar in the help window allows you to redisplay the very first topic called up from the `help` procedure, close the help window, or copy selected text to the clipboard.

To use the html_library from the **helpdlg.tcl** example script, you must have the file **html_library.tcl** in the current directory. That's not a very good restriction, so you probably want to set this up as a package (see Chapter 14) or simply include the file **html_library.tcl** into your Tcl scripts or use the `source` command but specify the directory during installation. In any case, you need to deal with this issue.

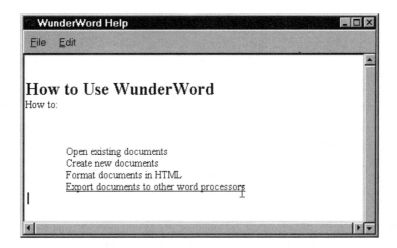

Figure 11.3 Showing HTML for on-line help.

The **html_library.tcl** script is located in the **contrib/html** directory on the CD-ROM. This directory contains HTML files that describe how to use the html_library.

Reading URLs

The **helpdlg.tcl** script only allows the ability to display HTML from files (see the HMlink_callback procedure). The World Wide Web, of course, allows for HTML documents from all sorts of locations. To help with this, Tcl comes with the Http package, which allows you to acquire data using the Hypertext Transport Protocol or HTTP. A **package** is a set of related Tcl routines, and the Http package is standard with Tcl 8.0 and higher releases.

Chapter 14 describes packages in greater detail. For now, you need to know that to use a particular package, you need to call the package require command, as shown here:

```
package require http 1.0
```

You can also skip the version number, 1.0, to get the latest version:

```
package require http
```

After you call the `package require` command, Tcl will automatically load any procedures you call from the Http package.

The main command you need to call is `http_get`, which gets the data from a URL. The basic syntax follows:

```
http_get url options
```

N O T E The `http_get` procedure is not forgiving. You need to place an ending / on most URLs. For example, **http://www.pconline.com/~erc** is not a valid URL to the `http_get` procedure, but **http://www.pconline.com/~erc/**, with a trailing /, is. Whether or not you consider this a bug (there is some debate), you need to be aware of this limitation.

The main option is `-command`, which specifies a Tcl procedure to call when the URL data are acquired. With most Web servers, it takes some time to get the URL data. So, with this `-command` option, `http_get` returns right away and then calls your Tcl script when the data arrive.

The Tcl script you pass with the `-command` option gets called with a special token variable that really points to a state array for the HTTP transfer. The Tcl script takes the following format:

```
proc http_callback { token } {
    upvar #0 $token state

    if { $state(status) == ok } {

        set data $state(body)

    } elseif { $state(status) == error } {
    } else {
        # reset state

    }
}
```

You can use the value of the `status` element in the *state* array to determine whether or not the transfer succeeded. If the transfer succeeded, you can use the `body` element of the *state* array to get at the URL data.

Displaying Progress

The Internet is not known for speed, so you may want to display a progress message while the data arrive. To set this up, use the `-progress` option to `http_get`. The `-progress` option needs to include a Tcl script, which gets called with three parameters: the special state token, the total amount of bytes expected, and the current amount of bytes received. You can use this to update a progress dialog window or to display the current amount of bytes received in a label widget (perhaps as part of a status bar).

The Tcl script takes the following format:

```
proc http_progress {token total_amt current_amt} {
    upvar #0 $token state

    # ...
}
```

If problems occur, you may want to specify a time out using the `-timeout` option and passing the number of milliseconds to allow for the transfer. If the timer times out, then the transfer is reset.

The Http package stores all the data about in-progress transfers in a *state* array, which you access via the `upvar` command in the callback procedures. The *state* array has a number of elements, shown in Table 11.1.

Table 11.1 Elements in the HTTP state array.

Element	Holds
body	The data from the URL; empty if using -
channel option.	
currentsize	Current number of bytes received.
error	Any error message.
http	Status from HTTP server.

continued

Table 11.1 continued

meta	Meta data about the document, e.g., content type.
status	Status of completed transfer: ok, reset, or error. Not set until complete.
totalsize	The number of bytes in the data, from the content length.
type	The content type.
url	The actual URL.

You can configure the Http package to deal with proxy servers (commonly used with Internet firewalls) with the http_config command. The -proxyhost option sets the proxy hostname, while the -proxyport option sets the port number.

Putting this all together, the following example acquires the raw data for an HTTP URL that you enter:

```
# Get URL data with http_get.

 # Requires Http package.
package require http

 # Create some widgets to show the data.
set frm .url_frm
frame $frm -bd 0
label $frm.url_label -text "Url: " -anchor e
entry $frm.url -width 40 -textvariable url

bind $frm.url <Key-Return> {
    global url

    .status config -text ""
    update

    http_get $url -command http_callback \
```

```
        -progress http_progress
}

pack $frm.url_label -side left -fill y
pack $frm.url -side right -expand 1
pack $frm -side top -fill x

set frm .text_frm
frame $frm -bd 0
text $frm.text -height 25 \
    -yscrollcommand "$frm.v_scroll set" \
    -xscrollcommand "$frm.h_scroll set"
scrollbar $frm.v_scroll -command "$frm.text yview"
scrollbar $frm.h_scroll -command "$frm.text xview" \
  -orient horizontal
pack $frm.v_scroll -side right -fill y
pack $frm.h_scroll -side bottom -fill x
pack $frm.text -side left -expand 1
pack $frm -side top -expand 1

label .status -bd 2 -relief sunken \
  -anchor w
pack .status -side bottom -fill x

 # Procedure to display progress of HTTP get.
proc http_progress {token total_amt current_amt} {

    .status config -text \
        "$current_amt/$total_amt bytes received"
}

  # Procedure to handle HTTP completion.
proc http_callback { token } {
    upvar #0 $token state

    .text_frm.text delete 1.0 end

    if { $state(status) == "ok" } {
```

```
        # Copy HTML data to text widget.
        .text_frm.text insert end "$state(body)"

} elseif { $state(status) == "error" } {
        .text_frm.text insert end "$state(error)"
} else {
      # reset state
        .text_frm.text insert end "HTTP transfer reset."
    }
}

# htppget.tcl
```

When you run the **htppget.tcl** script, you'll see a window like that in Figure 11.4.

Figure 11.4 Getting HTTP data with htppget.tcl.

Notice that the **htppget.tcl** script just grabs the raw HTML data. You can then combine this with the HMlink_callback procedure in **help.tcl** to create a Tcl Web browser. The **help.tcl** example just loads files.

Summary

Every application you write should provide on-line help. You may want to include some form of short help message that appears when you move the mouse over a widget. The short help message can be displayed in a status area at the bottom of the window or with pop-up tooltip style windows.

In addition to short help messages, your applications should also provide for full on-line help called from the *Help* menu. One of the easiest ways to do this is to use the html_library and create your help files in HTML format.

You can go even farther with on-line help and use the http_get command to get HTML data from a URL, just like Web browsers do.

Tcl Commands Introduced in This Chapter

```
http_config
http_get
```

Communicating Between Applications: Networking and Beyond

This chapter covers:

- Ways to communicate between applications
- The send command
- Networking with sockets
- Channels for socket and file commands

Communication Methods

Tcl provides a number of ways for applications to communicate with other applications, including the send command and TCP/IP network sockets.

In brief, the send command sends a Tcl script from one Tcl application to another, executing in the remote Tcl application. The send command is limited to Tcl applications only.

The socket command, on the other hand, allows you to create Internet TCP/IP sockets for communication with other Tcl applications or any network application. Once created, a socket link becomes a channel, a Tcl abstraction for files and communication links.

You can then work with that channel much the same as with files.

This chapter shows how to use Tcl to communicate with other programs.

584

Sending Commands to Applications

You can send a command from one Tcl script to another with the send command. With the other Tcl application executes the command and then returns the result as a text string to the calling application (everything in Tcl is text, remember?). Thus, send is similar to a remote procedure call. The calling application asks the remote application to execute the Tcl code.

As of this writing, the send command doesn't work on Windows. Sooner or later, send should be available on Windows. In the meantime, you can download a dynamic link library (DLL) that provides send on Windows based on dynamic data exchange (DDE). See the following URL for more on this: **http://www.sunlabs.com/~kcorey/tcldde.html**.

The basic syntax for send follows:

```
send options application command arguments
```

The application identifies the remote Tcl application based on its name. Because of this, each Tcl application is named. The tk appname command returns the name of your Tcl application:

```
set application [tk appname]
```

The default name is something like **wish8.0**. You can also change the name for your application with the tk appname command:

```
tk appname newname
```

If your application name begins with a dash, -, the send command will likely interpret this name as an option instead of the name as you intend. To get around this problem, you can use two dashes, --, to separate the end of the options and the beginning of the name. For example,

```
send -- -myname puts "Hello"
```

In this example, the Tcl interpreter is named *-myname*. It's generally a good idea to avoid names that start with dashes.

To get the names of all running Tcl applications, use the `winfo interps` command:

```
% winfo interps
wish8.0 app1 app2 tkdesk
```

The `send` command accepts a few options, including `-async` to send the command asynchronously (rather than waiting for completion) and `-display` of with an X Window display name.

For `send` to work, of course, you must have more than one Tcl application running.

To try out the `send` command, run two copies of **wish**. In each, set up a unique application name with the `tk appname` command. For example,

```
% tk appname app1
app1
```

In the second **wish** window, try the following name:

```
% tk appname app2
app2
```

Then, try to send a command from one interpreter to another, using the following command and assuming the second—remote—application is named *app2*:

```
send app2 {button .b -text Remote ; pack .b }
```

This should create a `button` widget in the second **wish** window.

The `send` command may generate an error like the following:

```
X server insecure (must use xauth-style authorization);
command ignored
```

If you see an error like this, you are facing `send`'s famous security issue.

Security Issues with Send

The ability to send commands to other applications opens up a whole new world of Tcl capability. But, it also opens up a gaping security whole. In UNIX, you need to use the **xauth** security system for controlling access to your X display, or send won't work between displays. In addition, the list of trusted hosts managed by the **xhost** program must be empty. You may still be able to use send between applications running on the same display, though, depending on your X display's security setup.

You can also compile the Tk source code with this security turned off, but this is not recommended. (Use a -DTK_NO_SECURITY compiler flag when compiling Tk.)

On Windows, the send command is disabled in the current release. Hopefully, a later version of Tcl will allow this handy command.

The send command, clever as it is, works only for communication between Tcl applications. Even though Tcl is clearly the most superior system available, some people still insist on writing code in other programming languages. Because of that, you may want to focus on a more general-purpose communications mechanism, such as networking sockets.

Networking Sockets

A **socket** is a network link between one application and another using standard Internet protocols, especially TCP/IP (transmission control protocol/internet protocol). Because TCP/IP is a standard means of communication, your options are a lot more open with sockets than with the send command.

Sockets allow reliable bidirectional communication, that is, you can send and receive data on the same socket. TCP/IP sockets will ensure that data packets get from one program to another.

Once created, a socket looks a lot like a file to your Tcl script. That is, you can use the read and puts commands to read data from and send data to your socket connection.

Sockets are identified by a network host address, called an IP address, and a port number. The IP address is typically a 4-byte number such as 192.42.6.1. The IP address identifies the machine you want to communicate with. The port number controls which port on the given machine. (This allows multiple sockets to exist on the same machine.)

Some network services—such as FTP, the file transfer protocol (20); HTTP, the hyper text transport protocol (80); and the X Window System (6000)—tend to use predefined port numbers. This allows programs to connect with the proper service on a given machine. In any case, if you communicate between programs with sockets, both sides of the communication must agree in advance which port number to use.

Socket-based communication is inherently client-server communication. One side of the link is the server, and the other side is the client. Servers are usually designed to remain active for longer periods of time and to provide some form of service. FTP servers allow you to transfer files, HTTP servers provide Web pages, and X servers provide windows. The Tcl code for creating clients and servers differ, with servers typically being harder to create. To get any work done with sockets, you first need to create them.

To create a networking socket, call the `socket` command.

The `socket` Command

The `socket` command creates a socket. To create a socket that connects with some network service, that is, to create a client socket, you can use the following syntax:

```
socket host port
```

The *host* parameter identifies the machine to connect. You can use a network IP address in a form like 192.42.6.1, or you can use a network host name, such as **www.pconline.com**. A special host name of `localhost` refers to the machine you're running on.

The *port* parameter is an integer that names the port number to use. Both sides of the communication must agree to use the same port number or you won't communicate. Generally, low-number ports are reserved by the system. (I tend to pick numbers in the 2000s. You should to pick numbers larger than 1024.) On UNIX, you can look in the file **/etc/services** for a listing of predefined services and port numbers.

When creating a client socket, you can use any of the options listed in Table 12.1. In most cases, you will not need these options.

Table 12.1 Client socket options.

Option	Usage
-async	Creates an asynchronous socket connection. That is, it returns right away even though the connection has not been made. This is not the same as nonblocking or blocking connections, which are described later.
-myaddr *address*	Provides the network name or IP address of the client-side network connection to use. This is for systems with more than one net work interface.
-myport *port*	Names a *port* number to use for the client side of the connection.

The `socket` command returns a channel identifier, much like that returned by the `open` command with files. You can then use this identifier to read and write data using the `read` and `puts` commands described in Chapter 6. For example,

```
set sockid [socket localhost 2345]
puts $sockid "Hello from Tcl"

close $sockid
```

To achieve full communication, one application creates a client socket and other a server socket.

Server Sockets

Server sockets require more complicated code than client sockets. Most of the extra work required is to handle incoming client connections.

To create a server socket, use the `-server` option on the `socket` command:

```
socket -server tcl_script port
```

In server mode, your application listens for incoming client connections on the given *port* number. When a connection occurs, the *tcl_script* gets executed and is passed such parameters as the new channel, the IP address of the client's host, and the client's port number. This means a server may have connections to multiple clients at any one time.

You can use the following as a guide for your Tcl script that gets called when an incoming connection is made:

```
proc accept { sock addr port } {


}
```

This may seem a little confusing at first, but it should be clear by the end of the discussion on sockets. There's a lot of material to cover before you can get started.

Server sockets can also use the -myaddr option, as shown in Table 12.1.

The -server option is a lot easier than in most other programming languages like Perl or C++. In most cases, you need to call the C functions socket, connect, bind, and listen.

N O T E

The server thus has two sets of sockets: the main socket that exists only to listen for incoming connections and individual sockets spawned off when a client connects. This second type of socket is used for communication.

Server-side sockets work for Tk applications only. If you are using **tclsh** instead of **wish**, you need to call the vwait command. **wish** provides an event loop that checks for incoming events. Without this, your Tcl script passed to the socket -server command won't ever get executed. (That's what vwait can do for you.)

N O T E

The vwait command waits until a given variable changes. While waiting, vwait enters the Tcl event loop that checks for channel input/output events. Before you call vwait, you set up some event-handling code, such as the Tcl code set with the -server option to the socket command or the fileevent command described in the section on Handling Asynchronous Data. The key to vwait then is that your event-handling Tcl code needs to set the proper variable to a new value to end the vwait wait loop. The syntax for vwait is

```
vwait variable_name
```

Now, for full communications, you need to have one process act as a client and another as the server. (Which is which doesn't really matter and depends on what you are trying to accomplish.)

Creating a Client and a Server

We can create a very simple client and server to show how to get started with Tcl's `socket` command. Another example the section on Sockets With Channel Commands should clarify the problem.

Our simple client just sends a message to the server:

```
set sockid [socket localhost 2345]

puts $sockid "Hello from Tcl"

close $sockid

# client1.tcl
```

Notice that we have chosen port number 2345 for our communication. The server also has to support the same port number, or your Tcl scripts will be like two ships that pass in the night.

A simple server script could take in text messages from clients and then print them out with the `puts` command, as shown next:

```
socket -server accept 2345

proc accept { sock addr port } {

    set data [read $sock]

    puts "Data received from $addr on $port is:"
    puts "$data"
}

# server1.tcl
```

The `socket` command in the **server1.tcl** example sets up a server socket with the `-server` option. The Tcl code to run when a client is connected is called `accept`, and the port number remains 2345.

The `accept` procedure gets in a socket to communicate with the client. The `accept` procedure also gets the IP address and port number for the actual socket. Note that this is probably not the main port number 2345, so we won't spend any time worrying about this number for our simple example.

To test this, start up two copies of **wish**. In one, `source` the **server1.tcl** script. Do this first, so the server is up and running before the client starts. Then, in the second copy of **wish**, use the `source` command to load the **client1.tcl** script. This should send a short message to the server. The **wish** running the **server1.tcl** script should print a message similar to the following:

```
Data received from 127.0.0.1 on 1028 is:
Hello from Tcl
```

After you establish a socket connect between two applications, you can read and write data on the socket much as you do for files, because sockets and files are both considered channels in Tcl.

Reading and Writing Data with Channels

Channels are a lot like files. (Actually, to Tcl, a file is a channel.) A **channel** is an input or output (or both) data stream. The key to channels is that you use the same commands on socket channels, such as `read`, `puts`, and `flush`, as you do on file channels, because sockets and files are both considered channels. This file-based abstraction makes it easier to write networking applications in Tcl.

Almost anywhere you use a file ID, you are really using a channel ID. Because sockets are channels, too, the basic file operations listed in Table 12.2 apply to sockets as well.

Table 12.2 Commands that work on channels.

Command	Usage
close $*channelid*	Closes open channel.
eof $*channelid*	Returns 1 at end of file; 0 otherwise.
flush $*channelid*	Forces all buffered data for channel to disk or out network channel.
gets $*channelid varname*	Reads line of text into *varname* and returns -1 on end of file.
gets $*channelid*	Reads line of text and returns the text or an empty string on end of file.
open *filename mode*	Opens a file and returns file ID.
puts -nonewline $*channelid string*	Writes data to channel.
read $*channelid*	Reads all data available on channel into memory.
read -nonewline $*channelid*	Reads entire data into memory and skips ending newline.
read $*channelid number_bytes*	Reads given amount of data into memory.
seek $*channelid offset starting_at*	Moves file pointer to given position.
tell $*channelid*	Returns current byte position in file.

For most of what you do, you can treat a socket as a channel. The main difference is that you call the socket command to create a socket, rather than open, which you use with files.

In addition to the commands listed in Table 12.2, Tcl offers some more channel commands that are especially useful for sockets. Table 12.3 lists some channel commands of use with sockets.

Table 12.3 Channel commands useful with sockets.

Command	Usage
fblocked $*channelid*	Returns 1 if channel is blocked awaiting input.
fconfigure $*channelid name value* ...	Configures channel.
fconfigure $*channelid name*	Returns channel configuration for *name*.
fconfigure $*channelid*	Returns entire channel configuration.
fcopy $*in_channelid* $*out_channelid*	Copies data directly from one channel to another, reducing the need for extra copying.

Because everything in Tcl is text (remember the mantra), Tcl programs tend to have problems working with binary data. The main problem is that the NULL character, 0, terminates a text string (this is an old C programming convention used in Tcl). But, binary data may very well have zeroes in the data stream. This causes problems with Tcl text strings. Starting with Tcl 8.0, you can use the binary command to transfer binary data. The fcopy command, listed in Table 12.3, also helps deal with binary data.

The binary format command builds a binary string from a set of formatting codes and data:

binary format *format_string value1 value2* ...

The binary scan command reverses the process and extracts parts from binary data, again, based on a set of formatting codes:

binary scan *value_to_scan format_string variable1 variable2* ...

The *format_string* argument contains the formatting codes. The values and variables associate with elements in the *format_string*.

The formatting codes are listed in Table 12.4.

Table 12.4 The binary command formatting codes.

Code	Meaning
aX	Use X characters, padding with NULL if necessary.
AX	Use X characters, padding with spaces if necessary.
bX	Binary data with X digits stored in low-to-high order, padding with 0. Each digit must be 0 or 1.
BX	Binary data with X digits stored in high-to-low order, padding with 0. Each digit must be 0 or 1.
cX	8-bit integer. X indicates how many numbers to use.
dX	Double-precision floating-point value in the system's native format. This is not portable across systems.
fX	Single-precision floating-point value in the system's native format. This is not portable across systems.
hX	Hexadecimal string with X digits stored in low-to-high order, padding with 0.
HX	Hexadecimal string with X digits stored in high-to-low order, padding with 0.
iX	32-bit integer, in **little-endian** order (least significant byte first), as used on Intel processors. X indicates how many numbers to use.
IX	32-bit integer, in **big-endian** order (most significant byte first), as used on most RISC processors. X indicates how many numbers to use.
sX	16-bit integer, in **little-endian** order (least significant byte first), as used on Intel processors. X indicates how many numbers to use.
SX	16-bit integer, in **big-endian** order (most significant byte first), as used on most RISC processors. X indicates how many numbers to use.
xX	Stores X NULL bytes in the data. Does not use an argument.

XX	Moves the cursor back *X* bytes in the string. This allows you to store values on top of values.
@*X*	Moves the cursor to bytes position *X* in the string.

All the codes are placed together in the format string. Each separate code implies that there is a separate argument to the `binary` command. For example, a format string of `b10b` implies two arguments of data, one for each *b*. That is, the following command requires two value arguments after the format string:

```
binary format b10b 10 01
```

Each formatting code may have an associated count to control exactly the contents of the binary data, shown as *X* in Table 12.4. You can omit the count for only one item, or use a count of 1. You can also use a count of * to apply to all the digits or characters in the argument.

The `binary scan` command reverses the process of `binary format`. For example,

```
% binary format b10b 10 01
% set val [binary format b10b 10 01]
% puts "First value is $variable1; second is $variable2"
First value is 1000000000; second is 0
```

The `binary scan` command returns the number of elements it parsed out of the input data.

Specifying binary data is difficult in a text-based language like Tcl. You can use the *ooo* syntax, which allows you to specify a character using its value in octal (base eight) notation. For example, \\000 is the NULL character, character 0. You can also specify characters by their value in hexadecimal (base 16) with the \\x*hh* syntax. For example, \\x10 for character 16.

The on-line documentation for the `binary` command provides a large number of useful examples. You'll find that you especially need to use the `binary` command when transferring binary data between sockets.

Controlling Channels

The main way to control channels is through the `fconfigure` command, which has many specialized options for various channels. For example, if you open serial ports, `fconfigure` has options to control the baud rate and other communication parameters as shown in Chapter 6. For sockets, `fconfigure` allows you to query the IP address, host name, and port number, as well as control the way the channel handles data.

Table 12.5 lists the options for `fconfigure` that apply to sockets.

Table 12.5 Socket options for `fconfigure`.

Option	Usage
`-blocking yes_or_no`	Determines whether or not channel can block awaiting input or output. Default is to allow blocking.
`-buffering buffer`	Sets channel buffering to one of `full` to buffer until internal area is full or flush is called, `line` to buffer until a newline is out put, and `none` to flush after every output.
`-buffersize size`	Sets size of internal buffer.
`-eofchar char`	Sets character to recognize as end-of-file.
`-eofchar` `{input_eof output_eof }`	Sets end-of-file characters.
`-peername`	Returns IP address, host name and port numbers for all client sockets connected to a server. Can only call this on a server socket.
`-sockname`	Returns list of IP address, host name, and port number. You can only read this data, not set it.
`-translation mode`	Translates end-of-line characters.
`-translation` `{ input_mode output_mode }`	Translates end-of-line characters.

A common option is to adjust the end-of-line translations. Tcl, based on its UNIX roots, likes a single newline character to act as the end of a line.

Windows likes a carriage return and a newline, whereas MacOS likes a single carriage return with no newline.

The allowable translation modes include `auto`, which translates any newline, carriage return, and newline or plain carriage return to an end of line; `binary`, which prevents any translations so as not to modify binary data; `cr`, which treats a carriage return as the end of line; `crlf`, which treats a carriage return and a newline as the end of line; and `lf`, which treats a newline as the end of line.

Handling Asynchronous Data

One of the most common requirements for client-server applications is the ability for the server to handle more than one client. A common way to deal with this is to provide a way to call your code when data are ready to be read on a channel, similar to an **event-driven process**. In Tcl, you can do this with the `fileevent` command (note the *ee*). The `fileevent` command sets up a Tcl script to call when a given channel becomes readable or writable. The syntax for `fileevent` follows:

```
fileevent $channelid readable tcl_script
fileevent $channelid writable tcl_script
```

With the default options, if you call `read` or `gets` on a channel, the Tcl commands will block until data are available to read. Using the `fileevent` command, you can break free from this restriction and call `read` or `gets` when data are available. For best results, set the channel into nonblocking mode with the `fconfigure` command.

The *tcl_script* you provide to `fileevent` gets called without any arguments, unless you pass them to `fileevent` originally. For example, if you want to pass the socket channel ID to your *tcl_script*, you can use the following as a guide:

```
fileevent $channelid readable "handle_socket $channelid"
```

Your Tcl script may get called on an error or end-of-file condition. Your script must therefore check for this or you could create an infinite loop.

WARNING

The `fileevent` command works for socket channels on Windows only, as of Tcl 8.0. Future releases should allow `fileevent` to work on file channels, too. The UNIX `fileevent` works on sockets and files.

Sockets with Channel Commands

To pull all this together, we can combine a number of channel commands with networking sockets to create interesting communicating applications. The following example provides just the barest glimpse of what you can do with Tcl's networking sockets. (If you want some hints about what more you can do, just think about the World Wide Web.)

The following example deals with a common case where you have an application and you want client applications to be able to connect to your application and send commands from clients to get executed in the server. The term *server* may be a bit misleading. If you have a word processor or computer-aided design package, you may want the ability for other applications to connect with your program and execute commands in the program—formatting documents or rotating the model of a house, for example. The advantage to Tcl is that because everything is text and you can use `eval` to execute commands, you can send over commands and evaluate them in the server without much work. Even though you may never have a system such as this, the example should provide more insight into Tcl's `socket` commands.

There are many uses for such a system and many ways to implement it. Using the `send` command, which was already described, is one way. Another way is to use Tcl's sockets.

Designing an Example Client

The client in this example is much easier to create than the server. For this example, the client will accept three commands, all part of one procedure (making a family of commands such as the `file` or `string` commands in Tcl).

The `client connect` command connects to a server on a given host and port. The `client send` command sends a set of Tcl commands to the server to get executed in a subinterpreter. (The subinterpreter prevents multiple clients from conflicting commands within the same server.)

Table 12.6 shows the simple `client` commands.

Table 12.6 Example client commands.

Command	Usage
`client connect` *`host port`*	Establishes connection to server.
`client send` *`command`*	Sends command to server to get executed.
`client disconnect`	Cuts connection to server.

N O T E

The `client` command is a procedure in the script file **client2.tcl**. It is not a standard part of Tcl.

The client code is relatively simple as shown here:

```
#
# Code for a remote client that sends
# commands to a single Tcl server.
#

# Global to store single socket connection.
set client_sock ""
global client_sock

# Handle socket-based client communications.
# These routines allow only one connection
# at a time.
#
# Usage:
# client connect host port
#     Establish a connection with a server.
```

```
# client send tcl_command
#     Sends tcl_command to server.
#     Blocks awaiting results. Returns results.
# client disconnect
#     Shuts down connection to server.
#
proc client { command args } {
    global client_sock

    switch $command {
        connect {
            if { $client_sock != "" } {
                close $client_sock
            }

            set host localhost

            catch {
                set host [lindex $args 0]
            }

            set port 2345
            catch {
                set port [lindex $args 1]
            }

            if { [string compare $port ""] == 0} {
                set port 2345
            }

            set client_sock [socket $host $port]

            fconfigure $client_sock -buffering line
        }
        send    {
            if { $client_sock != "" } {

                puts $client_sock $args
```

```
                # Wait for results.
                set results "ERROR"
                catch {
                    set results [gets $client_sock]
                }

                return $results
            }
        }
        disconnect {
            if { $client_sock != "" } {
                close $client_sock

                set client_sock ""
            }
        }
        default {
            # Do nothing...
        }
    }
}

# client2.tcl
```

The **client2.tcl** script creates a single procedure, `client`, that handles all the client side of the communications.

The `client connect` command establishes a socket connection to the server with the `socket` command and then uses the `fconfigure` command to set up buffering on the socket on a line-by-line basis. This assumes each Tcl command is a single line or can be executed as a single line. After the client connects to the server, the client can send any number of commands to get executed in the server.

The `client send` command sends a command to get executed in the server. This command assumes that there will be a response and waits for a line of data in response. This makes the client side of the connection synchronous in that the client awaits responses from the server.

Finally, the `client disconnect` command closes the socket connection.

Designing an Example Server

The server for this example is a bit more complicated than the client and gives us a chance to work with the `fileevent` command to accept commands from clients asynchronously.

The server task is handled by a single procedure called `server`. All you need to pass to the `server` procedure is the port number (and this is optional). That's all you need to do to use the server functionality. The reason why this works is that as a Tk application, the Tk event loop checks for connections on the socket. When a connection gets established, the `socket` command launches the procedure you pass on the command line. As such, the `server` procedure is relatively simple:

```
proc server { {port 2345} } {

    socket -server server_accept $port
}
```

The real work gets done in the `server_accept` procedure, a procedure you can keep hidden if you like. (Users of this code only need to call the server procedure. Everything else is taken care of.)

The `server_accept` procedure accepts an incoming client connection. When it is accepted, `server_accept` creates a new Tcl interpreter with the `interp` command. (See Chapter 5.) The `load` command loads up the Tk toolkit so that the newly spawned interpreter can actually create widgets on the screen—on the server's screen.

To allow for clients to send any commands at any time (once connected to the server), the `server_accept` procedure calls the `fileevent` command (see the preceding section on Handling Asynchronous Data) to set up a procedure, `server_read`, to get called when the socket has data (is readable). This command follows:

```
fileevent $sock readable [list server_read $sock]
```

This command sets up the `server_read` procedure to get called whenever there are data to read on the socket. The `server_read` procedure gets one parameter, the socket ID.

To ensure that `server_read` gets called when a whole command has arrived (and not for a partial command), you can call the `fconfigure` command to set up buffering on the socket on a line-by-line basis (same as for the client socket) with the following command:

```
fconfigure $sock -buffering line
```

The `server_read` procedure gets called whenever there is a line of input waiting to be read on a client socket connection. The `gets` command reads in the data and the `server_read` procedure checks against the end-of-file condition with the `eof` command. If everything is OK and there is a command, the `server_exec` procedure executes the command and uses the `puts` command to return the results to the client. A useful extension you could add to this script would be to call the `info complete` command to verify that the data received so far forms a complete Tcl command. If so, execute the command. If not, then store the data and await the end of the command. Chapter 9 covers the `info` command.

The basic syntax for the procedures in the **server2.tcl** script follows:

```
server port
server_accept sock addr port
server_exec sock command
server_read sock
```

All but the `server` procedure can remain hidden. The code for **server2.tcl** follows:

```
#
# Remote Tcl command server.
# Accepts incoming socket connections
# and then executes commands received,
# returning the results. This forms a
# command like send using sockets.
#
# To get going, call server with a port number.
#

# Procedure to set up server socket.
```

```
proc server { {port 2345} } {

    socket -server server_accept $port
}

# Accepts incoming client connections.
proc server_accept { sock addr port } {

    # Destroy any existing interpreter for socket.
    server_delete_interp $sock

    # Create an interpreter for the socket.
    interp create interp_$sock
    load {} Tk interp_$sock

    # Set up socket options for asynchronous input.
    fileevent $sock readable [list server_read $sock]
    fconfigure $sock -buffering line

}

# Reads data from client connection.
proc server_read { sock } {

    set cmd [gets $sock]

    # Check for errors.
    if { [string compare $cmd ""] == 0 } {
        if { [eof $sock] } {
            close $sock

            # Destroy interpreter.
            server_delete_interp $sock
        }
        return
    }
```

```
    # Execute command and send back results.
    server_exec $sock $cmd
}

# Executes command from client.
proc server_exec { sock cmd } {

    if { [interp exists interp_$sock] } {
        set results ""
        catch {
            set results [eval interp_$sock eval "$cmd"]
        } err

        puts $sock $results
    }

}

# Deletes interpreter.
proc server_delete_interp { sock } {

    if { [interp exists interp_$sock] } {

            interp delete interp_$sock
    }
}

# server2.tcl
```

Now, a remote Tcl execution script is not all that useful on its own (and would perform even more checking for errors). But, if you embed the Tcl interpreter into a C or C++ application you have, you could then allow for client programs to send commands—Tcl commands—To your application. The nasty part of the socket communication gets handled by the Tcl `socket` and `fileevent` commands.

Other Ways To Communicate

The send and socket commands aren't the only way for Tcl applications to communicate, but these two commands have the most support in Tcl.

On Windows, you can use Tcl extensions to engage in dynamic data exchange. You can also use the Tcl OLE extension to call OLE commands from Tcl. See the **contrib/win** directory on the CD-ROM.

Summary

Tcl provides a number of ways for applications to communicate.

The send command sends a Tcl command to a remote program for execution. Unfortunately, send is not yet implemented on Windows. The send command also works only between Tcl applications.

The socket command creates a client or server TCP/IP socket between two applications. Sockets work on all versions of Tcl.

Creating a client socket is easy. You can use the following as a guide:

```
set client_sock [socket $host $port]
```

The *host* specifies a host name or IP address. The *port* is a port number. Choosing numbers in the 2000s is a good idea.

To create a server socket, use the following code as a guide:

```
socket -server server_accept $port
```

The server_accept procedure then gets called whenever a client connects. The server_accept procedure gets three parameters: the socket, the IP address, and the port number of the client connection.

Tcl considers sockets and files to both be channels. The fconfigure command allows you to change options for a channel, such as a socket.

The fileevent command provides an easy way to handle asynchronous data arriving on a socket connection.

In Chapter 13, you'll see how to extend networking communication to the World Wide Web.

Tcl Commands Introduced in This Chapter

```
binary
fblocked
fconfigure
fcopy
fileevent
send
socket
tk
vwait
```

CHAPTER 13

Tcl and the Web

This chapter covers:

- Working with the World Wide Web from Tcl
- Writing Common Gateway Interface scripts with Tcl
- Writing Tcl applets, or "tclets", with a Web browser plug in

The World Wide Web

The World Wide Web has taken the world by storm. Billboards and TV commercials advertise Web addresses and just about every company seems to have a presence on the Web.

So far, we've seen how the `text` widget can display HTML output with the html_library. We've also seen how `text` widget tags can implement HTML links to other documents (in Chapter 11.)

The main missing area is how to make your Web pages dynamic. The two main ways to create dynamic Web pages include Common Gateway Interface scripts and client-side miniapplications called "applets". Tcl works well in both areas.

In this chapter, you'll see how to create interactive Web pages using both methods, starting with CGI scripts.

The Common Gateway Interface

Most Web pages are fairly static. Web browser programs, which run on your desktop, request a document from a Web server. The Web server serves up an HTML document, and the Web browser displays the document. The main form of interaction comes from links you click on. When you click on a link, the Web browser determines which Web server to send the request to based on the **universal resource locator** (URL), the equivalent of e-mail addresses for Web documents. The URL identifies the type of the request, such as http (Web), ftp (file transfer protocol), news (Usenet news), or mailto (send e-mail); the network name of the server machine; and the name of the data requested. In most cases, the data requested are a stream of text data that comes from an HTML file.

To add dynamics to Web pages, the main method is to create a Common Gateway Interface, or CGI, script. A **CGI script** is merely a program launched by the Web server, usually in response to a query or from a submit button on a Web form. Well-behaved CGI scripts output HTML data back to the Web browser to display feedback on the results of the program. CGI scripts allow you to extend the definition of the World Wide Web to include data sources other than HTML files.

For example, an on-line bookstore could provide the means to search for books based on the author's name, book title, or subject area. After you enter the necessary details of what you want to search for, you then click on a button—appropriately labeled *Search*.

At this point, the Web browser asks the Web server for a specially formatted URL, the URL of the CGI script. The fact that the URL is a script and the fact that the URL is formatted a certain way tells the Web server to launch an application. The actual formatting required differs by Web server software as well as local site-based configuration. The Web server launches the script and sends any results back to the Web browser for display to the user. (In our example, the results of the book search.) To get the CGI script to execute the URL, you must follow the naming conventions of your Web server software and perhaps your site administrator.

For example, the following could be a URL for a CGI script (the host name is not a real system, though):

```
http://www.efj.com/~erc/cgi-bin/tclform1.cgi
```

The protocol is HTTP, the (fake) host name is **www.efj.com**, the CGI script itself is **tclform1.cgi**, located in the **cgi-bin** directory under the **erc** user account. Some Web servers look for CGI scripts in **public_html** or **WWW** subdirectories of your user account.

CGI scripts form the primary means to connect Web servers to other sources of data, usually databases. The key point is that CGI scripts run on the server machine, not on your desktop. Applets, on the other hand, tend to run on the desktop, not the server. (Server applets run on the server.)

Table 13.1 lists the main factors differentiating CGI scripts and applets.

Table 13.1 CGI scripts vs. applets.

CGI Scripts	Applets
Run on the server	Run on the client
Output HTML data	Display any widget
Usually written in Perl or Tcl	Usually written in Java, JavaScript, or Tcl

For CGI scripts, Perl is the most-used language because of its handy tools and its ability to process text easily. Tcl also processes text well, and has neat tools, so Tcl forms a viable alternative to Perl for writing CGI scripts.

Web Forms

CGI scripts normally get executed from HTML-based data-entry forms. Web browsers convert the form definition to native widgets on the platform in use (Windows widgets on Windows, etc.). A special button, called the **submit button**, captures all the data and sends it to the Web server along with a request to run the CGI script.

As an example, a simple Web form follows:

```
<html>
<head>
<title>Form #1</title>
</head>
```

```
<body>

<FORM METHOD="POST"
 ACTION="http://www.efj.com/~erc/cgi-bin/tclform1.cgi">

<H2>Customer Order Tracking</H2>

Enter order number:
<INPUT NAME="orderno">
<p>

<INPUT TYPE="submit" VALUE="Look up">

</FORM>

</body>
</html>
```

The HTML <FORM> tag starts the form. The <INPUT> tag indicates a simple entry widget or the submit button.

Note the ACTION statement. This provides the URL for your CGI script. You'll need to customize this for your site.

When you call up this form in a Web browser, you'll see widgets like those shown in Figure 13.1.

CGI scripts get the data from the Web form in one of two ways, called the GET or POST methods. Good tools, like the **cgi.tcl** hide these differences.

You could write whole books on HTML, CGI, and the Web. For more on these topics, see Appendix A.

N O T E

The cgi.tcl Library

The easiest way to get started writing CGI scripts in Tcl is with the **cgi.tcl** library from Don Libes. This library allows you to create CGI scripts quickly and easily, as you'll see in the following examples. In addition, you can use the **cgi.tcl** library to create HTML documents.

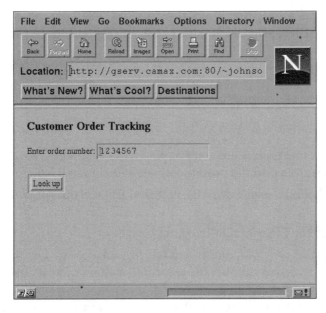

Figure 13.1 A simple data-entry form.

The **cgi.tcl** library provides a number of handy routines to handle Web form data and create HTML output. There's far more to the package than you'll ever need, but don't worry. With just a few simple procedure calls, you'll handle Web forms with ease.

Installing the cgi.tcl Library

The **cgi.tcl** library is not a standard part of Tcl, so you'll probably need to acquire it and install it on your system. Very few systems will have this already installed.

The **cgi.tcl** library is located in **contrib/cgi** on the CD-ROM. This directory contains extensive on-line documentation.

CD-ROM

There are two ways to install the **cgi.tcl** library. The **cgi.tcl** script needs the installation to perform some modifications based on the name of your **tclsh** executable, such as **tclsh8.0** or **tclsh76.exe**. In addition, you can choose the installation directory.

The official installation method works best on UNIX and will likely fail on Windows. Change to the directory with the **cgi.tcl** library and run the following commands:

```
./configure
make
make install
```

Note that you must run these commands on the Web server machine, so that installation scripts find the proper path and version of **tclsh**.

If this method doesn't work for you, you can use the simpler method:

1. Copy the file **cgi.tcl.in** to **cgi.tcl**.
2. Edit the very last line in **cgi.tcl**, to replace @CGI_VERSION_FULL@ with a version number (or you can comment out the line with a #).

Using this second method means that you must source in the **cgi.tcl** script in your CGI script files. This is the method shown in the following examples.

You need to install the **cgi.tcl** script in a directory that the Web server can find. (Each Web server is configured differently, and most allow you to restrict the file systems visible to the Web server for security reasons.)

WARNING

If you place the file **cgi.tcl** in an accessible directory, be sure to mark it read-only, so that malicious users cannot change the code to do nasty things.

When you have the **cgi.tcl** library installed, you can start to use its commands.

Using the cgi.tcl Library

The **cgi.tcl** library contains a huge set of Tcl procedures, so it is hard to know how to get started. Because of that, we'll stick to the basics. You can look up the advanced material in the on-line documentation in the **contrib/cgi** directory on the CD-ROM.

The basic method for processing a data-entry form follows:

1. Ensure that the Tcl interpreter **tclsh** will run your script.

2. Source in the file **cgi.tcl** or load the package.

3. Call `cgi_input` to get all the data-entry form values.

4. Call `cgi_import` to query each data-entry form value.

5. Create output—the result of the query, etc.—using `cgi_title`, `cgi_body`, `cgi_h1`, `cgi_p`, and so on.

The first step is to ensure that the Web server launches the proper interpreter for your script, the Tcl interpreter **tclsh** in this case. This differs by operating system.

WINDOWS

On Windows, you need to associate the extension, such as *.tcl* or *.cgi*, with the **tclsh** program (often named with a version number, such as **tclsh80.exe**) in the Windows registry. Chapter 1 discusses the Windows registry. (Remember that once you install Tcl, the registry likely associates the **wish** interpreter with *.tcl* files. If you change this from **wish** to **tclsh**, you may have problems running Tcl scripts that require Tk commands and widgets. So, you may want to use a different file extension for CGI scripts, such as *.cgi*.) When the Windows registry is set up, you may also need to configure your Web server software. Your Web server documentation should tell you how to do this. Even so, each Web server product differs, so you need to consult the Web server documentation.

U N I X

On UNIX, you need to mark the script as executable with the **chmod** command and then use the #! syntax in the very first line to provide the path to **tclsh** (often named with a version number, such as **tclsh8.0**) on your system. See Chapter 1 for details.

The next step is to get access to the Tcl procedures defined in the file **cgi.tcl**. There are three ways to include the source of the **cgi.tcl** script in your CGI scripts. First, you can simply include the entire file in your CGI scripts. This usually isn't good because of problems when you get an upgraded **cgi.tcl** script. Second, you can use the `source` command discussed in Chapter 1. Third, you can use the `package require` command as shown here:

```
package require cgi version
```

Replace *version* with the version number at the end of the *cgi.tcl* script, in the `package provide` command.

The following examples use the `source` command for simplicity.

NOTE It's a good idea to test a very simple CGI script that only calls `source` or `package require` to verify that you have everything properly installed. When you're sure that the **cgi.tcl** library is properly installed and accessible from a CGI script, you can then extend the script to perform all the tasks you need.

When you have access to the **cgi.tcl** commands, you need to call the `cgi_input` procedure, which extracts all the data-entry form element names and values:

```
cgi_input
```

After calling `cgi_input`, you can query the value of any named element from the form with the `cgi_import` procedure. For example,

```
set ordernum [cgi_import "orderno"]
```

Each element in the form is named. You pass the name to `cgi_import` to extract the value the user entered for the name.

If the name is typed in wrong, you'll get an error. In addition, you may not get a value back at all. Because of both of these problems, you need to program defensively. I always provide an initial value for each variable and bracket the call to `cgi_import` with `catch` to trap errors. For example,

```
set ordernum "0"
catch {
    set ordernum [cgi_import "orderno"]
}
```

This type of code helps prevent the dreaded server error.

The `cgi_import_list` procedure returns a list of named elements. You can use this list to verify the values available.

```
set varlist [cgi_import_list]
```

NOTE Not all named elements in the form may be available. For example, check buttons that are off may not return any value, whereas check buttons that are on have a value of "yes." Because problems are so hard to debug, it's best to code defensively, even if this is more work.

After you acquire all the form values, you then proceed to perform a database query or whatever you intended your script for in the first place. The main purpose for CGI scripts is to connect to some external data source, like a database. This task is up to you.

Finally, when you have all the results to display to the user, you need to create some HTML output. Even if you don't have meaningful results, you should still provide some feedback to the user. Because Web browsers support HTML data best, it's a good idea to output HTML.

The **cgi.tcl** script provides a number of handy routines to create HTML output. (In fact, you can use the **cgi.tcl** script as a good HTML generator and skip the CGI part.) To do this step, you need to know a bit—but not much— about HTML.

HTML documents come in two main sections: the header and the body. For these, you can use the cgi_head and cgi_body commands, respectively.

At this point, the **cgi.tcl** script requires some strange coding. You need to start the header with a <head> tag and end it with a </head> tag. The cgi_head procedure does this for you but requires that you to pass all the data between the <head> and </head> as a parameter to cgi_head. For example, all Web pages should provide a title, which you can add with the cgi_title command. The title goes inside the header as shown next:

```
cgi_head {
    cgi_title "This is my title"
}
```

If you had other commands for the header, these commands would appear as part of the same argument to cgi_head. The code looks a little strange, but it is easy to get used to.

The cgi_body command acts similarly, but you tend to have more commands in the body of the document, as shown here:

```
cgi_body bgcolor=white fgcolor=black {
    cgi_h1 "Your Order Number"
    cgi_p  "Your order number was: $orderno."
    cgi_p
}
```

This document body uses an H1 headline to display Your Order Number and a HTML paragraph, <p>, and to display the order number entered in the form.

Putting this all together, we have a simple script, **tclform1.cgi**, which handles the data entered in the **tclform1.htm** file, shown in Figure 13.1.

```
#!/usr/local/bin/tclsh8.0

# Source in the cgi.tcl script.
# You can also use packages.
source cgi.tcl

# Always set a default value for
# all variables just in case.
set orderno "0"

# Get values from Web server.
cgi_input

#
# Extract value of order number.
# The name must match the name in
# the Web page for this INPUT field.
#

set orderno [cgi_import "orderno"]

# Process input data.....

#
# Create HTML output to verify input.
#
cgi_head {
```

```
    cgi_title "Customer Order Tracking"
}


#
# Place all body output within cgi_body
# to create HTML's <body></body>.
#
cgi_body bgcolor=white fgcolor=black {
    cgi_h1 "Your Order Number"
    cgi_p  "Your order number was: $orderno."
    cgi_p
}

# tclform1.cgi
```

Note that you will need to customize the first line on UNIX systems to point to your **tclsh** executable.

When the user clicks on the *Look Up* button shown in Figure 13.1, the **tclform1.cgi** script gets run, producing output shown in Figure 13.2.

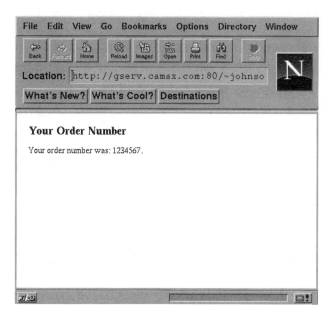

Figure 13.2 Output of first CGI script.

Placing CGI Scripts

Each Web server limits the areas where CGI scripts may be found. Oftentimes, CGI scripts are limited to directories such as **cgi-bin**. You need to consult your Web server manual for the specifics for your system.

A CGI script is a Tcl script but usually ends with a *.cgi* extension rather than *.tcl*. (This is by convention only. Again, your Web server may have different requirements. On Windows, you may need a *.tcl* extension to associate the script properly with the Tcl interpreter necessary for any Tcl script.)

Dealing With Errors

Web servers don't provide many useful error messages. The two most common errors are *Not found* and *Server error*. The *Not found* error means that the Web server didn't find your script. The *Server error* message means that your script had an error. *Server error*, unfortunately, does not tell you what the error was.

Because of this, I build up by CGI scripts slowly, one line at a time, so I know with more certainty that things work and what—if anything—went wrong. I constantly test each change to verify that the script still works. This is tedious but necessary, because of the lack of good debugging tools.

Working With More Complicated Forms

This example just barely introduces CGI scripts. We can also use a more complicated form like **tclform2.htm**, which follows:

```
<html>
<head>
<title>Form #2</title>
</head>

<body>

<FORM METHOD="POST"
 ACTION="http://http://www.efj.com/~erc/cgi-bin/tclform2.cgi">

<H2>Software Devlopment Buzzword Request</H2>

Software requested includes the following important
```

```
characteristics:
<p>

<INPUT NAME="web" TYPE="checkbox" VALUE="yes">
Web-Page Access
<br>

<INPUT NAME="gui" TYPE="checkbox" VALUE="yes">
Graphical User Interface
<br>

<INPUT NAME="oop" TYPE="checkbox" VALUE="yes">
Object-Oriented
<br>

<INPUT NAME="mod" TYPE="checkbox" VALUE="yes">
Modular
<p>

Performance must be:
<SELECT NAME="perform" SIZE=4>
<OPTION>No requirements
<OPTION>Low memory usage and fast performance
<OPTION>Fast performance
<OPTION>Low memory usage
<OPTION>The impossible, yesterday, for free
</SELECT>
<p>

Project name:
<INPUT NAME="projectname">
<p>

How would you solve the project's problems? Please
enter your suggestion below.
<p>

<TEXTAREA NAME="suggestion" ROWS=8 COLS=50>
```

```
Your evaluation of the requirements goes here.
</TEXTAREA>
<p>

<INPUT TYPE="submit" VALUE="Request Software">
<INPUT TYPE="reset" VALUE="Reset Form">
<p>
</FORM>

</body>
</html>
```

Again, you'll need to change the ACTION line to point to your scripts.

When you display this file in a Web browser, you'll see a form like that in Figure 13.3.

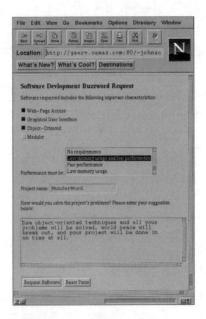

Figure 13.3 A second HTML form.

A Tcl script to process this form is a bit more complicated than **tclform1.cgi**. This script must handle different types of widgets. Because I programmed defensively, it's much longer than the first example:

```
#!/usr/local/bin/tclsh8.0

# More extensive Tcl CGI form.

#
# Source in the cgi.tcl script.
# You can also use packages.
#
source cgi.tcl

#
# Always set a default value for
# all variables just in case.
#
set web no
set gui no
set oop no
set mod no
set perform "No requirements"
set projectname "Unnamed"
set suggestion "None"

#
# Get values from Web server.
#
cgi_input

#
# Extract value of Web data.
# Each name must match the name in
# the Web page for the field.
#
catch {
    set web [cgi_import "web"]
}

catch {
    set gui [cgi_import "gui"]
```

```
}

catch {
    set oop [cgi_import "oop"]
}

catch {
    set mod [cgi_import "mod"]
}

catch {
    set perform [cgi_import "perform"]
}

catch {
    set projectname [cgi_import "projectname"]
}

catch {
    set suggestion [cgi_import "suggestion"]
}

#
# Create HTML output to verify input.
#
cgi_head {
    cgi_title "Software Request"
}

#
# Place all body output within cgi_body
# to create HTML's <body></body>.
#
cgi_body bgcolor=white fgcolor=black {
    cgi_h1 "Your Software Request"
    cgi_p
```

```
    cgi_p "Project $projectname requires:"

    cgi_bullet_list {
        if { $web == "yes" } {
            cgi_li "Web access"
        }

        if { $gui == "yes" } {
            cgi_li "Graphical user interface"
        }

        if { $oop == "yes" } {
            cgi_li "Object-oriented everything"
        }

        if { $mod == "yes" } {
            cgi_li "Modular design"
        }

     cgi_li "$perform"
     }

    cgi_p

    if { $suggestion != "None" } {
        cgi_p "Suggestions for implementation:"
        cgi_p $suggestion
    }
}

# tclform2.cgi
```

In the **tclform2.cgi** script, the cgi_bullet_list procedure creates a bulleted list with the HTML <UL> tag, and the cgi_li creates a list item, <LI>. The results of the **tclform2.cgi** script are shown in Figure 13.4.

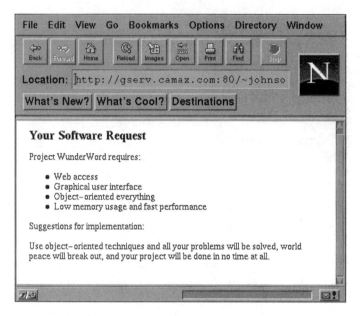

Figure 13.4 Running the **tclform2.cgi** script.

In addition to running CGI scripts on the server, you can also run Tcl applets on the desktop.

Writing Tcl Applets

An **applet** is a small application that gets executed from a Web browser on the desktop. So far, Java and JavaScript are the two most popular languages for writing applets.

To run an applet, you need to have a plug-in installed in your Web browser. Because Java and JavaScript generally come pre-installed, this is an extra burden if you use Tcl for creating applets.

For Tcl applets—also called **tclets**—you need the Tcl plug-in.

NOTE Because of copyright restrictions, you need to pick up the Tcl plug in from the SunScript Web site located at **http://sunscript.sun.com/products/**. The plug-ins support Netscape Navigator 3.0 and higher as well as Microsoft Internet Explorer 3.0 or higher, on a range of platforms. You will need this plug-in to create Tcl applets.

After you get everything installed, a Tcl applet is merely a Tcl script that runs from a Web page in a restricted, security-conscious environment. The same Tcl commands, with some restrictions, still apply.

Security Restrictions on Applets

Tcl applets run a restricted version of Tcl and Tk, removing commands listed in Table 13.2.

Table 13.2 Commands removed for Tcl applets.

Command

bell

cd

clipboard

exec

fconfigure

glob

grab

menu

pwd

send

socket

tk

tkwait

toplevel

vwait

wm

The Tcl interpreter running applets modifies some commands, listed in Table 13.3, to better enhance security.

Table 13.3 Commands modified for Tcl applets

Command	Restrictions
exit	Just exits applet.
file	Only allows a subset of `file` commands.
load	Only loads from $auto_path.
open	Can open Tcl script library files for reading only.
source	Only loads from $auto_path.
tclPkgUnknown	Allows packages to call up security policies.

In addition to restricting and changing the available commands, users can set up a **security policy**, a list of things that are allowed and those that are not. The on-line manual information on *safe* documents security policies.

Creating Tcl Applets

Writing Tcl applets is very easy, because you're merely writing Tcl scripts. For example, you can use the following script to start with:

```
# Tcl applet (tclet) for embedding in a Web page.

label .label -text "Inside Tclet"
button .button -text "Hello From a Tclet"
pack .label .button

# tclet1.tcl
```

It's very important to use a *.tcl* extension for Tcl applets, because this is how the Web browser knows which application to launch.

N O T E

The **tclet1.tcl** script creates widgets as children of the top-level widget named ".", as do most Tcl scripts. This "." widget is a special case for Tcl applets in that this window appears in the Web browser window.

The **tclet1.tcl** script isn't very interesting, but running it from a Web page is.

Connecting the Applet to a Web Page

To connect your applet to a Web page, you need to use the HTML <EMBED> tag (and have a browser that supports Tcl applets). The HTML <EMBED> tag allows you to specify a number of options, the most important of which is the src=*filename.tcl* option, to run a Tcl applet script named *filename.tcl*.

You can also specify a width and a height for the size of the window used by the applet. (This is the size of the toplevel widget named ".", because you cannot create toplevel widgets in applets.) This window appears inside the Web page.

Here's a simple HTML document that calls the **tclet1.tcl** script as an embedded applet:

```
<html>
<head>
<title>Tclet #1</title>
</head>
<body>
Here is a simple Tclet:
<p>
<embed src=tclet1.tcl width=220 height=65>
</body>
</html>
```

When you load this HTML file in a Web browser that supports Tcl applets, you'll see a window like that in Figure 13.5.

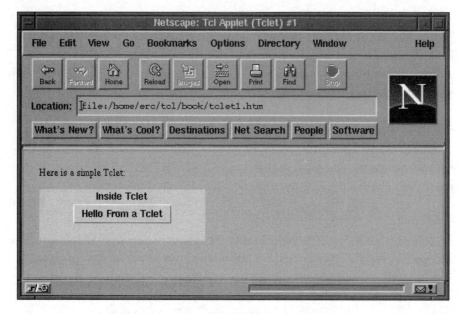

Figure 13.5 A Tcl applet in a Web document.

We can extend this example with a more complicated Tcl applet script, as shown here:

```
# Tclet example for a data-entry form.
#

frame .fr -borderwidth 1 -relief raised

  # Name
label .fr.l_name_first -text "First"
label .fr.l_name_last  -text "Last"

label .fr.l_name -text "Name: "
entry .fr.name_first -width 15
entry .fr.name_last  -width 30

set row 0
grid config .fr.l_name_first -column 1 \
    -row $row -sticky w
grid config .fr.l_name_last  -column 2 \
```

```
        -row $row -sticky w

set row [expr $row + 1]
grid config .fr.l_name -column 0 \
    -row $row -sticky e
grid config .fr.name_first -column 1 \
    -row $row -sticky snew
grid config .fr.name_last  -column 2 \
    -row $row -sticky snew


  # Street
label .fr.l_street -text "Street"
label .fr.l_address -text "Address: "
entry .fr.street -width 30

set row [expr $row + 1]
grid config .fr.l_street -column 1 \
    -row $row -sticky w
set row [expr $row + 1]
grid config .fr.l_address -column 0 \
    -row $row -sticky e
grid config .fr.street -column 1 \
   -row $row -sticky snew -columnspan 2

  #
  # City, State, Zip
  #
  # Note use of frm variable and
  # child frame widget.
  #
set frm .fr.city_frame
frame $frm -bd 0

label $frm.l_city  -text "City"
label $frm.l_state -text "State"
label $frm.l_zip   -text "Zip"

entry $frm.city  -width 20
entry $frm.state -width 2
```

```
entry $frm.zip    -width 5

grid config $frm.l_city  -column 0 \
    -row 0 -sticky w
grid config $frm.l_state -column 1 \
    -row 0 -sticky w
grid config $frm.l_zip   -column 2 \
    -row 0 -sticky w

grid config $frm.city    -column 0 \
    -row 1 -sticky snew
grid config $frm.state   -column 1 \
    -row 1 -sticky snew
grid config $frm.zip     -column 2 \
    -row 1 -sticky snew

  # Necessary to make frame properly fit.
grid columnconfigure $frm 0 -weight 1

set row [expr $row + 1]
grid config $frm -column 1 -row $row \
   -sticky snew -columnspan 2

  # E-Mail
label .fr.l_email -text "Email: "
entry .fr.email

set row [expr $row + 1]
grid config .fr.l_email -column 0 \
    -row $row -sticky w
grid config .fr.email   -column 1 \
    -row $row -sticky snew

  # Bottom part of form.
frame .controls -bd 0
button .controls.add_rec -text "Add New Record" \
    -command { add_record }
```

```
label .controls.status -text ""
pack .controls.add_rec .controls.status

pack .fr -side top -fill x -ipady 6 -ipadx 4
pack .controls -side top -pady 6

proc add_record { } {
    # This procedure would add a record.

    # Provide status on a job well done.
    .controls.status config -text "Record added."

    # Clear status after a while.
    after 1000 {.controls.status config -text ""}
}

# tclet2.tcl
```

The **tclet2.tcl** script was modified from the **dataform.tcl** script shown in Chapter 5. When you click on the *Add Record* button, you'll see a feedback message displayed for a short period of time.

An HTML document that calls up this Tcl applet follows:

```
<html>
<head>
<title>Tclet #2</title>
</head>
<body>
This Tclet presents a data-entry form.
<p>
<p>
<embed src=tclet2.tcl width=520 height=200>
</body>
</html>
```

When you run this more complicated example, you'll see a more realistic applet as shown in Figure 13.6.

Figure 13.6 A more advanced Tcl applet.

You can find a whole tutorial on Tcl applets on the Web at **http://sunscript.sun.com/plugintut/**.

Summary

Tcl works well as a tool for creating dynamic content in Web pages. You can use Tcl for CGI scripts with the **cgi.tcl** library.

With the plug-ins for Netscape Navigator or Microsoft Internet Explorer, you can also create Tcl applets that run on the desktop Web browsers.

Tcl Commands Introduced in This Chapter

```
cgi_body                    cgi_import_list
cgi_bullet_list             cgi_input
cgi_h1                      cgi_li
cgi_head                    cgi_p
cgi_import                  cgi_title
```

Advanced Applications

This chapter covers:

- Finishing the application
- Working with the window manager
- Setting up an icon
- Controlling the console window
- Getting the time with the `clock` command
- Updating widgets
- Supporting other languages
- Color schemes
- Start-up splash screens
- Cursors
- Using application builders
- Providing user customization
- The option database
- Libraries, packages, name spaces, and autoloading
- Installing your scripts
- Accessing the Windows registry

Finishing the Application

This grab-bag chapter focuses on how to finish off professional-looking applications with Tcl and includes a number of other miscellaneous topics.

636

We'll delve into issues for creating well-behaved applications, show how to refine the look for your interfaces, deal with cross-platform issues, allow for user customization, and install and package your code.

Creating Well-Behaved Applications

A well-behaved application is one that follows the standards of the platform it runs on, interacting as expected.

For UNIX applications, there are many rules controlling the interaction with the window manager. These rules don't apply so much on Windows, but you can still follow the rules to make well-behaved applications should your scripts ever run on UNIX.

Working With the Window Manager

On UNIX, the **window manager** controls the position, size and title bars placed on windows. You can adjust these settings with the wm command. On Windows, Tcl emulates the window manager by making the proper Win32 calls. Because the UNIX window manager does more than Windows, you don't need to call all these commands on Windows, but you can anyway, to ensure that your application remains portable across operating systems.

Table 14.1 lists the most useful wm command options. All these options apply to `toplevel` widgets. You can find out even more obscure options in the on-line documentation.

Table 14.1 The wm command.

Command	Usage
wm client *widget hostname*	Sets WM_CLIENT_MACHINE property for UNIX.
wm command *widget command_string*	Sets WM_COMMAND property for UNIX.
wm deiconify *widget*	Deiconifies *widget*, restores from wm withdraw, too. See Chapter 7.

`wm geometry` *widget*	Returns position of window manager window.
`wm geometry` *widget geometry_spec*	Sets window size and position. See Chapter 7.
`wm iconbitmap` *widget bitmap*	Sets icon bitmap.
`wm iconname` *widget name*	Sets icon name.
`wm iconposition` *widget x y*	Sets position of icon.
`wm iconwindow` *widget icon_widget*	Creates an icon window rather than an icon; UNIX only.
`wm maxsize` *widget width height*	Sets maximum size for *widget*.
`wm minsize` *widget width height*	Sets minimum size for *widget*.
`wm overrideredirect` *widget* `1`	Disables window manager from placing a border. See Chapter 7.
`wm overrideredirect` *widget* `0`	Allows window manager to place border. See Chapter 7.
`wm protocol` *widget protocolname tcl_script*	Handles given protocol, usually `WM_DELETE_WINDOW` or `WM_SAVE_YOURSELF`, with given *tcl_script*. See Chapter 7
`wm resizable` *widget width_ok height_ok*	Determines whether *widget* is resizable.
`wm state` *widget*	Returns one of `normal`, `iconic`, `withdrawn` or `icon`.
`wm title` *widget title_string*	Sets title for *widget*.
`wm transient` *widget master_toplevel*	Makes *widget* a dialog window for *master_toplevel*.
`wm withdraw` *widget*	Hides *widget*

Many of these options were described in Chapter 7 on dialog windows. In the following sections, you'll see what is required to create well-behaved applications (from the point of view of the window manager).

Determining the Window Position

On UNIX, the window manager creates and owns the title bar. This means that your windows usually appear farther down and a bit to the right of the position you provide with the wm geometry command.

You can use a trick with the wm geometry command to determine the position of the actual toplevel widget as opposed to the title bar position. The wm geometry command, without any geometry data, returns the position of the window manager's window. The winfo geometry command returns the position of the toplevel window. For example,

```
% wm geometry .
195x23+140+47
% winfo geometry .
195x23+146+74
```

Note the slight position difference. On Windows, the two positions will be exact, because Windows does not use separately owned title bar windows.

You can use this to determine the size of the window manager border on UNIX.

Changing the Title

To set the title for a toplevel widget, you can use the wm title command. For example,

```
wm title . "This is my title"
```

You want to set the title for all toplevel widgets.

Icons

When your application is minimized down to an icon, you want a nice picture—perhaps your product's logo—to make your application stand out.

You can control much about icons, but as of Tk 8.0, the icon commands work on UNIX only, not on Windows.

To set the name of the icon, you can use the following example:

```
wm iconname . "This is the icon name"
```

The icon name should be short, generally shorter than the title.

You can also set the `wm` icon bitmap. The `wm iconbitmap` command requires a Tcl bitmap (in X Bitmap format as described in Chapter 8):

```
# Icon bitmap

  #
  # Hide main window because some
  # window managers won't check a window
  # once mapped to the screen.
  #
wm withdraw .

  # Create icon. This must be in X Bitmap format.
wm iconbitmap . @tv.xbm

  # Show main window again when done.
wm deiconify .

# iconbit.tcl
```

When you run this script, the icon will look like that in Figure 14.1.

Figure 14.1 An icon bitmap.

The X Window System on UNIX allows for monochrome icons only. You can set up an icon window if you want a color icon.

To tell whether or not a window is minimized to an icon, you can use the `wm state` command:

```
set state [wm state .]
```

The state returned will be one of `normal`, `iconic`, `withdrawn` or `icon`. An `iconic` state is when the window is minimized. The `icon` state is when the window is an icon, as set with the `wm iconwindow` command.

With `wm iconwindow`, you can specify a Tcl `toplevel` widget that should act in place of an icon. This is also the way you get a color icon on UNIX.

Some window managers ignore icon windows. And, icon windows don't work on Windows either. Furthermore, your icon widgets will not likely get keyboard or mouse input. Because of this, I tend to stay away from icon windows.

Other Window Manager Initializations

All applications on UNIX should run two other commands, `wm command` and `wm client`. You can use the following as a model:

```
wm command . "$argv0 $argv"
wm client . [info hostname]
```

These commands come from the rules for well-behaved X Window applications. The `wm client` command specifies the name of the machine your script runs on. The `wm command` sets the command-line arguments, which can be used to restart the script, using the `WM_SAVE_YOURSELF` protocol.

In addition to the `WM_DELETE_WINDOW` window manager protocol described in Chapter 7, you may also want to support the `WM_SAVE_YOUR-SELF` protocol. The `WM_SAVE_YOURSELF` protocol allows window and session managers to save the state of applications and restart applications in another session. For example, you may want to save the current state of all running applications when you log out and then restart all the applications placing windows in the same position as before and editing the same files. On UNIX this is done is through the `WM_SAVE_YOURSELF` protocol.

When a `WM_SAVE_YOURSELF` message arrives, your application should write out the command-line arguments with `wm command`, as described previously. You are free to edit the command-line arguments to reflect the current state. This means that the command-line arguments should be sufficient to restart the program into the current state, whatever *state* means for your program.

When you call wm command, you should store the command-line parameters necessary to restart the program.

You can set up Tcl code to handle WM_SAVE_YOURSELF messages with the wm protocol command:

```
wm protocol . WM_SAVE_YOURSELF {wm command . "$argv0 $argv"}
```

There are a number of complications hidden by this command. In Tcl, the global variable *argv0* holds the name of the script. By setting *argv0* into the command line, you're assuming that the script is marked as an executable file. If not, then **wish** was executed to launch the script. In this case, you want to call wm command with the following arguments:

```
wm command . "wish $argv0 $argv"
```

This example stores a better command to restart the application. However, when the window or session manager restarts the application, the entire environment, especially the command PATH, may not be set up. (I've encountered many problems with this on Common Desktop Environment, or CDE, systems, such as Hewlett-Packard HP-UX workstations.) To get around this problem, you need to store the full path to the **wish** executable. You can get this path with the info nameofexecutable command:

```
% info nameofexecutable
/usr/local/bin/wish8.0
```

The info nameofexecutable command may or may not return a value, so you need to code defensively.

The next problem is that the application will likely be restarted with a different current directory. This means that the name of the Tcl script file, *argv0*, will probably be bad. To get around this, you can use the pwd command, which returns the current directory. For example,

```
#
# Get full path to this script
# (assuming full path was not provided).
#
```

```
set script [file join [pwd] $argv0]
```

Of course, this example makes a big assumption: that the Tcl script file came from the current directory. This may well not be a valid assumption. Assuming that our assumptions are valid, you can use the following script as a guide for restarting the application from window managers that support the WM_SAVE_YOURSELF protocol:

```
#
# Sets up WM_COMMAND for applications
# that are called from wish.
#
proc set_wm_command { widget } {

    global argv0 argv

    bell
    bell

    # Get full executable.
    set exe [info nameofexecutable]

    #
    # Get full path to this script
    # (assuming full path was not provided).
    #
    set script [file join [pwd] $argv0]

    if { $exe != "" } {
        wm command $widget "$exe $script $argv"
    } else {
        wm command $widget "$script $argv"
    }
}

wm protocol . WM_SAVE_YOURSELF { set_wm_command . }
set_wm_command .
```

```
button .b -text "I was restarted"
pack .b

# restart.tcl
```

You can use the **xprop** UNIX command to check what values are stored for the window manager. Clicking on the **restart.tcl** window from **xprop** yields the following results for the WM_COMMAND and WM_PROTOCOLS properties, which relate to the WM_SAVE_YOURSELF protocol:

```
WM_COMMAND(STRING) = { "/usr/local/bin/wish8.0",
"/home/erc/tcl/c_api/restart.tcl" }
WM_PROTOCOLS(ATOM): protocols  WM_DELETE_WINDOW, WM_SAVE_YOURSELF
```

Only one top-level window in a given program should respond to WM_SAVE_YOURSELF messages. This should be your application's main window. In addition, many window managers send a WM_SAVE_YOURSELF message just before killing your program. Because calling wm command means that your program has responded to the WM_SAVE_YOURSELF message, you should call wm command last in the Tcl script you pass to wm protocol.

Even though these commands are necessary only on UNIX, you can also run these commands on Windows.

Controlling the Console

On Windows and MacOS versions of Tk, you see an extra console window when you start **wish**. This console window contains the stdin, stdout, and stderr file IDs that Tcl defines for all applications.

The console has some quirks. For example, when you double-click on a Tcl script file or run such a file from the MS-DOS command line, you won't see the console window at all.

You can control the console window with the console command.

The console hide command hides the console window:

```
console hide
```

The console show command shows the console window:

```
console show
```

If you want a console window from a running Tcl application, you can call `console show`.

The console also has its own sub Tcl interpreter. You can send your commands to this interpreter with the `console eval` command:

```
console eval your_command your_arguments...
```

If you call the `console` command from UNIX, you'll get an error such as:

```
invalid command name "console"
```

The `console` command is not defined on UNIX. Because of this, you should not call the `console` command if your script is running on UNIX. To determine whether or not the script is running on UNIX, use the global *tcl_platform* array. The value of $tcl_platform(platform) will be unix on UNIX systems.

Cross-Platform Issues

Just as the `send` command runs only on UNIX so far, there are a number of cross-platform issues to deal with when writing Tcl scripts. Of course, if you don't intend to run your scripts on more than one platform, this isn't an issue.

So far, Tcl is clearly written from a UNIX point of view. Tcl scripts and programs run best on UNIX. However, the Windows version gets better with each release. If you do write cross-platform scripts, you'll need to perform a lot of testing on Windows.

Windows and UNIX file names differ. You'll need to be careful about path names. The `file join` command described in Chapter 6 can help build portable file names.

Even though the file names differ, the basic interface conventions only differ slightly. See Chapter 4 for more on menu and interface conventions. Generally, you'll find that Tcl applications appear close enough to the Windows style guide.

Getting the Time with the `clock` Command

The `clock` command allows you to query the time and date without worrying about platform differences.

The `clock seconds` command returns the number of seconds since the system's start of the epoch. UNIX, a child of the seventies, starts on January 1, 1970. DOS and Windows start on January 1, 1980. If you don't use the value returned by `clock seconds` directly, you don't have to worry about the operating system differences.

You take the value returned by `clock seconds` and then call `clock format` to retrieve the month, day, hour, minutes, and so on, as shown here:

```
% set secs [clock seconds]
868094342
% set month [clock format $secs -format "%B"]
July
```

The `clock format` command takes a number of seconds—the system-specific number returned by `clock seconds`—and a format string, which tells `clock format` how to format the time. The format string contains any number of special directives, such as the %B in the previous example, that describe what aspects of the time you want returned. These special format directives begin with a percent sign, %, and are listed in Table 14.2.

Table 14.2 The values for the `clock format` command.

Value	Meaning
%%	Treat as a single % character.
%a	Abbreviated day of week: Mon, Tue, and so on.
%A	Full day of week: Thursday, Friday, and so on.
%b	Abbreviated name of month: Oct, Nov, and so on.
%B	Full name of month: October, November and so on.
%c	Date and time specific to your locale (current language in use).

continued

Table 14.2 continued

%d	Day of month, from 01 to 31.
%H	Hour, 24-hour format, 00 to 23.
%I	Hour, 12-hour format, 00 to 12.
%j	Day in year, 001 to 366.
%m	Month number, 01 to 12.
%M	Minute, 00 to 59.
%p	AM or PM.
%S	Seconds, 00 to 59.
%U	Week in year, 01 to 52. With %U weeks start on Sunday.
%w	Day of week as number from 0 for Sunday to 6 for Saturday.
%W	Week in year, 01 to 52. With %W weeks start on Monday.
%x	Date specific to your locale (current language in use).
%X	Time specific to your locale (current language in use).
%y	Year without century, 00 to 99.
%Y	Year with century, such as 1998.
%Z	Name of time zone.

Table 14.3 lists formatting directives available on UNIX but not on Windows.

Table 14.3 Values for the clock format command available on UNIX but not Windows.

Value	Meaning
%D	Date as %m/%d/%y.
%e	Day of month from 1 to 31 with no leading zeros.

%h	Abbreviated name of month.
%n	Put a newline in the output.
%r	Time with format %I:%M:%S %p.
%R	Time with format %H:%M.
%t	Put a tab in the output
%T	Time with format %H:%M:%S.

The default format is %a %b %d %H:%M:%S %Z %Y. Many of the values return numbers with a leading zero, such as 01. These are not octal numbers. The leading zero is for formatting.

WARNING

Because clock format uses the percent sign, %, as does the bind command, you must be careful. Don't put the clock format command inside an event binding.

In addition to using the value returned by clock seconds, you can also use the values returned by the file atime, file ctime, file mtime, or clock scan commands as the input seconds for the clock format command.

You can reverse the process used by clock format with the clock scan command. The clock scan command converts a formatted time string to a seconds value. You can pass in a number of time and date formats such as month/day/year. A very useful side effect of the clock scan command is that you can use it for time calculations, such as determining what day the first of the month falls for a particular month and year. For example,

```
% set month_num 10
10
% set short_year 99
99
% set first_secs [clock scan "$month_num/01/$short_year"]
938736000
% set first_of_month [clock format \
    $first_secs -format "%A %d %B, %Y"]
Friday 01 October, 1999
```

You now know that October 1, 1999 falls on a Friday.

Putting this all together, the **clock.tcl** script shows the `clock` command in action:

```
# Using clock to get the time.

  #
  # Get values the long way, in case you
  # need them separate.
  #
set secs [clock seconds]

set month_num [clock format $secs  -format %m ]
set month [clock format $secs  -format %B]
set day_of_month [clock format $secs -format "%d"]
set weekday [clock format $secs -format %A ]
set year [clock format $secs -format %Y]

puts "$weekday $day_of_month $month, $year"
puts "Month number=$month_num"

  # Get values the short way.
set date [clock format $secs -format "%A %d %B, %Y"]

  # Reverse process to get first of month.
set short_year [clock format $secs -format %y]
set first_secs [clock scan "$month_num/01/$short_year"]

set first_of_month [clock format $first_secs -format "%A %d %B, %Y"]
puts "First of the month was $first_of_month"

# clock.tcl
```

Updating Widgets

If you change some values and a widget does not appear to get updated, you can call the `update` command:

```
update
```

Tk widgets normally don't get updated until a script completes. This means that intermediate results that you want to display may not get seen by the user. If you face this situation, call `update`.

For example, if your code is accessing a Web page over a network using the Http package, performing a long-running calculation, or updating a database, you may want to display a progress message. To get this progress message to display, you'll need to call `update`.

The `update idletasks` command runs any action that has been deferred until the event loop is empty or idle. For example, most Tk widget layout is deferred until the event loop is empty. To force the update of these tasks, call `update idletasks`:

```
update idletasks
```

Supporting Other Languages

It may sound extremely basic, but users expect applications to display in their own language. The most well-behaved application isn't very well behaved if the users cannot read the menus.

Tcl and Tk provide limited support for other languages. As of version 8.0, Tk displays Western European languages best. For Asian languages, you need to get an extension to Tcl/Tk. (Such extensions exist for Chinese and Japanese. I have not seen extensions for Korean or other Asian languages.) In future versions, Tk will support the Unicode character set, which should allow the display of just about every language worldwide. (This is very similar to the approach taken by Java.)

For right now, Tcl works best with European languages like German, French, and Spanish. To support languages like this, you need to find a way to separate the text displayed from the rest of your program. This is called **internationalization**. After you separate the text, you can then add support for other languages, a process called **localization** because you're adding support for a given **locale**, a combination of language and territory. Locales are complicated by the fact that language conventions in one territory are not the same in all other areas that speak the same language. For example, French in Canada, French in Switzerland, and French in France are all French, but currency formats, keyboard layout, and other factors differ.

One of the simplest ways to separate the text of the interface in Tcl is to place the text for a given language in a configuration file that fills a global array. Your code then references the global array instead of the text directory. For example, you can use the following commands to fill in the text necessary for the *File* menu (discussed in Chapter 4):

```
set interface_text(file)    File
set interface_text(new)     New
set interface_text(open)    "Open..."
set interface_text(save)    Save
set interface_text(saveas)  "Save As..."
set interface_text(print)   Print
set interface_text(exit)    Exit
```

Then, when creating the menu and menu choices, refer to the *interface_text* array. For example:

```
frame .menubar -borderwith 1 -relief raised
menubutton .menubar.file -text $interface_text(file) \
    -menu .menubar.file.menu

menu .menubar.file.menu
menu add command -label $interface_text(new)
menu add command -label $interface_text(open)
```

The advantage of this approach is that you never reference the text message directly. This allows you to replace the values in the *interface_text* array with words in another language. To help with this, Table 14.4 lists the *File* menu terms in English, German, French, and Spanish.

Table 14.4 The File Menu.

English	German	French	Spanish
File	Datei	Fichier	Archivo
New	Neu	Nouveau	Nuevo
Open...	Öffnen...	Ouvrir...	Abrir...
Save	Speichern	Enregistrer	Guardar

Save As...	Speichern unter...	Enregistrer sous...	Guardar como...
Print	Drucken	Imprimer	Imprimir
Exit	Beenden	Quitter	Salir

Figure 14.2 shows the *File* menu, called *Datei* in German.

Figure 14.2 The German *File* menu.

Figure 14.3 shows the same menu in French.

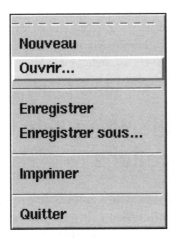

Figure 14.3 The French *File* menu.

And, Figure 14.4 shows the menu in Spanish.

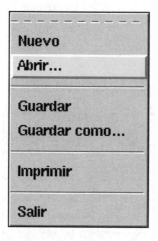

Figure 14.4 The Spanish *File* menu.

Appendix A lists books that will help you with common interface terms. Even so, you shouldn't use these terms blindly (as I have done). Instead, you should have a qualified person perform any translations to foreign languages.

In your code, you can use a variable to determine which language to use, or allow the user to choose a language during installation and use the `source` command to load in a file that fills in the array of interface text messages.

The LANG environment variable often tells you what language to use, but the value stored in the LANG environment variable differs by system. For example, French in France would be `fr_FR`, but some systems (notably Hewllet-Packard HP-UX workstations) place the word `french` in the LANG environment variable instead of `fr_FR`.

Creating a Distinctive Look for Your Applications

One of the most fun and rewarding tasks is to create a distinctive and professional look for your application. It's hard to specify exactly what you need to do, but in the end you want a professional look that makes you software easier to use.

The next sections cover some of the extras that enhance the look of your applications.

Color Schemes

You can improve the look of your applications by setting up a consistent color scheme for all the widgets. Each widget uses a number of colors, a background color, a foreground text color, colors for 3D bevels and shadows, as well as active and disabled colors.

Creating a Tan Color Scheme

Older Tk applications displayed a tannish color scheme based on the X Window color called **bisque**. You can use the `tk_bisque` procedure to restore that color scheme, as shown here:

```
tk_bisque
```

The `tk_bisque` procedure sets up a color scheme for all Tk widgets. Of course, you could do this yourself by setting the colors for each widget, but that tends to get rather tedious.

Creating Your Own Color Schemes

The bisque color may not appeal to you. In that case, you can create your own color scheme using `tk_setPalette`, which takes the following syntax:

```
tk_setPalette background_color
```

With a single background color, `tk_setPalette` will adjust the colors used by all widgets based on the background color. For example, you can try the following background colors:

```
tk_setPalette #4783b5
tk_setPalette lightsteelblue
tk_setPalette lightslategray
```

`tk_setPalette` also supports a longer syntax, allowing you to control each color used by a widget. This syntax follows:

```
tk_setPalette option color option2 color2 ...
```

You need to pass which options you want to set and the color for that option. The available options appear in Table 14.5.

Table 14.5 Color options for `tk_setPalette`.

Option

activeBackground

activeForeground

background

disabledForeground

foreground

highlightBackground

highlightColor

insertBackground

selectColor

selectBackground

troughColor

Determining Color Values

The `winfo rgb` command returns a list of the red, green, and blue values for a given color. You can pass a color name such as limegreen or the hexadecimal value such as #FF00004:

```
% winfo rgb . limegreen
12850 52685 12850
% winfo rgb . #FF0000
65535 0 0
```

These values come from UNIX and represent values from 0 to 65535, as used by the X Window System.

On Windows, you'll see similar values:

```
% winfo rgb . limegreen
12800 52480 12800
% winfo rgb . #FF0000
65280 0 0
```

You must pass the name of a widget, "." in this case, because some widgets may have different colormaps.

Start-up Splash Screens

Many applications present a splash screen dialog window on start-up. Usually, these dialog windows are windows that appear in the center of the screen and show a start-up message. Not only is this a good way to display your copyright message, but it also helps let the user know what is going on for applications that take a long time to start up.

Applications such as Microsoft Word, Netscape Navigator, and TkDesk display start-up windows, usually a variant on the About box that comes up from the *Help* menu discussed in Chapter 4. I especially like the splash screens on Navigator and TkDesk, which present status messages while the application starts up.

Following these examples, the **splash.tcl** script creates a sample start-up splash screen:

```
# Splash screen introduction dialog window.

  # Creates splash screen dialog window.
proc splash_create { image product copyright msg } {

    global tcl_version tk_version tcl_platform
    global tcl_patchLevel

    # Get rid of any existing dialog window.
    splash_remove

    toplevel .splash
```

```
wm withdraw .splash

# Center on screen.
dialog_position .splash

# Top area contains product info.
set frm .splash.top
frame $frm -bd 2 -relief groove

# Label for logo image.
label $frm.logo -image $image

# Label for product version number.
label $frm.product -text "$product"

# Message widget for copyright info.
message $frm.copyright -text "$copyright" -width 3i

# Label for Tcl version number.
label $frm.tclversion -text \
    "Tcl $tcl_version/Tk $tk_version, $tcl_patchLevel"

# Label for OS version.
label $frm.osversion -text \
    "$tcl_platform(os) $tcl_platform(osVersion)"

pack $frm.logo \
    -side top -fill x -pady 4 -ipadx 4 -ipady 4

pack $frm.product $frm.copyright \
    $frm.tclversion $frm.osversion \
    -side top -fill x

pack $frm -side top -fill x -padx 8 -pady 8

# Bottom area contains current message.
set frm .splash.bottom
frame $frm -bd 2 -relief groove
```

```
    # Label for message.
    label $frm.msg -text "$msg" -anchor w

    pack $frm.msg -side left -ipadx 6 -ipady 4
    pack $frm -side bottom -fill x -padx 8 -pady 8

    wm deiconify .splash
    update
}

  # Updates text message in splash screen dialog window.
proc splash_update { msg } {

    set name .splash.bottom.msg

    if { [winfo exists $name] } {
        $name config -text "$msg"
        update
    }

}

# Removes splash screen dialog window.
proc splash_remove { } {

    if { [winfo exists .splash] } {
        destroy .splash
    }
}

  # Centers dialog window in approximately screen center.
proc dialog_position { dlg } {

    set width  [winfo screenwidth  . ]
    set height [winfo screenheight . ]

    set x [expr ($width/2)  - 260]
    set y [expr ($height/2) - 260]
```

```
        wm geometry $dlg +$x+$y


}

# Test code.
image create bitmap ring -file rngbrod6.xbm

splash_create ring "WunderWord 10.0" \
    "Copyright 2001 Wunder Co.
All Rights Reserved." \
"Loading user preferences..."

#
# Show a set of messages spaced over
# time. In your programs, you can
# call splash_update when starting
# a new part of the initialization.
#
proc splash1 { } {
    splash_update "Creating bitmaps..."

    after 1400 splash2
}

proc splash2 { } {
    splash_update "Initializing interface..."
    after 1400 splash3
}

proc splash3 { } {
    splash_update "Loading data files..."
    after 1400 splash4
}

proc splash4 { } {
    splash_update "Connecting to server..."
    after 1400 splash5
}
```

```
proc splash5 { } {
    splash_update "Done."
    after 1400 splash_remove
}

after 1400 splash1

# splash.tcl
```

The **splash.tcl** script provides three main procedures you can call: splash_create, splash_update, and splash_remove. The splash1 through splash5 procedures just wait a small amount of time and then display new messages in the splash screen window. If you were using this for real, the initialization would take up some of the time, so you would not need to call the after command, which is used here to simulate the passage of time.

The splash_create procedure creates the splash screen window, a dialog window placed near the center of the screen. You pass in a logo image (in this case the file **rngbrod6.xbm**, available on the CD-ROM with the **splash.tcl** script file), a product name, a copyright statement, and a message. The message gets displayed in a small frame at the bottom of the dialog window. The rest get displayed in a frame at the top of the dialog window, as shown in Figure 14.5.

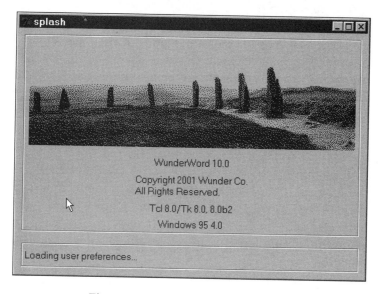

Figure 14.5 A splash screen window.

The `splash_update` procedure displays a new status message in the bottom of the splash screen window, such as *Connecting to server* or *Initializing interface*. You can use whatever messages are appropriate for the initialization of your scripts. This lets the user know that your program is doing something and that progress is being made. You can see a new update message in Figure 14.6.

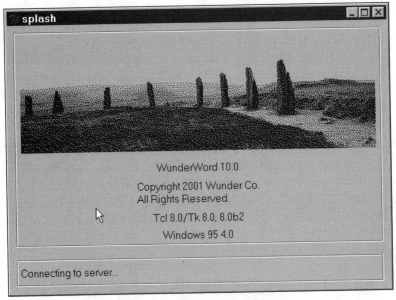

Figure 14.6 A splash screen window with a new message.

Note the use of the `update` command in the `splash_update` procedure. This ensures that the new status message gets displayed to the user right away.

The `splash_remove` procedure gets rid of the splash screen window. You should call this when your start-up code completes.

A common method for starting a complicated Tcl application is to first hide the main `toplevel` window with the `wm withdraw` command, display a splash screen window, initialize the interface, get rid of the splash screen window, and then show the main window with the `wm deiconify` command. This allows your application time to set up everything in the hidden main window as well as show progress through the initialization.

Cursors

You can change the mouse cursor shape with the `-cursor` option supported by most widgets. You can request just a cursor shape, or you can ask for a shape with a particular foreground and background color, as shown in the following syntax:

```
widgetname configure -cursor cursorname
widgetname configure -cursor { cursorname foreground background }
```

The latter form, where you can specify the colors, works only on UNIX, not on Windows.

The available cursor names come from the X Window System's **cursor** font and are shown in Figure 14.7 along with the corresponding cursor names.

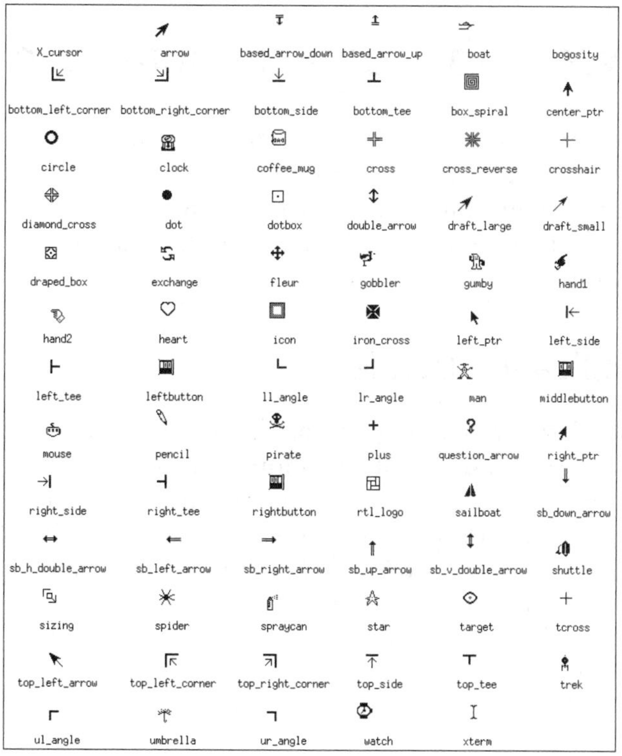

Figure 14.7 The available cursors.

Table 14.6 lists the most useful cursors.

Table 14.6 The most useful and best-looking cursors.

Cursor	Shape
crosshair	Cross hairs
left_ptr	Arrow pointing to upper left
right_ptr	Arrow pointing to upper right
top_left_arrow	Left-pointing arrow
watch	Busy-wait watch or hourglass
xterm	Text-entry "I-beam" cursor

Easier Ways To Create the Interface

Just about every chapter in this book covered some aspect of creating graphical interfaces and every section showed how to do this by hand, writing your procedures and placing widgets. Sometimes this task can be very time-consuming. To help with this, you may want to use an application, or GUI builder.

Using Application Builders

An application builder is a program that helps you create the interface for your programs. Application builders allow you to lay out widgets graphically, rather than calling the `grid` or `pack` commands in your scripts. The application builder interface lets you stretch widgets and place them with a mouse and then writes out the Tcl code necessary to create the widgets, so you don't have to do the tedious part.

There are a number of application builders for Tcl, including Visual Tcl, shown in Figure 14.8 and mentioned in the introduction.

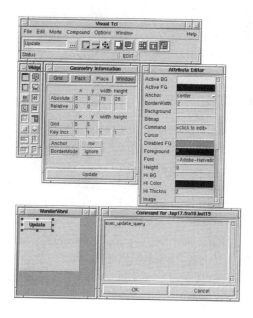

Figure 14.8 The Visual Tcl application builder program.

Other application builders include SpecTcl, XF, and GUIBuilder.

Application builders are located in the **contrib/scripting/builders** directory on the CD-ROM. SpecTcl is available on the Internet at the following URL: **http://sunscript.sun.com/products/spectcl.html**.

Even though application builders promise to ease the task of creating the user interface, I normally don't use them because I've found them all to be too constricting for my tastes. It's worth it to try some out and see if they work for you.

Providing User Customization

Modern user interfaces allow the user the ability to change fonts, colors, and window layouts and even to customize menus and buttons. Oftentimes, you'll provide this ability from the *Options* menu.

User Preferences

Whether you provide an *Options* menu or not, a relatively small amount of code allows you to store and retrieve user preferences.

In any case, the easiest way to store user customizations is with a Tcl array. You can write out the array and all its values to a file formatted as a series of Tcl set commands and then use the source command to load in the file the next time the software runs.

The reason for storing user preferences in an array is that you can iterate through all the elements in the array with the array names command. This makes it easy to add more options to save. As long as the values are stored in one array, you can store any number of options and extend this set at will.

Saving the options in Tcl format means that you can use the source command to load in the options file, again making things easier.

The following code contains procedures to save user preferences to disk, load the preferences back up, and get the user's home directory on Windows or UNIX. The home directory is used as a good place to store the user preferences. The GetHomeDirectory procedure uses the HOME environment variable on UNIX and the HOMEDRIVE and HOMEPATH environment variables on Windows. (However, not all versions of Windows provide these environment variables.)

The **userpref.tcl** script follows:

```
# Loading and saving user preferences.

proc UserPrefSave { filename arrayname } {
    upvar #0 $arrayname array_link

    # Open file.
```

```
    set fileid [open $filename "w"]

    set names [array names array_link]

    puts $fileid "# PROGRAM OPTIONS. DO NOT EDIT."
    puts $fileid "global $arrayname"

    foreach name $names {
        set var [format "set %s(%s)" $arrayname $name]

        puts $fileid "$var \"$array_link($name)\""
    }

    close $fileid

}

proc UserPrefLoad { filename } {
    catch {
        source $filename
    }
}

proc GetHomeDirectory { } {
    global tcl_platform env

    set dir "."

    catch {
        if { $tcl_platform(platform) == "unix" } {
            set dir "$env(HOME)"
        } else {
            set dir "$env(HOMEDRIVE)$env(HOMEPATH)"
        }
    }

    return "$dir"
}
```

```
    # Set up some user preferences.
set wunderword(foreground)  black
set wunderword(background)  lightsteelblue
set wunderword(font_family) Times
set wunderword(font_size)   12
global wunderword

    # Generate file name for saving.
set filename [file join [GetHomeDirectory] wunder.tcl]

    #
    # Save user preferences to wunder.tcl in
    # the user's home directory.
    #
UserPrefSave $filename wunderword

# userpref.tcl
```

You can use the **userpref.tcl** script as a guide to storing and loading user preferences for your applications.

In addition to storing user preferences, you can use Tcl's option database.

The Option Database

The **option database** is a fancy way of saying X resource files. Under the X Window System, users can modify the text, colors, fonts, and so on in applications by editing X resource files. Applications then load these text files at runtime.

X resource files are used extensively on UNIX to customize the colors and fonts used by applications. An X resource file has the format of name: value, where name specifies the name of a widget or class of widgets. For example,

```
! Example X resource file.
*foreground: maroon
*Button*foreground: blue
*b*foreground: red
```

```
*l*foreground: orange
```

```
! res.ad
```

Asterisks are wild cards in X resource files. These resource commands state that in lieu of other options to the contrary, widgets should have a foreground color of maroon. Widgets with class *Button* (that is, `button` widgets) have a foreground color of blue. Widgets named *b* have a foreground color of red, and widgets named *l* have a foreground color of orange. In general, the most specific rule is the one used. That is, the rule for widgets named *b* is more specific than the rule for widgets of class *Button*.

Sometimes, though, the last applicable rule in the resource file is the one that is used.

On UNIX, X resources are often stored in a file name that matches an application class name. *Tk* is the class name for Tk applications. In this case, a class resource file would be named **Tk** and usually resides in your home directory. *XTerm* is the class name for the **xterm** program, and so on. In addition to class resource files, the default X resource file name is called **.Xdefaults** and stored in your home directory. The Common Desktop Environment loads in resources to memory to a root window property called RESOURCE_MANAGER, ignoring the **.Xdefaults** file.

See Appendix A for more information on X resource files.

Tk also supports X resource files. For instance, the common widget `activeforeground` option corresponds to the *activeForeground* resource. In addition, each widget also has a class name in the resource files. To see the resources available, you can look in the on-line documentation on each widget.

To load in an X resource file, use the `option readfile` command:

```
option readfile res.ad
```

The `option readfile` command reads in the resource file and creates an option database. You can then query values from the option database for values of colors, fonts, and so on, from the database using the `option get` command:

```
option get widget resource_name class
```

For example,

```
% option get .b foreground *
red
```

Use a * if you don't know the class. *Tk* is the default class name for Tk applications.

If *.b* is a button widget, the value returned should be red. (This is from the most specific rule about widgets named *b*.)

The option clear command clears out the option database:

```
option clear
```

The option clear command doesn't fully clear everything out, because the option database will reinitialize from the RESOURCE_MANAGER property or **.Xdefaults** file with the next option command.

The option add command adds a new value into the option database:

```
option add pattern value priority
```

The *priority* is optional and defaults to 80, a high priority. The *pattern* is a resource name such as *b*foreground or *foreground (without the colon), and the *value* is the value for the resource such as red or blue. For example,

```
% option get .b foreground *
red
% option add *b*foreground limegreen
% option get .b foreground *
limegreen
```

Commands such as tk_setPalette, described previously in this chapter, call option add to place new values in the option database.

Problems Using X Resource Files

X resource files, used by the option command, are common on UNIX but are very hard for all but power users to modify because of the obscure syntax. Consequently, I find it better to provide an interface for changing defaults and then save the defaults to disk as described previously in the section on User Preferences. In addition, X resource files are not common on Windows at all. And, prior to version 8.0, Tk on Windows did not support the `option` command. For these reasons, I generally stay away from X resource files and the `option` command.

Packaging Your Code

Some of the final tasks in putting together your programs include creating installation scripts and packaging your code. Because the way you install you Tcl programs depends on how you package the code, we'll delve into that subject first.

Up to now, most of the scripts are contained in one *.tcl* file. A few examples, such as the menu and menu bar examples in Chapter 4, used the `source` command to load in other *.tcl* files. Both of these methods are valid for packaging your code. Other options include libraries and packages.

Libraries

A **library** is a set of Tcl procedures stored in files in a directory. Through the use of **autoloading**, the Tcl interpreter will load these files on demand. That is, when you first call the procedures in the files, the Tcl interpreter uses the `source` command to load in the files in which the procedures are defined. Each library directory contains a **tclIndex** file, which tells the Tcl interpreter which procedures correspond to which files.

The Great Unknown

Whenever the Tcl interpreter encounters an unknown command, it will try to execute the procedure named `unknown`, passing the unrecognized command and its arguments to `unknown`.

Because `unknown` is a Tcl procedure, you can redefine `unknown` if you want different behavior. By default, `unknown` will try to find the unrecognized command from a library or package, load in the Tcl procedure, and then execute it. If the unrecognized command is a program, `unknown` will try to run the program via `exec`.

Thus, when your code first calls a procedure that has not been loaded, the unknown command will try to load it. The file containing the procedure must be in one of the directories contained within the *auto_path* variable. And, the procedure must be indexed within a **tclIndex** file in one of the directories.

Autoloading

Tcl's automatic loading of procedures is based on the global variable *auto_path*. The *auto_path* holds the list of directories in which to search for a given procedure.

On Windows, the default *auto_path* holds the following directories:

```
c:\Program Files\Tcl\lib\Tcl8.0
c:\Program Files\Tcl\lib
c:\Program Files\Tcl\lib\Tk8.0
```

If you install Tcl in some other location than **c:\Program Files**, such as **c:\Tcl** (which I recommend because of the spaces in the name **Program Files**), the *auto_path* will look something like:

```
c:\Tcl\lib\Tcl8.0
c:\Tcl\lib
c:\Tcl\lib\Tk8.0
```

The version number, 8.0 in this example, depends on the version of Tcl you have installed.

On UNIX, you'll see an *auto_path* like the following:

```
% puts $auto_path
/usr/local/lib/tcl8.0
/usr/local/lib
/usr/local/lib/tk8.0
```

Again, the version number, 8.0 in this example, depends on the version of Tcl you have installed.

If you don't want the unknown command to try to load up unknown procedures automatically, you can set the global variable *auto_noload* to any value:

```
set auto_noload any_value
```

In addition to loading unknown Tcl procedures, the unknown procedure will also attempt to run unknown programs. To prevent unknown from executing UNIX or Windows commands, set the global variable *auto_noexec* to any value:

```
set auto_noexec any_value
```

Table 14.7 lists some commands that also relate to automatic loading.

Table 14.7 Autoloading commands.

Command	Usage
auto_execok *command*	Returns 1 if *command* is an executable program in your PATH.
auto_load *command*	Tries to load the Tcl procedure *command* from the *auto_path* list of directories.
auto_reset	Removes all information cached by *auto_execok* and *auto_load*. The next attempt to load a procedure will reinitialize all this information from disk.

After covering the theory behind Tcl libraries and the unknown command, you can now set up a library.

Setting Up a Library

To set up a library, you need to:

1. Place all the Tcl files for the library into a directory.
2. Prepare the **tclIndex** file in the directory.
3. Extend the *auto_path*, if necessary, to include the new directory, when your application runs.

Placing all the Tcl files in the directory is easy, as is preparing the **tclIndex** file. To create a **tclIndex** file, you need to call the `auto_mkindex` procedure in **tclsh** or **wish**:

```
auto_mkindex directory files_to_include
```

For example:

```
auto_mkindex /home/erc/tcl *.tcl
```

This command indexes all procedures that end in a *.tcl* extension in the directory **/home/erc/tcl**. The `auto_mkindex` procedure then creates the **tclIndex** file, which looks something like the following:

```
# Tcl autoload index file, version 2.0.
# This file is generated by the "auto_mkindex" command
# and sourced to set up indexing information for one or
# more commands.  Typically each line is a command that
# sets an element in the auto_index array, where the
# element name is the name of a command and the value is
# a script that loads the command.

set auto_index(parray) [list source [file join $dir parray.tcl]]
set auto_index(unknown) [list source [file join $dir init.tcl]]
set auto_index(auto_load) [list source [file join $dir init.tcl]]
```

This **tclIndex** example shows three procedures from the Tcl standard library: `parray`, `unknown`, and `auto_load`. The *auto_index* array contains an element for each procedure. The value of each element is the command necessary to load in the procedure if it is not yet defined.

The `auto_mkindex` command creates the **tclIndex** file. You can create the **tclIndex** file prior to installation—in fact, you should. If you create the **tclIndex** file prior to installation, then the installation program just has to copy all the files in the library directory, including the **tclIndex** file, to the target installation directory.

If your new library resides in a directory not in the default list of directories in the *auto_path* global variable, then you need to extend the *auto_path* at runtime within your Tcl script. For example,

```
lappend auto_path /home/erc/tcl
```

You need to run a command like this inside your Tcl script and be sure to run it prior to using any of the procedures defined in your library, or you'll see an error.

Packages

Packages are similar to libraries but add a few other features, such as version numbering. Unlike the automatic loading of procedures from libraries, packages require explicit loading, with the package require command. Usually, packages are loaded in their entirety, rather than use the automatic loading mechanism that loads each routine when it is first used.

Packages provide version numbering, which allows you to release a new and potentially incompatible version of a package while still maintaining the previous version.

To use a package in your code, you need to call the package require command with the name of the package and, optionally, a version number:

```
package require package_name version_number
```

For example, to use the Http package described in Chapter 11, you need to call the following command:

```
package require http 1.0
```

Or you can skip the version number:

```
package require http
```

If you require an exact version number, you can use the -exact option:

```
package require -exact http 1.0
```

Once you call the package require command, you can use any of the procedures defined in the package.

674

The Tcl scripts that define the package must call the `package provide` command in each Tcl script file that makes up the package. The `package provide` command requires the following syntax:

```
package provide package_name version_number
```

For example, using the same Http package, all Tcl script files that make up the package need to call the following command:

```
package provide http 1.0
```

The `package names` command lists the packages that are available. This is not the list of all possible packages, but rather the list of all packages that have been loaded into the Tcl interpreter either automatically or via the `package require` command. The **wish** interpreter starts with *Tcl* and *Tk* packages by default. If you call `package require`, you then add another package to the list returned by the `package names` command, as shown here:

```
% package names
Tk Tcl
% package require http 1.0
1.0
% package names
http Tk Tcl
```

Setting Up a Package

Setting up a package is a lot like setting up a library. To set up a package, you need to:

1. Create your Tcl scripts for the package. Each script file must call the `package provide` command.

2. Place all the Tcl files for the package into a directory. The name of this directory should be the package name and the version number, for example **http1.0**.

3. Prepare the **pkgIndex.tcl** file in the directory with the `pkg_mkIndex` procedure.

4. Extend the *auto_path*, if necessary, to include the new package directory, when your application runs. Or, you can install the package directory as a subdirectory under a standard package directory held in the *tcl_pkgPath* global variable.

The first step in creating a package is to create all the Tcl script files. Each script file must call the `package provide` command. For example,

```
package provide http 1.0
```

You must do this in each script file that makes up the package.

 A package can also contain a binary dynamic (shared) library that can be loaded with the `load` command. See the on-line documentation on the `load` command and the `pkg_mkIndex` procedure for more on this topic.

After you've created all the files that make up a package, place all the files in a directory. Unlike for libraries, the directory name is significant. The directory name should contain the name of the package as well as the version number, for example, **http1.0**.

The next step is to prepare the **pkgIndex.tcl** file in the package directory with the `pkg_mkIndex` procedure. The **pkgIndex.tcl** file is very similar to the **tclIndex** file used by Tcl libraries.

The `pkg_mkIndex` procedure requires the following parameters:

```
pkg_mkIndex directory pattern
```

The *directory* is the directory in which you placed the Tcl scripts that make up the package. This should be a relative directory name. For example, I usually build the **pkgIndex.tcl** file in the directory above the package directory. The *pattern* describes what Tcl files to look for procedures in the package, for example, *a*.tcl* or **.tcl*. The `pkg_mkIndex` procedure creates the **pkgIndex.tcl** file.

For example, if your package is located in a subdirectory named **bendy1.0**, you can call the `pkg_mkIndex` procedure as shown here:

```
pkg_mkIndex bendy1.0 *.tcl
```

The **pkgIndex.tcl** file ends with *.tcl*. To avoid checking the index file for packages, I normally delete the **pkgIndex.tcl** file before calling pkg_mkIndex.

N O T E

After you have the **pkgIndex.tcl** file, the next step is to decide where to install the package. You have two options. If the package is installed in a subdirectory under a standard package directory, then the Tcl interpreter will automatically find the package. The second option is to install the package in any directory. In this case, you need to append the directory to the *auto_path* global variable, similar to the case with libraries discussed previously. You can append the package directory itself to the *auto_path* global variable, or the package directory can be a subdirectory of one of the directories listed in the *auto_path* global variable.

Installing a Package In the Standard Directories

The global *tcl_pkgPath* variable contains the list of standard directories in which the Tcl interpreter searches for packages. If there is more than one directory listed in the *tcl_pkgPath* variable, then you should install your package in the second directory. If your package contains binary dynamic (shared) libraries, then you should install your package in the first directory. In both cases, the package directory should be a subdirectory of one of the directories listed in the *tcl_pkgPath* variable.

Your Tcl code should not change the global *tcl_pkgPath* variable, either.

N O T E

Installing a Package in Any Directory

To install your package in any arbitrary directory, you need to append the directory to the global *auto_path* variable. You can also install the package in a subdirectory of any directory listed in the *auto_path* variable.

For example, if your package is called *bendy*, with a version number of 1.0, and you installed the package in the **/home/erc/tcl/bendy/bendy1.0** directory, to access this package you'd need the following code:

```
lappend auto_path /home/erc/tcl/bendy/
package require bendy 1.0
```

Notice that the package was installed in the **/home/erc/tcl/bendy/bendy1.0** directory, but the *auto_path* is appended with the **/home/erc/tcl/bendy/** directory, the parent directory for **/home/erc/tcl/bendy/bendy1.0**.

You should now be able to call the procedures in this example package.

Problems with Packages and Libraries

Packages and libraries seem like neat ways to package and distribute your code. You can provide easier updates, and these methods encourage reusing the code in separate Tcl programs. There are a few problems, though, especially with the added administrative burden. The main problem is that with either packages or libraries, your program must properly set up the *auto_path* variable or your code won't be found. You can get around this by installing your code in the standard Tcl or Tk library directories or a subdirectory of one of these. But, this may require your end users to have administrator privileges to be able to copy files to what will likely be restricted directories.

Another problem is that it's hard to get packages and libraries to work. (Try it.) Additional problems, and advantages, are listed in Table 14.8.

Table 14.8 Methods for packaging your code.

Method	Advantages	Disadvantages
One *.tcl* file	• Simple to administer.	• Must update whole file at once.
	• Only one file to keep track of.	• Leads to very large files.
		• Tcl interpreter must load entire file even though you may not use all of the procedures.
Use source command	* Simple to create	• Many file accesses to load in sourced files.
		• Must keep track of more files.

continued

Table 14.8 continued

Libraries	• Loads procedures on demand	• Must keep track of more files.
	• Encourages code reuse.	• Must set up **tclIndex** file.
	• Partitions code into smaller, more maintainable pieces	• Must keep track of directories and *auto_path*
Packages	• Loads on demand.	• Must keep track of more files.
	• Supports versioning.	• Must set up **pkgIndex.tcl** file.
	• Encourages code reuse.	• Must keep track of directories and *auto_path*

I've used all the methods listed in Table 14.8. None is wholly satisfactory. To keep things simple, I now usually concatenate all the *.tcl* files into one large script file for a given program. Even so, I definitely reuse Tcl code from one program to another, by keeping the code in small files during development and then concatenating all at the end into one file. This generally makes things much simpler for installation and administration.

In fact, a number of freeware Tcl applications seem to follow the same philosophy of using libraries or packages during the development of the application and then concatenating all the code to simplify installation for the end user.

Name Spaces

Another problem with libraries and packages and any Tcl code in general is keeping the procedure and global variables names separated. If two packages (or libraries, etc.) define a procedure named redisplay, then the last one loaded wins. When you then call the redisplay procedure, you may get behavior that you did not intend. As you use more and more procedures written by others, the problem of conflicting names arises repeatedly. Even if you work alone, you may start using code from sources like **cgi.tcl**, html_library and the Http package discussed in Chapters 11 and 13. The more Tcl code you have, the more likely name conflicts will occur.

To help with this, Tcl provides name spaces.

A **name space** is a collection of procedures and variables connected by a name. Within a name space, a variable named *x* will not interfere with other variables named *x* outside of the name space. This means that name spaces are similar to local variables within procedures.

Name spaces add a lot more, however. You can export only some of the procedures within a name space and keep the other procedures hidden.

Name spaces are available in Tcl starting with version 8.0.

N O T E

To create a name space, use the `namespace eval` command:

```
namespace eval my_name {
    # Put code inside name space here...
}
```

This command creates a new name space named *my_name*. All the commands between the curly braces are within the name space.

Inside a name space, you write your Tcl code as you would without a name space. The commands and variables in the name space work together as one unit.

Outside a name space, you can call procedures inside a name space, but you must use a special syntax with the name space name and a double colon, `::`. For example, to call a procedure named `Puts` in a name space called *Hello*, you'd use the following double-colon syntax:

```
Hello::Puts
```

Global procedures outside of any name space (actually these are within the global name space) have a blank name. For example,

```
::puts
```

You can use the double-colon naming scheme or the normal naming scheme without double colons as you see fit.

To access procedures and variables within the name space, you must use the double-colon naming scheme. Or, if you access procedures and variables in a name space frequently, you may want to import the procedures in the name space to avoid having to type the pesky : : syntax for every procedure call. To do this, use the `namespace import` command:

```
namespace import pattern
```

For example, to import all the names within the name space called *Hello*, you can use the following command:

```
namespace import Hello::*
```

You can also import specific procedures or variables, such as

```
namespace import Hello::Puts
```

The `namespace import` command can import only the names of things that are exported within the name space with the `namespace export` command. This allows the name space to keep some procedures and variables hidden from the outside world. (That is, they are reasonably hidden. You can still access variables and procedures in a name space using the full double-colon notation.)

Call `namespace export` within a name space. You pass the names of the things to export. For example,

```
namespace export Puts
```

This command, executed within a name space, exports the name `Puts`. (With just that command, we don't know whether `Puts` is a procedure or a variable.

To tell where a command comes from, you can use the `namespace which` command:

```
namespace which -command command_name
namespace which -variable variable_name
namespace which name
```

The -command and -variable options are not required but rather allow you to separate procedures from variables if both have the same name. For example,

```
% namespace which puts
::puts
```

Don't depend on the namespace which command though, because it mostly echoes back its arguments with a double colon in front. The namespace origin command does better:

```
% namespace origin Puts
::Hello::Puts
```

The namespace current command returns the name of the current name space:

```
% namespace current
::
```

Technically, the global name space has a blank name. The double colon is for convenience.

N O T E

Variables in Name Spaces

The variable command acts sort of like the global command, but it works within a name space. You can pass an optional value, which is used to initialize the variable. The syntax follows:

```
variable variable_name value
```

For example,

```
variable message "Hello World"
```

Inside a procedure in a name space, you can use the `variable` command like the `global` command to access variables global within the name space. For example,

```
namespace eval Hello {
    variable message "Hello World"

    proc Puts { } {
        # Access variable named message.
        variable message
    }
}
```

A Name Space Example

To pull all this together, the following simple example creates a name space and shows how to call the most-used name space commands:

```
# Use of name spaces.

namespace eval Hello {
    variable message "Hello World"

    proc Puts { } {
        variable message

        puts "$message"
    }

    # Export Puts but not message.
    namespace export Puts
}

# You can use the full name.
Hello::Puts
```

```
# Or you can import frequently used names.
namespace import Hello::*

Puts

# You can still access nonexported items
# in a name space using the full name.
set Hello::message "Wow, I changed it"

Hello::Puts

# name.tcl
```

Name Spaces and Callbacks

When you set up Tcl code to execute for the -command option on a button widget or set up an event binding, that Tcl code gets executed in the global context. This can cause problems when trying to run code within a name space as part of the -command or binding Tcl script.

To get around this, you can use the fully qualified name of each procedure and variable. For example use Hello::Puts rather than just Puts. You need to use the full name with the name space, double colon, and procedure name.

Name spaces are a very useful way to keep your code separated from other Tcl code and avoid naming conflicts. You can even nest name spaces within name spaces, as well as evaluate Tcl commands in the context of another name space, but it's very easy to get confused. I'd suggest staying away from these parts of the namespace command. The on-line documentation on namespace and variable is very helpful if you'd like to do this.

Installation and Wizards

Windows and Macintosh users expect graphical installation programs to guide users through the task of installing new software. UNIX users would love to have the same help, but they rarely get it. No matter how nice or how bare bones your installation program is, you still need to install your

Tcl scripts on end-user systems. This section discusses the basic issues for installing your Tcl programs.

Installing a Tcl script itself is fairly easy, but it differs based on the operating system. The basic operation is copying the main Tcl script file to its final destination on the user's system. The harder part is installing all the support files needed. These support files include on-line help files (see Chapter 11) and perhaps Tcl scripts that make up a package or library (described previously in this chapter). You may also need icon bitmap files as well as general image files. All these files need to get installed somewhere on the user's machine. In addition, your Tcl script needs to know the location of all these support files.

 As of Tk version 8.0, the file dialog windows discussed in Chapter 7 do not allow you to select a directory.

N O T E

You can use the `file copy` command to copy these files to their final destinations. But, you then need to update your Tcl script to point to the new location. To do this, you can divide your script into two parts. The top— very short—part merely sets up configuration variables with the Tcl `set` command, such as the directory where the support files are located. This task is made easier if you install all the support files in the same directory (or underneath the same directory). Then you only need to keep track of the top-level directory under which all the support files can be found.

The bottom part is your true Tcl script file. You can use the file commands covered in Chapter 6 (`open`, `read`, `puts`, `close`, etc.) to combine the Tcl script file with a short header into the final destination script file.

Most Tcl applications require at least one file beyond the main Tcl script file, so you almost always have to mess with installation.

Installing on Windows

On Windows, Tcl scripts should have a *.tcl* extension. If you maintain this requirement, then users can double-click on your script file to start the program. Thus, installing on Windows is fairly simple, even though you still need to configure the location of the support files.

If you have an installation program like Install Shield or other installation frameworks available, you may want to use those, so you have a standard Windows installation program.

Installing on UNIX

On UNIX, you need to find the location of the **wish** executable and then customize the very first line of the Tcl script using the `#!/usr/local/bin/wish` syntax discussed in Chapter 1.

You can make this **wish** line part of the configuration header that points to the location of the support files.

Dealing With Interpreter Names

Another problem faced on UNIX is that the name of the interpreter differs by release. You may have worked with **wish8.0**, but your user may still have only **wish4.2** or simply **wish**. To build up the `#!` syntax, you need to know the exact name of the **wish** interpreter to run.

If you write your installation scripts in Tcl, then you can use the `info nameofexecutable` command to track down the name of the **wish** executable. This is essentially cheating: you ask the user to launch your installation script with **wish** and then use the `info nameofexecutable` command to get the information on the full path to the **wish** executable. This is also a convenient place to check for the right versions. For example, the `font` command discussed in Chapter 3 requires Tcl 8.0 or higher. You can check against the global *tcl_version* variable. Your Tcl scripts may have similar dependencies.

Installing Tcl

To run any Tcl script, you need to have Tcl (and most likely Tk) installed. Because Tcl does not come with most operating systems (Linux is one of the few exceptions), many of your users will need to install **wish** on their systems as a requirement for running your applications. (See Appendix B for more on installing Tcl/Tk.)

One way to get around this need to install Tcl/Tk is to create a C application with the Tcl interpreter linked inside. You can also use software called Embedded Tk (ET) to combine the Tcl/Tk runtime libraries in with your code. Both topics are covered in Chapter 15.

Accessing the Windows Registry

The **registry** contains the configuration of your Windows system. Installation programs will often add entries to the registry to allow the Windows Explorer to launch the right application when the user double-clicks on a data file. (This is not the only reason to change the registry, but it is a common one.)

On Windows—naturally—you can access the registry from the `reg-istry` command. This is a package, so you must call the `package require` command before using the `registry` command:

```
package require registry 1.0
```

After you've called `package require`, you can call any of the commands listed in Table 14.9.

Table 14.9 The registry command.

Command	Usage
registry delete *keyname*	Deletes *keyname* and all values underneath.
registry delete *keyname valuename*	Deletes *valuename* in *keyname* only.
registry get *keyname valuename*	Returns data for *valuename* under *keyname*.
registry keys *keyname*	Returns all subkeys for *keyname*.
registry keys *keyname pattern*	Returns list of subkeys that match *pattern*.
registry set *keyname*	Creates given *keyname*.

`registry set keyname` `  valuename data type`	Creates *valuename* under given *keyname* with optional data *type*.
`registry type keyname valuename`	Returns type of *valuename* under given *keyname*.
`registry values keyname`	Returns name of all values under *keyname*.
`registry values keyname pattern`	Returns name of all values under *keyname* that match *pattern*.

WARNING

Before changing any values in the registry, you should be very sure about what you're doing. If you make a mistake, you can destroy your version of Windows.

The Windows registry is based on key names and values in a hierarchy. At the top of the hierarchy for a given machine sit the root names listed in Table 14.10.

Table 14.10 Windows registry root names.

Root Name

HKEY_CLASSES_ROOT

HKEY_CURRENT_CONFIG

HKEY_CURRENT_USER

HKEY_LOCAL_MACHINE

HKEY_USERS

Under these root names come key names, which go downward like a directory hierarchy. At the bottom level, much like files in a directory, are value names. Each value name has a value. (The term *value name* comes from the Tcl documentation on the registry command.)

You can access the registry for a given machine host name or start from one of the root names listed in Table 14.10 on the current machine. The registry key names must follow the formats listed in Table 14.11.

Table 14.11 Valid key name formats for the Windows registry.

Format	Usage
rootname	Top-level access to the registry.
rootname\keypath	Access to a particular part of the registry.
\\hostname\rootname\keypath	Access to a particular part of the registry on the given machine *hostname*.

The registry actually sounds more complicated that it is. To help make some sense of the registry, you can use the following script as a guide:

```
# Accessing the Windows registry.

package require registry 1.0

  # Prints a single value and type in the registry.
proc registry_print { keyname valuename } {

    set type [registry type $keyname $valuename]
    set value [registry get $keyname $valuename]

    set output [format "%10.10s    %s" $type $value]
    puts "\t $output"
}

  # Queries all keys underneath parent key, prints values.
```

```
proc query_keys { parent_key } {

    set keys [registry keys $parent_key]
    set values [registry values $parent_key]

    # Go through under keys.
    if { $keys != "" } {

        foreach key $keys {
            set keyname "$parent_key\\$key"

            query_keys $keyname
        }
    }

    # Go through values.
    if { $values != "" } {
        puts "$parent_key"

        foreach value $values {
            registry_print $parent_key $value
        }
    }
}

console show

set keyname HKEY_LOCAL_MACHINE\\Software\\Classes\\TclScript
query_keys $keyname

# registry.tcl
```

The **registry.tcl** script prints out all values in the registry that descend from a single key, in this case, the most interesting key related to Tcl in the registry.

For each key found under the parent key, the query_keys procedure calls itself (this technique is called **recursion**) with the new key. This enables the query_keys procedure to traverse down to all subkeys under the starting parent key.

An odd part about the registry is that a key can have both a value and subkeys. For each value name found, the `registry_print` procedure gets the value associated with that name on that key and then prints the value, as well as the data type of the value.

Table 14.12 lists the registry data types supported by Tcl.

Table 14.12 Registry data types supported by Tcl.

Type	Meaning
binary	Binary data.
none	No defined type; binary data.
sz	Data is a text string.
expand_sz	Data is a text string that needs to be expanded with the value of environment variables enclosed in percent signs, such as %USER%.
dword	32-bit number.
dword_big_endian	32-bit number, stored with the opposite byte order of data with dword type.
link	Symbolic link.
multi_sz	List of text strings.
resource_list	Device-driver resource list.

When you run the **registry.tcl** script on a typical Windows NT system, you'll see output like the following:

```
% source registry.tcl
HKEY_LOCAL_MACHINE\Software\Classes\TclScript\DefaultIcon
        sz    C:\WINNT\System32\tk80.dll
HKEY_LOCAL_MACHINE\Software\Classes\TclScript\shell\edit\command
        sz    notepad "%1"
HKEY_LOCAL_MACHINE\Software\Classes\TclScript\shell\edit
```

```
        sz    &Edit
HKEY_LOCAL_MACHINE\Software\Classes\TclScript\shell\open\command
        sz    C:\Tcl\bin\wish80.exe "%1"
HKEY_LOCAL_MACHINE\Software\Classes\TclScript
        sz    TclScript
```

Always be careful before changing the registry. See Appendix A for books that cover more on this subject.

The Future of Tcl and Tk

Tcl and Tk aim to be the equivalent of Visual Basic for the Internet. As such, the language has been evolving with more networking commands. With version 8.0, Tcl and Tk are the most robust yet, especially on non-UNIX platforms, traditionally a weak area for Tcl.

I expect to see more and better tools for working with Web pages and protocols, better integration with Java, and enhanced platform support, especially on Windows. Future versions should also support Unicode characters to allow for the ability to display text in almost any language worldwide. This will be a great help for displaying Asian text, a current weakness in Tk.

Even without these future advances, Tcl and Tk provide a very useful application development platform.

I mostly use Tcl and Tk to create cross-platform test programs for object-oriented C++ software (a topic discussed in Chapter 16). Tcl has proven mostly adequate for most tasks. This may appear like I'm putting down Tcl, but if you think about the fast turn-around time, easy scripting, ability to link with C and C++ applications, and cross-platform support, Tcl forms an incredibly powerful tool. Tcl isn't suitable for all tasks, but it certainly works well for thousands of users worldwide. The real key advantage is the easy way you can link Tcl to your C and C++ applications. Future developments aim at making as easy a connection to Java applications.

Where to Go from Here

By now, you should be familiar enough with Tcl and Tk that you are ready to write applications. The best way to go on is to combine experiments with

692

reading the on-line manual information. This book—long as it is—is not a Tcl reference. Instead, I wanted this book to be a getting-started guide using real-world problems as examples.

Don't forget the Tcl on-line manuals. The information in these manuals is very helpful, and you'll refer back to the manuals again and again as you develop Tcl applications.

Appendix A lists a wide variety of other resources where you can get even more information to help you create Tcl applications.

The CD-ROM contains a lot of Tcl documentation as well as a plethora of Tcl freeware. The task before may have already been solved by someone else with the source code already residing on the CD-ROM. (It's worth checking out.)

This chapter concludes the discussion of Tcl and Tk. The next chapters delve into combining Tcl with C and C++ programs. If you don't intend to link Tcl to your C or C++ applications, you can skip ahead to Appendix A, which provides a number of places you can go to for further information on Tcl, Tk, and related topics. It's very easy to link Tcl with C or C++, so you should find the next chapters useful even if you weren't planning on combining Tcl with C or C++.

Summary

This chapter covers a grab-bag set of techniques to help you finish your Tcl applications. One of the keys in doing this is creating well-behaved applications.

On UNIX, users expect programs to provide icons for the window manager. Use the `wm iconbitmap` command to set up an application's icon. The `wm iconname` sets the name displayed with this icon. You should use a short name, or the user may not see the whole name.

On Windows and MacOS systems, the `console` command controls whether the extra console window is visible (`console show`) or not (`console hide`).

You can get the time with the `clock seconds` command and format the time with `clock format`.

Another facet to finishing your applications is creating a professional look. You can use the `tk_setPalette` command to set up a palette of colors for use with all Tk widgets. This is helpful if you create a number of color schemes. One such color scheme is the set of bisque colors that older versions of Tk used. To restore the older bisque colors, use the `tk_bisque` command. Splash screen dialog windows alert users that your program is initializing and provide a convenient venue for advertising your wares.

The `option` command controls the option database, which you can use to store user preferences.

As you create your code, you'll want to collect your procedures. Tcl supports a number of methods for doing this, including ad hoc methods. Two of the best methods are using either Tcl libraries or packages. The `namespace` command can help avoid naming conflicts between procedures.

And, the `registry` command allows you to access the Windows registry.

Tcl/Tk Commands Introduced in This Chapter

```
auto_execok
auto_load
auto_mkindex
auto_reset
clock
namespace
option
package
registry
tk
tk_bisque
tk_setPalette
unknown
update
variable
wm
```

Embedding Tcl in Your C and C++ Applications

One of the primary benefits of Tcl is the ability to easily extend the language using commands written in C. The Tcl interpreter itself is merely a set of C functions that you can call from your programs. This allows you to use Tcl as a form of macro extension language in your applications, the way some applications use Visual Basic.

Furthermore, I often use Tcl as a test harness for C++ applications. I create Tcl commands that create C++ objects and other commands that execute object member functions. Tcl then acts as the glue tying everything together. Another common approach is to use Tcl/Tk to create an application's interface and write the majority of the application in C or C++. This is very useful for existing applications, which are likely to be written in C or C++, not Tcl.

Even though Tcl and Tk provide a rich set of commands, you'll often want to extend this set to new commands, especially if you embed the Tcl interpreter into your applications as a sort of macro language. **Chapter 15** shows how to embed the Tcl interpreter in your programs. **Chapter 16** covers adding new commands to that interpreter and using Tcl for testing C++ applications.

Embedding Tcl in Your Applications

This chapter covers:

- Calling Tcl from C
- Creating your own Tcl interpreter
- Compiling and linking on Windows and UNIX
- Adding Tk into your interpreter

Application-Specific Languages

Tcl was originally created to allow you to embed the interpreter within your C programs. You can use Tcl as an application language, much like a macro language for a spreadsheet program.

Just about every major application, from AutoCAD to Microsoft Excel includes an extension or macro language, tuned to the application. These application-specific languages allow you to extend and customize the base package, automating common tasks.

The main advantage of application-specific languages is that you can automate tasks and go beyond what the designers of the application provided for in the interface, because you get programmable access to the underlying functionality. The main disadvantage of these application-specific languages is that, for older applications in particular, the application-specific languages provide strange, nonstandard syntax and tend to be clumsy to use.

So, instead of inventing your own language and creating your own parser, you can use Tcl as your application-specific language. Tcl provides an easy-to-learn syntax, which is documented in a number of books, training courses, and on-line resources. The Tcl interpreter is a C library that you can link to your applications. And of course, Tcl runs on Windows, MacOS and UNIX systems.

That's just one-half of the equation. An application-specific language needs to provide access to the application's underlying functionality. In Tcl, you do this by writing custom commands in C or C++ and then registering these commands with the Tcl interpreter, the topic of Chapter 16. This chapter shows the first part: how you can embed the Tcl interpreter in your application and can call Tcl commands from C.

Calling Tcl from C

Tcl is really a library of C functions. Tk is another library. You normally don't notice this because the **wish** program obscures this fact. This program is merely a set of very simple routines linked with the Tcl and Tk libraries. Based on this model, you can write C or C++ programs that call on the power of Tcl. The most common approach is to write the user interface in Tcl and call the Tcl scripts from your custom interpreter.

You add commands to the base set provided by the Tcl language. These new commands execute whatever new functionality you need. This usually works best if you divide your new C commands into low-level functions. Tcl provides the glue that connects the low-level functions together.

Taking a step back, what you do is build a new Tcl interpreter (i.e., **wish** or **tclsh**), embedded in your application. The reason you want to build this new interpreter is to add your own commands written in C or C++. Now, the term "interpreter" may be stretching things. You may be writing a spreadsheet application and embedding the Tcl interpreter as a macro language. From Tcl's point of view, you're building an enhanced Tcl interpreter.

To write your commands in C or C++ you need to:

1. Initialize the Tcl interpreter inside your C or C++ application.

2. Write the C or C++ code for any new commands. You must follow special conventions outlined in Chapter 16.

3. Register the new commands with the Tcl interpreter, so that it can execute your new commands. To do this, call `Tcl_CreateCommand` or `Tcl_CreateObjCommand`, passing in the textual name of your new command as well as a C function pointer to the code that executed the command.

4. Compile all your new C code and link the whole thing together with the Tcl and perhaps Tk C libraries.

This chapter covers many C and C++ programming issues necessary to embed the Tcl interpreter into your programs. If you're not familiar with C programming, or don't need to add new commands, then Chapters 15 and 16 won't be of much use, other than to find out more about how the Tcl interpreter works in the underlying code.

When To Code in Tcl and When to Code in C

In your applications, every part you can write in Tcl will be easier to modify. But, Tcl code does have its limitations, such as the fact that Tcl is an interpreted language, leading to inherent performance problems. The right mix of Tcl and C code is up to you—do what makes sense for your applications.

There's a lot of power in the Tcl interpreter, power you can harness in your applications.

The Simplest Tcl Interpreter

From a Tcl-centric point of view, an interpreter contains three parts:

*   Initializing the interpreter.
*   Feeding input to the interpreter, usually in some form of command loop.
*   Cleaning up before termination.

Of course, if you embed Tcl within your application, there are a number of parts missing—your entire application, for one! You'll need to mesh the Tcl calls with your application calls in the manner most appropriate for your needs.

For simple Tcl interpreters, all the initialization you need to do for the Tcl interpreter initialization is to call `Tcl_CreateInterp`:

```
#include <tcl.h>
Tcl_Interp* Tcl_CreateInterp()
```

All the available functions in the Tcl library are defined in the header file **tcl.h**.

`Tcl_CreateInterp` allocates memory for a `Tcl_Interp` structure, a structure that holds all the information about the current state of the Tcl interpreter. After calling `Tcl_CreateInterp`, you'll need to register any new commands you create. See Chapter 16 for more on this. For now, all you need to do is call `Tcl_CreateInterp`.

`Tcl_CreateInterp` returns a newly allocated `Tcl_Interp` structure, which has only a few fields, as shown here:

```
typedef struct Tcl_Interp{
    char *result;
    void (*freeProc) (char *blockPtr);
    int errorLine;
} Tcl_Interp;
```

`Tcl_CreateInterp` actually creates a much larger structure that shadows the `Tcl_Interp` structure used in your code. This structure is private to the Tcl library. The important point about the `Tcl_Interp` structure is that just about every Tcl function requires a pointer to the structure returned by `Tcl_CreateInterp`.

After you've initialized the Tcl interpreter, you can start feeding commands. The `Tcl_EvalFile` function reads in a file and executes the Tcl commands in the file. This is one way you can run the Tcl files necessary for your application, such as the user interface. Your C or C++ application starts up, initializes Tcl, and then runs your Tcl scripts from `Tcl_EvalFile`. `Tcl_EvalFile` takes the following parameters:

```
int Tcl_EvalFile(Tcl_Interp* interp,
    char* filename)
```

`Tcl_EvalFile` returns an integer code, one of the error codes listed in Table 15.1.

Table 15.1 Tcl error codes.

Code	Meaning
TCL_ERROR	An error occurred.
TCL_OK	Everything is hunky-dory.
TCL_RETURN	A request that the current procedure return.
TCL_BREAK	A request to exit the innermost loop.
TCL_CONTINUE	A request to jump to the top of the inner most loop.

Tcl_EvalFile should return only TCL_ERROR or TCL_OK. The other values appear when you're executing one command at a time with Tcl_Eval, as covered below.

These codes are the same as the ones in Table 9.1 in Chapter 9, except that the values are C language defines rather than Tcl strings.

N O T E

Getting the Results

If you get an error from Tcl_EvalFile, the result field in the Tcl_Interp structure will contain an error message in char* (string) format.

Don't free the result string. If you want to keep this string around, make a copy of it. The Tcl interpreter owns the memory for this string and may overwrite the contents at any time.

N O T E

The object-based commands introduced in Tcl 8.0 aim you away from reading the result field directly. Instead, you can call Tcl_GetObjResult:

N O T E

```
Tcl_Obj* Tcl_GetObjResult(Tcl_Interp* interp)
```

Chapter 16 covers the object-based C functions.

If `Tcl_EvalFile` returns `TCL_OK`, then the `result` field will hold the returned data from the script (usually passed by the Tcl `return` command).

To evaluate a single Tcl command instead of a whole file, use the `Tcl_Eval` function, which takes the following parameters:

```
int Tcl_Eval(Tcl_Interp* interp,
    char* command)
```

You must pass a writable variable for the *command*. A literal string won't work. Tcl writes into this *command*, although it usually restores any chages when complete.

Avoid the following code:

```
status = Tcl_Eval(interp, "puts ouch"); /* Wrong */
```

Instead, use something like the following:

```
char   command[100];

strcpy(command, "puts ouch");
status = Tcl_Eval(interp, command);
```

In addition to `Tcl_Eval`, you can use `Tcl_VarEval` to build up a command from a variable number of arguments, which uses the following syntax:

```
int Tcl_VarEval(Tcl_Interp* interp,
    char* string,
    ...
    NULL)
```

Because `Tcl_VarEval` takes a variable number of arguments, you must provide a sentinel value to tell the function where the end of the list lies. This sentinel value is `NULL`, as shown here:

```
status = Tcl_VarEval(interp,
    "puts",
    "ouch",
    NULL);
```

You can use literal strings with `Tcl_VarEval`, because it creates a new command string from the full set of arguments. However, don't forget the NULL sentinel value.

The Byte-Code Compiler

Starting with version 8.0, the Tcl interpreter compiles your scripts to an internal byte-code format. Prior to version 8.0, the Tcl interpreter parsed every single command, perhaps multiple times if the command was in a `for` command loop. With the byte-code compiler, all the Tcl code is parsed when loaded and then executed from the byte codes. This dramatically improves the performance of your scripts, without you having to do anything.

The byte-code compiler executes at runtime, that is, when your scripts are read in. Because of this, you don't have to compile your code in advance as you must with C, C++, or Java code.

With the byte-code compiler, the Tcl interpreter breaks the mantra that everything is text. Instead of keeping all numbers as text strings and then converting to and from numeric format—a slow operation, especially when repeated over and over again—the byte-code compiler keeps numbers as both numbers and strings.

Strings are still kept around to provide compatibility with older commands written in C. This is great if you have large amounts of C code written using the older string-based routines (as I do).

The Tcl interpreter keeps values stored as strings and in the native type (integer, and so on). The string value is regenerated only as needed. This means that if you can avoid converting back to strings, you can really improve the performance of the commands you write. The data structure used to store the dual value (string and native binary representation) is called `Tcl_Obj` and is delved into in Chapter 16. The drawback of the

`Tcl_Obj` format is that you need to use a new set of "object-based" routines, which correspond to the older routines.

Thus, instead of calling `Tcl_Eval`, you can call `Tcl_EvalObj`, starting with Tcl version 8.0:

```
int Tcl_EvalObj (Tcl_Interp *interp,
    Tcl_Obj *objPtr)
```

When you're done with your Tcl interpreter, free it with the `Tcl_DeleteInterp` function:

```
void Tcl_DeleteInterp(Tcl_Interp* interp)
```

You'll usually call `Tcl_DeleteInterp` at the end of your program.

 UNIX systems should free all memory allocated by your program on exit, making `Tcl_DeleteInterp` redundant. Windows 3.1, though, does not free all memory on exit. Therefore, it's important to call `Tcl_DeleteInterp` before exiting your application, if you called `Tcl_CreateInterp`.

 All Tcl definitions are found in the include file **tcl.h**, which should be installed with your copy of the Tcl libraries.

Pulling this all together, one of the simplest Tcl interpreters in a C program follows:

```
/*
 tclint.c, a simple Tcl interpreter.
*/

#include <stdio.h>
#include <stdlib.h>
#include <tcl.h>
```

```
int
main(int argc, char** argv)

{    /* main */
    Tcl_Interp* interp;
    int         status = TCL_OK;


interp = Tcl_CreateInterp();

if (argc > 1) {
        status = Tcl_EvalFile(interp, argv[1]);

        /* Print result string. */
        if (interp->result != NULL) {

        printf("TCL: [%s]\n", interp->result);
        }

}

/* Free memory for interpreter. */
    Tcl_DeleteInterp(interp);


/* Report errors. */
    if (status != TCL_OK) {

        printf("TCL Error: %d\n", status);
        exit(1);
    }

return 0;

}    /* main */
/* tclint.c */
```

Compiling and Linking Your New Interpreter

How you compile and link depends on which operating system you use.

Compiling and Linking on UNIX

On UNIX, you need to link in the Tcl and **m** (math) libraries. The actual library name for the Tcl library may vary on your system (e.g., **libtcl8.0.a**).

You may also need options for the C compiler to tell it where the Tcl include files and libraries are located. If your Tcl include files are located in **/usr/local/tcl/include**, for example, you'll need the following command:

```
cc -o tclint -I/usr/local/tcl/include \
    tclint.c -ltcl8.0 -lm
```

If your Tcl libraries are also located in a nonstandard directory, such as **/usr/local/tcl/lib**, then you'll need the following command to compile and link the example interpreter program:

```
cc -o tclint -I/usr/local/tcl/include \
  tclint.c -L/usr/local/tcl/lib -ltcl8.0 -lm
```

You can use the following makefile on UNIX to compile all the C examples in Chapters 15 and 16:

```
# Sample makefile for UNIX and Linux.

# Name of C compiler.
    # Generic UNIX
#CC= cc -g
    # HP
#CC= cc -Aa -g
    # Linux
CC= gcc -g
```

```
# Name of C++ compiler.
    # Generic UNIX
#CPLUS= CC -g
    # GNU C++
CPLUS= gcc -g

# Location of Tcl libraries.
TCL_LIBS= -L/usr/local/lib -ltk8.0 -ltcl8.0

# Location of Tcl include files.
TCL_INCS= -I/usr/local/include

# Location of X Window libraries.
    # Genric UNIX
#X_LIBS= -lX11
    # Alternate location.
X_LIBS= -L/usr/X11R6/lib -lX11

# Location of X Window include files.
    # Genric UNIX
#X_INCS=
    # Alternate location.
X_INCS= -I/usr/X11R6/include

# Shared library link directives, if needed.
# Linux uses -ldl, for example.
#SHARED_LD =
SHARED_LD = -ldl

INCS= $(TCL_INCS) $(X_INCS)
LIBS= $(TCL_LIBS) $(X_LIBS) -lm $(SHARED_LD)


all: revcmd revobj tclapp tclint tkapp linkvar objtest

revcmd.o:    revcmd.c
    $(CC) $(INCS) -c revcmd.c
```

```
revcmd:      revcmd.o
     $(CC) -o revcmd revcmd.o $(LIBS)

revobj.o:      revobj.c
     $(CC) $(INCS) -c revobj.c

revobj:      revobj.o
     $(CC) -o revobj revobj.o $(LIBS)

tclapp.o:      tclapp.c
     $(CC) $(INCS) -c tclapp.c

tclapp:      tclapp.o
     $(CC) -o tclapp tclapp.o $(LIBS)

tclint.o:      tclint.c
     $(CC) $(INCS) -c tclint.c

tclint:      tclint.o
     $(CC) -o tclint tclint.o $(LIBS)

tkapp.o:      tkapp.c
     $(CC) $(INCS) -c tkapp.c

tkapp:      tkapp.o
     $(CC) -o tkapp  tkapp.o $(LIBS)

linkvar.o:      linkvar.c
     $(CC) $(INCS) -c linkvar.c

linkvar:      linkvar.o
     $(CC) -o linkvar  linkvar.o $(LIBS)


objtest.o:      objtest.cxx
     $(CPLUS) $(INCS) -c objtest.cxx

objtest:      objtest.o
```

```
      $(CPLUS) -o objtest objtest.o $(LIBS)

# makefile.unx
```

You'll need to customize the **makefile.unx** file to point to your C compiler, Tcl and X Window System `include` files, Tcl and X Window System libraries and any shared library link commands, such as `-ldl` on Linux.

Once you've customized **makefile.unx**, you can use the following UNIX shell command to build the **tclint** example:

```
make -f makefile.unx tclint
```

Compiling and Linking on Windows

On Windows, your setup will vary depending on the compiler and integrated environment you use. No matter what compiler, you use you need to build a Win32 application and to link in the Tcl library, usually named something like **TCL80VC.LIB** or **TCL80.LIB**. The *VC* in **TCL80VC.LIB** stands for Visual C++, Microsoft's compiler. Use **TCL80.LIB**, without the *VC*, if you use the Borland compiler. The version number, *80* in this case, depends on the version of Tcl you have installed.

I use the Microsoft Visual C++ compiler. A makefile that you can use on Windows NT and Windows 95 follows:

```
# Makefile for MS Visual C++

#
# Change MSDEV to be directory you have
# installed MSVC++.
#
MSDEV=C:\MSDEV

#
# Change TCLDIR to location where Tcl is installed.
#
TCLDIR=C:\TCL
```

```
#

# You may need to change the name of the

# library files. The "vc" stands for Microsoft

# Visual C++. Most of the Tcl code was originally

# compiled with Borland C, which uses a different

# format for connecting to shared libraries.

#

#TCL_LIBS= tk.lib tcl.lib
TCL_LIBS= $(TCLDIR)\lib\tk80vc.lib $(TCLDIR)\lib\tcl80vc.lib


MSLDIR=$(MSDEV)\lib
MSLIBS= $(MSLDIR)\libc.lib $(MSLDIR)\oldnames.lib \
     $(MSLDIR)\kernel32.lib
LIBS= $(TCL_LIBS) $(MSLIBS)

CC=$(MSDEV)\bin\cl
CPLUS=$(MSDEV)\bin\cl
CFLAGS= /nologo
LINK_FLAGS= $(CFLAGS) /DEBUG:none

LINK=$(MSDEV)\bin\link

WINDOWS_ENTRY = -entry:WinMainCRTStartup
LD_WINDOWS = /SUBSYSTEM:windows /MACHINE:IX86
LD_CONSOLE = /SUBSYSTEM:console


INCS= -I$(MSDEV)\include -I$(TCLDIR)\include

all: tkapp.exe \
     tclapp.exe \
```

```
        tclint.exe \
        linkvar.exe \
        objtest.exe \
        revcmd.exe \
        revobj.exe

revcmd.obj:     revcmd.c
    $(CC) -c $(INCS) $(CFLAGS) /Tprevcmd.c /Forevcmd.obj

revcmd.exe: revcmd.obj
    $(LINK) $(LINK_FLAGS) $(LD_CONSOLE) \
    /OUT:revcmd.exe revcmd.obj $(LIBS)

revobj.obj:     revobj.c
    $(CC) -c $(INCS) $(CFLAGS) /Tprevobj.c /Forevobj.obj

revobj.exe: revobj.obj
    $(LINK) $(LINK_FLAGS) $(LD_CONSOLE) \
    /OUT:revobj.exe revobj.obj $(LIBS)

tclapp.obj:     tclapp.c
    $(CC) -c $(INCS) $(CFLAGS) /Tptclapp.c /Fotclapp.obj

tclapp.exe: tclapp.obj
    $(LINK) $(LINK_FLAGS) $(LD_CONSOLE) \
    /OUT:tclapp.exe tclapp.obj $(LIBS)


tclint.obj:     tclint.c
    $(CC) -c $(INCS) $(CFLAGS) /Tptclint.c /Fotclint.obj

tclint.exe: tclint.obj
    $(LINK) $(LINK_FLAGS) $(LD_CONSOLE) \
    /OUT:tclint.exe tclint.obj $(LIBS)


tkapp.obj:      tkapp.c
    $(CC) -c $(INCS) $(CFLAGS) /Tptkapp.c /Fotkapp.obj
```

```
tkapp.exe: tkapp.obj
    $(LINK) $(LINK_FLAGS) $(LD_CONSOLE) \
    /OUT:tkapp.exe tkapp.obj $(LIBS)


linkvar.obj:     linkvar.c
    $(CC) -c $(INCS) $(CFLAGS) /Tplinkvar.c /Folinkvar.obj

linkvar.exe: linkvar.obj
    $(LINK) $(LINK_FLAGS) $(LD_CONSOLE) \
    /OUT:linkvar.exe linkvar.obj $(LIBS)


objtest.obj:     objtest.cxx
    $(CPLUS) -c $(INCS) $(CFLAGS) /Tpobjtest.cxx /Foobjtest.obj

objtest.exe: objtest.obj
    $(LINK) $(LINK_FLAGS) $(LD_CONSOLE) \
    /OUT:objtest.exe objtest.obj $(LIBS)

# makefile.vc
```

This **makefile.vc** contains rules to build all the example C programs in Chapters 15 and 16. You'll need to customize where you installed Tcl and Visual C++.

You can compile the **tclint** example, using the following command at the MS-DOS prompt:

```
nmake -f makefile.vc tclint.exe
```

Running the Example Interpreter

Our simple Tcl interpreter needs a script file to execute. You can use the following short script or create your own:

```
#
# Test of our simple Tcl interpreter.
```

```
#
puts "Inside Tcl interpreter."

set var 55
set var2 [expr $var + 83]
puts "var2 holds $var2"

# Data to pass back to program
return "Hello out there"

# simple.tcl
```

When you run this new interpreter with this Tcl script file, you should see output like the following:

```
Inside Tcl interpreter.
var2 holds 138
TCL: [Hello out there]
```

The *TCL* line lists the data from the `result` field of the `Tcl_Interp` structure.

You cannot run the **tclint.c** interpreter on Windows 3.1, as the DOS shell cannot execute Win32s applications (you must execute these programs fully within the Windows environment). But, on Windows NT and 95, with the enhanced DOS Command Prompt, you can run the **tclint.c** interpreter.

Creating More Complex Applications

The **wish** and **tclsh** interpreters do a lot more than our simple Tcl interpreter in **tclint.c**. Because of this, you may want to take advantage of the initialization functions inside the Tcl and Tk libraries, called `Tcl_Main` and `Tk_Main`, respectively. These initialization functions set up all sorts of Tcl commands, such as the `unknown` procedure, from a Tcl library directory. In addition, the values of `argc` and `argv` get placed in Tcl global variables, along with all the initialization needed—quite extensive for Tk especially. Most applications that embed Tcl call `Tcl_Main` or `Tk_Main` rather than creating the interpreter directly with `Tcl_CreateInterp`.

714

To take advantage of all this, you don't call `Tcl_CreateInterp` from your `main` function. Instead, you call `Tcl_Main` for Tcl-only applications and `Tk_Main` for Tk applications (see the following section on Tk). With both of these functions, you pass in an application initialization function to call, usually a function called `Tcl_AppInit`.

The `Tcl_Main` and `Tk_Main` functions call `Tcl_AppInit` (or whatever function you pass in) just before entering the command loop. Inside your `Tcl_AppInit` function, you can initialize any commands you create (see Chapter 16 for more on this topic) and set up any data necessary for your program.

The basic format for `Tcl_AppInit` follows:

```
int Tcl_AppInit(Tcl_Interp* interp)
{

/* Insert your code here... */

return TCL_OK;
}
```

Usually, you'll want to invoke a function called `Tcl_Init` from within your `Tcl_AppInit` function, as shown here:

```
#include <tcl.h>

int Tcl_AppInit(Tcl_Interp* interp)
{
    int     status;

    status = Tcl_Init(interp);

    if (status != TCL_OK) {
        return TCL_ERROR;
    }

    /* Insert your code here... */

    return TCL_OK;
```

```
}

int
main(int argc, char** argv)
{
    Tcl_Main(argc, argv, Tcl_AppInit);
    return 0;
}

/* tclapp.c */
```

The `Tcl_Init` function sets up the unknown procedure and autoloading, covered in Chapter 14. See the on-line manual information on `Tcl_Init` for more on this subject.

For `Tcl_Main`, pass in the command line, in the form of *argc* and *argv*. You also need to pass a function to execute, normally `Tcl_AppInit`.

You can build this program using the makefiles provided previously.

When you run the **tclapp** program, you effectively have the same functionality as **tclsh**, the Tcl interpreter. The **tclapp** program does not have the Tk toolkit, so you cannot create any widgets.

Adding in Tk into Your Programs

The Tk add-on to Tcl weighs in much larger, code-wise, than Tcl itself, because graphical interfaces require much more code than the very simple Tcl language. If you use the `Tcl_AppInit` method, all you need to do is call `Tk_Main` instead of `Tcl_Main` (as called in the code in **tclint.c**, above), and link with both the Tk and Tcl libraries. You may need other libraries on your system.

To start up Tk functions, your `Tcl_AppInit` function should call `Tk_Init` as well as `Tcl_Init`. You can use the example file, **tkapp.c**, for the minimalist C program with Tk functionality. The code follows:

```
/*
 tkapp.c, Test of Tcl_AppInit().
```

```
*/

#include <stdio.h>
#include <stdlib.h>
#include <tcl.h>
#include <tk.h>

int Tcl_AppInit(Tcl_Interp* interp)
{
    int     status;

    status = Tcl_Init(interp);

    if (status != TCL_OK) {
        return TCL_ERROR;
    }

    /* Initialize Tk values. */
    status = Tk_Init(interp);

    if (status != TCL_OK) {
        return TCL_ERROR;
    }

    /* Insert your code here... */

    return TCL_OK;
}



int
main(int argc, char** argv)
{
    Tk_Main(argc, argv, Tcl_AppInit);
    return 0;
}

/* tkapp.c */
```

With this code, you effectively get the **wish** interpreter built into your program. Of course, you'll probably want to customize your program. This can be used as a basis for writing your interface in Tcl/Tk and calling a Tcl script from your C code, like that in **tkapp.c**. To execute a particular Tcl script file, you can add a call to `Tcl_EvalFile` described previously.

On Windows 95, I found that I needed to pass a Tcl script to the **tkapp** application to get it to display a window.

WINDOWS

Linking with Tk

You can link the **tkapp.c** program in much the same way as the **tclint.c** program, only you now need the Tk library as well. You can use the makefiles shown previously to compile and link on Windows and UNIX.

On UNIX, you'll need the Tcl, Tk, X11 (X Window System), and math (**m**) libraries. You can use a command like the following to compile and link the **tkapp.c** program:

U N I X

```
cc -o tkapp tkapp.c -ltk8.0 -ltcl8.0 -lX11 -lm
```

You may need special options to tell the compiler and linker where your include and library files reside, as with the Tcl example (**tclint.c**). On a system like Linux, for example, you may require options for the libraries and include files. In addition, you may need to link in specific versions of libraries, such as tcl8.0 and tk8.0, as shown here:

```
cc -o tkapp -I/usr/local/tcl/include \
   tkapp.c -L/usr/local/tcl/lib -ltk8.0 \
   -ltcl8.0 -L/usr/X11R6/lib -lX11 -lm
```

You can use the makefile presented previously to compile and link **tkapp**.

WINDOWS

On Windows, you'll need to link with the Tcl and Tk libraries, usually **TCL80.LIB** and **TK80.LIB**, and need to have the corresponding Tcl and Tk DLLs in your path, or your new program will fail.

The **tkapp.c** uses a `main` function instead of `WinMain`. This makes our example program more portable to UNIX, but means that initializations done on the Windows version of **wish** don't get done in **tkapp.c**. On Windows, **wish** creates an extra window called *Console* for your input. This makes **wish** act more like UNIX where terminal windows are still the norm. If you embed Tcl and Tk in your applications, it's not likely that you'll need such a Console window, because this goes against the Windows interface style guidelines.

You can get around this by creating your own `WinMain` function. The **wish** version of `WinMain` is located in the file **win\winMain.c** in the Tk sources (see the **tcl/tk8.0** directory on the CD-ROM). You can copy this function, or create your own, using the following as a guide for the function parameters:

```
int APIENTRY
WinMain(hInstance, hPrevInstance, lpszCmdLine, nCmdShow)
    HINSTANCE hInstance;
    HINSTANCE hPrevInstance;
    LPSTR lpszCmdLine;
    int nCmdShow;
{
/* Insert your code here ... */

}
```

The **wish** `WinMain` function calls `TkConsoleCreate`, which creates the console window, creates an *argv*, *argc* list of command-line parameters from the *lpszCmdLine* parameter, and then calls `Tk_Main`.

Without a `WinMain` like that of **wish**, the **tkapp.c** program won't show a console window and requires you to provide a Tcl script to execute (or you won't see anything).

CROSS-PLATFORM

The difference between `main` and `WinMain` creates a problem if you're trying to write cross-platform applications. Luckily, the difference in the code is not that great.

Running the tkapp Program with Tk

Try running the new Tcl interpreter with the **hello.tcl** script file from Chapter 1, or with any script file you care. The scripts should execute much as they do for **wish**.

Installation Issues

If you link with shared Tcl and Tk libraries, then you need to ensure that every user installs the proper shared libraries. For Windows, this is easy: the user can install the binary release of Tcl/Tk and therefore gets the shared libraries (called **Dynamic Link Libraries** on Windows).

On UNIX systems, you may need to include shared libraries or the Tcl/Tk source code to allow users to create their own shared libraries. Or, you can link statically.

You may also discover a problem at runtime, where **tkapp** cannot find the Tk or Tcl **init.tcl** file. Many Tcl and Tk commands are really procedures written in Tcl, and both `Tcl_Main` and `Tk_Main` try to load in these procedures, part of the standard library of procedures that comes with Tcl/Tk.

Pointing to the Proper Tcl/Tk Procedure Libraries

The main problem is making sure programs like **tkapp** can find the installed Tcl/Tk procedure libraries. If you get an error that the Tcl or Tk **init.tcl** script or a similar script such as **tk.tcl** could not be found, this is a likely suspect. This error will have a form similar to *Application-specific initialization failed: can't find a usable tk.tcl.*

To get around this problem, you can define the `TCL_LIBRARY` environment variable to point to the directory containing the library of Tcl procedures. Set the `TK_LIBRARY` environment variable to point to the directory containing the library of Tk procedures. For example, on Windows you can use commands like the following:

```
set TCL_LIBRARY C:/tcl/lib/tcl8.0
set TK_LIBRARY  C:/tcl/lib/tk8.0
```

On UNIX with the C shell, **csh**, you can use commands like the following:

```
setenv TCL_LIBRARY /usr/local/lib/tcl8.0
setenv TK_LIBRARY  /usr/local/lib/tk8.0
```

With the UNIX Korn shell, **ksh**, you can use commands like the following:

```
TCL_LIBRARY=/usr/local/lib/tcl8.0; export TCL_LIBRARY
TK_LIBRARY=/usr/local/lib/tk8.0;   export TK_LIBRARY
```

The directories you specify depend on where you installed the Tcl/Tk run-time files.

 Use forward slashes to separate directories on Windows as well as UNIX when setting the TCL_LIBRARY or TK_LIBRARY environment variables.

N O T E

For the TCL_LIBRARY and TK_LIBRARY environment variables to work, of course, users must first install Tcl/Tk on their systems. This means that end users must install these libraries of Tcl procedures to run any Tcl script. This can be a big issue with your applications. One way to get around this is to use the software called ET (embedded Tk).

Embedded Tk

ET allows you to embed calls to Tcl code within C programs in a function called ET, as shown next:

```
int
main(int argc, char **argv)
{
    Et_Init(&argc,argv);

ET( button .b -text {Inside ET}; pack .b );

Et_MainLoop();
}
```

You then use a preprocessor, **et2c**, that converts the code inside the call to the ET function into real C code. You also need to link the resulting file with the code in **et.o**, a UNIX-compiled object file you create when you install ET.

ET is located on the Internet at **http://users.vnet.net/drh/ET.html** and on the CD-ROM in the **contrib/et** directory.

CD-ROM

Summary

This chapter introduced the C language functions you need to embed Tcl within your application.

You can create a Tcl interpreter with `Tcl_CreateInterp`. The returned data value, a pointer to a `Tcl_Interp` structure, will be used in just about every Tcl function call. Instead of calling `Tcl_CreateInterp`, most applications call `Tcl_Main` or `Tk_Main`, which creates an interpreter and initializes many of the Tcl routines necessary for most usage.

The `Tcl_EvalFile` function executes a script file of Tcl commands. `Tcl_Eval` evaluates a single command, as does `Tcl_VarEval`, which builds up the command from a list of text strings.

In most of your applications, the main work to initialize your commands should be done within a `Tcl_AppInit` function. You can redefine this function to set up any Tcl commands you need and perform any other initialization you feel appropriate.

In Chapter 16, you'll extend your Tcl interpreter with new commands. You'll find this essential for virtually all applications.

Tcl and Tk Library Functions Introduced in This Chapter

Tcl_AppInit	Tcl_EvalFile
Tcl_Main	Tcl_EvalObj
Tcl_Init	Tcl_GetObjResult
Tcl_CreateInterp	Tcl_VarEval
Tcl_DeleteInterp	Tk_Main
Tcl_Eval	

Extending Tcl

This chapter covers:

- Making new Tcl commands in C
- Using the string-based and object-based C functions
- Returning data and error messages
- Evaluating arguments and handling string data
- Registering your new commands

Making New Commands

You can write new procedures entirely in Tcl, using the proc command. If you need to add something beyond the capabilities of Tcl and Tk, you're out of luck, unless you start writing commands in C.

This chapter covers how to create new commands in the form of C language functions, which will extend the base Tcl language into new areas—whatever areas you desire.

You'll find that extending Tcl is essential if you try to embed Tcl within an application. In most cases, the application already provides some significant functions. You can then use Tcl commands to provide user access to those functions, by writing small functions to connect Tcl to your C code. These small **wrapper functions** are generally easy to write and open up a surprising capability because you're adding your new commands to the already richly endowed Tcl language.

The best plan is to extend Tcl by adding primitive operations. Each primitive operation should become a new Tcl command, written in C.

724

Combine these primitive operations with Tcl procedures, not C code. By taking this approach, you'll find that your resulting code becomes reusable in ways you never imagined, rather than locking yourself into a single method of execution.

Your C functions also need to add in the application glue code to combine your application with Tcl. For example, if you create a spreadsheet program, you'll need to add Tcl commands to access cells in a spreadsheet. You'll probably add a set of new math functions. If you have a factory control application, you might want to add Tcl commands to turn on and off factory devices.

The key when adding new Tcl commands is to use the lowest level of code possible. This provides greater flexibility on the Tcl side, allowing you to combine these new low-level functions with existing Tcl commands.

This chapter covers how to create new Tcl commands in C and goes over a number of Tcl utility functions to aid in making your commands. Furthermore, it covers a very common case I've experienced: using Tcl to test C++ applications.

Creating Your New Tcl Commands

To recap, to write your commands in C or C++ you need to:

1. Initialize the Tcl interpreter inside your C or C++ application, usually from `Tcl_AppInit`.

2. Write the C or C++ code for any new commands. You must follow special conventions outlined in the following sections.

3. Register the new commands with the Tcl interpreter, so that it can execute your new commands. To do this, you call `Tcl_CreateCommand` or `Tcl_CreateObjCommand`, passing in the textual name of your new command as well as a C function pointer to the code that executes the command.

4. Compile all your new C code and link the whole thing together with the Tcl and perhaps Tk C libraries.

All commands in Tcl are implemented as C functions. Each C function takes a standard set of parameters, including a pointer to the `Tcl_Interp` structure, a pointer to any extra data you may want to pass, as well as the arguments to the command.

Starting with Tcl 8.0, there are two ways you can write your C functions: using an **object-based** approach, where each argument is stored in its native format, or the older **string-based** approach, where each argument is stored only as a text string. The object-based approach usually provides better performance because you don't have to convert values to and from strings.

Which approach you take depends on your needs. The object-based approach requires more complicated code but can greatly improve the performance of your new commands. The string-based approach is easier to code but has slower performance and forces you to convert values to and from text strings.

In the following examples, I'll show both the string- and object-based approaches.

Creating a Command: The String-Based Approach

With the string-based approach, each command function takes the following parameters, as defined in the `Tcl_CmdProc` data type:

```
typedef int Tcl_CmdProc(
    ClientData clientData,
    Tcl_Interp *interp,
    int argc,
    char *argv[]);
```

Much like the traditional `main` function, the *argv* array holds all the arguments to the command as text strings, and *argc* contains a count of the number of values in *argv*.

N O T E

The *argv* value includes the command name in `argv[0]`. This allows you to have multiple Tcl commands share the same C function if you want.

For example, you can use the following as a template for your own commands:

```
int MyCommand(
  ClientData client_data,
  Tcl_Interp* interp,
  int argc,
  char *argv[])

{

  /* Your code goes here... */

  return TCL_OK;

}
```

Your function can do whatever it wants. It must, however, return a code, as listed in Table 16.1.

Table 16.1 Tcl error codes for your command functions.

Code	Meaning
TCL_ERROR	An error occurred.
TCL_OK	Everything is hunky-dory.
TCL_RETURN	A request to make the current procedure return.
TCL_BREAK	A request to exit the innermost loop.
TCL_CONTINUE	A request to jump to the top of the inner most loop.

In most cases, the value returned will be TCL_OK or TCL_ERROR. This value returned tells the Tcl interpreter whether or not the command succeeded. In addition to this return code, many Tcl commands return data as well. To handle this, you need to set a result.

Returning a Result

Each Tcl command should place some data as the result of the command. If an error occurs, the error message should become the result.

In older versions of Tcl, you could write the result directly into the result field of the Tcl_Interp structure. With the advent of the byte-code compiler, you should only go through the established functions to store result data, whether you use the string- or object-based approaches.

The way to set the result data depends on whether or not you are using the new object-based functions. Sticking with the string-based functions, the easiest way to set result data is to reset the data and then append new data.

Tcl_ResetResult resets the result value and takes the following parameter:

```
Tcl_ResetResult(Tcl_Interp* interp)
```

Don't call this routine if you don't want to destroy any previous result data. In your Tcl commands, chances are you do want to reset the result string. Then, you can append new strings onto the result by calling Tcl_AppendResult, which takes the following parameters:

```
Tcl_AppendResult(Tcl_Interp* interp,
    char* string,
    ...
    (char *) NULL)
```

Like Tcl_VarEval shown in Chapter 15, Tcl_AppendResult takes a variable number of parameters. You can append more than one string to the result. You must end the input with NULL, the sentinel value that tells Tcl_AppendResult that the input is complete.

For example, we can create a simple Tcl command to reverse two arguments passed to it. A trial run of this command follows:

```
% reverse a b
b a
% reverse [expr 10+1] 12
```

```
12 11
% reverse a
ERROR: reverse requires two arguments.
```

To implement this new `reverse` command, the C code needs to check the number of arguments and generate an error. If enough arguments are provided, then the first and second arguments should be reversed and placed in the result. The initial code for this command follows:

```c
#include <stdio.h>
#include <stdlib.h>
#include <tcl.h>

/*
Implements a Tcl command named "reverse",
which reverses the first two arguments
and returns the reversed data.
*/
int RevCommand(
  ClientData client_data,
  Tcl_Interp* interp,
  int argc,
  char *argv[])

{    /* RevCommand */

    /* Reset result data. */
    Tcl_ResetResult(interp);

    /* Check number of arguments. */
    if (argc != 3) {
        Tcl_AppendResult(interp,
            "ERROR: reverse requires two arguments.",
            (char*) NULL); /* Sentinel. */

        return TCL_ERROR;
    }
```

```
/* Reverse arguments. */
Tcl_AppendResult(interp,
    argv[2], " ", argv[1],
    (char*) NULL); /* Sentinel. */

return TCL_OK;
```

```
}   /* RevCommand */
```

Even though this command returns an error code if it detects problems, it does not return any special error code information for use by the Tcl interpreter.

Returning an Error

When you function returns TCL_ERROR, you can also add in additional information with the Tcl_SetErrorCode function:

```
Tcl_SetErrorCode(Tcl_Interp* interp,
    char* info,
    ...
    (char *) NULL)
```

The values you pass are the ones listed in Table 9.2.

You can also call Tcl_AddErrorInfo with stack trace information, if you want. See the on-line documentation for more on this.

Registering New Commands with the Interpreter

After you've written your new Tcl command, you need to register the command with the Tcl interpreter, so that this command can be used in Tcl scripts. To do this, call Tcl_CreateCommand:

```
Tcl_Command
Tcl_CreateCommand(Tcl_Interp* interp,
    char* commandname,
    Tcl_CmdProc* function,
    ClientData client_data,
    Tcl_CmdDeleteProc* delete_function)
```

`Tcl_CreateCommand` associates a *commandname*, such as `reverse`, with a function pointer. The *function* is the C function you wrote for your command and takes the parameters shown in the section on Creating Your New Tcl Commands.

Function pointers are inherently dangerous. If you pass the wrong value, the Tcl interpreter won't know and will try to execute the code at whatever address you pass, leading to interesting and wrong results.

WARNING

The *client_data* is any value (integer or pointer) that you want passed to the *function* and *delete_function*.

You can normally skip the *delete_function*. This is intended as a clean-up function before your command gets deleted from the interpreter. See the on-line documentation on `Tcl_CreateCommand` for more on this.

N O T E

To put this all together, you can register the new `RevCommand` function for handling the `reverse` Tcl command within the `Tcl_AppInit` function, as shown here:

```
/*
 revcmd.c
 Tcl sample command to
 reverse two arguments.
*/

#include <stdio.h>
#include <stdlib.h>
#include <tcl.h>

/*
Implements a Tcl command named "reverse",
which reverses the first two arguments
and returns the reversed data.
*/
int RevCommand(
  ClientData client_data,
```

```
    Tcl_Interp* interp,
    int argc,
    char *argv[])

{    /* RevCommand */

    /* Reset result data. */
    Tcl_ResetResult(interp);

    /* Check number of arguments. */
    if (argc != 3) {
        Tcl_AppendResult(interp,
            "ERROR: reverse requires two arguments.",
            (char*) NULL); /* Sentinel. */

        return TCL_ERROR;
    }

    /* Reverse arguments. */
    Tcl_AppendResult(interp,
        argv[2], " ", argv[1],
        (char*) NULL); /* Sentinel. */

    return TCL_OK;

}    /* RevCommand */

int Tcl_AppInit(Tcl_Interp* interp)
{
    int    status;

    status = Tcl_Init(interp);

    if (status != TCL_OK) {
        return TCL_ERROR;
    }

    /* Register your commands here... */
```

```
    Tcl_CreateCommand(interp,
      "reverse",
      (Tcl_CmdProc*) RevCommand,
      (ClientData) NULL,
      (Tcl_CmdDeleteProc*) NULL);

    return TCL_OK;
}

int
main(int argc, char** argv)
{
    Tcl_Main(argc, argv, Tcl_AppInit);
    return 0;
}

/* revcmd.c */
```

You can compile and link the **revcmd.c** program using the makefiles presented in Chapter 15.

When you run the new reverse command, it reverses the two arguments, as shown here:

```
% reverse a b
b a
```

When you try the reverse command without any arguments, you'll see the following error:

```
% reverse
ERROR: reverse requires two arguments.
```

You get the same error if you pass more than two arguments:

```
% reverse a b c
ERROR: reverse requires two arguments.
```

To verify that your new command, and not a Tcl command, is running, you can try the **tclsh** interpreter and verify that the `reverse` command does not exist in the standard Tcl language, as follows:

```
% reverse a b
invalid command name "reverse"
```

WARNING

If you name your program, such as **revcmd**, the same name as the new Tcl command, you may get strange results with the standard Tcl interpreters **wish** and **tclsh**. The reason for this is that the `unknown` command, discussed in Chapter 14, tries to execute unknown commands as programs on your system. This is not what you expect.

Creating Commands: The Object-Based Approach

The object-based approach uses concepts very similar to the string-based approach. Generally, you have a parallel set of C functions with *Obj* in their names. These functions correspond to the same functionality of the string-based routines.

Like the string-based approach, to create an object-based Tcl command, you need to create a C function that accepts a standard set of parameters. These parameters are slightly different from the string-based parameters, as defined in the `Tcl_ObjCmdProc` type definition:

```
typedef int
(Tcl_ObjCmdProc)
    (ClientData clientData,
    Tcl_Interp *interp,
    int objc,
    Tcl_Obj* objv[] )
```

Your command function then accepts these parameters:

```
int RevObjCommand(
```

```
    ClientData client_data,
    Tcl_Interp* interp,
    int objc,
    Tcl_Obj** objv )

{    /* RevObjCommand */

  /* Your code goes here... */

return TCL_OK;

}    /* RevObjCommand */
```

The main difference from the string-based approach is that command-line arguments are in the form of an array of `Tcl_Obj` structures, each of which has the following format:

```
typedef struct Tcl_Obj {
    int refCount;
    char *bytes;
    int length;
    Tcl_ObjType *typePtr;
    union {
        long intValue;
        double doubleValue;
        VOID *otherValuePtr;
        struct {
            VOID *ptr1;
            VOID *ptr2;
        } twoPtrValue;
    } internalRep;
} Tcl_Obj;
```

The `Tcl_Obj` structure holds dual values: the value in its native format and a string representation. The `bytes` field holds the string representation, which is computed only as needed. The `length` field holds the length of the string in the bytes field.

The `internalRep` field holds the value in its native format.

`Tcl_Obj` structures are dynamically allocated and shared as much as possible, using reference counting. Normally, you don't have to worry about this much, except that you should access only a `Tcl_Obj` via the officially defined function calls.

To create a new empty `Tcl_Obj`, call `Tcl_NewObj`:

```
Tcl_Obj* Tcl_NewObj()
```

To create an object from a text string, call `Tcl_NewStringObj`:

```
Tcl_Obj* Tcl_NewStringObj(char* string, int string_length)
```

To copy an object, call `Tcl_DuplicateObj`:

```
Tcl_Obj* Tcl_DuplicateObj(Tcl_Obj* obj)
```

All these functions preserve the proper reference counting. You can find out more about reference counting and memory management in the on-line documentation entry for `Tcl_NewObj`.

Setting the Result with the Object-Based Approach

There are also object-based functions for setting the result data. For example, if you have a `Tcl_Obj` and want to use it as the result, you can call `Tcl_SetObjResult` instead of `Tcl_AppendResult`:

```
void Tcl_SetObjResult(Tcl_Interp* interp,
        Tcl_Obj* result_obj)
```

The `reverse` command example we've used so far reverses the two arguments to the command and returns the reversed data. With the object-based approach, this is more difficult than appending text strings to the result.

One method could be to generate text strings from the arguments and then reverse them.

`Tcl_GetStringFromObj` retrieves a text string from a `Tcl_Obj`:

```
char* Tcl_GetStringFromObj(Tcl_Obj* obj,
    int* length_return)
```

`Tcl_GetStringFromObj` returns the value held in the `Tcl_Obj` as a text string. You should not modify or free this string, because the Tcl object manager owns the memory. The *length_return* is set to the length, in bytes, of the returned text string.

After the data are in string format (not the most efficient format, of course), you can create a results Tcl_Obj with the Tcl_NewStringObj function, covered previously. Tcl_NewStringObj creates a new Tcl_Obj from a text string.

That covers handling one of the two arguments. The second argument can be appended to the first. To do this, call Tcl_AppendStringsToObj:

```
void Tcl_AppendStringsToObj(Tcl_Obj* obj,
    char* string,

    ...
    (char *) NULL)
    ,
```

Like Tcl_AppendResult, Tcl_AppendStringsToObj takes a variable number of arguments. NULL acts as the sentinel value, telling Tcl_AppendStringsToObj where the data end.

When you have a Tcl_Obj with all the data, you can set it as the result of the reverse command using Tcl_SetObjResult.

Manipulating Lists with the Object-Based Approach

Another approach for the example reverse command, as well as a very common case, is to return data as a list. Tcl provides a number of commands that manipulate lists, so multi-item result data should probably be returned as a list to meet user expectations.

With the object-based approach, you can create a new list object with the Tcl_NewListObj function:

```
Tcl_Obj* Tcl_NewListObj(int objc,
    Tcl_Obj* objv[])
```

Tcl_NewListObj creates a new Tcl_Obj list and optionally fills in this Tcl_Obj list with an array of Tcl_Obj structures you pass, along with a count of how many elements are in the array. To call Tcl_NewListObj to create a new empty list object, you can use the following code:

```
    Tcl_Obj*    result;

    result = Tcl_NewListObj(0, NULL);
```

After you have a list object, you can append elements with
Tcl_ListObjAppendElement:

```
int Tcl_ListObjAppendElement(
     Tcl_Interp* interp,
     Tcl_Obj* list_obj,
     Tcl_Obj* element_obj)
```

Tcl_ListObjAppendElement returns TCL_OK on success and TCL_ERROR
on errors.

For our reverse command example, you can reverse the arguments
using code like the following:

```
int RevObjCommand(
  ClientData client_data,
  Tcl_Interp* interp,
  int objc,
  Tcl_Obj** objv )

{    /* RevObjCommand */
    Tcl_Obj* result;

    /* Reverse arguments by creating an object list. */
    result = Tcl_NewListObj(0, NULL);

    Tcl_ListObjAppendElement(interp, result, objv[2] );
    Tcl_ListObjAppendElement(interp, result, objv[1] );

    Tcl_SetObjResult(interp, result);

    return TCL_OK;

}    /* RevObjCommand */
```

Registering a Command with the Object-Based Approach

To register a command that you've written using the object-based approach, you should call Tcl_CreateObjCommand instead of Tcl_CreateCommand:

```
Tcl_Command Tcl_CreateObjCommand (
        Tcl_Interp* interp,
        char* commandname,
        Tcl_ObjCmdProc* function,
        ClientData clientData,
        Tcl_CmdDeleteProc* deletefunction)
```

Like Tcl_CreateCommand, with Tcl_CreateObjCommand you pass in the name of the new command as well as a function pointer to the C function you wrote for the command.

An Example Command Using the Object-Based Approach

Putting this all together, the following **revobj.c** program implements the example reverse command, using the new object-based commands.

```
/*
 revobj.c
 Tcl sample command to reverse two arguments,
 using "object" based commands.
*/

#include <stdio.h>
#include <stdlib.h>
#include <tcl.h>

/*
Implements a Tcl command named "reverse",
which reverses the first two arguments
and returns the reversed data.
*/
int RevObjCommand(
  ClientData client_data,
  Tcl_Interp* interp,
  int objc,
```

```
  Tcl_Obj** objv )

{    /* RevObjCommand */
    Tcl_Obj* result;

    /* Check number of arguments. */
    if (objc != 3) {
        /* We cheat and use string-based result. */
        Tcl_AppendResult(interp,
            "ERROR: reverse requires two arguments.",
            (char*) NULL); /* Sentinel. */

        return TCL_ERROR;
    }

    /* Reverse arguments by creating an object list. */
    result = Tcl_NewListObj(0, NULL);

    Tcl_ListObjAppendElement(interp, result, objv[2] );
    Tcl_ListObjAppendElement(interp, result, objv[1] );

    Tcl_SetObjResult(interp, result);

    return TCL_OK;

}    /* RevObjCommand */

int Tcl_AppInit(Tcl_Interp* interp)
{
    int    status;

    status = Tcl_Init(interp);

    if (status != TCL_OK) {
        return TCL_ERROR;
    }

    /* Register your commands here... */
```

```
Tcl_CreateObjCommand(interp,
  "reverse",
  (Tcl_ObjCmdProc*) RevObjCommand,
  (ClientData) NULL,
  (Tcl_CmdDeleteProc*) NULL);

  return TCL_OK;
}

int
main(int argc, char** argv)
{
    Tcl_Main(argc, argv, Tcl_AppInit);
    return 0;
}

/* revobj.c */
```

Finishing Your Commands

In addition to the basic functions for registering new commands and setting the result data, the Tcl library provides a host of functions for fleshing out your command functions.

The following sections briefly cover some of the more important functions. The on-line documentation is very useful to help you choose which functions to call.

Allocating Memory

Any memory your program allocates and passes to Tcl routines should be allocated with the Tcl_Alloc or Tcl_Realloc functions:

```
char* Tcl_Alloc(int amount)
```

```
char* Tcl_Realloc(char* ptr, int amount)
```

Use Tcl_Alloc and Tcl_Realloc in place of the C functions malloc and realloc, respectively.

Free any memory allocated with `Tcl_Alloc` or `Tcl_Realloc` by calling `Tcl_Free`:

```
void Tcl_Free(char* ptr)
```

Use `Tcl_Free` in place of the standard C function `free`.

N O T E One of the reasons for the special memory allocation functions is the differences between how the Borland and Microsoft compilers work on Windows. Because Tcl uses dynamically linked libraries on Windows, and because the compiler you use can result in different kinds of memory allocations, you could experience problems if you allocate memory using the standard C functions.

Allocating Text Strings

Because everything in Tcl is text, you'll find that you need to allocate text strings. Tcl's C library comes with a number of routines for creating, copying, and appending dynamically allocated text strings.

For this task, Tcl uses a data type called `Tcl_DString`, short for dynamically allocated string. Inside this structure, Tcl takes care of all the memory management. This is very handy because Tcl strings tend to get very long (and you'll use many such strings).

When first declaring a `Tcl_DString`, you need to call `Tcl_DStringInit` to initialize all the data in the structure:

```
Tcl_DStringInit(Tcl_DString* ds)
```

To append data to the string, call `Tcl_DStringAppend`:

```
char* Tcl_DStringAppend(Tcl_DString* ds,
    char* string,
    int length)
```

To extract the value, call `Tcl_DStringValue`:

```
char* Tcl_DStringValue(Tcl_DString* ds)
```

Note that `Tcl_DStringValue` returns a pointer to the data. Don't write to these data directly, call `Tcl_DStringAppend` instead.

To get the length of a dynamic string, call `Tcl_DStringLength`:

```
int Tcl_DStringLength(Tcl_DString* ds)
```

When you're done with a dynamic string, call `Tcl_DStringFree` to free any allocated memory:

```
Tcl_DStringFree(Tcl_DString* ds)
```

Converting Strings

Tcl provides a number of handy routines for converting string data to and from numeric data. `Tcl_GetInt` converts a string to an integer:

```
int Tcl_GetInt(Tcl_Interp* interp,
    char* string,
    int* return_value)
```

If an error occurs, `Tcl_GetInt` returns `TCL_ERROR` and stores an error message on `interp->result`. Otherwise, `Tcl_GetInt` returns `TCL_OK`. The converted value is returned in *return_value*.

With the object-based approach, you can call `Tcl_GetIntFromObj`:

```
int
Tcl_GetIntFromObj(Tcl_Interp* interp,
    Tcl_Obj* obj,
    int* return_value)
```

Like `Tcl_GetInt`, `Tcl_GetIntFromObj` returns `TCL_OK` or `TCL_ERROR`.

`Tcl_GetDouble` and `Tcl_GetBoolean` act similarly:

```
int Tcl_GetDouble(Tcl_Interp* interp,
    char* string,
    double* return_value)
```

```
int Tcl_GetBoolean(Tcl_Interp* interp,
```

```
    char* string,
    int* return_value)
```

For the object-based approach, there's also `Tcl_GetDoubleFromObj` and `Tcl_GetBooleanFromObj`:

```
int Tcl_GetDoubleFromObj(Tcl_Interp* interp,
    Tcl_Obj *obj,
    double* return_value)
```

```
int Tcl_GetBooleanFromObj(Tcl_Interp* interp,
    Tcl_Obj *obj,
    int* return_value)
```

Accessing Tcl Variables in Your Commands

One of the key tasks you'll need to do in your commands is access Tcl variables. To access the value of a variable, call `Tcl_GetVar`:

```
char* Tcl_GetVar(Tcl_Interp* interp,
    char* varname,
    int flags)
```

The flags can be any of the bitmasks listed in Table 16.2. You can OR together one or more of these masks.

Table 16.2 Bitmasks for `"` and `"`.

Mask	Meaning
TCL_GLOBAL_ONLY	Look up the value only as a global variable.
TCL_LEAVE_ERR_MSG	If an error occurs, a message is placed in `interp->result`.
TCL_APPEND_VALUE	For `Tcl_SetVar`, appends value to existing value.
TCL_LIST_ELEMENT	For `Tcl_SetVar`, converts data to list element before writing.

To set a variable value, call `Tcl_SetVar`:

```
char* Tcl_SetVar(Tcl_Interp* interp,
    char* varname,
    char* data,
    int flags)
```

In addition to `Tcl_GetVar` and `Tcl_SetVar`, you can use a few other routines. Look up `Tcl_GetVar2` and `Tcl_SetVar2`, for array variables, in the on-line documentation, as well as `Tcl_ObjGetVar2` and `Tcl_ObjSetVar2`.

Evaluating Arguments

In addition to working with text strings, you may need to evaluate the arguments passed to your command function. To convert an expression (of the form given to the `expr` Tcl command) to a `double` value, use `Tcl_ExprDouble`:

```
int Tcl_ExprDouble(Tcl_Interp* interp,
    char* expression,
    double* return_value)
```

`Tcl_ExprDouble` handles errors like `Tcl_GetInt`. If everything succeeds, `Tcl_ExprDouble` returns `TCL_OK` and the result of the expression in *return_value*.

`Tcl_ExprDoubleObj` acts the same for the object-based approach:

```
int Tcl_ExprDoubleObj(Tcl_Interp* interp,
    Tcl_Obj* obj,
    double* return_value)
```

`Tcl_ExprBoolean`, `Tcl_ExprLong`, and `Tcl_ExprString` also work similarly, for the string-based approach:

```
int Tcl_ExprBoolean(Tcl_Interp* interp,
    char* expression,
    int* return_value)
```

```
int Tcl_ExprLong(Tcl_Interp* interp,
    char* expression,
    long* return_value)
```

```
int Tcl_ExprString(Tcl_Interp* interp,
    char* expression)
```

Tcl_ExprString acts slightly different in that it stores the results of the expression in interp->result.

For the object-based approach, you can call Tcl_ExprBooleanObj, Tcl_ExprLongObj, and Tcl_ExprObj:

```
int Tcl_ExprBooleanObj(Tcl_Interp* interp,
    Tcl_Obj* obj,
    int* return_value)
```

```
int Tcl_ExprLongObj(Tcl_Interp* interp,
    Tcl_Obj* obj,
    long* return_value)
```

```
int Tcl_ExprObj(Tcl_Interp* interp,
    Tcl_Obj* obj,
    Tcl_Obj** return_value)
```

Tcl_ExprObj creates a new object that is the result of the expression. It's important to manage memory properly, as described in the on-line documentation for Tcl_ExprObj. (This is a not-so-subtle trick to get you to read the on-line documentation.)

Looking Up Objects

Tcl uses text names for all objects, rather than the more common pointers in C and C++. This means that any object or structure created in your C and C++ code must have a name. You also must be able to look up the name and return the object or structure pointer.

Tcl provides hash table routines that can help in this regard, if your application doesn't support object lookup by names. See the on-line documentation for `Tcl_InitHashTable` and `Tcl_GetHashValue` for more information.

Linking Variables Between C and Tcl

You can make a connection between global C and Tcl variables with `Tcl_LinkVar`. `Tcl_LinkVar` connects a C and Tcl variable, ensuring that when one changes, the other will also change.

On the Tcl side, variable linking is accomplished through a trace on the variable, as discussed in Chapter 9. Every time the variable is read in Tcl, the latest value is queried from the C program.

`Tcl_LinkVar` takes the following parameters:

```
int Tcl_LinkVar(Tcl_Interp* interp,
    char* variable_name,
    char* address_of_C_variable,
    int type_of_variable)
```

The *variable_name* is the name of the Tcl variable you want to associate with the C variable. The *address_of_C_variable* is a pointer to the C variable, and the *type_of_variable* is a special flag value, telling `Tcl_LinkVar` what type of variable you have. Table 16.3 lists the types supported by `Tcl_LinkVar`.

Table 16.3 Types supported by " .

Flag	C Type	Meaning
TCL_LINK_INT	int	Integer variable.
TCL_LINK_DOUBLE	double	Double-precision floating point.
TCL_LINK_BOOLEAN	int	Integer treated as a boolean, 0 for false, 1 for true.
TCL_LINK_STRING	char*	Text string; you must allocate space for the string with `Tcl_Alloc`.

You can also OR the flag `TCL_LINK_READ_ONLY` so that the value cannot be changed from Tcl, only from C. For example, to connect a C `int` variable named *global_int* to a Tcl variable called port, you can use the following code:

```
int      global_int;

Tcl_LinkVar(interp, "port",
    (char*) &global_int, TCL_LINK_INT);

global_int    = 2345;
```

Trouble-Shooting `Tcl_LinkVar`

I've noticed a few quirks when using `Tcl_LinkVar` inside C programs. The following guidelines are the result of bitter experience:

- For string variables, allocate memory for the string first and then fill in a default value. After that, call `Tcl_LinkVar`.
- For numeric variables, initialize a default value after calling `Tcl_LinkVar`.

This may sound odd, but I had a lot of problems getting `Tcl_LinkVar` to work.

With a text string variable, you can use the following sequence:

```
char*   global_string = NULL;

global_string = Tcl_Alloc( 1024 );
strcpy( global_string, "localhost" );

Tcl_LinkVar(interp, "hostname",
    (char*) &global_string, TCL_LINK_STRING);
```

Note that you pass the address of the *global_string* pointer to `Tcl_LinkVar`.

If the variable changes in the C program and you need an immediate update in the Tcl script, call `Tcl_UpdateLinkedVar`:

```
void Tcl_UpdateLinkedVar(Tcl_Interp* interp,
      char* variable_name)
```

Normally, `Tcl_UpdateLinkedVar` is not needed, because the Tcl inter-preter rereads the C variable every time the variable is read in Tcl.

To break the link between the C and Tcl variable, call `Tcl_UnlinkVar`:

```
void Tcl_UnlinkVar(Tcl_Interp* interp,
      char* variable_name)
```

To show how to use `Tcl_LinkVar`, the following C program creates three global variables and a command that changes the variables. The **linkvar.c** program follows:

```
/*
 linkvar.c, test of Tcl_LinkVar
 in a Tk application. Creates three
 global variables linked to Tcl variables.
 */

#include <stdio.h>
#include <stdlib.h>
#include <string.h>
#include <tcl.h>
#include <tk.h>

/*
 Declare global variables.
 */
int     global_int;
char*   global_string = NULL;
double  global_double;

/*
 Implements a Tcl command named "set_vars",
 sets the variables to values to show change
 in Tcl interface.
 */
```

```c
int SetVarsCommand(
  ClientData client_data,
  Tcl_Interp* interp,
  int argc,
  char *argv[])

{    /* SetVarsCommand */

    /* Reset result data. */
    Tcl_ResetResult(interp);

    /* Increment global numeric values. */
    global_int    += 2;
    global_double += 42.0;

    /* Reset string value. */
    strcpy( global_string, "localhost" );

    Tcl_UpdateLinkedVar(interp, "float" );
    Tcl_UpdateLinkedVar(interp, "hostname" );
    Tcl_UpdateLinkedVar(interp, "port" );

    return TCL_OK;

}    /* SetVarsCommand */

int Tcl_AppInit(Tcl_Interp* interp)
{
    int    status;

    status = Tcl_Init(interp);

    if (status != TCL_OK) {
        return TCL_ERROR;
    }

    /* Initialize Tk values. */
    status = Tk_Init(interp);
```

```
if (status != TCL_OK) {
    return TCL_ERROR;
}

/* Insert your code here... */

/* Link variables. */

/*
 * For string variables,
 * allocate/initialize before link.
 */
global_string = Tcl_Alloc( 1024 );
strcpy( global_string, "localhost" );

Tcl_LinkVar(interp, "hostname",
    (char*) &global_string, TCL_LINK_STRING);

/*
 * For int and double variables,
 * initialize after link.
 */
Tcl_LinkVar(interp, " port",
    (char*) &global_int, TCL_LINK_INT);

Tcl_LinkVar(interp, "float",
    (char*) &global_double, TCL_LINK_DOUBLE);

global_int    = 2345;
global_double = 42.0;

/* Register command to set variables. */
Tcl_CreateCommand(interp,
 "set_vars",
 (Tcl_CmdProc*) SetVarsCommand,
 (ClientData) NULL,
 (Tcl_CmdDeleteProc*) NULL);
```

```
    return TCL_OK;
}

int main(int argc, char** argv)
{
    Tk_Main(argc, argv, Tcl_AppInit);

    return 0;
}

/* linkvar.c */
```

You can compile and link the **linkvar.c** program using the makefiles presented in Chapter 15.

The **linkvar.c** program goes with a **linkvar.tcl** script file that shows the interaction between the C program and the Tcl script:

```
# Tcl example for linkvar.c

label .l_port -text Port
entry .port -textvariable port

label .l_host -text Hostname
entry .host -textvariable hostname

label .l_float -text Float
entry .float -textvariable float

grid config .l_port -column 0 -row 0 -sticky w
grid config .port   -column 1 -row 0 -sticky snew

grid config .l_host -column 0 -row 1 -sticky w
grid config .host   -column 1 -row 1 -sticky snew

grid config .l_float -column 0 -row 2 -sticky w
grid config .float   -column 1 -row 2 -sticky snew

button .set  -text Set  -command { set_vars; update }
```

```
button .exit -text Exit -command { exit }

grid config .set  -column 0 -row 3 -sticky snew
grid config .exit -column 1 -row 3 -sticky snew

# linkvar.tcl
```

To run the **linkvar** program, you can use the following command:

```
linkvar linkvar.tcl
```

The **linkvar.tcl** script creates a number of entry widgets that allow you to change values from the Tcl interpreter. The *Set* button calls the new set_vars command, defined in **linkvar.c**, which sets the value of the variables from the C program, to show the other side of the system.

Tcl_LinkVar is an effective way to connect variables between Tcl and C. Because it uses traces, performance may suffer. If this is an issue, you should create a new Tcl command in C to get and set the values you need.

Using Tcl to Test C++ Programs

Tcl works very well as a testing framework for C++ applications. That's because C++ objects (no relation to Tcl's object-based internals) are self-contained units that hold data and operations that act on the data. I've found that Tcl works very well to create a framework where you can allocate C++ objects and then execute member functions, all from a few Tcl commands. It's surprisingly easy.

Not only is this technique easy to implement (if a bit tedious), it provides a number of advantages for testing your C++ programs:

- You can create objects of any class at any time.
- You can query data in objects from Tcl.
- You can change values in objects.
- You can automate testing by using Tcl scripts. You have the full Tcl language available for implementing control over the flow of the script and examining returned data for correctness.

- You can create a graphical interface for your testing. There are some interesting tricks you can do with this to automate the creation of dialog windows for a given class as well.

In a typical C++ program, you create a number of C++ objects at runtime, mostly allocated dynamically with the new operator. Each object is a semi-independent unit. You can call functions on that object to modify that object's internal state. If you think about Tk's widgets, you'll notice the similarity. Each widget is created at runtime and acts semi-independently. Each widget has a set of commands that operate on it. And, each widget name is registered as a new Tcl command. We can treat C++ objects similarly.

Allocate each object with new. Then, register a command for each object. (This means that each object requires a name.) Each of these object commands should have a number of subcommands that allow you to execute member functions on the object.

I also try to enforce some uniformity on the naming of the subcommands. This makes working with such a system much easier. For example, to return the value of a given data member on an object, you can use the following syntax:

```
object_name data_member_name
```

Try to use the same name as the actual data member, or the name of the access function that returns the data member's value. Because you're testing a C++ application, keeping the names as close to the names used in the actual class can help you better find out what is happening in the class code.

To set a value into that same data member, you can pass a value as well:

```
object_name data_member_name new_value
```

To restore data member values to some preset initial state, you can provide a reset subcommand:

```
object_name reset
```

To get a list of all the data members (it's easy to forget for complicated objects), you can have a members subcommand:

```
object_name members
```

You can use some tricks with the ability to query an object for its members, as I'll show later.

To execute a member function, make a subcommand for that function:

```
object_name function any_parameters
```

Finally, to help debug, you can provide a `print` subcommand that prints out all data in the object (this is more useful on UNIX than Windows because of the console) and a `help` subcommand that lists all the available options for the Tcl command on that object:

```
object_name print
object_name help
```

To implement all this, you'll need to write a function that executes this new object command. This command function needs to accept a number of Tcl arguments and deal with all the subcommands. This may seem complicated, but it is very straightforward to create.

Also, you don't have to write a function for each object. Instead, you can share the function between all objects of the same class.

The key to this technique is using the client data parameters that, up to now, we've ignored.

The **client data** parameter to each command function allows you to pass a pointer to any arbitrary data you want to pass to that command.

We can use the client data parameter to pass a pointer to a C++ object. This is how you can share the command function between a number of objects of the same class.

You need a separate Tcl command to create objects of each class. You also need a function to delete objects (the delete function that we've also ignored up to now).

To help make this clearer, I'll show an example using a contrived C++ class. For real applications, you'll need much more involved code. I hope, though, that this example shows the power of Tcl for testing C++ applications.

The Example C++ Class

For the example C++ class, we just provide a few data members:

```
class FlowControl {
public:
    FlowControl()  { Reset(); }
    ~FlowControl() { Reset(); }

    int Power() { return _power; }
    void SetPower(int power) { _power = power; }

    double Flow() { return _flow; }
    void SetFlow(double flow) { _flow = flow; }

    void Reset() { _power = 0; _flow = 0.0; }

    void Print(char* name) {
        printf("%s Power %d Flow %f\n", name, _power, _flow);
    }

private:
    int _power; // 1 for on, 0 for off.
    double _flow;  // Amount of flow.

}; // FlowControl
```

For this example, all member functions are defined in line. This is not necessary, of course.

Creating a Tcl Interface to the C++ Class

The next step is to create a Tcl interface to the C++ class. For this, we need three functions: one to create, one to delete, and one to handle the object command.

Creating and Deleting the Object

The creation function serves for a Tcl command that creates objects of the
FlowControl class:

```
extern "C"
int FlowControlCreate(
    ClientData client_data,
    Tcl_Interp* interp,
    int argc,
    char** argv)

{    // FlowControlCreate

    // First argument is name of object.
    if (argc < 2)
    {
        Tcl_AppendResult(interp, "Wrong # args: should be ",
            argv[0], " object_name", 0);
        return TCL_ERROR;
    }

    // Create new object.
    FlowControl*    obj = new FlowControl();

    // Register command to handle object.
    Tcl_CreateCommand(interp,
    argv[1],      // Argument is name of new object.
    (Tcl_CmdProc*) FlowControlCmd,
    (ClientData) obj,
    (Tcl_CmdDeleteProc*) FlowControlDelete );

    // Command returns the name of the created object.
    Tcl_AppendResult(interp, argv[1], (char*) NULL);
    return TCL_OK;
}
```

All these functions are marked as extern "C" to ensure that the calling
sequences will work with the Tcl library, which is written in C. (This basi-
cally turns off C++ name mangling.)

As a new object is created, the `FlowControlCreate` function registers a new Tcl command for the new object, calling `Tcl_CreateCommand`. (This example uses the string-based approach to writing Tcl commands.)

The creation Tcl command requires at least one parameter: the name of the new object to create.

Notice how a pointer to the new object is passed as the client data for this new Tcl command. This is how the object gets passed to the `FlowControlCmd` function.

The creation function is registered as a Tcl command in the `Tcl_AppInit` function:

```
// Register command to create FlowControl objects.
Tcl_CreateCommand(interp,
 "FlowControl",
 (Tcl_CmdProc*) FlowControlCreate,
 (ClientData) NULL,
 (Tcl_CmdDeleteProc*) NULL );
```

Note that the name of this command is `FlowControl`—made the same as the class name for simplicity.

The delete function frees memory:

```
extern " C"
void FlowControlDelete(
    ClientData client_data)

{    // FlowControlDelete

    // Extract the object from client data.
    FlowControl* obj = (FlowControl*) client_data;

    if (obj != NULL) {
        delete obj;
    }

}    // FlowControlDelete
```

A delete function is especially important if you later add commands to delete the C++ objects.

Handling the Object Command

The third function is most important. This function is called for each named object command and handles the subcommands:

```
extern " C"
int FlowControlCmd(
    ClientData client_data,
    Tcl_Interp* interp,
    int argc,
    char** argv)

{   // FlowControlCmd
    char        string[1024];   // Temp. string

    // First extract the object from client data.
    FlowControl* obj = (FlowControl*) client_data;

    if (obj == NULL) {
        Tcl_AppendResult(interp, "invalid object",
            argv[0],
            NULL);
        return TCL_ERROR;
    }

    // Must have at least 2 arguments:
    // obj name and command.
    if (argc < 2) {
        Tcl_AppendResult(interp, "Wrong # args. "
            "Try help sub command for list",
            NULL);

        return TCL_ERROR;
    }
    // Determine subcommand.
    if (strcmp(argv[1], "help") == 0) {
        Tcl_AppendResult(interp,
            "FlowControl objects support: \n",
```

```
            "obj help\n",
            "obj print\n",
            "obj members\n",
            "obj reset\n",
            "set flow [obj Flow]\n",
            "obj Flow new_flow_value\n",
            "set power [obj Power]\n",
            "obj Power new_power_value\n",
            NULL);

} else if (strcmp(argv[1], "print") == 0) {

    obj->Print( argv[0] );

} else if (strcmp(argv[1], "members") == 0) {
    // Append data as list items.
    Tcl_AppendElement(interp, "Flow" );
    Tcl_AppendElement(interp, "Power" );

} else if (strcmp(argv[1], "reset") == 0) {

    obj->Reset();

} else if (strcmp(argv[1], "Flow") == 0) {

    // Check for value argument.
    if (argc < 3) {
        // Get value.
        sprintf(string, "%f", obj->Flow() );
        Tcl_AppendResult(interp, string, NULL);
    } else {
        // Set value.
        double   value = atof( argv[2] );

        obj->SetFlow( value );

        // Return value, too.
        Tcl_AppendResult(interp, argv[2], NULL);
```

```
        }

    } else if (strcmp(argv[1], "Power") == 0) {

        // Check for value argument.
        if (argc < 3) {
            // Get value.
            sprintf(string, "%d", obj->Power() );
            Tcl_AppendResult(interp, string, NULL);
        } else {
            // Set value.
            int value = atoi( argv[2] );

            obj->SetPower( value );

            // Return value, too.
            Tcl_AppendResult(interp, argv[2], NULL);
        }

    } else {
        Tcl_AppendResult(interp, "Invalid sub command. " ,
            " Try help sub command for list",
            NULL);

        return TCL_ERROR;
    }

    return TCL_OK;

}    // FlowControlCmd
```

The rather long `FlowControlCmd` starts out by extracting the object pointer from the *client_data* parameter. This is how the individual object gets passed to a generic function that can work on any object of the given class, `FlowControl` in our example.

After extracting the C++ object and checking for simple errors, the `FlowControlCmd` function determines which subcommand was used.

Most of the subcommands are rather simple, such as `print` and `reset`. Having the support for these commands in the C++ class definition really helps.

The `Flow` and `Power` subcommands check whether the user is setting a new value or merely returning the current value. Because this function uses the string-based approach, all values must be converted to and from text strings. This isn't that hard in this example.

If you add new data members to the `FlowControl` class, then you need to add more subcommands like `Flow` and `Power` to the `FlowControlCmd` procedure. Member functions can be executed similarly.

The `members` subcommand returns a list of all data members formatted as a Tcl list. To do this, it calls `Tcl_AppendElement`:

```
void Tcl_AppendElement(Tcl_Interp* interp,
        char *list_element_to_add)
```

If you add new data members to the `FlowControl` class, you also have to add new list items to the `members` subcommand.

The Example C++ Program

The full **objtest.cxx** program follows:

```
/*
 C++ test program using Tcl to create C++ objects.
*/
#include <stdio.h>
#include <string.h>
#include <stdlib.h>

#include <tcl.h>
#include <tk.h>

  // Example class.
class FlowControl {
public:
```

```
    FlowControl()  { Reset(); }
    ~FlowControl() { Reset(); }

    int Power() { return _power; }
    void SetPower(int power) { _power = power; }

    double Flow() { return _flow; }
    void SetFlow(double flow) { _flow  = flow; }

    void Reset() { _power = 0; _flow = 0.0; }

    void Print(char* name) {
        printf("%s Power %d Flow %f\n", name, _power, _flow);
    }

private:
    int _power; // 1 for on, 0 for off.
    double _flow;  // Amount of flow.

};  // FlowControl

/*
 You need a command to execute member
 functions in an object.
*/

/*
Tcl command for FlowControl objects. Accepts the
following subcommands:

obj help
obj print
obj members
obj reset
set flow [obj Flow]
obj Flow new_flow_value
set power [obj Power]
obj Power new_power_value
```

```
*/

extern "C"
int FlowControlCmd(
    ClientData client_data,
    Tcl_Interp* interp,
    int argc,
    char** argv)

{   // FlowControlCmd
    charstring[1024];// Temp. string

    // First extract the object from client data.
    FlowControl* obj = (FlowControl*) client_data;

    if (obj == NULL) {
        Tcl_AppendResult(interp, "invalid object",
            argv[0],
            NULL);
        return TCL_ERROR;
    }

    // Must have at least 2 arguments:
    // obj name and command.
    if (argc < 2) {
        Tcl_AppendResult(interp, "Wrong # args. "
            "Try help subcommand for list",
            NULL);

        return TCL_ERROR;
    }

    // Determine subcommand.
    if (strcmp(argv[1], "help") == 0) {
        Tcl_AppendResult(interp,
            "FlowControl objects support: \n",
            " obj help\n",
            " obj print\n",
```

```
            " obj members\n",
            " obj reset\n",
            " set flow [obj Flow]\n",
            " obj Flow new_flow_value\n",
            " set power [obj Power]\n",
            " obj Power new_power_value\n",
            NULL);

    } else if (strcmp(argv[1],"print") == 0) {

        obj->Print( argv[0] );

    } else if (strcmp(argv[1],"members") == 0) {
        // Append data as list items.
        Tcl_AppendElement(interp,"Flow" );
        Tcl_AppendElement(interp,"Power" );

    } else if (strcmp(argv[1],"reset") == 0) {

        obj->Reset();

    } else if (strcmp(argv[1],"Flow") == 0) {

        // Check for value argument.
        if (argc < 3) {
            // Get value.
            sprintf(string," %f", obj->Flow() );
            Tcl_AppendResult(interp, string, NULL);
        } else {
            // Set value.
            double   value = atof( argv[2] );

            obj->SetFlow( value );

            // Return value, too.
            Tcl_AppendResult(interp, argv[2], NULL);
        }
```

```
    } else if (strcmp(argv[1],"Power") == 0) {

        // Check for value argument.
        if (argc < 3) {
            // Get value.
            sprintf(string,"%d", obj->Power() );
            Tcl_AppendResult(interp, string, NULL);
        } else {
            // Set value.
            intvalue = atoi( argv[2] );

            obj->SetPower( value );

            // Return value, too.
            Tcl_AppendResult(interp, argv[2], NULL);
        }

    } else {
        Tcl_AppendResult(interp,"Invalid sub command." ,
            " Try help sub command for list",
            NULL);

        return TCL_ERROR;
    }

    return TCL_OK;

}    // FlowControlCmd

/*
You need a command to delete each object.
This is called by the Tcl interpreter.
You can also add explict delete commands.
*/
extern" C"
void FlowControlDelete(
    ClientData client_data)
```

```
{   // FlowControlDelete

    // Extract the object from client data.
    FlowControl* obj = (FlowControl*) client_data;

    if (obj != NULL) {
        delete obj;
    }

}   // FlowControlDelete

/*
You need a command to create objects of each class.
*/
extern" C"
int FlowControlCreate(
    ClientData client_data,
    Tcl_Interp* interp,
    int argc,
    char** argv)

{   // FlowControlCreate

    // First argument is name of object.
    if (argc < 2)
    {
        Tcl_AppendResult(interp,"Wrong # args: should be" ,
            argv[0]," object_name", 0);
        return TCL_ERROR;
    }

    // Create new object.
    FlowControl*    obj = new FlowControl();

    // Register command to handle object.
    Tcl_CreateCommand(interp,
    argv[1],    // Argument is name of new object.
    (Tcl_CmdProc*) FlowControlCmd,
```

```
        (ClientData) obj,
        (Tcl_CmdDeleteProc*) FlowControlDelete );

    // Command returns the name of the created object.
    Tcl_AppendResult(interp, argv[1], (char*) NULL);
    return TCL_OK;
}

extern" C"
int Tcl_AppInit(Tcl_Interp* interp)
{
    int     status;

    status = Tcl_Init(interp);

    if (status != TCL_OK) {
        return TCL_ERROR;
    }

    status = Tk_Init(interp);

    if (status != TCL_OK) {
        return TCL_ERROR;
    }

    // Register command to create FlowControl objects.
    Tcl_CreateCommand(interp,
        "FlowControl",
        (Tcl_CmdProc*) FlowControlCreate,
        (ClientData) NULL,
        (Tcl_CmdDeleteProc*) NULL );

    return TCL_OK;
}

int main(int argc, char** argv)
{
    Tk_Main(argc, argv, Tcl_AppInit);
```

```
    return 0;
}

/* objtest.cxx */
```

You can compile and link this program using the makefiles provided in Chapter 15.

Testing the C++ Program with Tcl

The **objtest** program contains the Tcl interpreter and the Tk toolkit, like **wish**. When you run the **objtest** program, you can create new objects of the FlowControl class using the FlowControl command:

```
% FlowControl obj1
obj1
% FlowControl obj2
obj2
```

The FlowControl command calls the FlowControlCreate C function, shown in **objtest.cxx**, previously.

After the program is created, you can query data from the objects:

```
% obj2 Power
0
```

You can also modify the data in the objects:

```
% obj2 Power 1
1
% obj2 Power
1
```

You can reset the object and print the internal data:

```
% obj2 reset
% obj2 print
obj2 Power 0 Flow 0.000000
```

If you don't know what to do, you can use the `help` subcommand:

```
% obj2 help
FlowControl objects support:
obj help
obj print
obj members
obj reset
set flow [obj Flow]
obj Flow new_flow_value
set power [obj Power]
obj Power new_power_value
```

You can also copy values from one object to another:

```
% obj2 Power 1
1
% obj2 Flow 55.234
55.234
% obj2 print
obj2 Power 1 Flow 55.234000
% obj1 Power [obj2 Power]
1
% obj1 Flow [obj2 Flow]
55.234000
% obj1 print
obj1 Power 1 Flow 55.234000
```

This ability allows you to better test object interactions. So far, there's been nothing to get really excited about, except that you can now create test scripts to rerun tests automatically, thus saving you a lot of time and effort. In addition, though, because of the Tk connection, you can make graphical interfaces for your test scripts.

Creating Dialog Windows for the Class—Automatically

For each class you connect to Tcl, you can create Tk dialog windows to help you get a better grasp on the values in the objects. You can extend this to create a generic Tcl procedure that can create a dialog window for any object. This saves you a lot of work in creating dialog windows.

The key to this is that each object must follow a set of conventions for the subcommands. For example, you can query the list of data members for an object with the `members` subcommand. You can set a new value into a data member by using the data member and the new value. By following conventions like these, you can write procedures that can interact with any object, regardless of its class.

The basic algorithm to do this follows.

For each object, we create a new dialog window, a `toplevel` widget. Inside each dialog window, we place an `entry` widget for each data member. A `label` describes the `entry` widget, using the name of the data member. (This may not seem like the most user-friendly text—and it isn't. But, because it shares terminology with the C++ class, it allows you to more easily go back to the C++ code and track down any problems discovered.)

When the program is created, you need to query each data member's value and place this value into the `entry` widget, using the `insert` option.

A *Close* button destroys the dialog window. A *Print* button calls the `print` subcommand. And, a *Reset* button calls the `reset` subcommand.

The *Reset* button raises an interesting issue: if the object changes in the underlying C++ code, you need to re-synchronize the values with the values in the Tcl dialog window. You can use the `-textvariable` option for each `entry` widget and set up a variable. You can even use `Tcl_LinkVar` to connect that variable to the underlying C++ code. But, this results in a lot of extra work. If instead you provide the ability to do a manual synchronization, then you can write the entire procedure in Tcl.

The Tcl code to do this follows:

```
#
# Synchronizes display with internal state.
# args holds list of entry_name and member_name
# for each entry widget.
#
proc Synchronize { objname args } {

    foreach element $args {
        # First item is entry name
```

```
        set entry_name  [lindex $element 0]
        set member_name [lindex $element 1]

        set value [$objname $member_name]
        $entry_name delete 0 end
        $entry_name insert 0 $value
    }
}
```

The Synchronize procedure expects the object name as well as a list of lists in the args parameter. Each element in the list is a list itself with the name of the entry widget and the data member name that corresponds to the entry widget.

 You can accomplish this same goal in a number of ways. One way is to name each entry widget with a name based on the data member name. That way, knowing either the data member or the entry widget name allows you to regenerate the missing piece of data. The Synchronize procedure is just one way to accomplish the goal.

Putting this all together, the following Tcl script provides generic procedures to create a dialog window for a C++ object, resynchronize data values, and set values into objects when the user presses the **Return** key on an entry widget.

The Tcl script follows:

```
# Test script for C++ testing.
# For use with objtest.cxx.
#

 #
 # Creates dialog window for test objects.
 # Assumes members subcommand returns
 # list of data members.
 #
proc TestObjDialog { objname } {

    set top .$objname
```

```
toplevel $top -class Dialog
wm withdraw $top

set row 0
label $top.name  -text $objname
grid config $top.name -column 0 -row $row -sticky w
incr row

# Create list of all entries for syncronization.
set ent_list {}

# Create an entry widget for each member.
set members [$objname members]

foreach mem $members {
    label $top.l_$mem -text $mem
    entry $top.e_$mem

    # Fill in current value.
    $top.e_$mem insert 0 [$objname $mem]

    bind $top.e_$mem <Key-Return> \
       "SetObjValue $top.e_$mem $objname $mem"

    grid config $top.l_$mem -column 0 -row $row \
        -sticky w
    grid config $top.e_$mem -column 1 -row $row \
        -sticky snew -columnspan 2
    incr row

    set item [list $top.e_$mem $mem]

    lappend ent_list $item
}

button $top.close -text "Close" \
    -command "destroy $top"
grid config $top.close -column 0 -row $row \
```

```
            -sticky snew

    button $top.print -text "Print" \
        -command "$objname print"
    grid config $top.print -column 1 -row $row \
        -sticky snew

    button $top.reset -text "Reset" \
        -command "$objname reset; 
            Synchronize $objname $ent_list"
    grid config $top.reset -column 2 -row $row \
        -sticky snew

    wm deiconify $top
}

    # Procedure sets value from entry.
    # Assumes each object accepts:
    #       object_name member_name new_value
    #
proc SetObjValue { entryname objname member } {

    set value [$entryname get]
    $objname $member $value
}

    #
    # Synchronizes display with internal state.
    # args holds list of entry_name and member_name
    # for each entry widget.
    #
proc Synchronize { objname args } {

    foreach element $args {
        # First item is entry name.
        set entry_name  [lindex $element 0]
        set member_name [lindex $element 1]
```

```
        set value [$objname $member_name]
        $entry_name delete 0 end
        $entry_name insert 0 $value
    }
}


#
# Create FlowControl objects.
#
FlowControl obj1
FlowControl obj2

# Create dialogs for these objects.
TestObjDialog obj1
TestObjDialog obj2

# objtest.tcl
```

The **objtest.tcl** script, especially the `TestObjDialog` procedure, seems complicated but it really isn't. The majority of `TestObjDialog` goes through each data member one at a time creating `label` and `entry` widgets. Pressing **Enter** or **Return** in the `entry` widget is bound to code that will set the value into the underlying C++ object.

When you run the **objtest.tcl** script, you'll see two dialog windows, each of which looks like that in Figure 16.1.

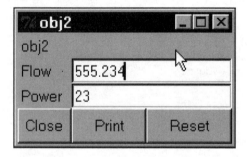

Figure 16.1 A dialog window created for an object.

Remember to press **Return** after entering each new value.

As you add more C++ classes to your test code, you'll need to create the three C functions shown in the **objtest.cxx** program for each new class. That's it. The `TestObjDialog` procedure should work for any number of classes that support the same conventions. Thus, after you set up the testing framework, it's relatively easy to extend this to new C++ classes.

Now, you could extend this much farther. If you had the ability to query a data member for its type, you could then create widgets other then `entry` for a given data member. For example, boolean values should have a `checkbutton` widget rather than an entry widget. There's a lot you can do with this.

There are a few extensions to Tcl to help mesh C++ code. One is called MIT Object Tcl (in fact, more than one is called Object Tcl) and is available on the Internet at **ftp://ftp.tns.lcs.mit.edu/pub/otcl/**. TclObj, another such method for combining Tcl with C++, is available at **http://www.uni-frankfurt.de/~fp/Tools/tclobj/**.

HUSH, which stands for Hyper Utility Shell, is a program like **wish** but offers a C++ interface to Tcl. HUSH is available at **http://www.cs.vu.nl/~hush/**.

Connecting Tcl to Java Applications

TclJava is the beginning of a connection between Tcl and Java. Located on the CD-ROM in the **contrib/java** directory, TclJava allows you to connect Java applications to Tcl. More information is also available on the Internet at **http://www.sunlabs.com/~kcorey/tcljava/**.

In another approach, Jacl, pronounced *jackal*, is a Tcl interpreter written in Java. Jacl is available at **http://simon.cs.cornell.edu/home/ioi/Jacl/**.

A major push for Tcl/Tk releases after 8.0 includes Java support and better ways to connect Tcl to Java. Future release should contain more and better connections to Java.

Summary

This chapter shows how to create your own Tcl commands using C functions. If you embed Tcl in your applications, chances are you'll need to create a number of Tcl commands. Each Tcl command gets executed by a C function that takes a set number of parameters, including the arguments passed to the Tcl command. There are two ways to write your C functions: the older string-based approach and the newer object-based approach. The object-based approach is more complicated but executes with better performance.

Each command function must return an error code, usually TCL_ERROR or TCL_OK, and fill in results for the Tcl command. You can use Tcl_ResetResult to clear the result and Tcl_AppendResult to store in new result data.

Inside your new command function, you can use Tcl_GetVar to access the value of a variable and Tcl_SetVar to store in new data to a variable.

You must register each new command with Tcl_CreateCommand or Tcl_CreateObjCommand. Tcl_CreateCommand and Tcl_CreateObjCommand both associate a command name, such as reverse, with a C function pointer, such as RevCommand. Typically, you'll register new commands in your Tcl_AppInit function.

Tcl and Tk Library Functions Introduced in This Chapter

Tcl_AppendElement

Tcl_AppendResult

Tcl_AppendStringsToObj

Tcl_CreateCommand

Tcl_CreateObjCommand

Tcl_DStringAppend

Tcl_DStringFree

Tcl_DStringInit

Tcl_DStringLength

Tcl_DStringValue

Tcl_DuplicateObj

Tcl_ExprBoolean

Tcl_ExprBooleanObj

Tcl_ExprDouble

Tcl_ExprDoubleObj

Tcl_ExprLong

Tcl_ExprLongObj

Tcl_ExprObj

Tcl_ExprString

Tcl_GetBoolean

Tcl_GetBooleanFromObj

Tcl_GetDouble

Tcl_GetDoubleFromObj

Tcl_GetInt

Tcl_GetIntFromObj

Tcl_GetStringFromObj

Tcl_GetVar

Tcl_LinkVar

Tcl_ListObjAppendElement

Tcl_NewListObj

Tcl_NewObj

Tcl_NewStringObj

Tcl_ResetResult

Tcl_SetErrorCode

Tcl_SetObjResult

Tcl_SetVar

Tcl_UnlinkVar

Tcl_UpdateLinkedVar

APPENDIX A

For More Information

Tcl Information and Code on the Internet

This book comes with a CD-ROM containing the latest versions of Tcl and Tk, as of this writing. Over time, though, you can expect new version of Tcl and Tk, as this language continues to evolve. You can acquire even later versions from the following Internet sites.

The official Tcl FTP site is located at **ftp://ftp.sunlabs.com/pub/tcl/**. This is the machine provided by Sun, where John Ousterhout, creator of Tcl, now works. Sun provides a Web page at **http://sunscript.sun.com/**.

The main contributed application FTP site is **http://www.NeoSoft.com/tcl/contributed-software/**, which also mirrors the Sun site for Tcl updates.

A good starting point for general Tcl information is the set of pages from SCO, a PC UNIX vendor, at **http://www.sco.com/Technology/tcl/Tcl.html**.

You'll find an extensive set of on-line manuals for Tcl and Tk at **http://sunscript.sun.com/man/** and **http://www.elf.org/tcltk-man-html/contents.htm**.

Many problems you'll face as you learn Tcl have been faced by others. There are a number of on-line resources that answer **frequently asked questions**. These resources, called FAQs, are located at **http://www.teraform.com/%7Elvirden/tcl-faq/**.

I maintain the frequently asked questions list for using Tcl/Tk on Windows. This list is on the CD-ROM in the **doc** directory. The absolutely latest version is located on the Internet at **http://www.pconline.com/~erc/tclwin.htm**.

I also provide a number of on-line resources on Tcl, located at **http://www.pconline.com/~erc/tcl.htm**.

Usenet News

The **comp.lang.tcl** Usenet newsgroup is a great source of information on Tcl and Tk. Every day, many users pose questions and receive answers from a number of Tcl experts. Chances are that if you face a problem, someone else has already faced it and solved it.

Tcl/Tk Books

This book concentrates on how to create graphical applications with Tcl and Tk.

The main reference comes with Tcl in the form of on-line manual information, accessible on Windows or UNIX, as discussed in Chapter 1. In addition, there's a few more Tcl books you might find helpful.

> *Tcl and the Tk Toolkit*, John Ousterhout, Addison-Wesley, 1994. Written by the creator of Tcl, this book contains more reference materials for an older version of Tcl, Tcl 7.3 and Tk 3.6. Most of this material is still valid, but some is out of date.

> *Practical Programming in Tcl and Tk*, Brent Welch, Prentice Hall, 1997. This book covers the UNIX version of Tcl and Tk in great depth, with some mention of Windows and MacOS. It uses Tcl/Tk 8.0a2, the second alpha prerelease of version 8.0.

> *Exploring Expect,* Don Libes, O'Reilly and Associates, 1995. Written with Tcl and Tk, **Expect** is a UNIX package that allows you to place a graphical interface on top of many UNIX commands. Instead of typing away at the unfriendly command line, **Expect** users interact with a graphical interface.

User Interface Books

Tcl/Tk allows you to create graphical applications quickly, but it's hard to create truly good applications in any language without following some guidelines. For better or worse, the Windows and Motif interface guidelines (on Windows and UNIX respectively) rule the roost.

The following books can help you turn your Tcl/Tk applications into truly great programs.

About Face: The Essentials of User Interface Design, Alan Cooper, IDG Books, 1995. This is by far the best user interface book I've seen, even though the author violated a number of his own interface rules (don't we all?). I highly recommend it.

The Windows Interface Guidelines for Software Design, Microsoft Press, 1995. This book contains lots of good advice for creating Windows, and yes, UNIX applications. Because the Windows style guide is so close to the Motif style, you can normally follow the Windows style on both Windows and UNIX.

Visual Design with OSF/Motif, Shiz Kobara, Addison-Wesley, 1991. This book is clearly aimed at Motif programmers, so you'll need to do a little bit of mental translation. If you can, though, you'll find Kobara's advice very helpful and quite detailed. Much of this book covers the best widths of scrollbars and how to properly align buttons and labels to make much better-looking programs. Because the terminology all uses that of Motif resources, you'll need to convert to Tk options. But, you can translate Kobara's advice into Tk widget options for things like padding, border widths, and so on.

Object-Oriented Interface Design: IBM Common User Access Guidelines, Que, 1992. This covers the Common User Access Guidelines, which form the basis for both the Windows and Motif (UNIX) interface style guides. In addition, a long section in the back includes translations of common interface terminology, such as File, Edit, and so on, to other languages.

Windows Books

Programming Windows 95, Charles Petzold, Microsoft Press, 1996. This is the classic for Windows programming. It is the best Windows programming book, updated for Windows 95.

The Windows 95 Registry: A Survival Guide for Users, John Woram, MIS:Press, 1996. This book covers the ins and outs of this terribly technical subject. If you need to mess with the Windows registry, to associate *.tcl* and *.tk* files with the **wish** executable, you can find out information on the process in this book.

UNIX Books

Teach Yourself UNIX, 3rd edition, Kevin Reichard and Eric F. Johnson, MIS:Press, 1995. Aimed at the UNIX beginner, you'll find clear explanations for UNIX file permissions (used with the Tcl open command) and more on where globbing came from. Tcl was written with the UNIX and X Window System in mind. It's only later that Windows and Macintosh versions appeared. If you're unfamiliar with the basics of UNIX, you'll find this book helpful.

Advanced Programming in the UNIX Environment, W. Richard Stevens, Addison-Wesley, 1992. By far the best book on programming UNIX applications, Stevens' book is an essential part of my bookshelf. If you need to program advanced applications on UNIX, this book is essential.

Teach Yourself C, 5th edition, Al Stevens, MIS: Press, 1997. If you're new to C programming, this book will be a great help.

X Window Books

The X Window System has become the de facto graphics engine on UNIX. Although not written for UNIX alone, it is UNIX where X succeeded the most. Tcl and Tk on UNIX use X for all graphics. And, many of the concepts of Tk, like selections and events, come straight from X.

One of the trickier concepts of X is the separation between the window manager and the windowing system. Neither Windows nor the Macintosh make this separation, a fact that tends to confuse many when they migrate to UNIX.

In X, a window manager is a separate program. The user can run any window manager desired, but few ever change the default configuration.

Even so, every system seems to come with its own different window manager. The tough part of all this is that X enforces a nasty rule: the window manager controls the screen layout. For more on these issues, you can try the following books.

Advanced X Window Applications Programming, 2nd edition, Eric F. Johnson and Kevin Reichard, M & T Books, 1994. This book covers programming with the X library, or Xlib. You'll find a lot of similarities with the internals of Tk, because Tk also uses the X library. Tk even goes so far as to port a number of Xlib C functions to Windows and Macintosh systems. The extensive window manager section in this book will go a long way to providing a background for the Tk wm command. The sections on X events will help you understand the Tk bind command and all its permutations. Furthermore, I'm biased; I'd love for you to buy this book.

UNIX System Administrator's Guide to the X Window System, Eric F. Johnson and Kevin Reichard, M&T Books, 1994. If you use the Tk send command, you'll often need to delve into X Window security and the **xauth** command, covered in this book. If you use the option command for X resource files, you'll also like the sections on the multitude of locations X resource files can be found.

CGI and HTML Books

Foundations of World Wide Web Programming with HTML and CGI, Ed Tittel, Mark Gaither, Sebastian Hassinger, and Mik Erwin, IDG Books, 1995. This giant book provides a good background in all things HTML.

Introduction to CGI/Perl: Getting Started with Web Scripts, Steven E. Brenner and Edwin Aoki, M&T Books, 1996. This thin book provides a great introduction to Web pages and CGI scripts, although the emphasis is on Perl.

APPENDIX B

Installing Tcl And Tk

Installing Tcl and Tk on UNIX

The instructions for installing Tcl and Tk differ based on your platform. The UNIX instructions are a lot different from those on Windows. In addition, different UNIX versions may require that you to make minor modifications to Tcl files to get things to compile. This appendix starts out covering installation on UNIX and ends with installation on Windows.

What You Need

For Tcl, you'll need a C compiler and the standard libraries and header files that come with C compilers.

For Tk, you'll also need X Window System libraries, because Tk provides a handy front end to making graphical X Window programs. In addition, you need to set up the directories properly for the Tcl runtime library to find the certain files it needs.

Unpacking the Distribution

Tcl and Tk for UNIX come in two packages, one for Tcl and one for Tk. Each package is a compressed UNIX tar file, called **tcl80.tgz** and **tk80.tgz** for Tcl and Tk, respectively. These files are located in the **tcl** directory on the CD-ROM. Copy these files to a top-level directory, such as **/usr/local/src**.

Uncompress the files with the GNU **gunzip** program. For example,

```
gunzip tcl80.tgz
gunzip tk80.tgz
```

If you don't have the GNU **gunzip** program, it is available in the **contrib/gzip** directory on the CD-ROM.

The full Tcl and Tk sources have already been uncompressed and extracted under the **tcl** directory on the CD-ROM. You can copy all these files and subdirectories if you'd like. However, it's usually easier to use **gunzip** and **tar** to extract all the files at once.

The next step is to extract the files from the UNIX tar archives, using the **tar** command:

```
tar xvof tcl80.tar
tar xvof tk80.tar
```

This process creates two subdirectories: **tcl8.0** and **tk8.0**.

If you acquired the Tcl and Tk sources over the Internet, now is the time to check for patches. A **patch** is a file that corrects problems in source code. **Patch**, the program that updates the code, uses **context difference** files in the form of those generated by the UNIX utility **diff**. If there is a patch file, you'll want to apply the patch before compiling and installing Tcl and Tk. This will ensure that you have the latest versions of the code and all the up-to-date fixes.

On the accompanying CD-ROM, any latest patches for both Tcl and Tk have already been installed.

CD-ROM

Configuring Tcl

Now you're ready to configure Tcl for your system. Change to the **tcl8.0/unix** directory and look at the **README** file. This file goes over the basic installation instructions.

The next step is to run **configure**. This program searches through your system and builds a—hopefully—correct **Makefile** with all the necessary options to build Tcl on your system. To do this, use the following command:

```
./configure
```

After **configure** completes, you should edit the **Makefile** it generated. You may need to change some of the entries in the **Makefile**.

The key entries to look for are `prefix`, the general directory path prefix, and `exec_prefix`, the directory path where the resulting executables should go.

The default values for these entries are the following.

```
prefix =        /usr/local
exec_prefix =   /usr/local
```

Using the `prefix` and `exec_prefix` values, the Tcl executables, **tclsh** and **wish**, will get installed into **/usr/local/bin**. (The location for **wish** is set when you configure Tk.) The Tcl libraries will get installed into **/usr/local/lib**. The runtime files will go into **/usr/local/lib/tcl8.0**. All these settings are controlled by the `prefix` and `exec_prefix` values.

You may want to change these values to something different. For example, you may want to use **/usr/local/tcl** as shown here:

```
prefix =        /usr/local/tcl
exec_prefix =   ${prefix}
```

I built Tcl on a Linux system that had an older version of Tcl and Tk already installed. Because I didn't want to damage a working version of Tcl until I was sure the new version worked, I choose to install Tcl and Tk in alternate directories to allow for testing without overwriting any of the existing versions.

Compiling Tcl

The next step is to run **make**, to build all the source code:

```
make
```

When **make** is finished, if it works successfully, then you should have **libtcl.a** and **tclsh** built. The library, **libtcl.a**, is used when you want to embed the Tcl interpreter within your applications. (This library may be named differently, such as **libtcl8.0.a** on your system.) You may also build a shared library, such as **libtcl8.0.so.1.8.0**. Shared library names vary by platform.

Tclsh is the Tcl shell program (much like **ksh** or **csh**, two other shells) that allows you to execute Tcl programs as discussed in Chapter 2. (You'll probably make much more use of **wish**, the Tcl shell with Tk support, than merely **tclsh**, which does not support graphical applications with Tk.)

If **make** fails, then you need to edit the **Makefile** and correct whatever problem was discovered. Sometimes this is not an easy task.

To help with this, the file named **porting.notes** in both the Tcl and Tk directories, may contain useful information for your platform.

After Tcl is properly made, you can run **make install** to install the proper files in the directories you listed in the **Makefile**, as shown below:

```
make install
```

Installing Tk on UNIX

The process for installing Tk is almost exactly like that for Tcl.

1. Run **./configure** in the **tk8.0/unix** directory.
2. Edit the **Makefile** generated by configure to change the `prefix` and `exec_prefix` entries, if necessary.
3. Run **make** to build the programs and library.
4. When **make** completes successfully, run **make install** to install Tk.

Because there is a lot more code for Tk, generally, this process will take longer than for Tcl.

Cleaning Up After the Installation

After you are sure Tcl and Tk both work (running some of the examples from this book may help test your interpreters), then you can run **make clean** to clean up all the extra object modules and associated debris left over from compiling and installing Tcl.

Merely run the following command in both the **tcl8.0/unix** and **tk8.0/unix** directories:

```
make clean
```

WARNING

Do not run **make clean** until you have built both Tk and Tcl. Building Tk requires **libtcl.a** from the **../../tcl8.0** directory. So, if you run **make clean** too soon, you may need to rebuild parts of Tcl to get Tk to build.

Installing Tcl and Tk on Windows NT, Windows 95, or Windows 3.1

The main problem on UNIX is the difference between UNIX versions. The main problem on Windows is differences between compilers.

Tcl and Tk require the Win32 subsystem (Win32s on Windows 3.1). You'll also need either the Borland or the Microsoft compiler to build Tcl from source code. Each of these compilers uses a different format for the important **Makefile**, which is why you need to be concerned about these compiler differences.

Installing the Binary Version

If you can avoid it, don't compile the libraries. Instead, just install the binary version that comes on the CD-ROM as a self-extracting archive. Execute the **TCL80.EXE** program, and it will lead you through the installation.

The default location chosen by the installation program is **C:\Program Files\Tcl**. Because of the space in the name **Program Files**, I strongly urge you to install Tcl elsewhere, such as **C:\Tcl**. You can get around the space problem, but it's much easier to avoid the issue completely.

Wherever you install Tcl, the **lib** subdirectory will contain both the Tcl/Tk runtime files and *.LIB* files that allow you to link applications with the Tcl and Tk libraries. For Windows, Tcl and Tk use DLLs.

To create an application that uses a DLL, you need a small *.LIB* file that contains the proper entry points and initialization for the dynamic link library. The **tcl80.lib** and **tk80.lib** files are libraries set up for use with the Borland compiler. The **tcl80vc.lib** and **tk80vc.lib** files are libraries set up for use with the Microsoft compiler. Because these libraries are included, you almost never need to compile Tcl from sources.

Compiling from Source Code

Just in case you do need to compile Tcl from source code, the Tcl source code comes in two packages, like that for UNIX: Tcl and Tk. This source code is located in Windows ZIP files in the **win** directory on the CD-ROM. The file names are **tcl80.zip** for the Tcl source code and **tk80.zip** for the Tk source code.

You'll need a ZIP program that understands long file names, such as WinZip to extract these sources.

If you don't have a ZIP program, you can copy all the files in **tcl/tcl8.0** and **tcl/tk8.0**, including all sub directories, to your hard disk. However, it's far easier to use a ZIP program.

After you have the source code files on your hard disk, look for the **README** files in the **win** subdirectories (for both Tcl and Tk). These files contain the latest instructions for using both the Borland or Microsoft compilers.

With the Microsoft compilers, the typical command to build the libraries follows:

```
nmake -f makefile.vc
```

You'll need to run this command in both the **tcl8.0/win** and **tk8.0/win** directories to build the Tcl and Tk libraries, respectively. You may need to set up INCLUDE and LIB environment variables to tell Visual C++ where your C++ compiler support files are located.

The Tcl and Tk source code uses long file names, which will be a problem under Windows 3.1. Windows 95 and Windows NT both allow for longer file names.

When you're all done with this, you can copy the executables (**.EXE** files) and Dynamic Link Libraries (**.DLL** files) to your installation binary directory, such as **C:\TCL\BIN**. You'll need to add this directory to your **PATH**. At the same level as the **BIN** directory (e.g., **C:\TCL**), create a **LIB** directory with **TCL8.0** and **TK8.0** subdirectories under **LIB**. Copy the Tcl and Tk support files to these directories. See the **README** files for more on which files are necessary.

Installing Tcl on MacOS

In the **tcl/tcl8.0** and **tcl/tk8.0** directories on the CD-ROM, you'll find subdirectories for UNIX (**unix**), Windows (**win**), and Macintosh (**mac**) versions of Tcl. The source code differs only slightly on the different platforms. Most of the code is platform-independent.

If you need to use Tcl on a Macintosh, for example, look at the **README** file in the **mac** subdirectories for instructions.

APPENDIX C

How to Use the CD-ROM

The accompanying CD-ROM uses Rock Ridge extensions to the standard ISO-9660 format. This allows for longer file names than the old-fashioned DOS eight-character names with three-character extensions. This was necessary because many Tcl programs use long file and directory names. If you see file names such as **INTEGER-;1**, your system does not support the CD's Rock Ridge extended file names. All the files are still available, but it will require more work to correct the names when you copy files to your hard disk.

You'll find these main sub directories on the CD-ROM:

- **book**, which holds examples from this book, listed in **examples.htm**.
- **contrib**, containing Tcl freeware.
- **tcl**, the source code for Tcl
- **win**, Windows binaries for Tcl

For ease of access, the Tcl sources are also available in compressed format. Files ending in **.tgz** are gzipped UNIX tar files. Files ending in **.zip** are Windows ZIP files.

The **contrib** directory is divided into a number of major categories of Tcl freeware, including the following:

- **cgi**, which holds the **cgi.tcl** library for writing CGI scripts.
- **debug**, with Tcl debuggers.
- **docs**, documentation on Tcl in HTML (Web) format.
- **et**, which holds the embedded Tk software discussed in Chapter 15.
- **extend**, containing extensions to the base Tcl/TK.

- **gzip**, location of GNU program to uncompress *.tgz* files.
- **html**, includes the html_library discussed in Chapter 11.
- **scripting**, with tools to help you create Tcl scripts.
- **softdev**, containing tools for C, C++, and Java software development.
- **uudeview**, containing the **uuenview** program discussed in Chapter 8.

INDEX

800

U

upvar command 85–88
URL, see Universal Resource Locator

variable command 681–682
variables 33–34
    variable substitution 34–35
Visual Tcl xxvii–xxviii, 663

while loop command 69–70
widget
    cget 149–150
    -command option 143–145
    common options 108–110
    configure options 148–149
    definition of widgets 8, 104
    list of widget types 105
names 8–9, 187
-relief option 188–190
-textvariable option 145–148
units 152
see also colors, pack, grid
window manager
    handling Close menu choice
        415–417
    icons 414–415, 638–640
    positioning windows 408–411

overriding 437
titlebar 407, 638
with no borders 437
winfo command 247, 409–414, 438,
    523, 585, 654–655
WinMain function 718
wish interpreter 4, 15–16
    from Unix shell script 18–22
    from Windows Explorer 17
wm command 407–410, 414–417,
    437, 636–643
World Wide Web (WWW) 288–289
    applets 626–634
    Plume web browser 288–289
    Netscape Navigator web browser
        562–565
    Microsoft Internet Explorer web
        browser 562–563, 565–566
    see also Common Gateway
        Interface (CGI)

X Logical Font Description, XLFD
    133–137
    see also fonts
X resources and resource files
    666–669
xfd Unix command 140
xfontsel Unix command 140–141
xlsfonts Unix command 134